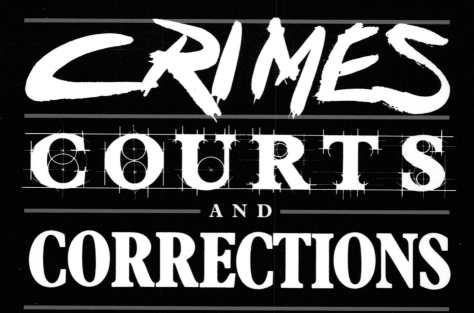

CRIMES
COURTS
AND
CORRECTIONS

AN INTRODUCTION TO CRIME
AND SOCIAL CONTROL IN CANADA

AUGUSTINE BRANNIGAN

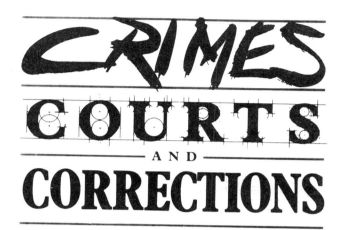

CRIMES COURTS AND CORRECTIONS

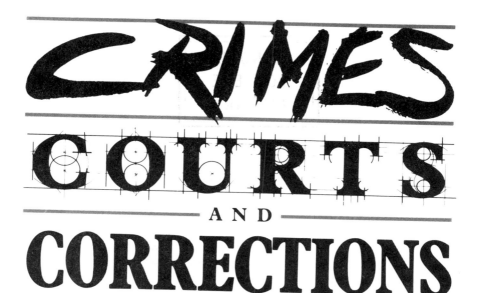

CRIMES

COURTS

AND

CORRECTIONS

AN INTRODUCTION TO CRIME
AND SOCIAL CONTROL IN CANADA

AUGUSTINE BRANNIGAN

Holt, Rinehart and Winston of Canada, Limited, Toronto

Canadian Cataloguing in Publication Data

Brannigan, Augustine, 1949–
  Crimes, courts and corrections

Bibliography: p. 000
Includes index.
ISBN 0-03-921623-3

1. Crime and criminals – Canada. 2. Criminal justice,
Administration of – Canada. I. Title.

KE8813.B73 1984   345.71'05   C83-099048-8

ACQUISITIONS EDITOR: Anthony Luengo
DEVELOPMENTAL EDITOR: Brian Henderson
COPY EDITOR: Greg Ioannou
DESIGN: Pronk & Associates
TYPESETTING AND ASSEMBLY: Compeer Typographic Services

Printed in Canada

2 3 4 5 88 87 86 85

CONTENTS

CRIMES

POLICING

CHAPTER THREE

The Police: Solutions to or Sources of Crime? 45

CHAPTER FOUR

Civil Rights and Safeguards from Abuse 69

JUSTICE AND STATUS

COURTS

CORRECTIONS

CHAPTER ELEVEN

Correctional Services in Canada 219

CHAPTER TWELVE

The Future of Canadian Justice 239

Preface

This book introduces the structures of justice and the control of deviance and harm in Canadian society. Crime and deviance directly affect the lives of thousands of Canadians and, vicariously through the news media, touch the lives and experiences of us all. Crime and deviance are also among those areas that, because of his or her moral sense, the average person feels he or she can speak about with some confidence and the ring of expertise. Likewise, crime and deviance are among the chief elements of what counts as news for us and of what counts as drama. There is nothing like a sensational robbery or mass murder to sell newspapers, and nothing like a good murder mystery to keep us entertained. This suggests that there is a parallel emotional charge for us in these events. We revel in indignation when they appear as news and in gratification when we consume them as entertainment. At the level of our perceptions of social life, it seems as though our individual feelings mirror the accounts of disorder paraded through the media: most Canadians seem to feel that violent crime is running out of control, that the courts are too lenient with offenders, that prisons don't work, that we should return to hanging murderers and that we need more law and order generally in our society. Although this critical public perception is not without foundation, it is far from accurate.

This study examines the major elements of the administration of justice, from law making to policing to the courts and corrections. We look at discretion and bias in the creation of laws and in the administration of justice, at police powers and civil rights and at the relationship between status and access to justice. We compare the treatment of crimes committed by the lower sectors of society to that of crimes committed by businessmen and the police. We deal with the trial process, eyewitness testimony and mistaken identification, and we review the effects of correctional services.

Throughout this exploration of the justice system, we adopt a critical approach, raising questions about the public perceptions and misperceptions of crime. We propose that many areas of justice that seem to function poorly probably are performing better than we think and that other areas that seem to be operating well are demonstrably not. Specifically, society seems to overestimate the prevalence of predatory and property crime while disregarding the harms from the legitimate activities of government and business. Clearly, certain interests are served if the public is riveted to the crimes of mass murderers and blind to the wholesale destruction of the environment in the name of free enterprise. This distortion is reinforced by the willingness of the media to feed the hysteria about the crime rate that accompanies infrequent but savage episodes of violent crime. However, the distortion is not entirely the fault of the media. The justice system itself contributes to our myopic view of what is harmful in our society by showing reluctance to prosecute the well-heeled criminal, whether he or she be a crook in the federal cabinet, an overzealous Mountie or a lawless business executive.

The distortion of our perceptions about the real sources of harm in our society is reflected in the sharp lines that many criminologists draw between the sociology of law, criminology, deviance and social control. Criminology is supposed to be confined to the explanation of criminal behaviours, while social deviance is limited to noncriminal activities. This distinction creates the false impression that we require separate theories for each type of behaviour, yet texts in both areas recurrently cover the same territory under different labels. Also, the distinction between crime and deviance, if taken for granted, eclipses the process by which certain groups succeed in having the harms they inflict controlled by regulatory laws or market forces rather than by the criminal process. If you dump poison waste in your neighbour's yard, you may face a criminal charge of wilful damage to property. However, if you dump hundreds of tons of lowly radioactive mine tailings into whole neighbourhoods (as was done in the Pickering-Oshawa area of Ontario), this amounts to little more than a regulatory offense, if that. Consequently, it is imperative that a sociology of law making accompany the study of crime and deviance, so we can understand how the elements that compose these fields were selected in the first place.

If the processes of social control that are mobilized to curb harmful behaviour have the effect of promoting or stabilizing this behaviour, then certain forms of justice (including unsound sentencing behaviour and penology, police strikes and the creation of biased laws that encourage civil disobedience) may become criminogenic and hence form part of the proper study of the causes of crime. The same applies to macroeconomic government policies that foster unemployment to reduce inflation. By creating personnel for property crimes and by generating stressful domestic environments, these policies are likewise criminogenic. What this suggests is that we should take a broad view of crime and harm and the social control apparatus that curbs and promotes them.

In undertaking a description of justice in Canadian society, our purpose is not confined to scientifically specifying what happens and why. From the point of its conception with Francis Bacon, science has had an emancipatory interest — an interest in improving human experience. This is doubly relevant in the study of social institutions where public policies, as opposed to the laws of society, form the subject matter. Since public policies can be changed by social action, many of the points raised in this treatment of justice are raised to promote discussion of optimal and alternative policies. This treatment provides no definitive answers or political elixirs to end suffering and misery. On the contrary, it is meant to raise questions about justice in Canada. It is meant to correct the common sense perceptions that Canadians have of their institutions. There is a complacency in English-speaking Canada that arises from the assumptions that if public institutions exist, they must exist for a purpose or public objective; that the purpose, as well as the people who carry it out, are good; and that the institutions are the best equipped to carry out public objectives. Evidence frequently suggests that these assumptions are unfounded. Although readers may not always agree with this and other conclusions, the key is raising the questions to promote dialogue and thoughtful social action.

Acknowledgements

This book is based on lectures given over a period of several years at the University of Calgary in courses on the administration of justice, criminology, deviant group behaviour and law and the liberal arts. I have had the benefit of conversations with and comments from a first-rate body of keen and hardworking students, who have made teaching both a pleasure and a challenge. I also have had the warm encouragement of friends and colleagues at the University of Calgary throughout this project. In addition, I must report an enormous gratitude to James L. Wilkins, who introduced me to socio-legal studies with the Crown prosecution project in 1977 through 1979. My studies of justice would never have been undertaken without his encouragement and without the opportunities he gave me to study research materials at the Centre of Criminology at the University of Toronto.

Drafts of chapters of this book were read by a number of colleagues, including Bill Avison, Ingrid Connidis, John Hagan, Chris Levy, Bill Rea, Bob Stebbins and Jim Wilkins. I am grateful to them for their suggestions, many of which I have adopted. If, despite all this good counsel, anything dubious remains, responsibility for that is mine alone.

In compiling and checking library sources, I had the able assistance of several researchers — especially Rhena Hymovitch and Shari Williams-Saunders. Shari also contributed in an outstanding way to the job of rendering something readable out of my awkward prose as well as checking many points of law in my arguments. Likewise, Anil Tiwari, Librarian at the Faculty of Law Library, provided great assistance in tracking down materials and bringing them to my attention.

The Department of Sociology provided facilities for the completion of this manuscript. The endless drafts of this project were typed and retyped cheerfully and accurately by my secretary, Gloria Hall. She has been an invaluable asset in preparing the manuscript and, frequently, an able commentator on it. Also, in working out bugs in the word processor, Tom Huang's computer wizardry has been invaluable. Last, I must give a special thanks to my wife, Terry, who has always been a source of encouragement in these late-night projects and to whom this book is dedicated.

Augustine Brannigan

CRIMES

CHAPTER 1

Laws and the Social Construction of Criminal Behaviours

Introduction to the Social Bases of Law

It is a mistake to argue that a law exists because it is just, just as it would be a mistake in natural science to say that a biological law exists because it is true. As in natural science, we should differentiate between the logic of discovery and the logic of justification: the former tries to document how a law was discovered, the latter tries to show how and whether a law is correct. So too with criminal laws: the question of how a law came about, that is, the forces underlying its invention, is a different question from whether it is a good law.

In their analysis of the grounds of good law in the English tradition, Sutherland and Cressey (1974: 4-8) describe four things that are required of good laws. The first of these is the political nature or politicality of law. Does the law reflect the will of the body politic that makes up the state and is it a legitimate state-manufactured law (as opposed to the law of the jungle, a mafia law, a church law, etc)? Second, is the law uniform? That is, does the law apply to all people equally; can anyone be exempted from the law because of irrelevant characteristics, such as social status, wealth or political connections? Specificity is the third characteristic. It refers to the accuracy with which laws describe forbidden behaviours. Good laws spell out what constitutes a violation in detail, while poor laws are too general. Lastly, laws must have a penalty or penal sanction to give gravity to the conviction of offenders. However, the penalty should be meaningful by being only as severe as the transgression.

These four characteristics are studied by students of jurisprudence and are rarely discussed by criminologists. Students of jurisprudence are more concerned with the logic of justification. Students of criminology are more concerned with the invention of new laws. The major issue discussed among contemporary criminologists is whether the laws have been invented to serve the interests of particular groups or whether the laws are derived from a situation of value consensus and are an expression of the collective will. Speaking generally there are few proponents of the idea that most or even the most important of our laws reflect the feelings of the majority of people in society. The contemporary debate is animated by the extent to which interest groups are able to dominate governments to ensure that the laws reflect their own interests. Marxists take the view that the state and the legal apparatus are an arrangement for the perpetuation of the capitalist system of production. Generally, criminal law is seen as a device to protect property and to prevent interference with the capitalist process of production (see Spitzer, 1975; and Thomas, 1982). By contrast, conflict theorists argue that whatever the economic basis of society, elites will struggle for control over the scarce resources of society and will employ law as a weapon to control dependent and subordinate classes and groups (Turk, 1969). Conflict theorists see no end to the cooptation of the law for the interests of elites with the passing of capitalism. Socialism, and indeed all social arrangements, will likewise be subject to a reliance on coersion through control of the legal apparatus.

This chapter examines examples of laws that reflect a number of perspectives. When we reflect on the diversity of things included as laws and the range of behaviours they relate to, it is naive to assume that all laws can be explained with reference to just one theory. The only thing that the proscription of murder and the regulation of the temperature of bathwater for babies, when and where trout can be fished and when and where goods can be sold have in common is that they are governed by laws. Likewise, the only thing that pliers, saws, screwdrivers and clamps have in common is being called "tools." Just as we would not expect a theory of tool invention to apply to every tool, so we should not expect the laws all to be cut from the same fabric. Some laws have clearly evolved from the influence of powerful political and economic forces in society. Others have been fostered by the success of moral leaders in the society, others by attempts to control minority groups, others by an expression of the collective will and still others by struggles within society to reform previous laws.

Political and Economic Influence in the Creation of Laws: Some Illustrations

One of the best examples of laws of this type is discussed by William Chambliss (1974) and concerns the introduction of poll taxes and registration taxes in Colonial East Africa in the period 1890-1930. One of the major problems facing English settlers in Uganda, Kenya and Tanganyika after colonization was that of getting large numbers of natives to leave their traditional lifestyles of herding and slash and burn agriculture to work on the large English plantations raising tea, coffee and sisal for export. The new agriculture depended on the creation of large pools of cheap labour and the legal code was at the forefront of the solution to this problem. The "poll tax" and "registration" laws required everyone of working age to pay a small tax, purportedly to support the colonial rule. Since the natives were subsistent agriculturalists, they had never previously participated in a money economy — until this law forced them into it. This situation was actively endorsed by colonial administrators. In 1895 Sir Harry Johnston stated:

Given abundance of cheap labour, the financial security of the Protectorate is established . . . . All that needs to be done is for the Administration to act as friends of both sides, and introduce the native labourer to the European capitalist. A gentle insistence that the native should contribute his fair share to the revenue of the country by paying his tax is all that is necessary on our part to ensure his taking a share in life's labour which no human being should avoid. (Cited in Chambliss, 1974: 9)

To guarantee the unwilling African's compliance with this "forced labour" arrangement, fines, imprisonment and corporal punishment were imposed on people who failed to pay the tax. Even this was not completely successful. Aaronovitch and Aaronovitch (1947) reported in *Crisis in Kenya* that more comprehensive and sterner guarantees were required. Labourers were required to register fingerprints so that runaways could quickly be returned to their plantation employers. Vagrancy laws prevented natives from leaving their reserves for anything but becoming wage labourers. In addition, wages were kept extremely low to prevent workers from generating sufficient cash to quickly pay off the poll tax and quit work.

This sort of situation was not limited to exotic colonial societies but was found even in England, the home of the common law tradition. Chambliss (1969) reviewed the history of the vagrancy law and showed that this residual type of social control was redefined and interpreted over time to serve the interests of the shifting power blocks in English society.

The English Vagrancy Laws

In 1274 a pre-vagrancy statute was passed that made it unlawful for travellers to live off the largesse of the abbies and religious monasteries and houses, for the biblical injunction to feed and house strangers and travellers was becoming a grave economic burden for religious orders. This, however, was not a true vagrancy law.

In 1349, a law was passed making it a crime to give alms or handouts to any beggars who were able, but unwilling, to work for a living. Consequently, beggars would be forced to take work to support themselves. The law also made it illegal for any man or woman without a trade to refuse work, and gave the individual who apprehended the latter the right to his or her service at a fixed wage for two years. This law overlapped with the Statutes of Labourers (1349-51) which fixed the price of labour, made it unlawful to accept more than this, made it unlawful to refuse work, and made it unlawful to flee one county to another to avoid offers of work or to seek higher wages.

According to Chambliss, the rationale for these laws was purely economic. The Black Plague had wiped out about half of the English population, creating a general labour shortage. The labour-intensive manorial system was put into jeopardy. The 1349 vagrancy law effectively minimized the ability of freemen to move about to maximize their economic self-interests. The net effect of the laws was to impress into jobs all those who were available to work and to make it difficult for anyone to move about to exploit wage differentials and thereby threaten the manorial reliance on peasant labour. The law had an obvious economic motive, despite being a vagrancy law.

Following 1349, punishments for vagrancy became more severe. The initial penalty of 15 days in jail changed to indefinite terms in the "stocks" until an employer could be found. With later population growth, the statute appears to have become dormant and unimportant.

In 1530 a new vagrancy statute was written to specifically cover what we would recognize as criminal and potentially criminal activities. It identified as vagrant those persons without any visible means of support, as well as those who lived by gambling and trickery. The punishments for vagrancy at this point were extremely cruel. Whipping and mutilation (e.g., cutting off the ears) were expanded in 1535 to include the use of the death penalty for repeat offenders. Chambliss argues that the vagrant was now conceived as a serious felon and not just a vagabond who did not want to work. In 1547, vagrants were branded on the chest or the forehead, indicating in a permanent way the view that such persons were inherently dangerous, rather than being mere nuisances. This was formalized in a 1571 law that laid down the conditions for first-, second- and third-time offenders (first — grievous whipping and burning "thru the gristle" of the right ear; second — impressed for two years forced work; third — death without benefit of clergy).

Chambliss argues that the change in the definition of vagrancy reflected the power of the new interest groups, the manufacturers and traders whose business in wool and cloth grew to international proportions in the 15th and 16th centuries. In 1400 there were 169 wool merchants in England. A century later there were 3000. Vagrants were prosecuted because of the threat they posed to the safe transportation of merchants' goods. The vagrancy act identified the vagrants as threats specifically on the highways:

> Whereas diverse licentious persons wander up and down in all parts of the realm . . . and do continually assemble themselves armed in the highways, and elsewhere in troops, to the great terror of her majesty's true subjects, the impeachment of her laws, and the disturbance of the peace and tranquility of the realm; and whereas many outrages are daily committed by these dissolute persons, and more are likely to ensue if speedy remedy be not provided . . . (Cited in Chambliss, 1969: 59)

The last notable change in the vagrancy laws occurred in 1743 when the vagrancy categories took a more modern twist, de-emphasizing the danger to trade of marauding bands and labelling the destitute wanderers and other marginal actors as threats to public order. The law was aimed at beggars, gamblers, runaways, vagabonds and the like. These were largely the sort of things found in the first Canadian criminal law on vagrancy: the people identified were less a specific threat to trade, and more an undifferentiated threat to normative life styles and the public peace and order (see Parker, 1983:26-27).

The vagrancy laws shifted their focus over time to include different categories of "enemies" or "delinquents." When the manorial system required labourers, the law was used to force labourers into the manorial system. When the merchants required freedom from threat of highway robbery, the law was re-tooled to serve this interest. And when the needs of the merchant class passed in importance, the law came to serve a more general interest in the control of marginal people.

Some of these same historical forces were important in the decision of the famous Carrier case, in which for the first time in English history a transporter or carrier who was legally bailed with the goods in his possession was found guilty of a felony for keeping them. This historic case shows again the way in which the criminal law can be manipulated to serve the interests of a specific group.

The Carrier Case of 1473

What was the problem in this case? A foreign merchant, probably an Italian, hired a man to carry some bales for him from London to Southampton. The carrier took the bales, legitimately, and broke them open, taking the contents—which was illegitimate. Under English law the merchant could bring a civil action for "trespass to goods." But under the common law governing criminal action, it was difficult to argue that any crime had happened. Certainly, a wrong had occurred, but not a crime. The common law required of theft the element of trespass. Presumably, to steal someone's property you would have to trespass first on his land. But the carrier had not trespassed to get the goods; he was given them voluntarily. Nonetheless the merchant successfully had a charge of felony laid, and the case was heard before the Star Chamber. At the outcome, contrary to the common law, the carrier was convicted against the opinion of the Chief Justice.

The problem is, how did this particular change come about? Jerome Hall's (1969) study of this case suggests three forces. First, there was a moral force underlying the decision. Though the King may have manipulated conditions to serve his own interests, the merchant was at least morally considered to have been victimized. Second, because of the political upheaval prior to the case (i.e., the defeat of the Lancastrians in the Wars of the Roses), Edward IV was distrustful of his ministers and tended to dominate and control them, as well as his judges. Notably, the case was heard in the Star Chamber, which was especially vulnerable to his personal influence. Third, because of his guarantee of safety to the foreign merchant, the King could have been held liable for the merchant's losses. Also, with the demise of the agricultural feudal system and the rise of the trade in wool, shipping and trading merchants were becoming increasingly influential, especially for Edward IV who relied on them for financial and political support. Also, Edward was himself a trader in wool, and wool was the major stuff of trade in the new society. Hence for a series of economic reasons, some of which were personal and others national, Edward appears to have exploited his power over the judiciary to gain a new interpretation of larceny, at the expense of the common law. In other words, he co-opted the criminal law in the interests of business.

The 1970 U.S. Drug Bill

These historical cases are distant in time and exotic in place. William Chambliss cites an example that hits somewhat closer to home (1974: 18-20). It concerns passage of the 1970 Comprehensive Drug Abuse, Prevention and Control Act in the USA. Of interest to us are the efforts made by the leading drug manufacturers to control the labelling of certain drugs as "dangerous." The statute was designed to control the distribution and use of "dangerous" drugs, and included a controversial provision allowing drug enforcement officers the right to enter private homes without notice or permission. Certain disturbing things became clear during the House of Representatives' hearings. First, there was substantial evidence to document the dangerousness of certain "legitimately" produced drugs; that is, products from leading pharmaceutical companies. Notwithstanding this, the legislators, under pressure from the lobbyists for the drug companies, managed to confine the focus of the state to drugs taken by youth and lower-class slum dwellers: cocaine, pot, heroin, and LSD. Consequently, the drug companies insulated their profits from possible interference by the federal drug regulations.

The law was drafted by the Nixon administration, with the assistance of, and after consultation with, the leading pharmaceutical corporations. This was passed in spite of the following sort of evidence. Each year in the USA the pharmaceutical industry produces tens of billions of amphetamines, meta-phetamines ("speed") and two closely related compounds: Valium and Librium. The widespread use of these compounds by middle-class housewives, students, businessmen and athletes has created several wide-spread negative effects:

a) the drugs create psychological dependence
b) continued use (especially of Librium and Valium) produces extreme depression
c) the Bureau of Narcotics and Dangerous Drugs cited Librium and Valium as precipitating factors in 36 suicides and 750 attempted suicides
d) evidence from the National Institute of Mental Health suggested that continued long-term use of these compounds often resulted in malnutrition, prolonged psychotic states, heart irregularities, convulsions, hepatitis, and brain damage.

Therefore, the drugs' harmfulness was well documented. (Chambliss, 1974: 19)

The second item of evidence concerned the diversion of drugs. Eight billion amphetamine pills were marketed legally, for the most part through prescriptions written by doctors. However, the Bureau of Narcotics and Dangerous Drugs estimated that about 75-90% of the illegally used "speed" was manufactured legally in the country, and therefore the drug companies were producing the bulk of the traffic in speed. Apparently there is widespread forging of prescriptions, duplication of prescriptions, and the distribution of open-ended prescriptions, which allow the "patient" to return at will to the drugstore to have a supply refilled. Also, the major drug companies were not terribly careful about who they sent the drugs to. According to Chambliss (1974: 19), one federal agent obtained 25,000 pills in the mail by signing his name as a doctor.

The third item of evidence concerned the actual utility of these pills in medical treatment situations. Most of the 53 submissions suggested a specific medical application, "for the early stages of a diet program." About 99% of all prescriptions were written for this purpose in spite of the fact that their utility in this regard was extremely limited. Instead of being used several times over a period of a week, the pills have undergone a widespread and consistent use. Apparently obesity has become an excuse to get high on "speed," and all this in spite of the testimony from one Vanderbilt Medical School doctor who testified that a few thousand pills would meet the real medical needs of the entire United States (Chambliss, 1974: 20). However, this would not meet the economic needs of the drug companies. Hoffman-LaRoche makes tens of millions of dollars annually from the profits on Valium and Librium alone, compounds that may be as harmful as "speed" or street narcotics.

Stuart L. Hills (1980: 118-20) in his commentary on the legitimate drug industry has pointed out how the pharmaceutical companies have co-opted the medical profession to encourage the use of these kinds of drugs for minor forms of "domestic unhappiness" caused by housework, not "fitting in," the challenge of attending college, boredom and the like.

In the end, the 1970 legislation was directed at and confined to the users and manufacturers of compounds like LSD, cocaine and marihuana, and was drafted with the assistance of those drug companies with large stakes in the production of "legitimate drugs," despite the evidence that these were at least as harmful as the so-called "dangerous" drugs marketed by independent entrepreneurs. This example again illustrates the fashion in which interest groups manipulate the law to serve their own ends.

Reforms

In the various case studies, the Colonial poll tax laws, the vagrancy laws, the Carrier case and the 1970 comprehensive drug bill, it is apparent that power blocks in the state have influenced the creation of criminal and administrative laws to maintain or protect their own political and/or economic status. Marxists have argued for a century that the ideas of the ruling class are the ruling ideas. Ideas, including laws, are determined by the all-important economic substructure of the society. The cases examined here appear to broadly bear out these critical observations.

However, what about reform movements and their influence in controlling the laws? After all, we tend to think that most modern changes in legislation are the results of enlightened individuals seeking to undo injustices of the past. This is presumably the motive behind much of the work of the Law Reform Commission of Canada and its various recommendations of changes in criminal law. However, not all reform movements have a liberal orientation. Furthermore, some reform movements ironically serve the interests of the very groups they are directed against. For example, Gabriel Kolko (1963) argues that the 1906 reform of the meat packing industries in the USA played into the hands of the larger capitalist entrepreneurs.

Readers of Upton Sinclair's novel *The Jungle* will be familiar with the dangerous and unsanitary working conditions found in the meat packing industries in Chicago at the turn of the century. "Everything but the squeal" was used in making the meat loaf, sometimes the hapless workers included. Partly as a result of Sinclair's book and partly as a result of the public's concern over the quality of the meat, there was a wide call for reform of the conditions in the industry. And, since the unsanitary conditions were producing unhealthy meat, there was a fall in reputation of the product that affected the export market in Europe, hurting the packers financially. The sanitation laws were passed with the cooperation of the large packers in an attempt to clean up the industry. One provision of the law required that the meat inspectors be paid for by the companies themselves, even though inspectors were government employees. This had a different effect on companies of different sizes. Large companies were able to spread their costs over a large volume of goods while many of the small companies went bankrupt or were bought out by the large outfits. Hence the law to regulate the industry had the effect of concentrating business in fewer hands (Chambliss, 1974: 17).

The inspectors gave the new meat a government seal of approval, boosting the reputation of the product and helping the export picture. Clearly this attempt to regulate the industry was subsequently co-opted to further the industry's objectives, and the "reform" inadvertently accelerated the centralization of the industry. However, other reform movements have not met with the same fate. Nonetheless, they tend to be self-serving for the groups who propose them.

Reforms of Lifestyles and Deviations: Laws as Symbols of Morality

Much of the sociological literature on law reform has centred on changes in law designed to regulate unsavoury lifestyles, habits and deviations. This literature argues that from time to time certain groups in a society effect changes in law that have a largely symbolic significance. Unlike the economic entrepreneurs who try to gain legal control over business regulations, these moral entrepreneurs, as Howard Becker (1963) calls them, seek changes in the law for symbolic ends. In other words, they seek passage of laws to degrade and criminalize the activities of other groups and consequently to upgrade, through invidious comparison, the moral superiority of their own group. Often, the laws they have passed are purely symbolic. That is, the laws do not change, but merely deprecate, the behaviour of the outgroups. The leading examples of this process are found in attempts to control elements of lifestyle and leisure, and surround the creation of laws against the use of liquor and drugs.

Prohibition

An important case is prohibition. The classic sociological study in this area is Joseph Gusfield's *Symbolic Crusade* (1963). The periods of temperance were different in the USA and Canada. In the USA, the 1919 Volstead Act made the 18th Amendment enforceable. This Act was repealed in 1933, ending prohibition. In Canada, a Prohibition Act was passed by the federal Parliament allowing provinces the right of separate ratification. Except for Quebec, provincial ratifications of the prohibition appeared over a two-year period, 1914-1916, and continued to 1924: even after 1924, when provinces began to opt out, there was widespread exercise of "local option," that is, decisions at the village, city, town or county level on whether to go "wet" (i.e., allow beverage rooms) or stay "dry." There was a one-year period from November 1919 to October 1920, when the law was not enforceable on inter-provincial trade, allowing persons in a dry province to import liquor from another province. We tend to equate prohibition with these well-known periods in the second and third decades of this century. However, the prohibition movement was a widespread 19th-century movement that effectively banned the trade in liquor in many local jurisdictions.

The very first North American attempt to introduce prohibition was initiated in New France by Bishop Laval in 1648. He tried unsuccessfully to free the Indians of alcohol and succeeded in having an order passed in 1657 prohibiting trade of liquor for furs with the Indians. This proved useless when the Dutch in New York filled the need and were threatening to displace the French traders.

James Gray's popular 1972 study of this episode in Canadian history indicates that the use of liquor among the white settlers of British North America was staggering. In Upper Canada in 1842 there were 147 distillers and 96 breweries serving a population of 500,000. This constituted about one manufacturer for every 2,000 men, women and children. In Winnipeg, in 1881, for the population of 8,000 people, there were 64 hotels with bars, 5 breweries, 24 wine and liquor stores. In 1882, the number of hotel bars jumped to 86, and there were 64 grocery stores selling bottled whisky, as well as a score of "wholesalers" in wagons (Gray, 1972: 5). We do not have figures for the volume consumption of alcohol in Canada over time, but our consumption is probably comparable to the Americans. Table 1, which shows total per capita volume of alcohol consumed, indicates that 19th-century and early 20th-century consumption was higher than today.

TABLE 1
Annual Consumption of Alcohol in the U.S.

1850	2.07 gallons / person over 13 yrs old
1911-15 (average)	2.56
1940	1.56
1957	1.91

Source: Gusfield, 1963: 132.

The dramatic change in drinking habits is also reflected in the type of alcohol consumed. In 1850, 90% of the volume consumed was distilled spirits (i.e. hard liquor) and 7% was beer. In 1957, 40% was spirits and 50% was beer.

With this volume of consumption, it is not surprising that many 19th-century pro-hibition movements did succeed. There was no single movement but a proliferation of temperance movements. In 1835, the Montreal Temperance Society was founded. In 1836 in Montreal there was a convention of 30 societies from numerous jurisdictions. In 1847, the Sons of Temperance was founded in New Brunswick, Nova Scotia and Lower Canada. The Independent Order of Good Templars flourished across British North America in the 1850s with a total membership of 20,000 as did the Women's Christian Temperance Movement and charters of numerous American groups. In 1855 Sir Leonard Tilley's provincial government of New Brunswick passed a total prohibi-tion law, but it was repealed. The Atlantic Provinces were following the lead of the New England States (Maine had passed a similar law in 1846); in 1853 the United Provinces of Canada (i.e., Ontario and Quebec) passed local option laws; in 1864 a new act was passed, the Dunkin Act, which strengthened the earlier statute. After Confederation in 1867, the Dunkin Act was replaced by a new act for all Canada, Canada's Temperance Act of 1878 (the Scott Act). It extended the right of local option to every province. Also, a nationwide plebiscite was held in 1898; the results favoured prohibition, but the voter turnout was very small. Prime Minister Borden noted only about half of the voters turned out and only slightly more than half voted of them (only about 25% of the total electorate) voted for prohibition, so he ignored the vote.

Who were the backers of these movements? According to Gusfield, they were pre-dominantly fundamentalist Protestant, white settlers, largely from rural areas, and ini-tially of middle-class background. They believed firmly in the old Protestant ethic and valued hard work, self-reliance and self-denial.

What theory accounts for their participation in the temperance movements and the ultimate enactment of the national prohibition laws? Gusfield argues that increasingly over the 19th century the traditional settlers of Canada and the USA experienced a loss of social status compared to the urban classes and a challenge to their traditional values with the increases of urban, non-Protestant, and non-Anglo-Saxon immigration. Consequently, their social status vis-à-vis others was tending to fall. The temperance movements were a form of status politics, not class politics, whose aim, unlike the vagrancy laws and the poll tax, was not economic gain but the reaffirmation of the prestige of a lifestyle. They tried to obtain these ends by getting others who were viewed as individual sinners or "backsliders" as well as alien groups like the urban Irish Catholics, or the beer-loving Germans, to accept the values of the temperate and the abstainers.

In the early period of the movements (1825-1875) the norms of the Protestant middle and upper class dominated the societies. The strategies of the movements were those of education, persuasion, and the reform of social conditions that caused exces-sive drinking. However, as the industrial capitalists rose to power with the success of American mining and railway conglomerations, the temperance movements' members fell in status with increases in urbanization, and non-English immigration, and the tactics changed from "assimilation" to coercive reform; that is, from a temperance movement to a prohibition movement. The fight for prohibition represented the attempt of the old middle class from rural and small-town communities to enforce their ideas on the rest of the population, even if only symbolically.

What is unclear about these laws is whether they radically altered drinking behaviour over the long run. In the USA, the federal government passed the Volstead Act, but did not approve the required expenditures to increase the civil service to assure it would be enforced. Local stills sprang up everywhere, and organized crime grew to replace the vacuum created by the temperance movement's lobbyists. While before prohibition every saloon required a license, prohibition actually multiplied the number of operating saloons. Now that it was illegal, no one was worried about the license, and everybody who wanted to open up a bar, but was previously restricted by the law, was now unrestrained, at least by the licensing boards. In Canada the volume of illicit liquor manufactured and consumed is nearly impossible to calculate.

However we can be fairly certain that Canadian palates did not do without alcohol just because of the law; just as we are fairly certain that nowadays people who want marihuana or hashish need not go without if they are prepared to flout the law. However, in rural areas, and especially in the west where the temperance movement was strongest, drinking fell to 20% by volume of what it had been earlier (Gray, 1972). Where did the 20% come from? Contrary to popular opinion, it was still legal to manufacture alcoholic beverages for the export market and for medicinal purposes. Much if not most of the Canadian liquor manufactured for export was illegally diverted to domestic sources or illegally exported south of the border. This was the experience of the early Bronfman operation in the fledgling distillery in Yorkton, Saskatchewan (Newman, 1978; Gervais, 1980).

Also, alcohol could be obtained by doctor's prescription from a pharmacy. James Gray (1972: 92) relates an instance from Calgary where a party of fishermen heading for a day at Banff, and fearful of "catching a chill" had a prescription filled for a quart of Scotch at the local pharmacy. Lastly, breweries were permitted to produce "temperance beer," a weak beverage ranging in strength from 0.5% to 4% depending on the year and the province. However, strong beer (5%-7% alcohol by volume) was often brewed and substituted in the taverns. Needless to say, the new laws dampened the rowdiness of the bars. No matter what was coming through the spigots, it was imperative to maintain an appearance of respectability to avoid the involvement of curious RCMP officers.

After 1924 the province-wide dry laws were repealed, though local option continued to keep many places effectively dry until the last two decades. The 1923-24 votes that removed prohibition replaced it with strict laws that turned over the retail distribution of liquor to provincial government control and regulated the operation of beverage rooms under provincial laws. Thereafter there were to be no more wide-open towns and no more rambunctious saloons. The new drinking laws forbade such things as standing on the table, singing in the bars and standing with a beer in hand.

If we contrast the reformist elements of the sanitation laws and the prohibition laws, we find that the sanitation laws, though designed to control the capitalist packers, actually played into the hands of these parties. In this case the state mediated what the individual producers could not impose on themselves. By contrast, the reformists who pushed for prohibition were responsible for the curtailment of the legal marketing of alcohol, but this served the symbolic interests of the temperance backers — the rural, traditionalist, fundamentalist classes, and, inadvertently, the interests of illicit entrepreneurs in organized crime. These laws scored a temporary symbolic victory over the newer elements in the ideological interests of a downwardly mobile sector of society. The temperance movement was an attempt to re-assert the righteous lifestyle of this formerly dominant group. Consequently, the rise of the prohibition laws was symbolic, not economic. Nonetheless, the *demise* of the laws reflected the economic interests of the legitimate brewers and distillers, and, with government in the business of distributing liquor, created an alliance between government and business by which government was given a share of the retail profits as well as the liquor taxes, and business, which had continued throughout this period to make liquor allegedly for export, was guaranteed a legitimate system of distribution in the home market. What this suggests is that to explain the rise of particular laws, we ought to examine the competing interest groups that arise to contest new laws and to reform old ones, and the moral as well as the economic elements that underlie the respective positions of such groups.

Law and the Manufacture of Fiends

In a case studied by Sutherland (1969), the "moral crusaders" appear to have been the newspapers and their general readership. Sexual psychopath laws were enacted in 1937 and thereafter in eleven northern states, California and the District of Columbia. They provided for indefinite incarceration in hospitals for the criminally insane for anyone pronounced by a psychiatrist to be a sexual psychopath. It turns out retrospectively that this diagnosis is not based on any known medical disease. Many psychiatric categories are only labels for things we do not like, not explanations of them. Nonetheless, a wide series of jurisdictions, with one eye to reforming sexual deviants, enacted laws based on this "disease." According to Sutherland, there was a three-fold process underlying the creation of these laws.

First, the laws are typically enacted after a state of fear and newspaper hysteria following several sex crimes committed coincidentally in quick succession. This was the case especially in Indiana, where the laws were enacted following four sex attacks (two involving murder). As Sutherland noted, in this case there was a rush to buy guns, guard dogs, locks and chains, reflecting widespread evidence of fear associated with the coincidence of crimes.

The second element in the development of these laws is the state of continued civic agitation in the community, fed by news coverage of related sex crimes in other areas and other times in history, and of sex-related behaviours and morality, including questions regarding striptease, letters to the newspaper editors and statements made by public figures. All this keeps the matter alive and invites a sort of collective indignation and a call for some institutional response.

The third phase in the development of these sexual psychopath laws, according to Sutherland, was the creation of committees to study "the facts" of the sex crimes and "the facts" of sexual psychopathology. These committees, though initially struck on the basis of collective terror, persist long after the fear and news stories subside. The typical outcome of these committees was a presentation of briefs to legislative bodies. Apparently, one factor that made these briefs so convincing was the testimony of a new class of medical experts. Hence, the community hysteria was legitimated by the identification of the crimes as a form of disease by the new class of professional psychiatrists.

Aside from the expertise of this new class of psychiatrists, the identification of this new criminal category had a general plausibility. It served the collective outlook of the various communities that had experienced several reprehensible sex attacks and sex-related murders; i.e., it "explained" otherwise unintelligible and unconscionable activities and provided a severe penalty (though disguised as a medical one) for this new type of human being, the sexual psychopath.

The creation of prohibition laws and the psychopath laws are similar in that both appeared as a result of a moral crusade to re-establish the significance of a particular lifestyle or mode of conduct. However, in one case the laws were initiated by a downwardly mobile traditional sector of society, while in the other case they were initiated by an outraged community fueled by newspaper reports and formulated by a proxy committee in association with the psychiatric profession.

There is a third type of moral crusade: that conducted by members of government

— politicians from certain cultural groups — who change laws without evidence of pressure from "outsiders," in order to control the disdainful leisure habits of certain unpopular minority groups. This was the case in the creation of the Canadian anti-opium laws, which have been the source of continuous interest since they were first explored by Shirley Cook in 1969.

The Social Context of the Anti-Opium Laws

The first anti-opium law was passed in Canada in 1908 as a result of Mackenzie King's study and report on the use of opium in Vancouver. As Deputy Minister of Labour, King had been sent to Vancouver to supervise compensation for losses to Asiatics after the 1907 anti-Asiatic riots. Prior to the Canadian episode, there had been previous anti-Asian riots in the USA. In 1871, 18 Chinese were murdered in riots and looting in Chinatown in Los Angeles and in 1885, scores of riots across Pacific towns resulted in the deaths of hundreds of Chinese. The anti-Asiatic riot in Vancouver in 1907 occurred in a year of economic recession. The Asians were blamed for creating a depression by accepting lower wages. A crowd of 30,000 gathered in downtown Vancouver. Fifteen thousand rioters attacked the Chinese ghetto, looting, burning stores, and attacking the inhabitants. The attackers were repulsed in the Japanese ghetto. The Chinese and Japanese Consulates later won $100,000 in damages from the Canadian government.

In retrospect, it appears that the riot was sparked by a rally of the militant Knights of Labour. The Chinese, who formerly were employed by the CPR, became available in large numbers for general manual labour after the completion of the railway, and while white workers were demanding $2 per day for cutting and clearing bush and timber, Asians were being organized by other whites to work for 50 to 75 cents per day. The situation was exacerbated in 1907 by the recession and higher white unemployment. Also, during this period, there was continued immigration of Asians from China, Japan and East India.

The first Chinese immigrants had arrived from California, following rumors of a Fraser River gold rush. By 1871, there were 2,000 Chinese in B.C. In 1881, the CPR began importing Chinese labourers to finish the Trans-Rockies extension of the railway. They set a figure of 17,000 but as the work neared completion, these 17,000 workers became unemployed. They looked for any other subsistent work in laundries, in kitchens, as home servants, gardeners, miners and lumberjacks, thereby coming into competition with white workers. Also, there was massive labour-management strife in B.C., and Asians were used to break strikes and undercut wage levels. Pressure mounted to reduce immigration, and as a result, the federal government instituted the head or immigration tax. Prior to 1900, the head tax was $50 per immigrant; in 1901, $100 per head; in 1904, $500 per head. In 1923 the Chinese Immigration Act (Exclusion Act) virtually ended Asiatic immigration. While 43,998 had immigrated during the period 1906-23, only 15 per year were allowed during 1923-1941 (Chan, 1983: 11).

Among the claimants, following the Vancouver Riot, were two merchants whose seven opium manufacturing plants had been destroyed and who were submitting claims for compensation. King found he could freely purchase opium over the counter, in spite of a provincial law forbidding this. He submitted a report of the situation to Parliament and in 1908, with hardly any discussion, the Opium Act was passed.

However, King continued his interest in the social problems created by opium use. He attended the Shanghai Opium Commission Conference in 1909 and became an expert in the global problem of opium export. In 1911, he sponsored a more severe bill—the Opium & Drug Act—presumably provoked by scores of letters from clergy, police, welfare workers, and concerned citizens, calling for more control of the Chinese opium trade. It has since been shown that these letters had been solicited. In 1912, the Hague Opium Conference was held to restrict exportation and trading in opium. After the First World War, all signatories of the Versailles Peace Treaty (1919) and members of the new League of Nations were also required to sign the Hague Opium Conference Treaty, and in 1920, Canada changed the laws regulating narcotics to parallel the international agreement. However, the change of the laws sparked anti-opium hysteria (1920-1923) fueled by sensationalist media attention to the danger of opiates. *Maclean's Magazine*, for example, ran five sensationalist articles in 1920 that purported to trace a number of evils to opium use including seduction of white women by Chinese and black men, corruption of youth, destruction of the family and erosion of Christian faith (see Hagan, 1977: 28-29). Many MPs, especially Vancouver based members, picked up on this sensationalism and managed to introduce a number of harsh features into the laws: specifically, whipping for the distribution of drugs to youth, deportation of alien dealers, denial of appeal of deportation orders and radical power of search and seizure.

Cook (1969) points to three interrelated causes which brought about these changes. First, the moral entrepreneurs focussed attention on only a fraction of the trade, excluding the involvement of high-status doctors. Second, they exploited views about the inherent dangers of all intoxicants as destructive of the moral fibre. Third, they exploited longstanding anti-Chinese feelings, based on stereotyping, as justification of the law.

The Focus on Low-Status Drug Distributors

From what we know about medical practice in the early decades of the century and from representations made to Parliament during the 1908-1912 and 1920-1923 periods, it is clear that the medical profession was probably responsible for as much opiate addiction as Chinese opium dealers. It has been pointed out that opium and similar derivatives were prescribed almost universally for every sort of ache and pain. It was often put into cough syrups, and was the chief ingredient in "Mrs. Windslow's Tonic," "Kopp's Baby Friend," "Dover's Powder," and "Hodnett's Gem" (Cook, 1969: 39; Chapman, 1976: 57). These were popular home cure-alls. Cold and headache tablets often contained cocaine and codeine. Reports to the House of Commons from members of the medical profession indicated that open-ended prescriptions for opiate-based medicines for diseases as diverse as epilepsy and asthma were made freely available. The narcotics law sidestepped this source of opium as legislators focussed exclusively on the Chinese dealers and their users. The higher status medical profession was handled under another law that lacked the same severe penalties and extraordinary rights of search, the 1908 Patent and Propriety Medicines Act, which also exempted any "remedy" that had ingredients printed on the label. Therefore, the law criminalized activities of a lower-status group while ignoring similar behaviour of a higher-status group. Presumably the lower-status use of the drugs was "leisure related" while the higher-status dispensation was "medicine" and, therefore, legitimate.

Cultural Attitudes to Drug Use

The creation of the initial narcotics legislation was buttressed by hysterical newspaper reports describing the purported widespread use and extremely dangerous effects of narcotics. Cook (1969) reports that, at the time of the hearings, Parliament relied not on social science surveys or techniques as indication of the extent of "the problem," but on newspaper clippings. For example, during the 1911 debate, King referred to a number of newspaper clippings including the following from the *Montreal Witness*, 23 November 1910. Entitled *Cocaine a Social Plague*, it quoted the views of a judge, Mr. R. Dupuis:

> This curse of cocaine has existed for a short time in the city. It is a real evil. It is a social plague and it goes on spreading so fearfully that it is time for society to take marked notice. Alcoholism and morphia are nothing compared to cocaine. It is the agent for the seduction of our daughters and the demoralization of your young men. . . ." (House of Commons Debates, 1910-1911: 2525. Cited in Cook, 1969: 40)

This practice of citing newspaper articles led to an uncritical acceptance of the "dope fiend" version of the drug user. Newspaper articles widely circulated the opinion that narcotics (including marihuana, which was added to the narcotics list in 1923) produced an instant moral depravity and complete loss of control. One Alberta judge, Emily Murphy, also known as Janey Canuck, wrote about the effects of marihuana:

> Persons using this narcotic, smoke the dried leaves of the plant, which has the effect of driving them completely insane. The addict loses all sense of moral responsibility. Addicts to this drug, while under its influence, are immune to pain, and could be severely injured without having any realization of this condition. While in this condition, they become raving maniacs and are liable to kill or indulge in any form of violence to other persons, using the most savage methods of cruelty without, as said before, any sense of moral responsibility. (Murphy, 1922: 333. Cited in Cook, 1969: 40)

This is either very potent marihuana or hysterics on Murphy's part. However, it should be pointed out that this attitude to intoxicants was not limited to narcotics. Minutes from debates on alcohol and tobacco show a similar hysterical view. Members of Parliament from various ridings submitted some startling opinions, including the notions that tobacco use stunted the physical and moral growth of young people, transforming them into cigarette fiends who could not distinguish right from wrong, and that it eroded their ability to effectively reproduce (Cook, 1969: 41).

These views of intoxicants appear to be based on a peculiar conception of the natural depravity of man. Church and state build up defenses against immorality, cruelty and sexual impulsiveness, and drugs wipe out all the protection from oneself that socialization produces. The drugs, whether cocaine, opium or marihuana (the legislators and popular columnists never bothered to study specific effects of specific drugs), all produced moral depravity. Everything that was considered immoral and reprehensible was viewed as a natural consequence of opium use (loss of virginity, promiscuity, miscegenation, violence, etc.).

The Racial Factor

The first anti-opium law was introduced the year after the anti-Asiatic riots of 1907. The Chinese were stereotyped and discriminated against. House of Commons Debates (1907-08) contained frequent complaints about these Chinese immigrants. "They come in swarms,'' refuse to marry, refuse to build schools, churches and houses, prefer to live in squalor and crowded hovels, etc. Many politicians thought that the opium trade should be eliminated simultaneously with the entire Chinese racial group. This view was supported in submissions made to Parliament by the Anti-Asiatic Exclusion League suggesting that the way to cure opiate addiction in whites was to deport the Asians (Cook, 1969: 43). Similar propaganda was offered in Murphy's book *The Black Candle* (1922). She suggested that the Chinese were trying to bring about the ruin of the entire Canadian society by getting the youth of Canada hooked on narcotics peddled by internationally directed Chinese drug rings. Authors, like Murphy, and many Vancouver politicians exploited the stereotypes of cool, calculating, Oriental drug dealers who were characterized as preying on the weaknesses of white women and encouraging their addiction in order to turn them to lives of sexual slavery.

The strength of these stereotypes, and the degree to which they relied on strong anti-Asian sentiments, is revealed by the fact that in 1921, when amendments were first suggested to the narcotics law requiring whipping, deportation, denial of the right of appeal, and extraordinary measures of search, these were temporarily defeated; when they were reintroduced in 1922 and directed specifically at Oriental traffickers, they were approved with enthusiasm. The senators allowed the extraordinary powers of search, except for private homes. The assumption they made was that the Chinese would not be exempted under this provision because they usually lived in ''shacks'' alongside stores, or apartments in their shops! Hence, the law would affect only the Chinese merchants, not the respectable Occidentals. The law was passed in 1922 and took effect in 1923.

Terry Chapman's examination (1976) of this period puts the observations about racism into greater historical perspective. There had been a great deal of animosity toward the Chinese ever since the CPR began to bring Chinese workers into Canada on a massive scale in the 1880s. The B.C. government tried to pass a law forbidding Chinese from owning land and stopping Chinese immigration. The federal government overruled these laws because they encroached on federal matters. To placate the people of B.C. they passed, as we have seen, the head tax on all Asian immigrants.

Also, there were two Royal Commissions, in 1885 and 1902, held to look into the question of Chinese immigration. Both received massive inputs from organized labour, which decried the slave wages the Chinese were accepting and the subsequent undercutting of white Canadian labourers. Unemployment of Canadian workers was universally blamed on the Asian immigrants. One of the conclusions of the 1902 commission stressed the demoralization of the manual worker and the disrepute attached to manual labour because of the willingness of the Chinese to work cheaply at jobs that had traditionally been done by white workers (Chapman, 1976: 28).

How was the leap made from labour tensions to opium legislation? The answer is that the labour movement during this period turned the economic problem of competing labour into a moral conflict. The position increasingly espoused by the labour movement was not merely that the Chinese were willing to work for less, but that this was indicative of their moral inferiority. In a petition to the federal government in 1899 (and included in the report of the 1902 Commission) labour argued:

> that the Chinese are non-assimilative, and having no intention of settled citizenship are in moral, social and sanitary status below the most inferior standard of Western life, and being used (the most of them being imported as coolies by labour-contracting organizations) accept less than the lowest living wages of

White labour, yet expend but little of their scanty earnings in the land of temporary adoption. (Cited in Chapman, 1976: 29)

This negative stereotyping of the Chinese was expanded. The press frequently carried
stories making reference to the Chinaman's heathenism, his loathsome habits (opium),
his numerical "invasion," the entrapment of women via opium addiction, as well as his
displacement of the organized white labourer. During this period, the notion of the
yellow peril became commonplace. The pro-white Anti-Asiatic League was formed under the banner "Canada for Canadians." The objectives of the League were to ensure
the maintenance of Western culture and Christian civilization. Politicians played into
the hands of these jingoists and racists.

For example, Prime Minister Borden, in his bid to get his Conservatives elected,
made this speech in Vancouver, September 24, 1907, just over two weeks after the
Anti-Asiatic riot of September 7:

> The Conservative party which brought B.C. into Confederation will make its
> aim that the province remains British and Canadian, inhabited and dominated
> by men in whose veins flows the blood of the great pioneering race which built
> up and developed not only Eastern, but Western Canada. (Printed in *The Cal-
> gary Herald*, 25 September, 1907. Cited in Chapman, 1976: 32)

A similar statement made by a Liberal member was carried in *The Calgary Herald*
of 23 July, 1907:

> Very soon we will have not only Asiatic labourers, but Asiatic employers as well,
> for they are fast coming in today. Even that is not the worst feature. If the flood
> keeps on we will have nothing but Asiatics in this part of the country. . . . (Cited
> in Chapman, 1976: 34)

It is true that about 95% of all the immigration via Vancouver was Chinese, Japanese and East Indian, and this large volume meant they did not have to assimilate, which
only exacerbated the stand-offish view of the Chinese that white Canadians had. Nonetheless they composed only 11.1% of the population in B.C.

In this climate all that was needed was some strange Oriental habit that could be
equated with the downfall of white Canadian society. Opium filled the bill.

The Narcotics Law in Perspective

We have argued that the status stratification system caused attention concerning the
use of narcotics to be focussed on the Chinese, the low-status distributors, and not the
medical profession. Narcotics and other intoxicants, such as tobacco, marihuana and
heroin, were all viewed in the same way, as potential causes of the most serious breaches
of the moral order. The abuse of narcotics was transformed by making this a moral
threat to the entire nation through associating the drugs with negative stereotypes of
Asians. Consequently, the moral crusade to control narcotics, undertaken initially by
Mackenzie King, was directed at a particular segment of society, the Chinese immigrants,
and relied on a sort of collective public hysteria about the grave deleterious effects of
these drugs on the national character. However, this belief won its wide popular support and its important political dimensions because of the economically based animosity towards Asians.

The massive influx of Asian labourers recruited to work cheaply on the railways could not be assimilated into the failing economic conditions of recession and inflation that marked the period following the completion of the railway and the first decade of the 20th century.

This interpretation reflects a point raised by Ian Taylor in his study of moral entrepreneurs (1982). Taylor argues that many crime waves, as well as anti-crime waves (for example, the prohibition movement), are mystifications of economic problems that misdirect our attention away from basic social conflicts or social contradictions. For instance, the alleged wave of muggings in England in the early 1970s fostered calls for more law and order policies and greater policing; yet massive unemployment contributed to the muggings, to the extent that any "wave" did occur. However, since the problem is defined socially as individual lawlessness, the conservative solution of more policing overlooks the economic unemployment that first generated the problem.

Other Restrictive Legislation Affecting Asians

The anti-opium law reflected a mobilization of hatred against an economically marginal group at a time when the stagnant economy could not absorb the immigrants. The economic tension also led to direct bars against Asian employment, as well as to a number of indirect actions that stereotyped and denigrated the threatening group. There was a range of punitive restrictions directed against the Asiatic population of Western Canada. These laws affected personal demeanor and voting and labour rights.

In 1876, B.C. law called for an annual $10 tax on Chinese with long hair kept in the shape of a "tail or queue." Two years later, the provincial law proposed that no one with hair over 5½ inches long could be eligible for work on the CPR. Health standards were cited as rationales in these laws. In the same year, the City of Victoria passed a law barring Chinese from employment on public work projects, and imposed a license fee for all Chinese working in the City. In 1900, B.C. law required immigrant workers, when asked, to write an application to the provincial secretary in some European language, to qualify for work. Failure to comply could result in a $500 fine, one year in jail and/or deportation. The law was overruled by Ottawa in 1900, but similar laws were passed (and overruled) in 1902, 1903, 1905, 1907 and 1908. Clearly, the white constituency was very supportive of these moves. These punitive laws were not restricted to the west. A 1914 Ontario law barred white women and girls from working in Chinese business establishments, and, in 1915, Quebec law required a massive license and inspection fee for all laundries, except those run by charitable organizations or by corporations. This effectively targeted the Chinese minority.

The B.C. Male Minimum Wage Act of 1925 set minimum wage levels well above the customary level of compensation typically accepted by the Chinese worker. In the same year, the federal Department of Marine and Fisheries restricted the number of licenses that could be given to non-English and non-Indian fishermen. There were restrictions barring Asians from entering nearly all the crafts and labour laws directed specifically at the Asians and barring them expressly from certain types of work in B.C. For example, the 1890 Coal Mines Regulation Act barred Chinese from mining. This was later quashed by Ottawa. There was also provincial legislation that prevented Asians from teaching in public schools, and caveats were attached to provincial work contracts that prevented contractors from hiring Chinese workers. This latter action was also quashed by Ottawa.

Voting Rights

In 1875, B.C. law deprived Chinese immigrants of the provincial vote. In 1895, this law was extended to cover all "Orientals and Asians." In 1896, the law was extended to cover municipal elections. Saskatchewan denied Chinese the provincial vote in 1905. And, in 1903, the Privy Council upheld the right of B.C. to deny the Japanese the vote. Similarly, in 1914, the Supreme Court upheld the right of B.C. to deny the Chinese the vote.

Voting affected the ability to do other things. One's name had to appear on the provincial voters' lists in order to get a B.C. liquor sale permit, or get a B.C. license to operate a pharmacy, or to study pharmacy or law at provincial institutions. Consequently, the voting restrictions effectively blocked certain avenues of educational and economic advancement (Adachi, 1976: 52). In 1919, the federal government passed a law that held that one could not vote in a federal election if one was barred from voting in a provincial election. These laws remained in effect until after the Second World War. The bar was lifted from Chinese Canadians in 1947 and from Japanese Canadians two years later (Adachi, 1976: 345).

Summary

This brief examination of several different laws illustrates that social causes or conditions dictate or influence the laws a society adopts. Laws do not respond to some external ideal of universal justice that transcends society and to which society naturally aligns itself. Only in mythology are laws passed from gods to mankind. In democracies, laws are passed by politicians, and are formed under a variety of conditions. We have focussed on several of these. First, we examined laws passed and changed in response to the economic aspirations of certain elite groups of society. This was reflected in the evolution of the vagrancy laws in England, and in East Africa. In the guise of controlling unruly public behaviour, vagrancy laws were a method of exerting control over marginal or rebellious elements of the labour force. Economic considerations likewise controlled the evolution of the law of theft in the Carrier Case where, contrary to the common law, the absence of the element of trespass was disregarded to register a conviction, thereby safeguarding the English trade in wool.

The second type of situation that contributes to the introduction of criminal law is law reform. Laws are frequently passed to correct a perceived harm. We examined cases in which the circulation of supposedly harmful drugs, as well as tainted meat, was brought under control by new laws. However, in the case of the regulation of the meat-packing industry, we saw that state intervention was actually in the interests of the elite members of the groups being regulated. The same cannot be said of those controlled under the 1970 U.S. Comprehensive Drug Bill and the initial Canadian Anti-Opium laws. In both cases, the criminalization of the behaviour was clearly denunciatory and discriminating. In the one case, the law was limited to ensure that it was not extended to regulate legitimate harmful drugs, while in the other case, it was designed to target low-status opium users, especially Chinese users. So even laws introduced as reforms of illicit conduct can have an underlying economic aspect. Also, in examining attempts to reform behaviour, we explored the role of moral entrepreneurship. This may be undertaken by specific interest groups, as in the case for prohibition led by the temperance movements, by newspapers and public-opinion makers, as in the advent of the American sexual psychopathy laws, or by individual entrepreneurs such as Mackenzie King and his anti-opium crusade. Our discussion of the social context of the anti-opium laws suggests that moral entrepreneurship is the *process* by which a call for change is undertaken. It is not an explanation of why such a change is sought. In the cases of prohibition and the narcotics legislation, the interests of various elements of society dictated the content of the laws sought. The laws were attempts by particular groups to have their interests and values reflected in legislation by denunciating in criminal law the kinds of behaviours already denounced in the group's religion, ideology or beliefs.

In the introduction to this chapter, we identified several elements that are relevant when determining whether laws are good laws. These were politicality, uniformity, specificity and penal sanction. These are not narrow concerns of jurisprudence but are important ideals in democratic forms of society. They provide grounds for making and for challenging laws. The question of politicality has arisen in most of the illustrations we have examined. The thrust of the vagrancy laws, the drug laws, and prohibition are of note in sociological studies because they smack of one-sidedness, of political domination of one group over another by virtue of its control over the legal apparatus. In other words, they raise questions about the politicality of the law. In addition, we find many of these laws objectionable because they defy the ideal of uniformity. For example, the punitive narcotics legislation pinpointed Asian users and avoided the high-status medical pushers; contemporary narcotics legislation targets potheads for criminal processing but fails to regulate corporate Valium pushers. The differences in penal sanctions reflect this differential labelling: entrepreneurs who import illicit narcotics face a minimum sentence of seven years while entrepreneurs who import Valium deduct the costs from their income tax and operate with impunity despite the harmfulness of their brand of narcotics.

Politicality and uniformity exist in a special tension in democratic states. To recognize that laws are political or conventional, and that they are self-serving for those groups who control their passage, is to detect a loss of innocence in man-made law that was never problematic when laws were given to society from above. To say that the laws are politically motivated is to raise the question of who is benefitting and who is suffering from them. The standard of uniformity tends to control the politicality of the law. While legal systems in every country are politically organized, the hallmark of democratic societies is the uniformity of law. This puts enormous importance on the legal standards by which criminal behaviour is judged. Obviously, to be judged criminal one must be more than simply a foreigner and more than merely unusual. The distinguishing elements of criminal behaviour have preoccupied students of law for centuries. They are the subject of our next chapter.

FURTHER READING

Ken Adachi, *The Enemy That Never Was*. Toronto: McClelland and Stewart, 1976.
Patrick Devlin, *The Enforcement of Morals*. London: Oxford University Press, 1959.
Troy Duster, *The Legislation of Morality: Law, Drugs and Moral Judgement*. New York: Free Press, 1970.

James Gray, *Booze, The Impact of Whiskey on the Prairie West*. Scarborough: New American Library, 1972.

H.L.A. Hart, *Law, Liberty and Morality*. Stanford: Stanford University Press, 1963.

Emily Murphy, *The Black Candle*. Toronto: Thomas Allen, 1922.

Phillipe Nonet and Philip Selznick, *Law and Society in Transition: Toward Responsive Law*. New York: Harper and Row, 1978.

C.E. Reasons and R.M. Rich (eds.), *The Sociology of Law: A Conflict Perspective*. Toronto: Butterworth, 1978.

M.E. Tigar and M.R. Levy, *Law and the Rise of Capitalism*. New York: Monthly Press, 1977.

Austin T. Turk, *Criminality and Legal Order*. Chicago: Rand McNally, 1969.

CHAPTER 2

The Elements of Criminal Behaviour

Introduction

In his history of the development of criminal law, C.R. Jeffrey (1957) points out that while a concern for morality is found in all human groups, the control of behaviour under a set of specifically criminal laws emerged in British society following the eleventh century Norman invasion. Prior to that time, wrongful behaviour, whether murder, theft or rape, was viewed as an interfamilial or intertribal affair, and was settled by acts of revenge or feud, or by payment of material compensation. Saxon law even specified the magnitude of penalty for various transgressions. The Normans, in an effort to enforce the centrality of English society under the authority of the King, redefined wrongful behaviour by members of feudal groups as a breach of the King's peace, and the King was made the victim of the wrongful act. Consequently, transgressors became answerable to the King and a system of circuit judges was devised to enforce the King's peace, and to assess penalties for his coffers. Today, while the victim of a harmful act typically has recourse against an assailant by invoking the criminal law in the fashion of the Normans, he or she can also bring a civil action or tort for the same transgression in the fashion of the Saxons. Criminal law is not a static entity; just as it came into being under the political struggle of the Normans and the Saxons, so it has continued to evolve.

Some of the central questions dealt with by legal scholars throughout common law history concern the criteria of criminal behaviour. What is it that distinguishes criminal behaviour from other behaviour? What are the necessary aspects of the criminal act? How do these distinguishing components interact? These questions tend to offset the notions of some sociologists of law who try to simply reduce criminal laws to the class bias of the lawmakers. While certain laws clearly reflect this type of influence, it is important to remember that the modern state is composed of numerous interest groups even within the major social classes. Consequently, any account of the social origins of law must be sensitive to the complexities of influence-group relationships. Behaviour is not criminal merely by virtue of its class or group origin. Nor is behaviour criminal just because it is called criminal. Contrary to the position of the labelling theorists (Becker, 1963; Glassner, 1982), if mere labels were sufficient to make behaviour criminal, we could never experience injustice nor criticize our system of laws. Part of our ability to do so comes from our sense of what makes laws good, and what makes conduct bad. In the last chapter we touched on aspects of the former question. This chapter describes seven distinguishing elements of criminal conduct.

Crime as Harm

Criminal behaviour is conduct deemed to be harmful. Typically, criminal behaviour involves causing pain, distress, or loss to other individuals, groups, or to one's self, or to property. The existence of this harm, usually associated with the imagery of a victim or an injured party, provides for an intuitive link between crimes in civil society and sins or evil in religious society. There is merit to the idea that crime is secular evil. It involves conduct that is hurtful and wrongful and, indeed, often the religious morality of a group determines what things they criminalize (Erikson, 1966).

In view of this criterion of harm, some critics of the criminal law have argued that many things currently under the control of the state are none of the law's business (Geis, 1974). Drug and alcohol use and addiction, prostitution-related activity like soliciting, homosexuality between consenting individuals, public nudity, suicide and suicide assistance, abortion and euthanasia are victimless crimes. They are victimless, it is argued, because the participants willingly and knowingly participate in these activities. However, critics of these victimless crimes point out that the costs of alcohol detoxification centres and of drug withdrawal clinics are borne by the public. Also, the increased medical costs that result from self-inflicted diseases like cirrhosis, and from injuries inflicted on others by the overindulgent are also borne generally. Consequently, the costs of many so-called victimless crimes are subsidized both by the anonymous taxpayer and by the insured person whose lifestyle results in few medical and personal insurance claims. However, these harms or costs result not from simple alcohol or drug use, but overindulgence and abuse. Offenses such as prostitution, gambling and heroin use also generate revenue for organized crime, which has more obvious victims. Loan sharking, bribery, and the infiltration of legitimate businesses are all bank-rolled by vice rackets such as prostitution (Whyte, 1955). However, this observation argues as much for the legalization of these vices as for their continued proscription, in that legalization would remove major sources of funding for organized crime.

Other victimless crimes, such as nudism, offend the public morality in a marginal though obvious way. It is one thing to pursue alternative lifestyle practices such as nudity or homosexuality in the confines of one's own home or one's own social club or social setting. However, "streaking" is a defiant public act. It flaunts a counter morality. It challenges the taken-for-granted expectations of public life, and attempts to disrupt the sense of civility or decency of public life. (See Law Reform Commission, 1978: 7-8.) However, the harm of streaking is nothing more than transient discomfort or even amusement. Legally speaking, this is not a criminal but only a mischievious act. In

R. v. Springer (1975), the accused was acquitted of a charge of committing an indecent act following a naked run through a football stadium in Regina. Since this was done as a joke, and there was little evidence of moral turpitude, there was no crime. The same reasoning applied in *R. v. Benolkin et al* (1977) where a group of three young men were acquitted on appeal of a charge of public nudity that arose from an incident of "skinny dipping on a sand bar in the South Saskatchewan River." Obviously being nude in public is not enough. Nudity has to be associated with some motive of sexual immorality, deviation or exploitation. However, the deviation need not be specifically sexual. Charges of public nudity and indecent exposure were frequently laid against members of the Sons of Freedom Doukhobor religious sect of Western Canada to control their collective defiance of Canadian law and traditional values. The more radical sect members resisted integration into traditional religious, economic and educational institutions, and when confronted by the police burned property, not exclusively their own, and frequently paraded nude through numerous towns, particularly in southern British Columbia. As a result of their activities, sect members faced charges of arson, morality offenses, as well as actions of neglect that resulted in the seizure of their children. In fact the provision of the Criminal Code covering public nudity was passed by Parliament to control the Doukhobors. In 1932, 725 naked parading Doukhobors were arrested, 150 children made wards of the government, and the remainder of the group sentenced to confinement in a special camp on Piers Island in the Strait of Georgia (Holt, 1964). Consequently, nudism can be variously harmless or harmful depending on the significance of the threat and the significance of the motive. Single individuals thumbing their noses at society by streaking through the Academy Awards, or college engineers defiantly leading "Lady Godiva" through a campus present little threat to the dominant morality. However, the collective nudism of a radical religious minority group associated with both a public defiance of authority figures and with episodes of arson, internecine murder and child neglect, is taken more seriously. Nudism, the very way in which the defiance was expressed, was targeted to attempt to control the entire countercultural lifestyle.

The same concern has been applied to public displays or advertisements of homosexuality or public advertisements of sex for sale. These are viewed as serious moral harms. They reflect a more all-encompassing challenge to the dominant morality, and their occasional public character is a source of grave alarm to heterosexual couples. While streaking is a transient repudiation of the norms of civility, prostitution and "flagrant" homosexuality represent entirely unorthodox ways of life and fundamentally different patterns of interpersonal affiliation. Since they are perceived to vary so greatly from conventions, they are deemed outrageous and harmful to the public, that is, the morality of the majority. Consequently, though individual participants may gravitate voluntarily toward these activities for a variety of reasons, they are deemed harmful, if not to the direct participants, then to the body politic. This harm is more symbolic than real. Notably, we control the particularly *public* manifestations of these activities. It is soliciting for the purposes of prostitution that is illegal, not prostitution *per se*. Section 158 of the Criminal Code of Canada indicates that acts of buggery and gross indecency that take place in *private* between persons who are both 21 years or more of age, or who are married, are not unlawful.

Critics of victimless crimes argue that they are victimless only because the victim is never heard from. The paramount case is abortion. While a woman has an obvious right to control the developments within her own body, this right is tempered first by the claim of the father to his potential offspring, and second, by the offspring itself.

Which of these rights must be given priority is the subject of much discussion. Right-to-life advocates interpret the fetus in terms of its potential as a human being. As a person the fetus would have legal protection from homicide. Indeed, under Canadian law, it is illegal to procure a miscarriage. However, the degree to which the matter is compounded by competing interests is reflected in the fact that it is legal to produce a miscarriage in a woman if, in the opinion of the therapeutic abortion committee of an accredited hospital, "the continuation of the pregnancy . . . would be likely to endanger her life or health" (Section 251 (4)). This allowance has opened the way for the exercise of the rights of women. Proponents of the women's movement view the exercise of the right of the woman to choose to terminate or continue pregnancy as primary. Consequently, they give a liberal interpretation to what things can endanger health. Since there is frequently substantial stress associated with pregnancy and mothering and with the change in lifestyle associated with mothering, proponents of the "right to choose" position find little block to abortion in Canadian law. The number, and the rate, of abortions in Canada have more than doubled from 1971 to 1979.

TABLE 1
Abortions and Abortion Rates in Canada 1971-1979

Year	Total Number of Reported Therapeutic Abortions	Abortion Rate per 1000 Females 15-44 Years Old	Abortion Rate per 100 Live Births	Number of Canadians Having Abortions in the U.S.A
1971	30,923	6.6	8.6	
1972	38,853	8.2	11.2	6,573
1973	43,201	8.9	12.6	5,501
1974	48,136	9.6	13.7	4,299
1975	49,311	9.6	13.7	4,394
1976	54,478	10.3	15.1	4,234
1977	57,564	10.6	15.9	2,300
1978	62,290	11.3	17.4	1,802
1979	65,043	11.6	17.8	1,071

Source: Statistics Canada, *Therapeutic Abortions 1979*, Ottawa: Minister of Supplies and Services, 1979, p. 16.

Note that in 1979 the reliance on American clinics dropped to a sixth of the 1972 figure. The real battles today occur when advocates of the rival positions compete for control of the administration of hospitals to establish or abolish therapeutic abortion committees. Since science cannot tell at what point a fetus becomes human, the matter unavoidably falls to the political process. The decision as to whether a fetus is human is a political decision, as is the decision as to when abortion is criminal and when legal. Canadian law has recognized elements in both positions, and rather than coming out either for abortion on demand or for a blanket condemnation of all abortions, has shifted the legal question to the medical domain by allowing doctors to determine on a case-by-case basis which right prevails. Because the resolution of the conflicting interests has resulted in attempts to control the boards of directors of accredited hospitals, the matter is again put into the political arena, though at a lower level. One of the costs of this solution has been significant variations in the availability and frequency of abortions between regions, as indicated in Table 2.

When considering abortion in the context of harm and victimless crimes, we have no absolute answers. Different parties have conflicting rights and freedoms. Freedoms

TABLE 2
Therapeutic Abortion Committees, Hospitals and Abortions by
Province, 1979

Province	Number of Therapeutic Abortion Committees	Number of Public General Hospitals	Number of Abortions	Abortions per 1000 Females 15-44 Years Old	Abortions per 100 Live Births
Nfld.	5	34	645	4.9	6.3
P.E.I.	2	8	46	1.7	2.4
N.S.	12	45	1,511	7.8	12.2
N.B.	8	33	447	2.8	4.1
Quebec	30	124	8,609	5.6	8.7
Ontario	109	199	30,671	15.2	25.2
Manitoba	8	77	1,624	7.0	10.0
Sask.	10	132	1,645	8.0	9.7
Alberta	26	116	6,872	13.9	18.6
B.C.	57	92	12,716	21.1	33.1
Yukon	1	–	113	19.5	22.6
NWT	2	3	141	13.7	11.0
	270	863	65,043	11.6	17.8

Source: Statistics Canada, *Therapeutic Abortions 1979*, Ottawa: Minister of Supplies and Services, 1979, p. 17, p. 56.

can be construed in different ways. For example, the Ayotollah Khomeini argues that Islam is freedom, Islam will make you free. But, Iranians are not permitted to "harm themselves" by seeking corrupting Western lifestyles, rock and roll music, alcohol, and denim jeans. The definition of harmfulness is intertwined with politics and morality.

While some idealists will despair that the perception of harm ultimately comes down to politicality, this is not such a bleak situation. The politicality of harmfulness reflects an ability to modify and rehabilitate our conception of crime as our morals, science and experience change and as different groups in society are able to change the public's sensitivity to what is defined as criminally harmful. Clearly over the last quarter century Canadians have witnessed a liberalization of many laws, including those controlling abortion and homosexuality. While these changes do not refect an outright endorsement, they nonetheless reflect concessions to counter moralities as their proponents come to political prominence and as we reassess the harm of victimless vice.

No Crime without Law

A second major criteria of criminal behaviour is the principle of *nullum crimen sine lege* (no crime without law). This principle respects the difference between simple harmfulness, which is indicated by our ethics, and harmfulness that is actually prohibited by the law. To be a criminal, it is not enough to be anti-social or sinful: the act must specifically be forbidden in a penal law. In others words, crime is not harmful per se, but is conventionally harmful. Many harmful things are not crimes. It was legal to hunt the bison to the point of extinction on the 19th century plains of North America, despite the dependency of numerous indigenous peoples on these herds. It is legal in the 20th century to hunt whales on the high seas to the point of extinction. It is lawful today to exhale carcinogenic cigarette smoke into the air other people must breathe, despite the known danger to non-smokers. It is lawful in some provinces for a dog to bite a person without redress, though two bites in Ontario is sufficient for extermination. It is lawful for companies and towns in some regions to discharge untreated sewage and poisonous industrial waste into drinking water. It is lawful for governments to artificially expand the money supply and to contribute to inflation while pensioners are maintained on fixed pensions. Consequently, not all evils are crimes.

Some harmful activities are downplayed because of the balance of powers in the state. However, the issue becomes dicey when the balance of power shifts and when previously non-criminal acts are retroactively viewed as crimes. Nearly all revolutions, whether from the political right or the left, have experienced this situation. Previously lawful activities are tirelessly redressed by the firing squad as the new revolutionary elites retrospectively define previously conventional activity as criminal. The common law tradition has resisted this impulse. As Nettler (1978:34) has indicated, the law in Western societies provides the individual with an inadvertent civil rights safeguard: the existence of a specifically proscribed set of criminal conducts shows the individual on which side of the law he or she stands. Pragmatically, this underscores the difference between what is socially disvalued or disliked and what is actually criminal. Again the principle of *nullum crimen sine lege* points to the politicality of the criminal law.

Actus Reus: The Physical Element

The *actus reus* is the guilty or wrongful act. It is the physical element of the crime. Generally, the *actus reus* of a crime consists of a certain type of conduct, a consequence of that conduct, and/or the circumstances surrounding it. In a case of murder, the act of pointing the gun and pulling the trigger is the conduct. An example of consequence might be cutting the brake cable of another's car, thereby ensuring the driver will come to harm. Circumstance is a more technical matter. It refers to the specific requirements spelled out in the law. For example, section 143 of the Criminal Code, which was in effect until 1983, dealt with rape. It read:

143. A male person commits rape when he has sexual intercourse with a female person who is not his wife
   (a) without her consent, or
   (b) with her consent if the consent
      (i) is extorted by threats or fear of bodily harm
      (ii) is obtained by personating her husband, or
      (iii) is obtained by false and fraudulent representation as to the nature and quality of the act.

Given this wording, to demonstrate in court that section 143 had been violated it would be necessary to establish the following circumstances: that the complainant was a female, that the accused was a male, that they were not married, that sexual intercourse occurred and following section (a), that the act of intercourse transpired without the woman's consent. Where there was no actual penetration, the *actus reus* might not substantiate rape, but attempted rape or indecent assault. If there had been consent, it would be necessary following paragraph (b) that the consent was invalid and meaningless because it had been obtained by threats, impersonations of the husband or by false advertising about the status of the act. For example, in *R. v. Harms* (1944) it was held that the accused's intercourse with a woman if obtained on the pretext that it would correct certain health problems from which she suffered, constituted rape because this pretext falsely misrepresented the nature and quality of the act. Presumably this interpretation would extend to patients who are administered "doses" of intercourse on psychiatric couches to alleviate "sexual maladjustment." The *actus reus* under paragraph (b) would require that consent to intercourse be given under the circumstance of false pretense.

In 1983 the crime of rape was eliminated from the Criminal Code and a new law was instituted. Sexual crimes became part of the assault laws. Assault is the application of force or the threat of force against another person without the person's consent or with consent obtained by force or fraud.

244. (1) A person commits an assault when
    (a) without the consent of another person, he applies force intentionally to that other person, directly or indirectly;
    (b) he attempts or threatens, by an act or gesture, to apply force to another person, if he has, or causes that other person to believe upon reasonable grounds that he has present ability to effect his purpose; or
    (c) while openly wearing or carrying a weapon or an imitation thereof, he accosts or impedes another person or begs.
(2) This section applies to all forms of assault, including sexual assault, sexual assault with a weapon, threats to a third party or causing bodily harm and aggravated sexual assault.

Where the *actus reus* of rape involved sexual intercourse, the new law covers any kind of assault involving sexual activity. Kissing, fondling or sexual intercourse without the consent of the victim could constitute an offense under section 244. Unlike the old section 143, under the new law, both males and females can be victims of sexual assault, both males and females can be charged with breaching section 244 and a spouse can be charged by the other spouse. These provisions are in marked contrast to the *actus reus* of rape which was confined primarily to a man who had sexual intercourse with a woman other than his wife without her consent. Unlike rape, a conviction for sexual assault does not require the corroboration of the testimony of the victim by other evidence, and the "recency" of the complaint cannot be used to assess its truthfulness. Previously, if the testimony of a victim of rape was uncorroborated by other evidence, the trial judge would instruct the jury about the danger of convicting the accused. Also, the delay in registering a complaint was sometimes held against the victim. The new law also clarifies the question of consent. If the victim of rape was perceived to have had consented to intercourse, this belief, no matter how improbable in light of the circumstances could be offered as a reasonable excuse to the charge, as in the Pappajohn case:

    The accused was charged with the rape of a woman whom he had engaged to sell some property. The evidence indicated that they spent the afternoon together and both had quite a lot of liquor to drink. They eventually went to his house to discuss the sale where according to the complainant the accused took off her clothes and repeatedly raped her. Also during the last hour she was bound and gagged but was able to escape. According to the accused once they reached the house they began to kiss and she removed her necklace in the living room. They then went to the bedroom where she permitted him to remove her clothes which he folded up. He also asked her to remove his cuff-links but she refused. He testified that he then undressed and they had intercourse. He testified that to stimulate sexual climax he engaged in bondage by tying her wrists and tying a bow-tie around her neck. Her behaviour then changed and she started crying but would take no assistance from him. He left the room and when he returned she was gone. In his statement to the police the accused stated that the complainant did "not violently" object when they first went to bed and did not "resist very much". The trial Judge refused to instruct the jury that if the accused honestly believed that the complainant consented, whether or not she did in fact consent, then he should be acquitted. The sole issue left with the jury was whether she did in fact consent. An appeal by the accused from his conviction to the British Columbia Court of Appeal was dismissed. . . . An honest but mistaken belief that the victim is consenting to the acts of intercourse is a defence to a charge of rape and such a belief is not required to be based on reasonable grounds. However, it is not every case of rape in which the accused asserts that the victim was consenting that requires the trial Judge to leave this defence to the jury. As with other defences there must be in the evidence some basis upon which the defence can rest, some evidence to convey a sense of reality to the defence. In this case there was a fundamental conflict between the stories told by the accused and the complainant. Her version excluded consent and any possible mistaken belief in consent. His version was of actual consent and no suggestion of any mistaken belief could arise. The other evidence did not support a defence of mistaken belief as opposed to actual consent. To require the putting of the alternative defence of mistaken belief in consent there must be some evidence beyond the mere assertion of belief in consent by defence counsel. This evidence must appear from, or be supported by, sources other than the accused in order to give it any air of reality. (*Pappajohn v. the Queen*, pp. 481-482)

The new legislation states that an accused may offer as an excuse to the charge his or her belief that the victim consented to the conduct; however, the judge is entitled to draw to the jury's attention the *honesty* of the belief, as well as its *reasonableness*. In contrast, the reasonableness of Pappajohn's belief was not an issue under the old rape law (though he was convicted nonetheless). Lastly, the new legislation strictly limits the introduction of evidence about the victim's previous moral reputation and allows the victim the power to bar publication or broadcast of identity in the media.

The maximum penalty for rape was life imprisonment. Now, the penalties for sexual assault depend on the seriousness of the case. There are three tiers of penalties reflecting the degree of harm of the crime. A simple sexual assault, like a simple assault, can be dealt with either as a summary conviction offense, which has a maximum penalty of six months imprisonment, or as an indictable offense with a maximum penalty of ten years. The second tier of penalties applies if bodily harm occurs, if the assailant carries, uses or threatens to use a weapon, if the assailant threatens to cause bodily harm to a third person, or if there is more than one party to the assault. The maximum penalty is 14 years imprisonment. The most serious level of assault, is aggravated sexual assault, which carries a maximum penalty of life imprisonment. It applies where sexual assault is accompanied by wounding, maiming, disfiguring or endangering the life of the victim.

The introduction of the sexual assault law fundamentally redefines the character of sexual offenses in Canada. Where the rape law stressed the sexual aspects of these offenses, the new law stresses the violent character of these crimes. They are now a species of assault. The law also revises the conduct of the criminal trial by minimizing the chance for the harrassment of the victim who testifies at the trial, and, in recognition of variations in the gravity of the crime, allows the courts to proceed on different levels of the charge depending on differences in the physical elements of the crime.

The *actus reus* of an offense refers to a certain illegal conduct, a consequence of this conduct or specific circumstances described in the law. The *actus reus* or physical element includes all the elements of the offense except for the *mens rea*.

Mens Rea: The Guilty Mind

The rule of *mens rea* refers to the requirement that, in a criminal act, the individual must be wilfully engaged in the commission of the act. In other words, one must foresee the consequences of one's behaviour and be aware of the circumstances that make the behaviour criminal. The implication here is that one does not inadvertently commit a crime; one must mean to do it. The mental element is construed in three ways: intention, knowledge and recklessness (Clarke, Barnhorst and Barnhorst, 1977: 25ff).

Intention

Intention is the most obvious form of the *mens rea*: it is the subjective monitoring and control of conduct. I pull the trigger because I intend to shoot. I light the fuse with the intent to explode a bomb. I break the window with the intent to enter a building. Intention here refers to the immediate control we possess over our conduct and the use of such control to fulfil our objectives and desires.

Intention is often distinguished from motivation. Motivation is considered the final product one aspires to, or the longer term objective. It refers to the end state that the commission of the act will achieve. Sutherland and Cressey (1966: 13) distinguish these two things in the following example. "If a man decides to kill his starving children because he feels they will pass on to a better world, his motive is good, but his intention is wrong." So, as he grinds up the glass into the hamburger, though he may have a heart of gold, he is nonetheless pursuing murder to attain his longer term objectives.

The distinction between intention and motivation is often questionable in cases of police deviance. Even though a national security force might be motivated to thwart illegal attempts to change the nature of the state by frustrating radical organizations, when such efforts take the form of burning the premises where meetings occur, kidnapping the participants and stealing their records and files, these activities are criminal inasmuch as they are known to contravene the law and are intentionally executed (McDonald Commission, 1981; Dion, 1982; Shearing, 1981). Members of the RCMP have faced charges for exactly these things.

A parallel situation occurred in July, 1979 in Calgary where a detective conspired with a known thief cum police informer to repeatedly burgle a private residence in order to gather incriminating evidence against the occupant. The thief entered the premises and removed articles that were irrelevant to the police investigation. During the third entry a photographer and reporter from *The Calgary Herald*, acting on a tip from the thief, staked out the house and took pictures of two detectives assisting the thief to break and enter. The thief was ultimately convicted of break and enter but the detectives were never charged. In fact, after seeing their photographs in the local paper, they launched a suit for damages, and the matter was settled out of court. In law, it is unclear whether their behaviour can be construed as criminal. The law regarding break and enter requires that the culprit undertake the act with the intention of committing an indictable offense — presumably theft. Section 306 (1) of the Criminal Code of Canada reads "every one who breaks and enters a place with intent to commit an indictable offense therein" is liable to a penalty of life imprisonment in the case of a private dwelling place, or 14 years otherwise. Similarly section 307 reads "every one who without lawful excuse, the proof of which lies upon him, enters or is in a dwelling-house with intent to commit an indictable offense therein is guilty of an indictable offense and is liable to imprisonment for ten years." Since the detectives' intention was to gather evidence and not to commit some offense in the dwelling place, it is questionable whether any conviction could be registered. In fact, it is the position of the police that this reasoning applies whether or not the law expressly speaks about the "intent to commit an indictable offense." In other words, all police deviance, if undertaken with the intent to catch criminals, must be allowed. In the case of illegal entry, this attitude expressly contravenes the citizen's right to be free from unreasonable search and seizure as outlined in the Charter of Rights and Freedoms. Canadian courts that fail to control deviant police acts because of the lofty motives of the officers obviously leave the door open for systematic abuse of process.

Jean-Paul Brodeur (1981) suggests that police reasoning in such unlawful acts invokes a new legal concept, the *finis reus*. The *finis reus*, a positive end the state seeks through unorthodox police practices, is cited as justification for illegal behaviour. Presumably it is meant to supercede the immediate unlawful intention of the police officer in favour of the longer term benefits to society. The problem with this special type of reasoning employed by overzealous police agencies is that it is without legal foundation (see McDonald Commission, Second Report, Vol. I, 1983: 359-402). Motivation, as in the *finis reus*, does not excuse intention.

Knowledge

The second method by which *mens rea* is determined is knowledge. A person may have the guilty mind even if he did not undertake an activity with clear intent to break a law, but if he finds that subsequently his conduct is in contravention of the law. Perjury is a good instance. Few individuals take the stand with the express intention to mislead the court. However, they may find that under questioning they begin to guard their statements and avoid incriminating admissions even though they know this results in a criminally inaccurate picture of the evidence. Another illustration of knowledge can be gathered from the former rape law. A man who impersonated a woman's husband in order to obtain the woman's consent for sexual intercourse, knowingly obtained such consent in a criminal way. The *mens rea* consisted of the knowledge that the consent was deceptively and falsely obtained.

Recklessness

Lastly, *mens rea* can be construed in recklessness. Persons who refuse to exhibit care and control of themselves and their possessions, and who consequently injure others can be held accountable for their behaviour just as though they had purposefully undertaken the injury. For example, someone who practices target shooting in a school yard, and who accidentally kills a child, can be held guilty of homicide, whatever the subjective intention, as a result of the recklessness and negligence of his or her conduct.

Exceptions

In Canadian law there are some important exceptions to the rule of *mens rea*. For example, there are a number of situations in which persons will be liable to murder charges if they cause the death of another while committing or attempting to commit treason, sexual assault, abduction, robbery, burglary, or arson or escape custody. This holds whether or not they intend to cause death and whether or not they are aware that a death will likely be caused by their behaviour. Specifically, if in the commission of one of these crimes or in the course of getting away the criminal means to hurt someone or to stop their breath for the purpose of committing the crime or of getting away, or is carrying a weapon that produces, even accidentally, another person's death, then the criminal will be liable to a charge of murder under section 213 of the Criminal Code. In these cases, the accused is liable to a charge of murder even though the specific intention to murder may be subjectively lacking.

Under the Narcotic Control Act, a person can be liable to a charge of trafficking in a narcotic if he sells or circulates a narcotic or any substance which he *represents* as, or *pretends* to be a narcotic. In other words, though you may intend to defraud by selling sugar or milk as heroin, the wording of the law makes you liable to actual trafficking in a narcotic despite your intention. This matter is compounded by the fact that you cannot offer as a lawful excuse for a crime the explanation that you were trying to commit another crime. It is no excuse for attempted murder that you were only trying to occasion bodily harm or wounding. Similarly, it is no excuse to claim attempted fraud for a charge of trafficking in narcotics (See Parker, 1983: 291).

There are some other considerations in weighing the significance of the guilty mind. The criminal law has responded to the growth of the psychological sciences in recognizing that the reliability of the mental element is subject to great variation, and that in certain cases the formation of the mind or the intention may not be sound or complete. This is the case in situations of duress, in situations of insanity, and in cases regarding the young.

Duress and Necessity

Necessity and duress are similar though not equivalent considerations. In certain situations, they may be offered as excuses that mitigate the degree of responsibility for the commission of a criminal act by pointing to the lack of real choice faced by the accused. Necessity concerns a situation in which natural forces curtail the choice of individuals and necessitate the commission of a crime. In the British case of *R. v. Dudley and Stephens* (1884), the accused were charged with homicide in a cabin boy's death. Several people abandoned a sinking ship for the safety of a small open rowboat. While adrift on the high seas, the accused killed and ate the dying cabin boy and thereby survived to be rescued. Their defense of necessity was rejected by the court, though they were convicted not of murder, but of manslaughter, and received relatively light jail terms. The court held that the evil avoided by the crime must be greater than the evil inflicted by it. The court was not moved by the argument that one life was sacrificed to save two lives since it was not clear that the death of the three was inevitable for no one could foretell the hour of rescue (Parker, 1983: 236).

Duress or compulsion is a more technical matter. The Criminal Code spells out certain circumstances in which a person, who is forced by others to commit a crime, may be excused because of duress or compulsion. Section 17 specifically states that such an excuse cannot apply to certain crimes (treason, murder, piracy, attempted murder, assisting in sexual assault, forcible abduction, robbery, causing bodily harm, or arson), that it only applies where the individual is facing threats of imminent death or grievous injury where such threats are made by someone immediately present at the time of the offense, and where the person is not participating with the group committing the offense.

In *R. v. Carker* (1967), the accused pleaded he had been compelled to trash his own prison cell during a riot "in the course of which a substantial body of prisoners, shouting in unison from their separate cells, threatened the accused, who was not joining in the disturbance, that if he did not break the plumbing fixture in his cell he would be kicked in the head, his arms would be broken and he would get a knife in the back at the first opportunity" (Clarke, Barnhorst and Barnhorst, 1977: 55). As in the previous case of necessity, the court rejected this defense of duress because Carker, being locked up in his own cell, was not facing threats of *immediate* harm or loss of life as required in section 17. His excuse of compulsion was rejected. This rather narrow reading of duress or compulsion overlooked the fact that Carker would probably have been attacked subsequently. However, this situation would not have been a certainty, for Carker could have spent the rest of his sentence in protective custody or could have been transferred to another institution.

Maturity and Culpability

The second illustration of the idea that criminal responsibility is a function of the ability to form an intention is associated with age. Where early English criminal codes hanged young and old alike for criminal infractions, we have evolved the notion that young people do not have the same capacity for evil intentions as older people. In Canada, prior to 1981, no person under the age of seven years could be convicted of an offense. Likewise, no child between the ages of 7 and 13 could be held responsible for a criminal act unless first, the child's competence to judge the nature and consequences of the child's conduct, and second, the child's ability to appreciate that it was wrong, were expressly demonstrated by a prosecutor. Furthermore, in some cases, the law expressly ruled out the culpability of children on the basis of age. For example, section 147 indicated that no male child under the age of 14 could be convicted of rape. Similarly, no person under the age of 14 was deemed capable of giving consent in sexual matters. However, the introduction of the Young Offenders Act (1981) changes the age of culpability and will replace the Juvenile Delinquency Act (1908).

The new law will raise the age of accountability from 7 to 12. No one under the age of 12 will be held responsible for a criminal act. The Young Offenders Act applies to those from 12 years of age to those under 18 years of age. Unlike the old Juvenile Delinquency Act, the Young Offenders Act does not apply to status offenses. Previously, adolescents who committed a crime were ruled to be in "a state of delinquency." However, under the notion of status offenses they were also liable to be found in a state of delinquency for being promiscuous or having some other vice. Consequently, adolescents were more liable to control than adults for doing the same things. The justification for this approach was that the delinquent was actually a misdirected child who required guidance and direction by the juvenile courts.

In keeping with this, the old Act allowed for indefinite periods of judicial control over the juvenile, made appeals nearly impossible, and made no provision for the delinquent to be represented by a lawyer. By contrast, while still recognizing the diminished accountability of juveniles, the Young Offenders Act allows rights of appeal, of bail, of public hearings, and of representation by counsel, and imposes finite limits on the period of control of offenders. It also permits the voluntary diversion of the offender to non-judicial settings, such as community service programs and special education programs, as well as counselling and restitution agreements, provided the offense is not serious. The Youth Court itself will have a variety of sentencing options for disposing of cases. Judges will be free to make absolute discharges, to impose fines of up to $1,000 (previously the limit was $25), to direct financial restitution, to provide service to the victims and to the community. However, in very serious cases such as sexual assault, manslaughter, or armed robbery, the judge could order the case to be heard in an adult court, provided the accused was at least 14 years old. Lastly, the new law applies only to Criminal Code offenses and violations of federal statutes. It does not cover provincial offenses involving, for example, traffic or liquor.

The new Act, though it confers more rights on the young offenders, also makes them more responsible for their behaviour, and provides a somewhat greater protection of society in that penalties are expressly more beneficial. A statement from the federal Solicitor-General argued that the new Act balances the wider interests of all those involved in youthful crime.

. . . it provides the same safeguards and guarantees of legal rights as are already provided to adults; . . . it establishes a system of youth courts, procedures and dispositions which are separate from those established for adults. In addition, it incorporates into its provisions a concern for the safety of the community and the opportunity for parents to get involved in proceedings which involve their children (Solicitor General, The Young Offenders Act, Highlights, 1981:3).

The success of the Youth Courts will take some time to appraise. The previous law could control juveniles until the 21st birthday, but was very limited in terms of sentencing options. The new law gives the accused wider freedoms in conducting a defense, but also puts the offender at greater financial liability in terms of fines and makes him or her more likely to face community-oriented corrections. Though passed, this Act will probably not be proclaimed until 1985.

Sanity and Culpability

Section 16 (4) of the Criminal Code states that "everyone shall, until the contrary is proved, be presumed to be and to have been sane." Usually, the burden of proving issues in criminal cases lies with the Crown. However, where insanity is a live issue, and where it constitutes a defense for a crime, the burden of proof lies with the accused. In Canada, the defense of insanity is based on section 16, which reads:

16 (1) No person shall be convicted of an offense in respect of an act or omission on his part while he was insane.

The section then outlines what constitutes insanity. A person is insane when he is in a state of natural imbecility or has a mental disease "that renders him incapable of appreciating the nature and quality of an act or omission or of knowing that an act or omission is wrong." Where someone suffers from delusions "but is in other respects sane," insanity is no excuse except if the delusions caused him to believe his conduct was lawful and justified.

The Canadian law is an amplification of the famous, though now dated, M'Naghten rule. In England in 1843, M'Naghten was found not guilty of murder by reason of

insanity. This decision was influenced by the testimony of physicians who treated individuals suffering from diseases of the mind that affect the faculties of reason and morality.
The Court argued that

> . . . to establish a defense on the ground of insanity, it must be clearly proved
> that, at the time of the committing of the act, the party accused was labour-
> ing under such a defect of reason from disease of the mind, as not to know the
> nature and quality of the act he was doing; or, if he did know it, that he did not
> know what he was doing was wrong (Parker, 1983: 250).

Critics of the M'Naghten Rule have charged that it makes far too much of the cognitive dimension of behaviour, and underplays the impulsive and emotional aspects. For
example, a person may know that the commission of an act is wrong, but might nonetheless experience an acute but transitory "irresistible impulse" to do it.

While psychiatrists may attest to the mental condition in which persons lose their
capacity to control their impulses, this testimony is virtually impossible to establish
with certainty. As Nettler argues so succinctly, "it requires finer psychological tools
than are presently available to be able to distinguish reliably between behaviour that is
uncontrollable and behaviour that is uncontrolled" (Nettler, 1978: 44). Consequently,
the doctrine of "irresistible impulse" only confuses the question of intent.

Nonetheless, there is some merit to the criticism that the wording of the M'Naghten
rule attaches undue importance to what persons know cognitively and to the criticism
that the rule suggests a simple-minded distinction between those with sick minds and
those with wicked intentions. The Canadian law is worded somewhat differently from
M'Naghten. Rather than referring to what the accused "knows," the law speaks about
an "appreciation" of the nature and the quality of an act. Appreciation alludes to the
mixture of cognition, feeling and reflection that characterizes subjective states, and this
wording is thought to be an improvement over the earlier rule. As well, the wording of
the Canadian law requires not only that there be some mental problem — natural
imbecility, disease of the mind or delusions — but that these problems make it impossible for the accused to assess the morality of the conduct. In other words, being crazy *per
se* does not give one a license to break the law with impunity. In *R. v. Craig* (1974) it was
established that the accused in a rape trial had a grave personality disorder; he was a
psychopath. A psychopath is an anti-social individual with a marked disregard for rules, a
lack of consideration for others, and a craving for excitement; he or she is self-centered,
impulsive, aggressive, remorseless, and incapable of enduring affection. Despite the
confirmation of this diagnosis, Craig was found guilty as charged for it was held that
while he did suffer from this disability, it did not follow that he was unable to appreciate that he was raping his victim. Furthermore, because psychopathology is a personality disorder, there is some question as to whether it is really a disease of the mind at
all, especially in view of the psychopath's ability to cope, even if only in a marginal way,
with most of the exigencies of everyday life.

With respect to delusions, section 16 (3) says that someone who is in other respects
sane, but who experiences delusions cannot offer the excuse of insanity "unless the
delusions caused him to believe in the existence of a state of things that, if it existed,
would have justified or excused his act or omission."

Suppose you believed that you had paid for a car and were removing it from a dealer's
lot. If this belief were shown to be a delusion, insanity could be offered as an excuse for
theft. However, if the act in question was not legal, even allowing for the truth of the
delusion, insanity would be no excuse. Clarke, Barnhorst and Barnhorst (1977: 48)
report an excellent illustration of this possibility:

In one of the few reported cases involving a specific delusion, the accused was under the delusion that he was suffering from a fatal and incurable disease. He and his wife made a suicide pact and each took poison with the intention of committing suicide. The wife died but the accused recovered from the effects of the poison. He was charged with counselling his wife to commit suicide. His defence was that, although he was sane in other respects, he was insane at the time of the offence because of his specific delusion that he was suffering from an incurable disease. The court held that despite the delusion the accused did not meet the legal test of insanity. He could not be acquitted unless the delusion caused him to believe in a state of things which, if it existed, would have justified or excused his act. Even if it had been true that the accused was hopelessly ill, this would not have justified his counselling his wife to kill herself. The court went on to find that the accused was capable of appreciating the nature and quality of his act and that he knew his act was wrong. Therefore, he was convicted.

Though insanity provides an exception to the rule of *mens rea*, acquittal on the grounds of insanity does not mean that the accused becomes a free person. Section 542 (2) of the Criminal Code directs that an acquittal on the grounds of insanity involves an order that the person "be kept in strict custody . . . until the pleasure of the lieutenant governor of the province is known." While jail may be a cheerless confinement, the term is usually definite and the ground rules for early release are relatively clear. The same cannot be said for those who are declared wards of the lieutenant governor and confined to hospitals for the criminally insane.

Concurrence of Action and Intent

In the criminal act, the physical and mental elements must be fused or concurrent. For example, it is possible for a person to form the intent to kill another person, and subsequently to actually cause the death accidentally. Though acquaintances might observe smugly that he had only carried out his wishes, there is no crime if the wish or intention is not the responsible factor behind the actual deed. If the deed truly was accidental, if for example someone just happened to accidentally run over an arch enemy, then the matter is only a coincidence, not a crime. If you remove the wrong coat from a coat check and only discover the mistake later, you may have complied with the physical requirements of theft; however, there is no concurrence, no fusion of the act with the intent. But if you realize the error and subsequently decide not to return the item to its owner, then there is a fusion of the criminal intent and the criminal conduct (Parker, 1983: 90-91).

This point was illustrated by an English case, *Fagan v. Commission of Metropolitan Police* (1969), that involved a traffic constable and a driver he was directing. The constable directed the driver into a parking space but found the driver had stopped the car on his foot. The car remained there either because the engine stalled or because it was turned off (depending on whose word you believe). The constable implored the driver to move but the driver swore and told the officer to wait. He only moved after repeated requests. He was arrested for assaulting a police officer. In court, the accused's lawyer argued that there could be no finding of guilt because there was no concurrence. The physical element, actually driving the car onto the constable's foot, occurred independently from the mental element, the intention to assault the officer. While the driver may have formed the intent to assault, this occurred after the accidental stop on the officer's foot.

This argument was rejected by the court in a judgement that suggested that the driver's failure to remove the car once the harm was recognized constituted a fusion of conduct and intention. Though the event may have been initiated by accident, it was maintained and prolonged wilfully by the driver (see Parker, 1983: 148-150).

Causality: The Relationship between Harm and Conduct

In criminal cases, the issue of causality is not raised in most situations because the relationship between one's conduct and the harm suffered by another is clear cut. However, in certain cases the harm is not immediate and is not direct. For example, in a 1974 U.S. court case, *Fuller v. Preis*, a woman sued the estate of a man who had caused an automobile accident involving the woman and her husband. The man whose estate was being sued had died in the crash, which evidence showed was caused by his intoxication. The woman's husband suffered extreme injuries as a result, injuries that rendered him an invalid. After several months in convalescence, the husband became depressed and committed suicide. The woman brought suit successfully and won a settlement from the estate of the deceased driver. The court recognized that there was a causal relationship between her husband's suicide (i.e., the harm) and the other man's impaired driving (the criminal conduct). In this case, the demonstration of causality was heard in a civil court, not a criminal court. In civil court, the test for truth depends on "the balance of probabilities," which either support or fail to support the complaint. In criminal court, the rule of truth is much stricter: "beyond a reasonable doubt." Presumably, such distant causality would be harder to establish in criminal court.

In *R. v. Wilmot* (1940), there was a similar driving situation. The accused, Wilmot, was involved in a fatal driving accident with a man on a bicycle. Wilmot was impaired when the bike collided with his car. The evidence showed that by the time of the impact, Wilmot had nearly come to a dead stop, and that the cyclist, who was carrying a carton of empty beer bottles on his handlebars, had swerved across the centre line, ramming the front of the car. Wilmot was charged with manslaughter for "causing the death of a human being by means of an unlawful act." The unlawful act was driving while impaired. At trial, Wilmot was acquitted on the issue of causality. The defense argued that the mere fact of Wilmot's intoxication was not enough to account for the death of the cyclist. It would have to be shown that the impairment was a direct cause or contributing cause of the death. In other words, though Wilmot was impaired, his driving performance had not contributed causally to the fatal outcome.

The issue of causality was also raised in *R. v. Dubois* (1960). In this case Dubois was charged with indirectly causing the death of a person. Dubois had started a fight with another man, Miron, in a tavern. Dubois left the tavern and "a few minutes later, Miron ran out and fired a shot at Dubois. The shot missed Dubois but killed Petit, an innocent passerby. Miron was convicted of manslaughter" (Clarke, Barnhorst and Barnhorst, 1977:24). However, Dubois, who never fired at anyone, was charged with murder on the grounds that his provocation of Miron had caused the death of Petit. In court, he was found not guilty because the causal relationship between the tavern fight and the accidental killing of Petit was too remote and coincidental. Though Petit might still be alive today had no fight occurred, his death was not a necessary or even likely outcome or effect of the fight. But there was an obvious link between the fatal shooting and the reckless firing of a gun by Miron.

Aside from the question of determining the measure of causality between individual conduct and individual harm, students of jurisprudence have considered the question of determining causation of harm from corporate activities. Faulty products cause deaths, disfigurements and injuries. Companies pollute the water we drink and the air we breathe, and saturate the environment with chemical contaminants and electronic radiations. Crown corporations as well as oil cartels affect the marketplace by artificially controlling the price of commodities. Though the harm from such activities is increasingly easy to detect, the questions of the culpability of a non-human corporation and the determination that harmful effects arise causally from group-mediated actions are sometimes difficult to assess.

If the lack of product safety has been a direct effect of a policy of financial restraint by a manufacturer, it may be easier to establish causality. However, most relevant cases are not so clear cut. For example, cigarette smoking is recognized universally in the scientific community as a contributing cause of cancer. However, since not everyone who smokes gets cancer and not everyone who gets cancer smokes, gaggles of tobacco company lawyers have been quick to point out that the chain of effects is questionable. Likewise, though a particular automobile may have hazardous operating features that contribute to accidents, since not every driver of this car is doomed to an accident, the link is contentious. These situations are aggravated by the fact that most manufacturing policies are functions of committee decisions and are subject, even within one company, to much interpretation and latitude as the decision is distributed through the division of labour. Even if a policy is dubious at one point, it may be harmful at another as it gets enacted or transformed in the production process. Tracing the resulting harm to some particular committee or person can be highly problematic, especially when no one is governed by any unlawful intentions. Analysts of this situation have recommended that the criminal law be structured to make corporate actors liable for their policies and for the way such policies are implemented so that they would become criminally liable for exercising "due negligence."

A corporation should be held criminally responsible for the conduct of its officers, agents and employees causing bodily harm if the harm is related to policies adopted by the corporation to achieve its objectives, to the corporation's accepted practices, or to the failure of corporate policy-makers to take steps to prevent its occurrence (Law Reform Commission of Canada, 1976a: 66).

The Law Reform working paper goes on to suggest that the penalty to such groups should be weighed with respect to the corporation's profits, assets and capacity to absorb a fine. Though the criminal law has been slow to target the harmful practices of corporations and companies, there is nonetheless some interest in this area, especially as the public becomes more aware of manufacturing-related diseases on the job, of industrially caused destruction of the environment and of artificial manipulation of prices in the market place. The success of criminal law in these areas is an open question (Goff and Reasons, 1978; Reasons, Ross and Paterson, 1981).

Just Deserts:
The Last Criterion of Criminal Behaviour

In order for criminal laws to have meaning, criminal behaviour must be liable to sanctions and restraints; otherwise the difference between criminal and legal behaviour would be meaningless. One of the distinguishing features of criminal acts is that they are deserving of punishment. Eating excessively and being grossly overweight are not the sort of things that beckon forth a criminal sanction. Nor is cheating at a game where there are no monetary stakes. Nor is failure to attend church. Nor is streaking. Nor is blasphemy and swearing. Nor is attempted suicide. When such behaviours have come under the purview of the law and have been the subject of criminal arrests, there has often been a storm of public controversy or disbelief. Attempted suicide, which was illegal at the turn of the century (Tremeear, 1902: S.238) was an indictable offense and punishable by imprisonment for two years. However, it made little sense to arrest unsuccessful attempters and to drag them from the emergency clinic to the city jail. Similarly, it seems pointless for the vice squad to scoop away copies of girlie magazines when demand shows endless lines of men trying to make purchases. However unsavoury we might find such activities, criminal sanction usually seems inappropriate. Advice from a relative, a minister, or a guidance counsellor is more in order.

On the whole, our reaction to things like obscenity or gross indecency is ambiguous. We want our laws to reflect the values we hold dear. Consequently, laws perform a symbolic role. They indicate those sorts of disreputable things we dislike and fear most. On the other hand, it makes little sense to jail a shopkeeper for selling smut and thereby expose him in jail to the most wanton sort of homosexual exploitation our society has devised. However, on a moment's reflection, we can find a good reason for doing this cruel thing. It will warn all the other pornography hucksters that sale of these materials is disreputable. So we sacrifice one dealer on the cross of expediency as a symbol of our disdain of obscenity with the hope that the pain and shame we inflict on him will restrain or regulate this disvalued thing called obscenity. In other words, the retribution we wreak on him for his sins will be a lesson for others. And if the courtroom is empty at the time of sentencing, we can console ourselves that, though the others might miss it, the lesson will not be lost on the individual convicted. Hopefully, contemplation of his fate will make a better person of him.

What is important has less to do with the scenario of obscenity painted here than with the conflicting expectations of criminal law that underlie it. While criminal behaviour may well deserve state-fostered punishment, what that punishment consists of and why the behaviour deserves it are matters about which there is a diversity of opinion. Specifically, criminal law is said to serve the objectives of restraint, retribution, symbolic rejection, deterrence and rehabilitation. By casting the net so widely, it must be impossible for jails, no matter how good or bad, to fail to meet at least some of the objectives of punishment. That, of course, is the problem: the objectives are often contradictory.

Restraint

Restraint is witnessed in the intervention by the police in a disruptive activity or in the termination of a criminal career. Arrest restrains (Nettler, 1978: 48). Juveniles are taken to their parents, criminals are taken to jail and disturbed people are taken to psychiatric hospitals. Hence, the mechanism of arrest and/or detainment ensures a return to a level of stability or tranquility undermined by the breach of the peace.

Retribution

Retribution is a more obvious objective of criminal law. In the English system of justice, where crimes are viewed primarily as offenses against the body politic as opposed to squabbles between individual culprits and victims, retribution and symbolism are intertwined. Though an individual victim or complainant may decide at some point in the proceedings that he or she wants the charges dropped, this is not that individual's decision. Though the individual may personally be the victim of an assault, this harmful act, as a crime, is an affront to the entire body politic and will be redressed on behalf of the whole society, whether or not the individual victim wishes to abandon the case before its completion. Furthermore, the victim typically does not benefit financially or materially from criminal proceedings: usually the opposite is true, especially where the victim is a witness. In other words, fines are paid to the state, not the victim. To receive compensation for damages, a victim typically must file a civil or tort action against the criminal, which must be initiated and pursued privately. An exception to it is section 653 (1) of the Criminal Code, which gives the judge in criminal court power to order financial restitution or return of stolen property to its rightful owner.

Punishment is not the same thing as vengeance. When we speak of the retributive function of punishment, we must remember that in the Western tradition the law provides punishment in accord with the gravity of the crime. The severity of the punishment is symbolic of its seriousness. All crimes specify a maximum level of fine and length of incarceration. Judges are empowered with a great latitude to give jail terms within the allowable range as merited by the facts of the case. In other words, judges have great discretion in weighing facts and circumstances, such as the age and record of the offender, the degree of harm involved and the public's concern for the type of crime so as to arrive at a punishment which fits the crime. Though critics have charged that this system is open to abuse through lack of *uniformity*, the discretion allows a highly flexible sentencing policy that best meets the requirements of balance in punishment. An important exception to the principle of definite sentencing involves the finding of an accused as a "dangerous offender." Where a person shows evidence of serious persistent violent behaviour, he or she may be committed to a penitentiary under section 688 of the Criminal Code "for an indeterminate period." The Code requires that such cases be reviewed by the National Parole Board after an initial three years of confinement and every two years thereafter in order to determine whether parole should be granted. The anomaly of this legislation is that accused persons can be jailed for substantially longer periods than they would have faced if convicted of the specific crimes that formed the basis for the dangerous offender status.

The Dangerous Offenders Act (1977) replaced the earlier Habitual Criminal Legislation (1947). Both laws provide for indefinite periods of "preventive detention." However, those committed to prison as habitual offenders prior to 1977 were not released with the new law. Michael Jackson's study (1982) of the experience of habitual criminals reveals that the application of the earlier law was extremely uneven. Approximately half of all commitments made in Canada under this law were made by the Vancouver courts. Those who were held in custody since 1977 have not been denied parole because they are dangerous (as the 1977 law requires) but for a variety of considerations including failures to observe non-criminal conditions of parole (such as abstinence from alcohol) and displays of contempt for the parole authorities. The Parole Board views confinement as desirable for the welfare of the criminals, most of whom are in their fifties or sixties. Despite this, Jackson argues that the habitual offenders he sampled had spent more time in jail than any other group of prisoners in Canada, including those convicted of murder (1982:7). Furthermore, given the requirements of the Dangerous Offenders law, very few habitual offenders could be committed today under the new law since few had any records of violent behaviour. Nonetheless, the new law was passed on the understanding that its provisions would be applied to habitual offenders who were still in custody. Jackson's report suggests this has not happened. He further suggests that the use of indefinite detention is arbitrary, that the continued incarceration of habitual offenders is unnecessary and that the control of habitual offenders under a defunct 1947 law violates the 1982 Charter of Rights protection against "cruel and unusual treatment or punishment." The Canadian habitual offender law was modelled after a similar law enacted in England in 1908. The English law was abolished in 1967 after numerous complaints such as those that now plague the Canadian situation.

Deterrence

Deterrence, another classical model of punishment, is based in Cesare Beccaria's rationalist theory of justice (1764). Criminals must be deflected from their goals by off-setting criminal gains with judicial penalties. The fine must always exceed the value of the theft. The suffering of confinement must offset the pleasure of criminal delights. This theory also is based on a model of retribution that balances the crime and punishment.

Deterrence is always spoken of at two levels. *Individual* or *specific deterrence* refers to the effect (if any) of an individual's penalty on his or her subsequent behaviour. *General deterrence* is the symbolic effect that punishment of one person has on the community at large — especially potential criminals. Presumably, contemplation of the fate of others prevents the novice or aspiring crook from committing the same folly, and/or at least getting caught at it. Whether there is any deterrent effect is difficult to determine. Nonetheless, punishments have a symbolic effect in that, like morality plays, they reconfirm what is evil in a society. This is more evident in the renaissance spectacle punishments at the public gallows, the auto-da-fé, stocks, the pillary, and public floggings. However, such scenes are not relegated to the past as the recent situation in Iran has so vividly reminded us. Even the USA has not been above the odd televised execution, as Gary Gilmore's case shows. A substantial part of the contemporary population find such displays objectionable, if not altogether barbaric. The functional theory of deviance holds that these executions and tortures have a ritual or agonistic aspect in that the audience or public, though they have no familiarity with the condemned, vicariously enact or participate in the execution and the degradation of the culprit in the name of society and what it stands for. Mercifully, our popular fictions and dramas have overtaken this function.

Rehabilitation

The last major model of punishment is rehabilitation. The concept of mass incarceration of convicted prisoners and the ideology of penological rehabilitation emerged together in 19th century Britain and the USA. Prior to this period, few criminals were confined to jails. They were hanged en masse, transported to the colonies, impressed into naval duty, or flogged or mutilated and released. With the growth of liberal thought, confinement was viewed as a more humane alternative (Foucault, 1977). The great, dark prisons of North America date from the mid-19th century. Early penologists thought that contemplation in isolation would facilitate a change of heart and so a rehabilitation of offenders (Reid, 1981: ch. 6; Rothman, 1971). However, solitary confinement and enforced monotony did not have the desired effects, and so the notion of rehabilitation through work developed. There was less than wholesale endorsement of this liberal attitude to penal punishment; the ambivalence among retribution, deterrence and rehabilitation that we experience today was widespread in the 19th century. The following letter, written in 1871, from John A. Macdonald, Prime Minister of Canada, to John Creighton, Warden of Kingston Penitentiary, is a good illustration of this point (quoted in Edmison, 1976: 366-67).

> Ottawa, October 31st, 1871
> Private
> My dear Creighton -
>   I have yours of the 25th which I have read with all the attention you bespeak. I can quite appreciate your anxieties in your office, it is a most responsible one, not without care but as you remark, it has also its bright side. I never had any doubt of and do not now doubt your ultimate success in making the Penitentiary a school of reform as well as a place of punishment, of course you feel that inexperience at first, that everyone does in a new situation. My only fear is that your natural kindness of disposition may lead you to forget that the primary [purpose] of the penitentiary is punishment and the incidental one reformation.
>   You say that you desire to feel that you are the means of making five or six hundred of your fellow creatures more happy than they have previously been in the Penitentiary. I could quite sympathize with your desire if it were to make them less miserable than they have been previously rather than more happy — happiness and punishment cannot and ought not to go together. There is such a thing as making a prison too comfortable and prisoners too happy . . . I am pleased to think that I have in any way strengthened your hands by the release of some prisoners, the power of release should however be exercised very sparingly. Severity of punishment and more especially, certainty that the sentence pronounced will be carried out is of more consequence in the prevention of crime than the severity of sentence . . . John A. Macdonald.

There is a great deal of truth in Macdonald's views on the role of certainty as opposed to severity of punishment, as we shall see in a later chapter. Nonetheless, the tension between the conflicting objectives of incarceration is quite clear. Criminal behaviour may well be conduct that is deserving of punishment, but what this means in practice is quite a contradictory and complex thing. An examination of the success of punishment is beyond the scope of this chapter. We shall return to this question later.

Summary

The criteria of criminal behaviour have several sources. The elements of harmfulness, the principle of *nullum crimen sine lege*, and the provisions for punishment emanate from the existence of the state and the political regulation of social life. The other elements, *actus reus*, *mens rea*, concurrence, and causation, reflect a more concrete understanding of how behaviour originates and how it is organized. These structural and psychological dimensions collectively provide a vivid sense of what we are talking about when we speak of criminal behaviour. And as our concept of *mens rea* indicates, this understanding is always evolving. However, what constitutes justice is only partially covered by the sociology of law and by jurisprudence. One must examine how justice is administered, and how the administration of justice determines what it is in the end that the society experiences. As we shall see, the administration of justice is constrained by occupational as well as by purely legal considerations.

FURTHER READING

K.L. Clarke, R. Barnhorst and S. Barnhorst, *Criminal Law and the Canadian Criminal Code*. Toronto: McGraw-Hill Ryerson, 1977.

W.K. Greenaway and S.L. Brickey (eds.), *Law and Social Control in Canada*. Scarborough: Prentice-Hall, 1978.

Edward Greenspan (ed.), *Martin's Annual Criminal Code*. Agincourt: Canada Law Book Ltd., annual.

A.M. Kirkpatrick and W.T. McGrath, *Crime and You*. Toronto: Macmillan, 1976.

Louis A. Knafla (ed.), *Crime and Criminal Justice in Europe and Canada*. Waterloo: Wilfred Laurier University Press, 1981.

Law Reform Commission of Canada, *Our Criminal Law*. Ottawa: Supply and Services, 1977.

Graham Parker, *An Introduction to Criminal Law*. Second Edition. Toronto: Methuen, 1983.

Roger Salhany, *Canadian Criminal Procedure*, Third Edition. Agincourt: Canada Law Book Ltd., 1978.

Robert Silverman and James L. Teevan, *Crime in Canadian Society*, Second Edition. Toronto: Butterworths, 1980.

Edmund Vaz and Abdul Lodhi (eds.), *Crime and Delinquency in Canada*. Scarborough: Prentice-Hall, 1979.

CHAPTER 3

The Police: Solutions to or Sources of Crime?

Introduction

The police are one of the most interesting and most studied groups in our society. We are preoccupied with the police and police culture. This is readily witnessed in our television series. Over the past decade we have watched the activities of the personnel of *Hill Street Blues*, *T. J. Hooker*, *Chips*, *Policewoman*, *Baretta*, *Hawaii 5-0*, *Rockford Files*, *Columbo*, *Starsky & Hutch*, *Streets of San Francisco*, *Kojak* and *Barney Miller*, not to mention the characters of *The French Connection*, *Serpico*, *The Onion Field* and *Magnum Force*. Police stories exemplify for us our collective morality and, in a more prosaic form, provide what the Shakespearean plays did for Elizabethan audiences, or the Greek dramas for Athenian audiences. However, the nature of policing is rarely captured accurately in these accounts. These accounts tend to create the impression that most police work is related to "fighting crime."

While this is highly entertaining in the short run, in the long run it appears that the entertainment community serves the ideological function of stabilizing and reproducing as crimes only certain types of illegal behaviours — those interpersonal predatory and property crimes that involve the constable on patrol. Little of upper world crimes, such as tax evasion, medical and legal malpractice or stock manipulation, is depicted. As a result, the public's perception of what sorts of crimes constitute major social issues is inadvertently influenced by what, in the eyes of the scriptwriter, whets the appetite of the consumer. Likewise, the social role of the police is edited to show policemen as heroes and antiheroes surmounting the challenges of wicked men, thoughtless administrators and ineffective laws. While it would be wrong to deny the romantic and heroic dimensions of the police role, our media perception has overblown these things. In this chapter we shall explore the role of the police, elements of police culture and the relationships between police deployment and the crime rate.

Policing in Historical Perspective

Historically, the forerunners to our modern police were far more involved in peacekeeping than in enforcing the law. The King's officers in the counties or shires were called reeves or shire-reeves (sheriffs). The sheriffs, their servants, and the city watchmen monitored the city and tried to prevent breaches of the peace. For example, the early watchmen of London were required to patrol the roads and bridges into London and to walk a beat at night, lantern in hand, calling "all is well" (see Reid, 1979: 371-72, 379). It was also their task to find shelter and employment for the homeless and unemployed, handle riots, find jobs to rehabilitate prostitutes, regulate the disposal and burning of garbage, and inspect bakers' and butchers' shops to see that the premises were kept clean. In Renaissance France, Louis XIV employed 40 lieutenants and police inspectors, who, through their paid informants, kept the King advised of the loyalty of the nobility, the clergy and the merchant class. It is estimated that one quarter of all the housemaids in Paris took police bribes to inform on their masters. However, the lieutenants did far more than political espionage. They built market places, paved streets, set up the Bourse stock exchange, moved a cemetery, provided crude street lighting, established a system of state pawnshops, created a hospital for children of the poor, founded a veterinary college, built schools for children of the unemployed, and organized fire and river rescues. They regulated trading practices, disallowing lead containers for wine and copper for milk; they censored public posters, inspected drains, had the streets swept clean, inspected unsafe buildings, licensed dogs, checked food prices and regulated sales in the off-seasons (e.g., prohibiting sales of oysters in summer) (Banton, 1974: 663). In other words, they tried to facilitate the harmonious conduct of civic life and among the many things this required was the arrest of suspected criminals. But this was only a minor function they performed.

Things have not changed drastically from early times, as we shall see. The modern concept of a police force can be traced to the Metropolitan Police of London, created by the English Parliament in 1829 at the insistence of Sir Robert (Bob) Peel. The early London police were called Peelers or Bobbies. The other English forces, and eventually most civic forces, were modelled on this decentralized type of policing (as opposed to the national police forces found elsewhere in Europe).

This does not mean that England, Canada and the USA do not have other kinds of police forces with some division of labour over the different activities that are policed or controlled. For example, in Canada we can distinguish at least seven different levels of policing.

On the federal level, there is the Royal Canadian Mounted Police. This force was established in 1873 as the North-West Mounted Rifles. The title was changed to North-West Mounted Police when the American government protested the creation of an armed guard on the undefended international border. The NWMP were responsible for enforcing Canadian law in the vast North-West Territories formerly held by the Hudson's Bay Company. The prefix "Royal" was added in 1904 by King Edward VII in view of the prestige of the force. In 1920, when the RNWMP were amalgamated with the Dominion Police, headquarters were moved from Regina to Ottawa and the title of the force was changed to the Royal Canadian Mounted Police. During the Great Depression, the Mounties assumed responsibility for provincial and municipal duties in all provinces but Quebec, Ontario and British Columbia. After 1950, the RCMP were commissioned in B.C. and in the new province of Newfoundland, except where municipalities were large enough to maintain their own local departments.

The second tier of policing is provincial. The Ontario Provincial Police and the Sûreté du Québec each have a total personnel of approximately 5,000. They enforce the Canadian Criminal Code, and the provincial liquor and highway laws. However, the RCMP still maintain offices in each province to investigate and prosecute cases of narcotics offenses and breaches of other federal statutes such as the Official Secrets Act. Because the RCMP work for the provincial Solicitors-General on a contract basis in all provinces except Ontario and Quebec, and because of the lack of cost control for the service as well as a lack of accountability to the provinces, many critics of the Mounties have called for each province to establish its own autonomous force. In the past, provincial officials have been unable to initiate internal RCMP reviews of questionable conduct by Force members despite the provincial financing of the service. Also at the provincial level, some provinces maintain separate highway patrol services, which operate under the auspices of the provincial Solicitors-General.

The third tier of policing is municipal. Provincial laws make it mandatory for villages and towns of a certain size to maintain a police force for the protection of people and property. All cities and most towns have their own forces. Often regional municipalities covering several counties with numerous hamlets, villages and towns will be covered by a regional police force. As well, for the adjudication of administrative laws governing such things as propriety over land and land use, counties maintain sheriffs and bailiffs.

There is also a series of residual police organizations: special categories of federal peace officers in customs, harbour and border patrol officers; private police forces working under civil contracts; plus the railway police. Clearly in view of the wide range of police organizations, there are probably several thousand "departments" and organizations in Canada. In the United States, it is estimated that there are 40,000 separate public police organizations, though most employ only a handful of men and often on a part-time basis (Banton, 1974: 666).

TABLE 1
Police Strength by Organization, 1976 and 1977

Force	Number of Police Including Cadets		Other Full Time Employees		Total	
	1976	1977	1976	1977	1976	1977
RCMP	14,012	13,955	4,650	4,283	18,662	18,238
Ontario Prov. Police	4,064	4,060	1,169	1,157	5,233	5,217
Sûreté du Québec	4,195	4,360	975	1,005	5,170	5,365
Municipal Police†	28,914	29,491	4,498	5,554	33,412	35,045
CNR Police	432	423	25	25	457	448
CPR Police	318	322	89	88	407	410
Harbour Police	237	236	97	78	334	314
	52,172	52,847	11,503	12,190	63,675	65,037

†Excludes RCMP and OPP contracts.
Source: Canada Year Book 1980-81, p.54.

In 1976 and 1977 the ratio of total police personnel per 1,000 population was approximately 2.75, and the ratio of police alone was 2.25. In 1968, the ratio was much lower: 2.1 for total personnel and 1.8 for policemen per se. In 1951 and 1961 the rate for police alone was .188 and .165 respectively (Chretien, 1982: 116). This shows a clear rise in the number of police independent of the rise in population. Notably, the costs of policing have also risen dramatically. From 1971 to 1981 there was a 270% increase in police expenditures. In 1979-80 approximately two billion dollars were spent on police services, the major portion going for salaries, which averaged $35,000 annually. This constituted about 66% of the total expenditure for criminal justice, the balance going to corrections (21%), the courts (9.5%), Crown Counsel (1.9%), Legal Aid (1.6%), and victim compensation (.2%) (Chretien, 1982: 111-114).

What is surprising is that this increase in police manpower has been independent of an increase in the number of serious crimes. The absolute number of crimes, as judged by the number of persons convicted of indictable and summary conviction offenses, decreased from 1966 to 1973. This decrease in absolute numbers is all the more significant since the population increased at over 1% per year during the same period. Per capita convictions fell in absolute as well as relative terms while the per capita number of police increased. The likelihood that the fall in convictions was a function of more police on the street is not borne out by studies of police deployment, as we shall see. Also, comparisons of the per capita number of police in various modern democracies show no clear correlation with the crime rate. Japan and France have much lower overall crime rates than Canada, yet France has many more police per capita while Japan has significantly fewer (Chretien, 1982: 117). Finally, statistics on convictions, the one type of information that contradicts the popular hysteria over the rise in the crime rate, have not been gathered by the federal government since 1973.

TABLE 2
Persons Charged & Convicted of Indictable Offenses,
1966, 1967, 1972, 1973

	1966	1967	1972	1973
charged	51,088	51,388	55,541	53,964
convicted	45,670	45,703	45,614	40,761

Note: Includes criminal code and federal statutes.
Source: Canada Year Book 1970-71, p.513; Canada Year Book, 1977-78, p.55

Number of Convictions for Summary Offenses,
1967, 1968, 1972, 1973

	1967	1968	1972	1973
criminal code	113,578	89,014	104,825	107,688
federal statutes	29,949	25,741	28,849	38,228
provincial statutes	1,382,451	1,529,313	1,281,582	1,151,535
municipal by laws	376,116	157,875	102,206	86,566
Totals	1,902,094	1,801,943	1,517,462	1,384,017

Source: Canada Year Book 1970-71, p.521; Canada Year Book, 1980-81, p.59.

The single major important exception to this table involves conviction for breaking and entering. If we examine the period from 1890 to 1970, the rate of convictions for murder is quite stable while the rate for robbery rises quite slowly over the period. By contrast, there is a marked rise in the frequency of breaking and entering (Chretien,

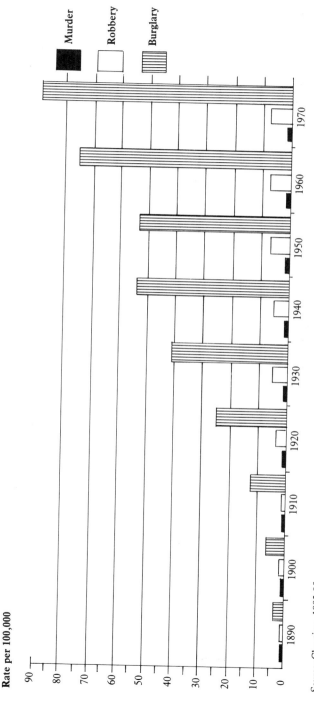

FIGURE 1
Convictions of Persons Aged 16 and Over
Canada: Selected Indictable Offenses

Source: Chretien, 1982:95.

1982: 95). This pattern appears to be unique to this crime and probably reflects the rise of urbanization, which has provided an increasing supply of targets as well as a supply of dislocated urban offenders. Nonetheless, two-thirds of break and enter cases result in either no losses or losses under $200 (*Selected Trends in Canadian Criminal Justice*, 1979).

How much police time is actually spent in criminal matters? Some sense of this may be gathered from examining the number of persons charged by the police, the kinds of things they are charged with, and the average number of charges per police officer.

TABLE 3
1977 Law Enforcement Record

Type of Offense	Incidents Reported	Persons Charged (including juveniles)
Offense Against Person[a]	116,249	42,227
Offense Against Property[b]	1,079,179	214,777
Prostitution	2,843	2,941
Gaming and Betting	3,487	3,680
Offensive Weapons	13,432	8,307
Other Criminal Code	438,825	107,403
Narcotics	63,131	55,803
Controlled Drug	2,807	2,196
Other Federal Statutes[c]	65,782	30,446
Provincial Statutes[c]	379,588	278,571
Municipal By Laws[c]	61,273	27,724
Criminal Statistics Subtotal	2,226,596	774,075
Criminal Code Traffic Offenses[d]	266,972	192,529
Federal Traffic Offenses	17,429[g]	17,429
Provincial Statutes[e]	118,161	57,204
Residual Provincial Traffic Statutes[f]	2,789,894[g]	2,789,894
Municipal By Laws	393,122[g]	393,122
Traffic Statistics Subtotal	3,585,578	3,450,178
Grand Total	5,812,174	4,224,253

Notes

[a]Includes murder, attempted murder, manslaughter, infanticide, rape, sexual offenses, wounding, and assault.
[b]Includes robbery, breaking and entering, theft, fraud, possession of stolen goods, etc.
[c]Excluding traffic.
[d]Includes criminal negligence, failure to remain at the scene of an accident, dangerous driving, refusal to give a breath sample, driving while impaired or disqualified.
[e]Includes failure to remain at the scene of an accident, dangerous driving, and driving while disqualified.
[f]None of these various traffic categories include parking violations.
[g]Absolute minimum estimates based on persons charged.

Source: Canada Yearbook 1980-81: 55-56. Figures are rearranged.

What does the table tell us? Out of a total of 23,257,700 Canadians in 1977, 4,224,253 faced some sort of criminal and/or driving-related charges. This is about 18% of all men, women and children, or about every sixth person. On the face of it, this is quite staggering, since we are not excluding those under 12 or 13, who make up over one quarter of the population. If we take them into account, this means that on average in a single year every fifth person is charged with something. It also means that each policeman charged or ticketed an average of 80 Canadians in 1977. This would seem to indicate that we are a very wicked lot and that we keep our police forces very busy. However, before we draw comparisons with Sodom or Gomorrah, we should realize that while the police are very busy, little of their business is expressly concerned with serious crime. Abolish the automobile and we would eliminate most "crime" as we define it.

This conclusion is consonant with the findings of the Ouimet Report (1969), which concluded that while there has been an astonishing 2500% increase in the crime rate in Canada between 1901 and 1965, 98% of this increase involved the less serious summary conviction offenses, and 90% of this 98% figure was due to traffic offenses. The Traffic Statistics subtotal indicates that about 82% of all persons charged in 1977 were charged with driving-related offenses. Indeed, two-thirds of all those identified in 1977 were faced with tickets written for residual provincial traffic violations (improper turns, faulty lights, failing to obey a traffic sign, speeding, etc.).

Even under the Criminal Code there is a great variance in how serious a charge is. Though we tend to think that all crimes in the Code are *mala in se* (evil in themselves), many are simply *mala prohibita* (wrong because they violate the rules). In accord with this distinction, crimes in the Code are either indictable offenses or summary conviction offenses, and, depending on the circumstances, some crimes can be prosecuted as either. The less serious crimes are summary conviction offenses (the Code limits penalties to a $500 fine and/or six months in jail). The more serious are indictable and can carry penalties in some cases up to life imprisonment. The question is, of all the Criminal Code charges in any year, what proportion are indictable and what proportion are summary convictions? While we do not have 1977 data for this question, 1973 data indicate that, excluding Alberta and Quebec, of the 145,909 persons convicted under the Criminal Code, only about one quarter had faced indictable offenses. Consequently, most criminal code cases concern the less serious type of offense (Canada Year Book, 1980-81: 56). This is borne out by the report of the Criminal Law Review committee, which revealed that over 26% of all criminal code violations in 1980 were for theft under $200 (bicycles, shoplifting, theft from automobiles, etc.). This was the single most frequent criminal code offense in 1980, followed by wilful damage and then by theft over $200. Together these constituted about 53% of all criminal code offenses (Chretien, 1982: 81). However, there is a grave discrepancy between this picture and the average citizen's perception of crime. In 1982 a Gallup survey asked people what percent of crimes they thought were violent. The average estimate was 54%. In point of fact, less than one criminal code crime in ten is violent (Chretien, 1982: 77, 80).

What does this tell us about police work? As indicated earlier, the historical activities of police forces had little to do with the heroic business of capturing dangerous crooks. Clearly, this is also the picture that emerges in modern forces despite the public perception of the nature of crime and police work. Our national statistics provide only one kind of evidence about how diverse the police role is. A number of other kinds of studies have examined the amount of time the police actually spend on law enforcement.

Studies of Citizen-Initiated Calls to Police

Wilson (1968a: 18) monitored all the calls received by the police department in Syracuse, N.Y. over a period of one week: June 3-9, 1966. First, he found that 22.1% of the calls were for information (e.g., asking about recovery of stolen property, what to do to secure house from burglars during vacation, traffic conditions, traffic laws). Second, he found that 37.5% of the calls were for services, such as calls for ambulances, police to drive a family member to hospital, for assistance to retrieve a treed cat or lost dog, to fix a fallen power line, for assistance in finding or reporting lost or found property. Third, he found that 30.1% of calls were for what he classified as order maintenance, that is, intervention in family arguments, neighbour arguments, presence of gangs and/or fighting in public, or to investigate victim allegations of already completed criminal activities. Lastly, Wilson found that 10.3% of calls actually required active police intervention to enforce the law, (e.g., to respond to a burglary in progress, to give pursuit to a thief, to investigate a prowler, to arrest a suspect on the scene).

In a similar study, Albert Reiss (1971) monitored the incoming calls to the Central Communications Center of the Chicago Police Department for one day in April, 1966. He reported a total of 6,172 calls. Of these he classified 58% as requests for assistance about criminal matters. These included matters-in-progress as well as investigative matters. The 58% figure can be further broken down into components. Twenty-six per cent of all calls related to breaches of the peace, 16% to offenses against property, 6% to offenses against the person, 5% to traffic violations, 3% to suspicious persons, and 2% to residual criminal matters. The rest of the calls, about 30%, were requests for assistance, such as calls for intervention in family and personal matters (domestics, suicides), medical problems, traffic accidents, etc. Evans (1973) reported a comparable study in Montreal in 1973 in which he found that 13% of police activity concerned anti-criminal matters.

There are differences between the Wilson and the Reiss samples. However, both show that the public requires far more of the police than the simple enforcement of the criminal law. In view of the complexity of the police role, Cumming, Cumming and Edell (1965) characterized the policeman as a hybrid "philosopher, guide and friend" (276-286).

The Emphasis of Police Work

The previous discussion about citizen-initiated calls quite correctly indicates that police work, though this is less true of detective work, is largely reactive as opposed to proactive. In other words, the police spend most of their time responding to citizen calls, rather than independently detecting crime. A minority of police work is, however, proactive as in the periodic round up of prostitutes in Canadian cities to test the soliciting law, or the entrapment of narcotics offenders by undercover agents, or the maintenance of police informers.

The second feature of police work discussed by criminologists is task orientation. What task does a policeman perform in the course of duty, or what task does the officer or department give emphasis to: law enforcement, order maintenance, or social service?

Law Enforcement. As indicated earlier, police are generally not heavily involved with those who commit serious crimes. It is estimated that in New York City during the early 1970s, the average police officer worked for more than a year without making a felony arrest and that the chance of apprehending a robber occurs once in a lifetime. In Los Angeles, in 1965, it was calculated that a patrol officer captured a burglar once every three months, and a robber once every 14 years. In Washington, D.C., it was reported that fewer than 10% of all the police officers were making over 50% of all arrests (Reid, 1979: 382). In other words, most of the arrests were made by a small segment of the force, and the majority of the force made very few arrests. In Toronto in 1973, it was estimated that an average patrolman laid charges against only 15 individuals per year (including non-Criminal Code arrests), while detectives laid 15.5 criminal charges per year (Evans, 1973).

Though these figures strike us intuitively as low, there is a variation between police departments on the degree of emphasis given to law enforcement, and this seems to be controlled by the degree of professionalization versus traditionalism in the department. James Wilson (1968b) compared the release rate of juvenile delinquents in two cities. He found that in the professional department, that is, the department marked by an emphasis on centralization of operation, recruitment on basis of achieved characteristics, and a stress on education and training, juveniles were arrested at the rate of 47% (hence, 53% released). In the more traditional department, emphasis was given to attributes such as height and weight, familiarity with the local culture and having relatives in the department. Here the arrest rate was only 30% (hence, 70% released without arrest).

Order Maintenance. The second police function, presumably more characteristic of traditional departments, calls for an emphasis on restoring disruptive situations to normalcy without arresting the citizens involved. Many criminologists argue that most of the criminal justice system consists in this sort of management of situational tensions: controlling of skid-row alcoholics, detaining the mentally ill, "cooling out" domestic disputes, "letting pass" public drunkenness or merely warning those who make noise or disturb the peace of their neighbours. Police departments that emphasize these informal methods of social control are oriented to the maintenance of order, not the intervention of the law to punish offenders. The order maintenance function is often in tension with the law enforcement function.

Social Services. Because they operate 24 hours a day and because the majority of clients they deal with have not been institutionally certified, police are required to offer what are effectively social welfare, psychiatric and psychological advisory services, such as counselling battered wives, talking to attempted suicide victims, mediating family tensions, finding lost children, and attending sudden deaths and fatal accidents.

These tasks create enormous role strains for the police and result in high levels of personal pathology, including alcoholism and divorce (see Vincent, 1979: ch. 5). The role of the police is further exacerbated by the fact that the police, until recently, have been relatively poorly paid, and the occupation has been regarded as having little status or esteem.

The stresses are observable in other ways. Since the occupation's task orientation is often very tenuously defined, the police must rely on public respect for the authority of their office. Consequently, since lack of respect is sometimes threatening, the police frequently respond with cynicism and antagonism toward the public. As outlined by Westley (1953) this is an important occupational source of police brutality. The low pay of the police, however, makes them also vulnerable to the vices of graft and corruption, though this is much less a problem in Canada than in the USA.

Some Aspects, Causes and Consequences of Police Culture

Criminologists have argued that, beside being an occupational group, the police constitute a distinctive subcultural group (Wexler, 1974). While most occupations evolve distinct subcultural characteristics, few come to dominate the self-concept of the practitioners as pervasively as does police work. A series of studies have discovered a number of characteristics of the police culture. Peter Manning (1971) developed several postulates or assumptions that he feels characterize the outlook of the police. The foremost was "people cannot be trusted; they are dangerous." This suspicion would not be very significant if it occurred in isolation, but it is only one of several characteristic traits. The second is a feeling of powerlessness. Contrary to the popular image of the police as a source of legitimate power and legitimate violence, the police themselves recurrently suggest they are frustrated in their attempts to enforce the law and keep the peace. They are hamstrung by the laws of evidence, bail and arrest, often resorting to violence to dole out justice, as shown in Westley's 1953 discussion of police abuse of citizens. They are frequently rejected by civilians, the very people they are supposed to serve. For example, in domestic cases, many battered wives are asked to swear out informations for arrest of their husbands, but few agree to do so. Furthermore, police investigations and case preparations are subject to court outcomes, plea bargains with prosecutors, and lenient judges. A third characteristic of police culture is low occupational perception of police work by citizens: the police believe the public undervalues their work. Surveys of police officers indicate that they rank police work as among the most important and most highly esteemed occupations (judges, doctors and the like). However, the public tends to view the police profession as moderate in prestige. When the relative prestige of the 90 most prominent occupations is calculated, police are ranked 47th, even below an army sergeant (Wexler, 1974: 130). A fourth characteristic of police culture is high solidarity — the police as a group are very close, compared with other occupations. Westley (1956) reported the results of a questionnaire dealing with this characteristic. He asked police whether they would ever report on stealing by fellow officers. Seventy-three per cent of his sample indicated that, under no circumstances would they squeal on a fellow officer. In fact, 77% suggested they would even perjure themselves rather than offer evidence against another police officer. Given the nature of police work, the repeated exposure to risks on the job, and the mutual reliance on one another, it is easy to understand how a strong bond grows between policemen.

Beside being highly cohesive, the police have traditionally been relatively isolated. They tend more than other professionals to spend their leisure time almost exclusively with other officers and their spouses. They are also resistant to establishing contacts with non-police families or individuals; after all, what is a police officer going to do on a Saturday night when somebody pulls out a marihuana cigarette? This resistance has been documented in the USA, the UK and Canada. For example, in Britain, Banton surveyed police regarding their social contacts with civilians. Fifty-eight percent of the police with five years experience reported incidents in which other people became reserved and guarded when their occupation became known. This percentage went up to 73% for police with over eleven years experience. It appears that the isolation of police becomes more acute the longer they stay on the force (cited in Wexler, 1974: 134).

These five elements of police culture — cohesiveness, isolation, suspicion of the public, feelings of powerlessness and problems of status — are not particularly of interest in themselves. However, they are important to understand two vices to which the police are subject — violence and corruption. Unlike other forms of vice in society, police vice is especially pernicious because it is almost invulnerable to restraint. How can one control the very group that has the monopoly on control? From the 1930s onwards, repeated attempts have been made to clean up corruption in large American cities. Typically, there is a short period of rehabilitation, some lower level officers are "sacrificed," the newspapers report the clean-ups cathartically, and, thereafter, the corruption gradually returns. Some of the central causes of resistance to rooting out corruption and police brutality are found in the characteristics of police culture. For example, Justice Morand's 1976 inquiry into police brutality in Toronto was repeatedly confronted by officers "closing ranks" and lying. In other words, the isolation and solidarity of the police, together with their disdain and suspicion of civilians, make them almost impossible to control externally.

Some Sources of Police Culture

A number of studies point to the importance of role or occupational conflicts and ambiguities in the causation of police culture. The assumption of these explanations is that there are a number of ambiguous or pathological elements in police work and that the characteristics of police culture have evolved as modes of accommodation to these pathologies or tensions. We shall examine some of these sources of police culture.

Ambiguities of Police Status. As previously mentioned, there is a great discrepancy between the officer's view of police work and the citizen's view. The police regard their work as a very high status occupation and demand some degree of deference from the public for it. However, neither the citizen's perception of high status nor shows of deference are always forthcoming. In fact, lack of citizen co-operation and citizen apathy are frequently cited as reasons for resigning on large American police forces. For those who stay, the perception of rejection has led to a desire for a display of deference even if it must be cajoled from the citizens. A sample of Toronto citizens in 1970 indicated that the most frequently acknowledged source of police abuse towards citizenry consisted of belligerent and aggressive policing (Courtis, 1974). Tension between citizens and police has led to the isolation of the police occupation. It is probably true that most professionals like to get away from their "clients," and many may experience a tension with them. However, the "clients" of the police are the entire public! Therefore, when they wish to get away from them, this leads to extreme isolation.

Ambiguities of Police Work. A survey of the Chicago Police Department indicated that the least-preferred police task was patrol duty. Among the reasons given for other choices, the most important was "the officer has a better sense of what is expected of him" (Reid, 1979: 386). In other words, the officer on patrol often faces contradictory expectations. Notably, the same Chicago police came under national scrutiny following the 1968 U.S. Democratic Convention, which was marked by massive demonstrations and abusive police overreaction. This was the first televised police riot. In many routine encounters, police face a clear choice: to arrest in accord with the *rule of law* or to restore the peace through a *discretionary decision* to not arrest, but to give a warning, or ignore a crime. Obviously such ambiguity of expectations allowed the runaway show of repressive physical abuse of lawful protest witnessed in Chicago in 1968. The problem the police face is that, while full enforcement is impossible, police manuals and police departments make a pretense of full enforcement. For example, La Fave (1965: 71) estimated from observations of one corner in Berkeley, California, that if traffic violations occurred throughout the city at the rate they occurred at this one corner, there would be 3 million daily violations of traffic laws in that city. That would require 14,000 traffic officers, nearly three time the actual size of the force to police traffic violations alone. Presumably, the police force would have to increase massively to engage in full enforcement, not just for traffic violations, but Criminal Code violations as well.

Pragmatically speaking, the police have always been called on, largely informally, to interpret the intent of the legislation they are supposed to enforce. This use of discretion leaves the police open to accusations of bias because of "selective" enforcement, even though selectivity is unavoidable. Few other professionals are thrust into such ambiguous situations. Rather than having clear guidelines to control decision making, the officer is plagued with dilemmas that require spur-of-the-moment choices and that are not clearly sanctioned by the law but are implicitly required in its administration. Given the ambiguous nature of the role, the officer is caught in a twilight zone between what is illegal and what he knows is immoral, and usually uses the former to control the latter. Despite the intolerability of full enforcement (it would create a police state) and its staggering costs, the public possesses a limited understanding of discretion. A survey in Toronto indicated that only slightly over half of the citizens interviewed thought that police had the discretion to not lay a charge when a law had been technically violated. However, the majority of these people thought that discretion only covered things like "minor offenses under parking and traffic violations" (cited in Wexler, 1974: 142). This is clearly a public misperception of how policing works. This ambiguity in police work and the public's failure to understand the complexities of police decisions tend to make the police cynical about the public and mistrustful of public judgements about the police. This facilitates the alienation and isolation of the police.

Another important ambiguity of police work is the question of when the use of force to control members of the public becomes illegitimate. In some jurisdictions the use of massive physical coersion has produced community outcries. For example, the U.S. Department of Justice filed a lawsuit in the federal court in Philadelphia alleging that police violence was so widespread on the Philadelphia force that it violated the civil rights of all the city's citizens (Reid, 1982: 340). Similarly, a community-based group has been created in Toronto (the Citizens' Independent Review of Police Activities) to monitor allegations of brutality by the Metro Toronto Police. The use of force by the police is another area of ambiguous discretion little clarified by Canadian law.

The third item that underlies the creation of the police culture is the *limitations of the police job*. There are two elements here: the procedural limits of criminal investigation and the disposition of criminal cases by the courts. Regarding procedural limits, the police are often hamstrung in their work when they see emphasis given to the accused's rights as opposed to the accused's harmfulness and the victim's suffering. Furthermore, once the case goes to court, the matter is largely out of police hands. The disposition of cases by judges is almost universally a source of frustration to the police (Wexler, 1974: 143-145). Police typically are disenchanted by the withdrawal of charges, the dismissal of charges for "technical" reasons, and light non-jail sentences — probation, discharges and suspended sentences. Their disenchantment is based on a feeling that the judge has only a limited access to the case. The police feel that they typically sort out all the less serious charges through their own discretionary decisions to arrest. Consequently, when an arrest is made, it is deemed to be more serious. For example, an arrest may follow several warnings. This, however, is irrelevant to the judge who re-sorts the cases to his or her own liking, as though the police were working on a full enforcement policy and as though the cases had not been preselected.

These situations lead to the sense of cynicism and powerlessness examined above among members of the police force. The police feel their efforts are eroded by the courts. Peter Manning (1971: 156) reports that it is almost universally felt by the police that "stronger punishment will deter criminals from repeating their errors." This view is less widely held among the judiciary.

Futility of Police Work. Many grave social situations do not lend themselves to simple legal intervention. The police are also first-line social workers, called on to deal with battered wives, alcoholic husbands, neglected children, suicidal teenagers and impoverished geriatrics. These groups frequently require the attention of the police, but their problems do not lend themselves to simple legal solutions. Should the police arrest a husband who is beating his wife or a mother who is beating her child? The arrest will probably aggravate the situation. Consequently, in these situations, the police feel powerless. They are also very cynical about the public's expectations of them in these social areas. Twenty-two per cent of police deaths and 40 per cent of police injuries in the USA are tied to domestic disturbances (Reid, 1982: 354). In Canada some 12% of police homicides from 1961 to 1980 arose from domestic disturbances (Juristat, 1982). So not only are these service areas futile, they are dangerous for the police. One attempt to clarify policy in the area of domestic intervention is the recent adoption of a practice of automatically laying criminal charges where there is evidence of assault. The utility of this policy can only be assessed with time.

Police Responses: Deviant Occupational Behaviour

Beside exploiting their roles to take graft (e.g. to avoid gambling joints or to ignore cars illegally parked in front of classy restaurants) and in addition to the frequent reliance on physical force to produce confessions and to dole out revenge (see Hagan, 1977: 148-150), the police appear to routinely trample over the rights of accused people. Mr. Justice Donald Morand's 1976 Royal Commission into Metropolitan Toronto Police Practices found "a sense of alienation from the public. . . . Some police officers believe that they are the only remaining barrier between the public who hired them and the anti-social persons who break society's laws." This alienation from the public appears to lead some officers to believe that their job is "not only to investigate crimes but to act as judge and jury" as well. Lorne Tepperman (1977: 28) argued that it was "largely this alienation from the public" that led to the kinds of abuses of power documented in a controversial 1970 study by the Canadian Civil Liberties Education Trust.

Justice Morand found that excessive force was used by police in 6 of 17 cases studied by him. Tepperman recounts some of the findings (1977: 28-29):

> In the most grisly case, Mr. Justice Morand came to believe the allegation by one victim that two police constables had, in a police station and overheard by other police constables, placed a claw-like device on his nose and on his penis with the intention of intimidating him. In subsequent investigations of these and other allegations, Mr. Morand was disturbed at the extent to which he found "the evidence of police officers mistaken, shaded, deliberately misleading, changed to suit the circumstances and sometimes entirely and deliberately false." Be-

TABLE 4
Police Treatment of Accused

	Percent of Sample
- accused denied right to phone call from custody	21%
- accused questioned by police before consulting lawyer	77%
- accused never advised of right to counsel	30%
- statement made/given before a lawyer is consulted	96%
- accused in custody three or more days before consulting a lawyer	34%†
- accused not advised of right to remain silent	62%
- statements given to police involuntarily	17%
- accused alleges injury inflicted by police	25%

†This study pre-dated the Bail Reform Act, which greatly facilitated the pretrial release of accused persons, and which provided a number of methods of release from custody.
Source: Based on Tepperman (1977: 29).

sides the occurrences of brutality carried out, apparently, by a few police against a few citizens, other police officers aware of such occurrences did not try to stop them and these incidences were covered up by both those directly involved and by other police when these allegations were investigated. It is impossible to tell how much these cover-ups account for the discrepancy between the findings of the Canadian Civil Liberties Education Trust study and the rarity of public acknowledgement of police brutality, but the Morand commission opens the door to further investigations along these lines.

The Morand commission was unprecedented in Canadian police history in encouraging public discussion and recognition of the problem of police deviance. Unfortunately, the later McDonald Commission on RCMP wrongdoings and the Quebec Keable Inquiry into the RCMP confirmed the propensity for lawlessness in Canadian policing. Similarly, admissions of police lying and police brutality were videotaped by Neil Proverbs in a sensational 1982 Toronto case (*Globe and Mail*, Nov. 4, 5, 6 and 9, 1982). In the Proverbs case, two senior police officers were recorded as saying that they frequently lied in the courts, altered notebooks to suit the requirements of prosecution and framed individuals with planted evidence. Though they later retracted such claims when the tapes were brought to court, similar incidents had already been documented by Justice Morand.

The most recent report on the Toronto police confirms that the unnecessary use of force by the Toronto police is a substantial problem. Richard Henshel (1983: 10) reports that "for a ten month period from mid-1978 to early 1979 there was almost a killing a month, mostly of members of minority groups. Widespread protest erupted in Toronto's ethnic communities, culminating in September of 1979 in the passage by Toronto City Council of a resolution of non-confidence in the Metropolitan Toronto Police Commission." Henshel (1983: 98-101), working in conjunction with the Citizens' Independent Review of Police Activities, reviewed the complaint procedures in Toronto and concluded that alteration of evidence by the police was common, that complaints to the police department of physical abuse were inadequately processed, that penalties to officers were inconsequential and that certain elements of the police service, specifically the hold-up squad, tortured suspects to get confessions. This last observation was already familiar to several criminal lawyers and has been brought to the attention of Amnesty International. It is an empirical question whether the situation in Toronto is unique and whether or not it is applicable elsewhere.

Police Deployment and the Crime Rate

Police violence and police disregard of due process are an ironic source of criminal activity in our society. However, critics of police work argue that normative police behaviour, not just infrequent cases of abuse, in a curious way is the greatest contributor to crime statistics. The kernel of this observation is that there is a relationship between the amount of crime reported to Statistics Canada in the Uniform Crime Reports and the organization of police work. Because of their great discretionary power and the conflicting demands of the role, police exercise a great control over how much criminal activity actually gets certified in the official records. For example, Piliavin and Briar (1964) suggested that the police decision to arrest juvenile offenders was not based simply on the offense having been committed. The juvenile's demeanour or show of respect for the police, as well as any exhibition of contrition or show of remorse or sorrow, determined whether the case was brought to court. Piliavin and Briar point out that these informal conditions of arrest probably resulted in a racial slanting of the arrest statistics. Since American urban black males demonstrate a demeanour that provokes the police (or is lacking in shows of deference and contriteness), they are arrested disproportionately to white kids involved in the same kinds of behaviours. This has an application to the Canadian scene in that Indian, Inuit and Métis people frequently find themselves at odds with the police in urban areas where their dress, personal hygiene, physical characteristics and location in run-down sections of the city make them especially vulnerable to police suspicion (Hagan, 1977: 151).

Black and Reiss (1970) in their study of police work in Washington, D.C., New York and Chicago, found results similar to those of Piliavin and Briar. Black and Reiss found that the best determinants of arrest were seriousness of crime (more serious, therefore, less discretion); degree of relatedness or familiarity (more distance, more arrest); deference and cooperation of complainant; and victim's demands/insistence on arrest as opposed to a warning. In examining the disproportionate arrests of blacks, Black and Reiss found that this was explained by two things. Blacks tended to get involved in more serious crimes than whites and black victims more frequently insisted on police charges against other blacks than did white victims with white assailants. Black and Reiss also reported a similar racially biased vindictiveness involving police brutality. While 33% of victims brutalized by white policemen were black, 71% of the citizens victimized by black police were black!

What does all this show? The officially reported rate of crime is tied to the police perceptions of the accused and the victim as well as the demands of victims for enforcement. The bias in the subsequent records of arrest reflects the bias of the citizens for intervention (Hagan, 1977: 151-154).

There are a series of other studies that do not focus on the conditions that produce arrest (e.g., deference, citizen demands for "justice"), but focus simply on the size of a police force as a determinant of the volume of the crime rates. The assumption here is simply that more police find more crime. This situation has an uncanny implication. If true, chiefs of police could call for more manpower, which would in turn certify more crime requiring even larger numbers of police. Hence, the rate of crime could soar without any change in the actual behaviour of criminals. Indeed our earlier tables suggested that there has been a significant growth in per capita police manpower with little change in convictions for serious crime.

Lynn McDonald (1969) examined the correlation between the change in the crime rate in Canada between 1950 and 1966 and the change in police strength over this same period. McDonald found that, except for convictions for break and enter, no significant correlation could be found for serious crimes measuring either charges laid or convictions for serious offenses. However, convictions for less serious offenses, including delinquency judgements, summary conviction offenses, traffic violations and parking tickets, increased in proportion to the increase in the police force size. One interpretation of this is that the force increased as a result of increased victimization; that is, more crimes were experienced, so more officers were needed. This does not appear to be the case because the increases witnessed are offenses more subject to police discretion (less serious crimes); and, secondly, they are the type of crimes more susceptible to out-of-doors monitoring, that is, they are more easily detected because they occur in public and are, therefore, more liable to be observed if the police numbers are increased. In other words, where there are more police, they tend to spot more "outside" crimes. Consequently, McDonald's study suggests that police deployment is not changing the behaviour of criminals, just officially certifying more of it. Some other studies argue that police monitoring actually changes the behaviour of criminals.

"Operation 25" was a study carried out in East Harlem in 1954. The number of policemen was more than doubled in the area for a period of several months. As a result, there was a significant decline in arrests for "street crimes" such as mugging, auto theft, and burglary. The problem with this study was that there was no measure of displacement of criminal activities to other neighbourhoods. Consequently, the results are suggestive, but inconclusive (cited in Hagan, 1977: 190).

The most exciting recent study of the relationship between crime detection and police deployment was reported by George Kelling et al (1974) in a study of the Kansas City police force experiment. This study is exceptional because it measured the crime rate in several ways including victimization studies. The study varied the nature of the police patrol and monitored changes in the crime rate. Fifteen police beats were matched for important community characteristics (such as density, socio-economic status and age composition) and then divided into five matched groups of three. In each group, one beat was designated as a control and was policed in the usual way with mixes of proactive, reactive, enforcement and peacekeeping activities. In the second beat, a proactive patrolling was employed. Squad cars were assigned to the streets at several times the normal frequency. Lastly, in the third beat, policing was limited to reactive enforcement. Police service was delivered solely at the request of citizens. The results showed that "for the one year experimental period no substantial differences were observed in criminal activities" (Hagan, 1977: 191). The amount of reported crime did not change; the rate of victimization did not change; the community satisfaction with police work did not change; and the level of citizen fear did not change. "The type and level of police deployment seemed to make no significant difference" (Hagan, 1977: 191) either in the activity of criminals judged by the number of victims, or in the official rates of crime judged by the number of occurrences and arrests. It should be emphasized that this is one of the more important studies on this subject because it uses control groups, matched communities, and several measures of changes in criminal activities including victim studies as well as official statistics. Kelling and Fogel (1978) suggest that the failure of preventive patrol stems from several sources. The dispatch-rapid response system contributes to the alienation of the police from their communities. There is no close tie of officers to a "beat," no casual interaction between officers and citizens, no exchange of information about potential crimes. Consequently, there is citizen resistance to "getting involved" that extends both to witnessing crimes and reporting being the victim of crimes. This resistance undermines the effectiveness of the preventive patrolling.

However, it would be erroneous to conclude from this that the police are dispensable. Every police strike is marked by a sharp increase in breaches of the peace (see Hagan, 1977: 192ff). In Montreal on October 7, 1969, an illegal walkout of police officers and firefighters precipitated a night of looting, gun battles, arson and rioting. The Royal 22nd Regiment was called on to restore order. A member of the Sûreté du Québec and a burglar were shot dead. In a shoot-out between Murray Hill limousine drivers, who had exclusive rights to airport fares, and 300 rival taxi drivers, 12 men were shot and limousines and buses were overturned and burned. On the same day, 25 banks were robbed. The provincial police were called into the city to control wandering vandals, but were too few to do anything but stand back and watch the rioting. Mobs formed on St. Catherine Street and vandalized windows and rooms in downtown hotels, department stores and restaurants. The mayhem was stopped only by the presence of the army. Police were forced back to work by the National Assembly in Quebec City with threats of fines, imprisonment and loss of unions.

Though some people think that the suspension of police services precipitates what Hobbes characterized as the natural state of man — the war of all against all — this is not inevitable. Police strikes create opportunities for individuals and groups already involved in criminal pursuits or already involved in a high state of friction. Also, the conspicuous absence of law enforcement in the first few days following a strike encourages defiant, rebellious and invariably intoxicated breaches of the peace by young men. This was witnessed in 1969 in Montreal, in the 1979 Bathurst, New Brunswick, strike and in the 1981 Halifax strike. However, as a strike continues, this type of public vandalism falls off, especially as merchants, bankers and private citizens take precautions to protect their property and persons. The Halifax strike, which lasted several months, was marked by flagrant breaches of the peace in only the first few days. Ironically, with the police off the job during the strike, the official crime rate began to fall. Whether the actual levels of victimization rose is an open question.

What can we conclude from all this? Kelling's work indicates that the the mode of deployment of the police does not appear to determine the level of crime as measured either by the official records or by victimization studies. Studies like that of McDonald, which show a relationship between the rate of petty crimes and the size of police forces, point out that this rise involves the certification of crime by the police (as opposed to the level of activity of criminals), especially as this certification involves less serious and highly visible crimes. Lastly, our experience of police strikes is associated with an increase in major crimes as criminals exploit the authority vacuum, and an acute but brief increase in disorderly conduct and vandalism as young people act out displays of defiance. Since most strikes are very short and troublesome, we tend to think that police work is a necessary dike holding back a sea of criminality. However, the persistence of such strikes shows we do not get washed away in a tidal wave of crime, but that they produce a shift of the burden of responsibility from the police to the citizens at large.

Police Deployment as Crime:
The RCMP Security Service Scandal

In 1976 former RCMP Constable Robert Samson gave testimony during his own trial for planting a bomb at a private residence in Montreal that he had done much worse things for the RCMP, including breaking into the office of a radical news service, the Agence de Press Libre du Québec and stealing documents. Subsequent investigation uncovered a host of crimes, wrongdoings and unauthorized activities committed by members of the RCMP security service. These included:

   a. Operation Ham: a break-in at the offices of the Parti Québecois in January 1973 to remove and photocopy membership lists and financial information.
   b. Over 400 break-ins, unauthorized by search warrants but with the knowledge of senior officers from 1970 to 1976, mostly in British Columbia by the Criminal Investigations Branch.
   c. Investigation of New Democratic Party "Waffle Wing" members on the premise that the party had been penetrated by political subversives; this operation was authorized by senior Mounties with knowledge of the Privy Council Office.
   d. Surveillance of federal Members of Parliament as well as persons seeking every kind of political office in Canada.
   e. Unlawful opening of the mails contrary to the Post Office Act over a period from 1950 to 1976 and undertaken with probable government knowledge.
   f. Unlawful destruction of property by burning a barn in May, 1972 at St. Anne de la Rochelle, Quebec, in order to prevent a suspected meeting of terrorists.
   g. In December, 1971 in Montreal, the Security Service issued a false communiqué with the forged signature of a Quebec radical with the expectation that the communiqué would excite political extremists to violence.
   h. From 1970 across Canada the Mounties gathered evidence from confidential medical files in an attempt to identify information that might discredit radicals. This was done in Ontario with knowledge of the provincial government.
   i. In the early 1970s, Security Service members kidnapped and unlawfully detained members of radical groups in attempts to intimidate them and turn them into police informers.
   j. For undisclosed reasons, members of the RCMP stole a case of dynamite and some electronic detonators on the night of April 27th, 1972 from the yard of a construction company after smashing the padlock. (See *Toronto Globe and Mail*, June 5, 1978; also see Henshel, 1979)

Since much of the RCMP behaviour had occurred in Quebec and since the Parti Québecois government had been the object of some of the RCMP "inquiries," the first commission to investigate the RCMP scandal was initiated under the direction of Jean K. Keable in Quebec. Michael Mandel (1983b: 3) reports that the federal Commission under the Direction of Mr. Justice D.C. McDonald was initiated in part by the RCMP itself in an effort to limit or contain the Keable Inquiry. Indeed, with the federal McDonald Commission of Inquiry into Certain Activities of the RCMP, the federal government could attempt to block the progress of Keable's inquiry while indicating its willingness to clear the air through its own Commission. Also, by having a Commission of Inquiry in place it was thought that criminal charges against individual Mounties could be postponed until the Commission completed its work. Subsequently the federal government lamented the fact that so much time had elapsed between the crimes in the early and mid 1970s and the completion of the inquiry in 1981, that evidence would be difficult to establish. Predictably, in fall 1982, the Solicitor General of Canada announced that the federal government planned no prosecutions arising from the McDonald Commission. This decision was made secretly by the Justice Department in summer 1982 (Mandel, 1983b: 1) and was confirmed in the summer of 1983 (McGuigan, 1983).

In the meanwhile the McDonald Commission had omitted the details of the most serious RCMP crimes on the grounds that their publication would prejudice subsequent criminal trials of individual RCMP members (McDonald Commission, Third Report, 1981:517-520). And so between them, Solicitor General Kaplan and Commissioner McDonald kept the RCMP's dirtiest laundry out of the public domain and out of the courts. Criminal prosecutions proceeded only in Quebec.

Nonetheless, the basic conclusion of the McDonald Commission was that there had been a breakdown in the rule of law in the RCMP Security Service in the early 1970s. In other words, in undertaking to uphold the laws of Canada, members of the RCMP had put themselves above the law and had committed a series of acts that, if undertaken by any other citizens, would have resulted in substantial periods of incarceration. These activities were, after all, not on the order of the highway patrolman who speeds to catch a speeding motorist. These were crimes of arson, breaking and entering, theft, contravening the Post Office Act, kidnapping and forcible detention and invasion of privacy. Despite this, few RCMP officers have been charged. In fact the government of Ontario blocked private prosecutions of Mounties brought by the victims by staying the proceedings (*Re Dowson and the Queen, 1982*). Of those charged and convicted, most have faced reduced charges and all have received non-jail sentences. Jean-Paul Brodeur (1981:131ff) who was a consultant for two years with the Quebec's Keable inquiry, reported that internal records of the illegal RCMP activities were rewritten for submission to external agents. For example, the original report of the APLQ break in referred to "illegal entry," "theft," and "crime." The redrafted report substituted the terms "entry without warrant" and "removal of documents." The Mounties likewise tried to suppress the idea that their behaviour was illegal in the dynamite theft by characterizing the event as an "unauthorized seizure of dynamite" (Brodeur, 1981:133). In both cases there was an attempt to create the impression that the search warrants would have automatically been extended and that seizure of private property would have been permissible if authorized.

Probably the most significant implication of the re-description of these crimes was that when Mounties ultimately did face criminal prosecutions for these activities, they faced charges on the downgraded offenses contained in their own revised reports. Specifically, the breaking, entering and theft committed by three policemen (one each from the RCMP, the Sûreté du Québec and the Montreal Police Force) at the APLQ resulted in charges of contravening a federal statute contrary to S.115 of the Criminal Code by failing to obtain a search warrant. Where break, enter and theft carried a 14-year maximum penalty, S. 115 carries a maximum of two years. The low minimum attached to S. 115 allowed the accused policemen to qualify for the most lenient sentence upon conviction: an absolute discharge. The discharge wipes out evidence of a criminal record and allows people who have been convicted of crimes to be held as something other than criminals, and to keep their jobs as law enforcement officers. What is ironic is that this disposition was possible only because the charge was virtually dictated by the accused via the revised RCMP reports (Mandel, 1983b: 2). Judges have consistently awarded this type of penalty to convicted RCMP criminals.

From its inception the McDonald Commission was charged with bias. In 1978 the Law Union of Ontario, an association of progressive lawyers and legal workers, through lawyer Paul Copeland tried to arrange a court order to prevent the three Commissioners from sitting on the Inquiry. They pointed out that all three had strong affiliations with the Liberal Party. Mr. Justice David McDonald had been appointed to the bench in Alberta by a Liberal government and had been a devoted Liberal Party supporter, having once served as president of the Alberta Liberal Party. Donald Rickard was known to be a friend and business associate of the Solicitor General, Francis Fox, the Minister in charge of the RCMP. The third Commissioner, Guy Gilbert, was a loyal Quebec Liberal who "flamboyantly stated his confidence in the RCMP and the patriotic importance of protecting the image of the Liberal Party in Quebec since the election of the PQ, and whose annual donation of money to the Liberals continued throughout the Commission's deliberations" (Mandel, 1983b: 4). Critics of the Commission pointed out that since the extent of ministerial knowledge of illegal activities would be an important issue in the inquiry, it was imperative that the Commissioners be above any suspicion of protecting their Liberal colleagues in the federal cabinet. The order of prohibition sought by Copeland on behalf of the Law Union failed. The Ontario Court of Appeal argued that a Royal Commission, because it was not a judicial inquiry settling claims between two parties, could not be subject to review on the basis of bias (*Re Copeland and McDonald et al, 1979*). In other words, there is no bar in law against the government's stacking of a Royal Commission since in principle the purpose of such an inquiry is to investigate facts and advise governments and not to determine liability or guilt.

The final reports of the Commission ran to several volumes and covered several thousand pages. All the ministers of the Crown were exonerated of any direct involvement in the unauthorized activities. After much pulling of teeth, the Commission received cabinet minutes that suggested that the Prime Minister knew of illegalities committed by the RCMP but did not know the type of illegalities. Likewise one-time Solicitor General Warren Allmand "suspected" illegalities. Jean-Pierre Goyer, George McIllraith and Francis Fox knew of certain activities but did not know they were illegal. As Mandel (1983b: 4) points out, "this novel defense of ignorance of the law must have come as a pleasant surprise to all these legally trained Ministers." In the end the breakdown in the rule of law was found to have been limited to the RCMP and government ministers were on the whole cleared of responsibility. This was the section of the report best received by the government.

The reports of the Commission cover several major areas. First, they deal with the role of the security service within the RCMP and recommend that it be replaced by a civilian service. Secondly, they deal with the legal questions that arise from police illegalities and possible police defenses in such cases. On the whole they dismiss defenses of mistake of law, mistake of fact, lofty motives, necessity, duress, "just following orders" and the like. In the final volume they deal with specific wrongdoings and they suggest remedies. We shall deal with the areas covered in the final volume.

The wrongdoings fell into three different categories. First, there were cases "not requiring further action." These involved RCMP misrepresentations to the government of RCMP surveillance of radicals on university campuses, attempts by the RCMP to control information given to the 1966 Royal Commission on Security, attempts to recruit informers, failure to inform the Solicitor General of illegal acts, misleading the Solicitor General regarding the policy on mail interception, misrepresentation of its investigation of the Royal American shows in Western Canada to provincial and federal officials, the theft and subsequent destruction of private property during the surveillance of a foreign agent, and the misrepresentation to the Solicitor General of information about financial support given to the defector, Igor Gouzenko, from 1946 to 1962. For the most part, the Commission found that the failures of communication between the Force and various government officials were not purposefully deceptive, arose for unaccountable reasons or were inconsequential. Accordingly, the Commission recommended that no action be taken against individual Mounties.

The second type of activity reviewed by the Commission was one for which the Commissioners recommended internal disciplinary action. First, the Commission dealt with a case in which one particular officer felt that RCMP use of information from the National Revenue Department was probably unlawful; the officer refused to seek a legal opinion about the practice because of his expectation that it would make the unlawfulness explicit and hence would undermine the Force's reliance on revenue files, contrary to the Income Tax Act. As the Commissioners commented, this showed "a complete disrespect for the law and the legal process" (Third Report, 1981: 349). This attitude permeated other areas. For example, the second circumstance studied by McDonald involved the illegal use of master keys for automobiles. Master keys were developed by General Motors to allow dealers access to all GM products. Because of the illicit use of such keys, the Criminal Code in 1970 required that anyone possessing a master key have a provincial license. From 1970 to 1978, the RCMP used such master keys in criminal investigations to secretly search vehicles for evidence. This practice was only brought under control in 1978.

The third area requiring disciplinary action involved the destruction of the files relating to "Operation Checkmate." This operation involved the use of illegal activities to discredit, impede, deter or undermine political radicals. According to the Mountie who destroyed the files, they were "very sensitive" and "very explosive" and if brought to public attention would have brought the Security Service into disrepute. The Commissioners commented that in their opinion, "the explanation given by Mr. Yawarski for recommending in 1974 the destruction of the Checkmate files . . . amounts to nothing less than an intention to reduce the possibility of the Government of Canada learning of acts which he himself had come to consider to have been 'wrong' " (Third Report, 1981:367). Had Operation Checkmate involved illegal acts, the destruction of the records would amount to obstruction of justice. The RCMP's obstruction of justice by misinforming agencies of the federal and provincial government and the amazing gaps in memory of senior RCMP officers were on the whole the subject of little comment by the Commissioners (see for example, Third Report, 1981: 374-75).

The third area of inquiry in the final report dealt with "cases referred for possible prosecution and disciplinary action." These included breaches of the confidentiality of the National Revenue files, the Unemployment Insurance Commission files, breaches of the Post Office Act, unlawful attempts to recruit informers, breaking and entering, theft and invasion of privacy. The Commission did not publish its chapters on these cases because of possible criminal charges against those involved. In fact several such charges have been laid in Quebec at the suggestion of the Keable Inquiry, though no one has been jailed or fined as a result.

What has been the federal government's response to the McDonald Commission? At the level of individual Mounties, it has shown no interest in prosecution. In fact after receiving the final Commission reports in January 1981, it delayed publication for eight months and commissioned two legal opinions, which challenged McDonald's conclusions about RCMP crimes. These were released simultaneously with the publication of the Royal Commission in an attempt to discredit the conclusions of its own hand picked Commissioners (Mandel, 1983b: 7). The opinion of the government seems to be that whatever the police need to do in order to do their job is *ipso facto* legal. In other words, the end of law enforcement justifies any means. A consequence of this would be that anyone victimized in the course of police work has no protection and no redress under the criminal law. This is of course both morally reprehensible and legally incorrect. Nonetheless, the same mentality was at work in 1983 and 1984 in the preparation of the new security service. The Government is implementing the recommendation to create a civilian security service, but it is also making provisions both to legalize the sorts of crimes that gave rise to the McDonald and Keable inquiries and to loosen the new agency's public accountability. This would not be quite so distressing if such an agency were directed solely at foreign spies and subversives. However, the history of the RCMP in the area of national security reveals that the Mounties have maintained files on tens of thousands of Canadians, have targeted legitimate political organizations like the Parti Québecois and the NDP as well as members of the peace movement, Jehovah's Witnesses, progressive union leaders and those political elements that are trying to democratize social life and increase government accountability (see Mann and Lee, 1979: 107-121). This suggests that it would be politically regressive to model the new security service on an agency in which a totalitarian attitude towards the political left has been combined in the past with a pervasive breakdown in the rule of law.

Summary

The role of the police in a democratic society is precarious. We require the maintenance of order and coercive law enforcement as well as various social services. We require the exercise of discretion yet demand a fair and even application of law. This contributes to the ambiguities attributed to and the contradictory expectations that are held by the police. They are required to proceed in the face of situations marked by structural limitations in controlling crime as well as social futility in dealing with the problems of those in crisis and without hope. These factors contribute to a distinctive occupational subculture characterized by cohesiveness, isolation, suspicion, feelings of powerlessness and misgivings about status and worth. This subculture in turn may foster certain deviant responses, including a vigilante attitude among certain officers. Yet, when the police themselves become a source of deviance, accountability to the public is fraught with problems. The police control the investigation of complaints against police. The police exercise the discretion to discipline internally or to lay charges. If charges are laid, as in the RCMP break-in at the APLQ, the police control which charges they or their associates will face. The success of commissions of inquiry into police practices are mixed. They create bad publicity but the extent to which external publicity changes internal practices is an open question. For example, the aftermath of the McDonald Commission has seen attempts to normalize and legitimate police crimes. Civil rights is one of the major areas in the justice system that appears to limit or countervail the illegitimate elements of social control. In theory, the legal rights of the citizen offset the overzealous conduct of police. This is the subject of the next chapter.

FURTHER READING

Craig L. Boydell and Ingrid A. Connidis (eds.), *The Canadian Criminal Justice System.* Toronto: Holt, Rinehart and Winston, 1982.

Robert Dion, *Crimes of the Secret Police.* Montreal: Black Rose Books, 1982.

Richard V. Ericson, *Making Crime: A Study of Detective Work.* Toronto: Butterworths, 1981.

Richard V. Ericson, *Reproducing Order: A Study of Police Patrol Work.* Toronto: University of Toronto Press, 1982.

Brian Grosman, *Police Command: Decisions and Discretion.* Toronto: Macmillan, 1975.

W.E. Mann and John Alan Lee, *RCMP vs The People.* Toronto: General Publishing, 1979.

Peter Manning, *Police Work: The Social Organization of Policing.* Cambridge, Mass.: MIT Press, 1979.

McDonald Commission, *Commission of Inquiry Concerning Certain Activites of the RCMP*, Second Report: Freedom and Security Under the Law (Vols. 1 and 2), Third Report: Certain RCMP Activities and the Question of Governmental Knowledge. Ottawa: Supply and Services, 1981.

W.T. McGrath and M.P. Mitchell (eds.), *The Police Function in Canada.* Toronto: Methuen, 1981.

Ruben G. Rumbaut and Egon Bittner, "Changing conceptions of the police role: A sociological review", pp. 239-288 in Norval Morris and Michael Tonry (eds.), *Crime and Justice, An Annual Review of Research.* Chicago: University of Chicago Press, 1979.

Clifford D. Shearing, F. Jennifer Lynch and Catherine J. Matthews, *Policing in Canada: A Bibliography.* Ottawa: Solicitor General, 1979.

Philip C. Stenning, *Legal Status of the Police*, Law Reform Commission of Canada. Ottawa: Supply and Services, 1982.

Claude L. Vincent, *Policeman.* Toronto: Gage, 1979.

CHAPTER 4

Civil Rights
and Safeguards
from Abuse

The last chapter examined the controversial 1970 study by the Canadian Civil Liberties Educational Trust, which suggested that a number of the civil liberties of Canadians were being systematically ignored and abused by the police. Specifically, it revealed that arrested persons were frequently denied access to a telephone to call a lawyer, were not advised about the right to silence, were made to give incriminating statements, and were interrogated without benefit of counsel.

It should be pointed out that this study was somewhat unreliable because it was based, for the most part, on the opinions of convicted persons, persons who in view of their experience would be least sympathetic with the justice system. Also it was noted that the figures would probably be lower today because the Bail Reform Act (1971) gives the police a variety of options to expedite the release of arrested persons, and puts the onus on the state to show why an arrested person should be confined to jail before trial. Consequently we only rarely find people incarcerated "three or more days." However, aside from these points, many critics of the Civil Liberties study questioned whether the various items sampled were civil rights at all (Wilkins and Jeffries, 1971-72). Critics argued that under Canadian law, denial of access to a telephone and failure to give warnings were not contraventions of rights because these things were not guaranteed or protected by Canadian legislation. Obviously, there is great confusion in the minds of Canadians about their rights, a confusion that can probably be traced to the influence of American mass media — the television police dramas and their depictions of American civil rights. The various rights of citizens in Canada require closer examination.

Two Fundamental Principles of Criminal Procedures

The basic principle of the criminal trial in the English tradition is the presumption of innocence. "The law presumes a man is innocent until the contrary is proved. The burden of proving guilt is on the prosecution, and the trier of fact (judge or jury) must be convinced 'beyond a reasonable doubt' " (Parker, 1983: 365). Proving "beyond a reasonable doubt" is a matter of some debate. It does not mean removing every possible uncertainty in all the minor details of a case. It does not mean that the jury must be 100% convinced or that the case must be *absolutely* watertight, but only that no reasonable doubt of guilt or innocence can be ignored and left unresolved.

The second fundamental rule, which touches more closely on matters of civil rights, is that the accused is not required to say anything at any point of an investigation in his or her own defense. Other then pleading guilty or not guilty, the accused is not required to utter a word to the courts or to the police (Parker, 1983: 365). A corollary of this fundamental principle of English justice is that a person cannot be forced to make self-incriminating statements. This affects the "right to remain silent" but only to a point. As the eminent English judge, Lord Devlin, stated, "the balance on which the English system works is that it combines the suspect's right to silence with the opportunity to speak" (Devlin, 1958: 59-60). Usually, this is pertinent to a trial in which an accused considers taking the stand to rebut the prosecution's case where the accused believes the charges are unfounded. Though the accused does enjoy the right to remain silent, the exercise of that right may be construed as consistent with guilt (i.e. the accused will not testify because he will be trapped in prevarication and evasion during cross-examination).

The right to silence may backfire in other contexts. This is illustrated by the 1978 case of *Moore v. The Queen.* Moore was a cyclist who rode his bike through a red light in the city of Victoria, and was stopped by a motorcycle patrolman. The officer asked for Moore's name and address (to write him a ticket for ignoring a red light), but Moore refused to give this information. This made it impossible to issue a ticket for this relatively minor driving infraction. The officer arrested and handcuffed Moore on the more serious charge of obstructing a police officer (Criminal Code, Section 118) by refusing to identify himself. The Supreme Court of Canada denied Moore's appeal and upheld the British Columbia Court of Appeal's order for a new trial. The Court ruled that "the constable had no power to arrest the accused whom he found committing a summary conviction offense except if arrest was necessary to, *inter alia,* 'establish the identity of the person'." Even though the legislation covering bicycles does not spell out that cyclists must identify themselves to the police, the cyclist's refusal made it impossible for the constable to uphold the provincial laws. Consequently, the insistence on the right to silence in this case constituted an obstruction of the constable's efforts to enforce the laws. It was pointed out, however, that the constable's persistence did *not* entail any admission of incriminating evidence on Moore's part. Moore's guilt was established by the eyewitness evidence of the constable, not Moore's admission of his identity, so there was no denial of his right to silence.

Civil Rights Guarantees: USA vs Canada

Though the USA and Canada share many of the basic attributes of English justice, such as the adversarial system, trial by jury, rules of arrest, rules of lawful search and exclusionary rules for hearsay evidence, there is a great difference in the area of the protection of individual rights. The United States follows the model of the French enlightenment and has enshrined the basic premises of justice in a written constitution and a robust Bill of Rights.

The American Supreme Court has brought down numerous decisions based on interpretations of the Constitution. For example, the landmark civil rights decisions of the 1960s regarding racial desegregation were based on judicial enlightenment, not legislative changes. The Supreme Court has also made a number of radical decisions that safeguard the "due process" standards in the USA and produced substantial changes in police practices, notably the advisement of the accused's rights. By contrast, the Canadian situation was relatively bleak. The Supreme Court of Canada did not confirm the fundamental right of an individual to a defense lawyer in criminal matters until this ruling was made by the Manitoba Court of Appeal in the Ballageer case in 1969. While Canada passed a Bill of Rights in 1960, there was only one case in which the Supreme Court of Canada declared that the Bill of Rights negated other legislation (the Drybones case in 1969). Aside from this case, the Supreme Court of Canada appeared to have developed the opinion that if the only ground for an appeal was that the appellant had been denied something expressly guaranteed by the Bill of Rights, and if there was no other ground in common law, then this was insufficient for the Court to consider the matter. It should be noted that the 1960 Bill of Rights was not bound up with the basic Constitution as is the Canadian Charter of Rights proclaimed by Parliament in 1982. The latter is more like the American case, where the Bill of Rights is an integral part of the American Constitution.

In the Drybones case, Joseph Drybones, an Indian, was found drunk on April 8, 1967 in the Old Slope Hotel in Yellowknife, NWT. He was charged with being an "Indian who was unlawfully intoxicated off a reserve" contrary to S.94 of the Indian Act, and was convicted. However, Drybones successfully appealed his conviction to the Supreme Court of Canada. The Supreme Court argued that the Indian Act was at variance with the Bill of Rights because it made Indians unequal before the law. The Indian Act called for a minimum $10 fine, up to $50 maximum and/or up to three months in jail. The Liquor Ordinance of the NWT called for a maximum imprisonment of 30 days for being found drunk in public. Under the liquor law whites faced no minimum penalty and a maximum 30-day penalty while Indians faced a $10 minimum and a harsher maximum penalty! There are no reservations in the NWT, so any Indian found drunk anywhere could be liable to prosecution under S.94, but this is beside the point. It is also illegal to have liquor on a reservation, and again, this is beside the point. Section 94 was struck down by the Supreme Court because it was inconsistent with the Bill of Rights. We might expect similar decisions regarding the rights of Indians who marry non-Indians. Since a woman loses Indian status by marrying a non-Indian, while a male Indian does not, we should expect that the Supreme Court of Canada will strike down this section of the Indian Act because it is at variance with both the 1960 Bill of Rights and the new Charter of Rights and Freedoms.

However, a challenge to the Indian Act under the equality provisions of the Bill of Rights failed in the cases of two Indian women, J.C. Lavell and Yvonne Bedard. Both had lost Indian status as a result of marriage to non-Indians, and both failed in their attempts to have the Supreme Court invalidate the relevant sections of the Indian Act, as had happened in the Drybones case. Justice Ritchie reasoned that the provisions of the Indian Act that regulated how and by whom reserves were used was based in Section 91(24) of the British North American Act. To overturn the relevant sections of the Indian Act on the basis of the 1960 Bill of Rights would in effect make the Bill of Rights superior to the original Canadian Constitution, something clearly not intended by the 1960 legislation. It remains to be seen whether the same argument will apply under the new Charter of Rights and Freedoms. Notably, aboriginal rights were entrenched in the 1982 Charter. However, what these rights included was not spelled out. The repatriation of the British North America Act included making this Canada's official constitution by way of the new *Constitution Act 1982*. Consequently the special status of natives has been adopted directly in the Charter, and indirectly in the Constitution. Paradoxically, special native status could block equality rights in cases like Lavell and Bedard. Nonetheless, the federal government has committed itself to eliminating sex discrimination from the Indian Act (see John C. Munro, 1982).

The 1973 decision in Lavell and Bedard showed that the 1960 Bill of Rights, despite the Drybones case, could be quite a limited document. Also, what many civil libertarians find distressing about the Drybones case is that it was the only case in which the 1960 Bill of Rights influenced other Canadian legislation, but its influence was not based on any consideration of "due process" but on "equality before the law." In other words, the Bill of Rights did not have an impact on procedural matters (due process), which is the area of dramatic impact made by the Supreme Court in the USA, where the protection of civil rights through the preservation of "due process" has resulted in the absolute exclusionary rule. This requires that evidence against a person gathered in a way that ignores the rule of law (due process) — that is, evidence that is illegally gathered — must be excluded altogether from the trial in court. The Canadian judiciary has resisted this blanket rule but has evolved a related partial exclusionary rule in the cases of evidence obtained by admissions or confessions given by the accused to persons in authority. This is the rule of voluntariness. A person's statement may be used to convict him or her of a crime, despite the right of silence, if the person gives the statement voluntarily. Certain social scientists have suggested that these differences reflect the different political ethos in each country. In the US, the police and the laws are constituted for the people and by the people and hence the police must be exemplary in their behaviour, otherwise their evidence will be excluded. In Canada, citizens tolerate a more autocratic and secretive government and bureaucracy that is responsible only indirectly to the citizenry, as well as to the Queen, through Parliament. These differences are vividly illustrated in the different regulations regarding warnings given by the police to suspected persons. Warnings are of interest here because they relate directly to the common law right to silence. As we shall see, the situations regarding warnings differ significantly in the USA, Britain and Canada.

USA: The Miranda Case (1966)

In 1966, the US Supreme Court quashed the conviction of Ernesto Miranda on charges of kidnapping and rape and handed down a set of warning rules to be followed by all American policemen. Miranda had been arrested by police, taken into custody for questioning and subsequently identified in a police line-up by two victims. During his interrogation he was not informed that he had the right to have an attorney present. As a result of this interrogation, police obtained from Miranda a written confession of rape and kidnapping. The confession claimed to be given voluntarily and made by Miranda with full knowledge of his constitutional rights. The confession was admitted at trial and Miranda was convicted of kidnapping and rape, and received 20-30 years on each count (to be served concurrently). His conviction was upheld in the Arizona court of appeal because, it was reasoned, Miranda did not ask to have an attorney present. Presumably an attorney would have informed the accused of the Fifth Amendment protection in the American Constitution, which states that no one can be compelled to give evidence against himself. There would have been no confession if due process had been followed. In a very close and highly controversial decision, the US Supreme Court overturned the Arizona decisions and quashed the original conviction. Miranda's confession was ruled inadmissible because it had been obtained illegally; that is, it had been obtained without the prior giving of a caution or warning (in accord with the spirit of the Fifth Amendment) and had been obtained where the accused was without benefit of counsel (in accord with the spirit of the Sixth Amendment) (Reid, 1982:294-296).

The Court also discussed the institutional contexts in which Miranda-type confessions were taken, and decried the strong psychological pressures brought to bear on arrested persons to make inculpatory statements and the interrogation methods advocated in police manuals to obtain confessions. Chief Justice Warren attacked such things as the stress on secrecy, on the interrogation of the accused in isolation and in unfamiliar surroundings without the support of family or friends, and the presumption of guilt. Police manuals advised interrogators to show an air of confidence in the guilt of the accused as though the purpose of the interrogation was to clear up minor details. Warren attacked such practices as giving suspects misleading legal advice ("judges go easier if you confess"), confronting the suspect with false confessions made by accomplices, and interminable questioning (see Parker, 1983: 379ff). Clearly these police practices could lead even innocent people to say things that, under normal circumstances, they would not. Warren also described some of the positive effects of a lawyer's presence during interrogation.

> If the accused decides to talk to his interrogators, the assistance of counsel can mitigate the dangers of untrustworthiness. With a lawyer present the likelihood that the police will practice coercion is reduced and, if coercion is nevertheless exercised, the lawyer can testify to it in court. The presence of a lawyer can also help to guarantee that the accused gives a fully accurate statement to the police and that the statement is rightly reported by the prosecution at trial (*Miranda v. Arizona*, 1966: 1009).

As a result of the Miranda case, the Supreme Court spelled out what sort of procedural safeguards would have to be followed. The judgement reads in part:

> As for the procedural safeguards to be employed, unless other fully effective means are devised to inform accused persons of their right of silence and to assure a continuous opportunity to exercise it, the following measures are required. Prior to any questioning, the person must be warned that he has a right to remain silent, that any statement he does make may be used as evidence against him, and that he has a right to the presence of an attorney, either retained or appointed. The defendant may waive effectuation of these rights, provided the waiver is made voluntarily, knowingly and intelligently. If, however, he indicates in any manner and at any stage of the process that he wishes to consult with an attorney before speaking there can be no questioning. Likewise, if the individual is alone and indicates in any manner that he does not wish to be interrogated, the police may not question him.

Consequently, US police forces carry warning cards that repeat almost verbatim the terms of the Miranda decision. However they also provide for the right of the accused to waive his or her rights and to volunteer a statement. If the warnings are not administered or if there is no evidence of a voluntary waiving of rights, the evidence will be inadmissible. This is quite drastic. Clearly, in weighing the rights of the accused to be treated fairly, and the rights of society to be protected from criminals, the American situation gives more weight to the former, though later decisions of the US court have tended to narrow the scope of the Miranda rules.

The English Case: The Judges' Rules, 1918 and 1964

In contrast to the American situation, the British take a more conservative approach. The British system, unlike the American, does not use the absolute exclusionary rule. The admissibility of evidence that has been obtained without a warning of liability is subject, within limits, to judicial discretion. In 1918, the judges of King's Bench in England issued a set of administrative guidelines in a pamphlet titled "Judges' Rules and Administrative Directions to the Police." These rules were intended to guide the police in obtaining evidence while respecting the rights of individuals to not be compelled to incriminate themselves. While the rules do not have the force of law, the decision of the admissibility of evidence lies largely in the hands of the judge, and hence the rules are viewed as strongly advisory. As the revised Rules (1964) themselves advise, non-adherence is not unlawful but very unwise on the part of the policeman. "Non-conformity with these rules may render answers and statements liable to be excluded from evidence in criminal proceedings." The ruling on the admissibility of the defendant's statements or confessions is done via a proceeding called a *voir dire*. The *voir dire*, often referred to as "the trial within a trial" is evidence heard in the absence of the jury, in order to allow the judge an opportunity to rule on its admissibility. If he rules that it is admissible, the same evidence is repeated with the jury present. The key issue in the context of warnings given by English police pertains to the freedom of individual suspects from being compelled to make statements prejudicial to their own best interests. While individuals may wish to give information that could hurt them in a criminal trial, they must be seen to offer it voluntarily. Warnings are deemed to demonstrate that admissions of guilt were given freely.

The Judges' Rules describe the entitlement of the police to question the public about criminal matters, the point at which warnings should be issued and repeated, and the wordings of these warnings. The rules also describe how statements should be taken and how they should be witnessed. While these do not have the force of law, they nonetheless constitute a robust set of guidelines, and they have been instrumental in the Canadian context with regard to warnings (see Kaufman, 1979: 386).

The Judges' Rules (1964)

1. When a police officer is trying to discover whether, or by whom, an offence has been committed he is entitled to question any person, whether suspected or not, from whom he thinks that useful information may be obtained. This is so whether or not the person in question has been taken into custody so long as he has not been charged with the offence or informed that he may be prosecuted for it.

2. As soon as a police officer has evidence which would afford reasonable grounds for suspecting that a person has committed an offence, he shall caution that person or cause him to be cautioned before putting to him any questions, or further questions, relating to that offence.

The caution shall be in the following terms:

You are not obliged to say anything unless you wish to do so but what you say may be put into writing and given in evidence.

When after being cautioned a person is being questioned, or elects to make a statement, a record shall be kept of the time and place at which any such questioning or statement began and ended and of the persons present.

3. (a) Where a person is charged with or informed that he may be prosecuted for an offence he shall be cautioned in the following terms:

Do you wish to say anything? You are not obliged to say anything unless you wish to do so but whatever you say will be taken down in writing and may be given in evidence.

(b) It is only in exceptional cases that questions relating to the offence should be put to the accused person after he has been charged or informed that he may be prosecuted. Such questions may be put where they are necessary for the purpose of preventing or minimising harm or loss to some other person or to the public or for clearing up an ambiguity in a previous answer or statement. Before any such questions are put the accused should be cautioned in these terms:

I wish to put some questions to you about the offence with which you have been charged (or about the offence for which you may be prosecuted). You are not obliged to answer any of these questions, but if you do the questions and answers will be taken down in writing and may be given in evidence.

Any questions put and answers given relating to the offence must be contemporaneously recorded in full and the record signed by that person or if he refuses by the interrogating officer.

(c) When such a person is being questioned, or elects to make a statement, a record shall be kept of the time and place at which any questioning or statement began and ended and of the persons present.

4. All written statements made after caution shall be taken in the following manner: (a) If a person says that he wants to make a statement he shall be told that it is intended to make a written record of what he says. He shall always be asked whether he wishes to write down himself what he wants to say; if he says that he cannot write or that he would like someone to write it for him, a police officer may offer to write the statement for him. If he accepts the offer the police officer shall, before starting, ask the person making the statement to sign, or make his mark to, the following:

I,............., wish to make a statement. I want someone to write down what I say. I have been told that I need not say anything unless I wish to do so and that whatever I say may be given in evidence.

(b) Any person writing his own statement shall be allowed to do so without any prompting as distinct from indicating to him what matters are material.

(c) The person making the statement, if he is going to write it himself, shall be asked to write out and sign before writing what he wants to say, the following:

I make this statement of my own free will. I have been told that I need not say anything unless I wish to do so and that whatever I say may be given in evidence.

(d) Whenever a police officer writes the statement, he shall take down the exact words spoken by the person making the statement, without putting any questions other than such as may be needed to make the statement coherent, intelligible and relevant to the material matters: he shall not prompt him.

(e) When the writing of a statement by a police officer is finished the person making it shall be asked to read it and to make any corrections, alterations or additions he wishes. When he has finished reading it he shall be asked to write and sign or make his mark on the following certificate at the end of the statement:

I have read the above statement and I have been told that I can correct, alter or add anything I wish. This statement is true. I have made it of my own free will.

(f) If the person who has made a statement refuses to read it or to write the above mentioned certificate at the end of it or to sign it, the senior police officer present shall record on the statement itself and in the presence of the person making it, what has happened. If the person making the statement cannot read, or refuses to read it, the officer who has taken it down shall read it over to him and ask him whether he would like to correct, alter or add anything and to put his signature or make his mark at the end. The police officer shall then certify on the statement itself what he has done.

5. If at any time after a person has been charged with, or has been informed that he may be prosecuted for an offence a police office wishes to bring to the notice of that person any written statement made by another person who in respect of the same offence has also been charged or informed that he may be prosecuted, he shall hand to that person a true copy of such written statement, but nothing shall be said or done to invite any reply or comment. If that person says that he would like to make a statement in reply, or starts to say something, he shall at once be cautioned or further cautioned as prescribed by rule 3(a).

6. Persons other than police officers charged with the duty of investigating offences or charging offenders shall, so far as may be practicable, comply with these rules.

Canada: Limbo between English Administrative Rules and Precedent

In Canada, we have neither the rigid procedural laws found in the US nor the detailed extra-legal guidelines furnished by the judiciary of Britain. We are torn between informal use of the British Judges' Rules and a growing body of case law that is beginning to spell out the law regarding warnings and the admissibility of evidence and the question of its "voluntariness." Generally, Canadian courts advise that a caution is necessary to ensure the voluntary quality of a statement. However, the absence of a caution does not bind the hands of a court. All the surrounding circumstances must be investigated to determine whether a defendant's admissions were voluntary and, therefore, admissible.

Most professionally trained peace officers in Canada are instructed to administer warnings to suspects in criminal investigations, and are given guidelines. However since these are largely a matter of local initiative, the guidelines tend to be loose, and only weakly cognizant of the suspects' right to silence. This however is changing, since under the new Charter police are required to advise the accused of the right to counsel.

The Right to a Caution in Review

Having examined the state of legislation and judicial practice in Canada, we can return to the claims of the Canadian Civil Liberties Educational Trust. Can we say that arrested persons who received no warnings and who made inculpatory statements to the investigating officer were deprived of due process of law and denied their civil rights? Rather than having a clear-cut answer, the situation is quite ambiguous. First of all, we could answer no, Canada does not have rigid legal safeguards comparable to those found in the US. In other words, we have no Miranda rules. Formerly a provision in the 1960 Bill of Rights guaranteed the right not to be deprived of liberty without the due process of law, but what constitutes "due process of law" can be interpreted quite narrowly. The rule of law in Canada does not require that police give warnings, so failure to caution is not an abrogation of due process in the strict sense.

A weaker claim might be made by answering yes, failure to warn before taking a statement is a denial of rights, but not an illegal one. It is a denial inasmuch as the police ignored the Judges' Rules. The problem with this outlook is that we are pressed to hang our protection on a set of transplanted administrative rules that even in England can be disregarded by the police without criminal liability.

The last possible answer is at once the most realistic and the least optimistic. Were the convicted persons deprived of their rights? Maybe. If these people had gone to trial and contested the admissibility of statements on the basis that these had been induced by the pressure of custody, they might have been ruled involuntary and hence inadmissible. Such a motion would vindicate the common law protection against being compelled to give self-incriminating evidence. Nonetheless, as noted throughout, the right to silence can be waived if done so voluntarily. The problem with the last solution is that since the vast majority of arrested persons plead guilty, there is rarely any question of the voluntariness and admissibility of guilty or inculpatory statements. In summary, we will never know whether the subjects of the Civil Liberty study were wrongfully and illegally deprived of their civil rights. In terms of admissibility, all we can address are the judicial criteria under which such claims would have been adjudicated had the matter been raised in court.

There is one further question. What difference would such a deprivation make? In Canada, the illegality of the manner in which evidence is gathered has no bearing on the guilt or innocence of the accused established by such evidence. These matters are viewed as quite independent. The reasoning is this: because a policeman broke a law does not mean that the suspect is then absolved from the illegal behaviour discovered by that policeman. By contrast, the American judiciary has linked these by providing for the exclusion of illegally gathered evidence. The American court has reasoned that, without such controls, there would be no curbing the illegal acts of the police. American decisions might be traced to egregious violations of human dignity by law enforcement officers. For example, in the *Rochin v. California* case (1952), drug enforcement officers illegally entered the premises of Rochin's home, saw Rochin swallow two pills, and tried to forcibly open his mouth to retrieve them. When this failed, they took him to the hospital to have the contents of his stomach forcibly pumped out. He was later convicted of possession of morphine. In a judgement quashing the conviction, the judge noted: "This is conduct that shocks the conscience, illegally breaking into the privacy of the petitioner, the struggle to open his mouth and remove what was there, the forcible extraction of his stomach's contents — this course of proceeding by agents of government to obtain evidence is bound to offend even hardened sensibilities. These are methods too close to the rack and the screw" (see Reid, 1979: 338-39). In Canada, Rochin would have been convicted and invited to sue the officers for trespassing and assault; in view of the conviction, the damages would be trifling.

The Law Reform Commission (1975a: 22) in its draft proposal for a new evidence code suggested that evidence should be excluded if it was obtained under such circumstances that its use would tend to bring the administration of justice into disrepute. Such a decision would weigh all the surrounding facts of the case and would result in great judicial power in controlling the introduction of evidence. This has been advocated as an attempt to redress the impunity with which the police can ignore the rule of law. The gravity of such a situation has been raised in several cases of denial of right to counsel, and a protective measure was subsequently incorporated in Section 24(2) of the Charter of Rights. We shall deal with this below. However, we shall first examine the right to counsel in Canada and the associated issues of the rights to call a lawyer and the right to be informed of such rights. While the right to counsel is clearly provided for in the 1960 Canadian Bill of Rights, as well as the 1982 Charter of Rights and Freedoms, how this was translated into practice under the 1960 legislation was quite a complex affair.

The Right to Counsel in Canada

The Canadian Civil Liberties study in 1970 reported that 21% of those surveyed were denied access to a telephone call while in custody, and 30% claimed they were never advised of their right to counsel. What is the Canadian law with respect to these situations? Unlike the American context in which the Miranda warning not only issues a caution against self-incrimination but also advises of the right to a lawyer, and if you cannot afford one, the right to a state-appointed lawyer, the cautions used by Canadian police forces prior to 1982 did not advise the accused of the right to counsel. This was done in some jurisdictions by a court official, the duty counsel, who speaks to accused persons before bail hearings to assist them in making application for legal aid. Typically, this interview occurs after the police have sought a statement from the person in custody.

The right to counsel has been provided in the common law tradition, and was formally enshrined in the 1960 Bill of Rights in sections 2c(ii) and 2d.

1960 Bill of Rights

1. It is hereby recognized and declared that in Canada there have existed and shall continue to exist without discrimination by reason of race, national origin, colour, religion or sex, the following human rights and fundamental freedoms, namely:
   (a) the right of the individual to life, liberty, security of the person and enjoy-

ment of property, and the right not to be deprived thereof except by due process of law;

(b) the right of the individual to equality before the law and the protection of the law;

(c) freedom of religion;

(d) freedom of speech;

(e) freedom of assembly and association; and

(f) freedom of the press.

2. Every law of Canada shall, unless it is expressly declared by an Act of the Parliament of Canada that it shall operate notwithstanding the Canadian Bill of Rights, be so construed and applied as not to abrogate, abridge or infringe or to authorize the abrogation, abridgement or infringement of any of the rights or freedoms herein recognized and declared, and in particular, *no law of Canada shall be construed or applied so as to*

(a) authorize or effect the arbitrary detention, imprisonment or exile of any person;

(b) impose or authorize the imposition of cruel and unusual treatment or punishment;

(c) *deprive a person who has been arrested or detained* (i) of the right to be informed promptly of the reason for his arrest or detention, (ii) *of the right to retain and instruct counsel without delay,* or (iii) of the remedy by way of habeas corpus for the determination of the validity of his detention and for his release if the detention is not lawful;

(d) *authorize a court, tribunal, commission, board or other authority to compel a person to give evidence if he is denied counsel, protection against self crimination or other constitutional safeguards;*

(e) deprive a person of the right to a fair hearing in accordance with the principles of fundamental justice for the determination of his rights and obligations;

(f) deprive a person charged with a criminal offence of the right to be presumed innocent until proved guilty according to law in a fair and public hearing by an independent and impartial tribunal, or of the right to reasonable bail without just cause; or

(g) deprive a person of the right to the assistance of an interpreter in any proceedings in which he is involved or in which he is a party or a witness, before a court, commission, board or other tribunal, if he does not understand or speak the language in which such proceedings are conducted.

The difference between 2c(ii) and 2d should be clarified. The first section states that no law of Canada shall be applied so as to deprive a person who has been arrested or detained of the right to retain and instruct counsel without delay. This applies to the immediate situation following detention or arrest right up to the point of trial and usually covers part of the period during which police are still involved in the investigation. Section 2d covers the trial phase and guarantees that no one can be made to give evidence at a trial or other legal tribunal if he or she is denied legal counsel or is denied protection against self-incrimination.

The phrase "without delay" in section 2c(ii) was usually interpreted as without *undue* delay, but not instantaneously. Even the point at which police denial of *access* to counsel constituted a denial of the *right* to counsel was subject to much interpretation. A number of important cases clarified, to some extent, what the right to counsel in Canada actually involved.

Canadian Cases on Right to Counsel

Most cases in which right to counsel was at issue involved driving offenses. In the first important test of the right to counsel, *Regina v. Gray* (1962), the accused was stopped by a police officer on suspicion of impaired driving and taken to the police station. Gray requested an opportunity to contact his lawyer but was refused any opportunity to do so. He was charged and tried for impaired driving. The County Court Judge in BC who heard the case ruled that this denial by police before the accused was examined by the doctor and before formal charging, was a denial of a right guaranteed under S. 2c(ii), and he acquitted Gray. However, he argued that acquittal should not be advisable or automatic in every case, but only where the abrogation of the right prejudiced the accused. He did not clarify what circumstances constituted prejudice.

In *R. v. Steeves* (1964), the accused contacted his lawyer about a car accident he had just been involved in. The lawyer accompanied Steeves to the RCMP office to report the circumstances. When the police issued a warning and began to seriously question Steeves about the accident, his lawyer advised him to remain silent on certain questions. Steeves was then placed under arrest and taken for questioning to a private interrogation room. The lawyer was actively prevented from accompanying Steeves. As a result of the statements made by Steeves while being held incommunicado, a hostile witness was identified and called to testify against Steeves.

At trial the magistrate ruled such evidence inadmissible and the charge was dismissed. On appeal by the Crown to the Nova Scotia Supreme Court, it was argued that, while the accused may have been illegally denied the right to counsel, this did not mean that he was denied opportunity to make a full defense at trial and that he could not receive a fair hearing. Indeed, at the original interview, he could have refused to say anything, but he waived this right. Consequently, the Court ruled that the original magistrate erred in excluding the evidence gathered by the RCMP. A new trial was ordered allowing Steeves' admissions.

This case is noteworthy because it shows that even though the court recognized that a violation of the right to counsel occurred, this did not mean that evidence gathered as a result of an illegal act would be automatically inadmissible even though it would clearly affect the accused. The Court, however, was not unsympathetic with Steeves' plight. Judge Coffin pointed out a series of relevant cases in which failure of officials to uphold the law gave Steeves some criminal as well as civil remedies, such as a suit for damages, but not a remedy that amounted to acquittal for his own transgressions.

The 1966 case of *O'Connor v. The Queen* was somewhat more complex than the Steeves case. O'Connor was stopped by police who had reason to believe he was impaired while driving. He was compelled under the breathalyzer law to give a sample of breath at the police station. After he had complied and the policeman saw the results of the test, O'Connor was informed that he was under arrest and would be confined to a cell for the night. At this point, he requested to call his lawyer. He was allowed to call but his attempt proved abortive; he was denied any further calls, and was subsequently convicted under the breathalyzer law. This conviction was appealed to the Ontario Supreme Court. Mr. Justice Haines argued that the evidence from the tests should have been excluded and he ordered a new trial. The Crown successfully appealed this motion to the Ontario Court of Appeal, and this was in turn appealed to the Supreme Court of Canada. The latter Court upheld the conviction, pointing out several things. First of all, it argued that the Steeves rule applied. While there may have been a denial of right to counsel when the police refused a second telephone call, this did not automatically mean that an accused person had the right to an acquittal by virtue of exclusion of the breathalyzer evidence. In other words, denial of right to counsel without delay (as per S. 2c of the Bill of Rights) does not mean that an accused cannot make a full defense and have a fair trial. The questions of full defense and fair trial turn on the aspects of the court hearing: the right to counsel *at trial*, the right to call witnesses, the right of protection from unreliable evidence, the right to cross-examine witnesses. Denial of S.2c did not undermine S.2e (the right to a fair hearing). As in the Steeves case, it was observed that, if it could be established that a denial of S.2c had actually occurred, O'Connor could seek a civil remedy. Secondly, it was noted that O'Connor asked to consult a lawyer *after* he had given breath samples. Had he consulted his lawyer beforehand, it is doubtful whether the advise of counsel could have affected the outcome since it is illegal to refuse a sample without lawful excuse. Having contacted the lawyer, what legal excuse could apply? The next case is more intriguing because it deals with this question.

The case of *Brownridge v. The Queen* (1972) is a very ambiguous victory for civil libertarians. Brownridge was stopped by the police on suspicion of impaired driving and compelled to give samples of his breath for analysis. At the police station, he indicated that he wanted to speak to his lawyer and, in fact, told the policeman he would comply with the request for samples only if his lawyer advised him to do so. The police prevented him from making such a call and laid a charge for refusing a sample. Two hours later he was allowed to call and he contacted a lawyer, who advised him to take the test. At this point, the police declined Brownridge's offer of breath samples, presumably because it was too late under the breathalyzer law to take such samples, and he was subsequently convicted of refusing a sample. Mr. Justice Haines set aside the conviction in the Ontario Supreme Court, but this decision was reversed by appeal of the Crown to the Ontario Court of Appeal. When the matter was heard in the Supreme Court of Canada, the original conviction was quashed by a 6-3 decision. What is disconcerting about the decision for the majority is that it was a split majority decision. Justices Ritchie, Fauteux, Martland and Spence argued that the refusal of police to allow Brownridge contact with his lawyer did not *per se* constitute grounds for quashing a conviction. What was relevant was that this request for contact and the denial of access constituted a "reasonable excuse" to refuse a breath sample. The breathalyzer law allows refusal where there is a reasonable excuse.

S.235 (2) Every one who, *without reasonable excuse*, fails or refuses to comply with a demand made to him by a peace officer under subsection (1) is guilty of an indictable offence or an offence punishable on summary conviction and is liable
(a) for a first offence, to a fine of not more than two thousand dollars and not less than fifty dollars or to imprisonment for six months or to both;
(b) for a second offence, to imprisonment for not more than one year and not less than fourteen days; and
(c) for each subsequent offence, to imprisonment for not more than two years and not less than three months.

The Court held that it could not have been demanded of Brownridge that he delay contact since it was advice about the test that constituted the very reason he wished to contact a lawyer. In their minority opinion, Justices Laskin and Hall held that consideration of the breathalyzer law was secondary to the Bill of Rights. Even if the words "without reasonable excuse" were not part of that law, the right to counsel without delay would nevertheless be operative and would apply even if this entailed delay in the administration of the breathalyzer. They argued that, strictly on the basis of S.2c of the Bill of Rights, the accused was entitled to have the charges stayed or the conviction set aside. In other words, the requirements of the Bill of Rights supercede those of the breathalyzer law (without negating them, as in Drybones). It also implied duties on the part of the police in such cases. Justice Laskin noted:

> On this view, it does not lie with an arresting police officer to determine in his discretion or on a superior's instructions whether or when to permit an arrested person to contact his counsel. The right to retain and instruct counsel without delay can only have meaning to an arrested or detained person if it is taken as raising a correlative obligation upon the police authorities to facilitate contact with counsel. This means allowing him upon his request to use the telephone for that purpose if one is available. I am not concerned in this case with determining how many calls must be permitted. Here, on the facts, the accused was prevented from making even one. I am content to say for the purposes of this case that the accused's right under S. 2c(ii) would have been sufficiently recognized if, having been permitted to telephone, he had reached his counsel and had spoken with him over the telephone. I would not construe the right given by S. 2c(ii), when invoked by an accused upon whom a demand is made under S. 223(i), as entitling him to insist on the personal attendance of his counsel if he can reach him by telephone. I refrain from enlarging on the matters mentioned in this paragraph of my reasons because it is better that this be done when particular cases call for it (*R. v. Brownridge*, 1972: 436).

Justice Laskin also pointed out that it was the refusal of the policeman to allow Brownridge to contact his lawyer that made Brownridge hesitant in submitting a sample: in other words, the police officer's illegal act constituted the grounds for the officer to find that Brownridge was delinquent. That denial caused Brownridge's refusal.

> A police officer cannot turn his violation of an accused's rights into an exercise of lawful powers of his own so as to support a charge of a criminal offence which ordinarily arises if those powers are flouted. Where the accused's rights have primacy, as is the case here, the police officer cannot assert his own powers as being then lawfully exercised when that assertion amounts to a denial of the rights of an accused (p.438).

This case differs significantly from the earlier cases. In the previous cases, statements of guilt had been given and/or samples had been obtained. Brownridge was not charged with impaired driving or "over 80," but with "refusing a sample." The *actus reus* was the refusal, not some earlier offense; and the demand for the exercise of a liberty under the Bill of Rights was isomorphic with refusal behaviour under s.235. In the O'Connor case, the evidence was already gathered by the time a lawyer was sought, and the issue turned on whether that evidence could be used to show impairment. In Brownridge, the issue is whether the exercise of a civil right can be construed in the self same behaviour as evidence of refusal to give a sample. As well, since the evidence was already gathered, the appeals have a different nature. O'Connor appealed on the basis that, since he was denied the rights of S. 2c (right to counsel without delay), he was subsequently denied S. 2e (right to a fair trial). Only in this way could an argument be made linking the police crime with the accused's crime. In Brownridge, the question was whether the Bill of Rights superceded the breathalyzer law.

The most recent case to deal with these issues is *Hogan v. The Queen* (1975). When asked for a breathalyzer test, the accused requested to call a lawyer. Unlike O'Connor, this request was made before the test. The police refused Hogan this request and told him that if he refused to give a sample of breath, he would face a charge of refusing a sample. The facts show that the police refusal was flagrant, for Hogan's lawyer was at the police station and Hogan could hear him in an adjoining room making inquiries. Hogan gave the following evidence (*Hogan v. The Queen*, 1975: 68-69).

Q. What happened then?
A. I was taken into the breathalyzer room and introduced to Constable MacDonald and I was sitting waiting for the test when I heard my counsel.
Q. What do you mean you heard your counsel?
A. I could hear him through the door my counsel asking if I was at the police station, my counsel was present.
Q. I see, you recognize your counsel's voice?
A. Yes, I do.
Q. You know it well?
A. Yes.
Q. So you heard his voice asking to see you, before the test was completed?
A. This was before the first test was given, yes.
Q. I see and what did you do at that point?
A. I requested to Constable MacDonald to see my counsel before taking the test and I was told that I didn't have any right to see anyone until after the test and if I refused the test I would be charged with refusal of the breathalyzer.
Q. I see, so he told you no when you asked to see your counsel?
A. That's right.
Q. Why did you want to see counsel?
A. I wanted to see counsel to see whether I had to take the test or not.
Q. And then I gather the test was given to you?
A. Yes, I took the test rather than be nailed with refusal.
Q. I see, in other words you took the alternative?
A. Yes.
Q. It was offered to you by Constable MacDonald?
A. Yes.
Q. And that alternative was offered to you in reply to your request for counsel?
A. Yes, it was.
Q. Was counsel present when your test was finished?
A. After I left the room I saw my counsel.
Q. I see and where was he?
A. Counsel was just outside the door to the breathalyzer room.
Q. At any time was he present during the test?
A. No, he wasn't.

Unlike Brownridge, Hogan reluctantly cooperated and was convicted of "over 80." As in the Steeves and O'Connor cases, the abrogation of the right resulted in the collection of evidence whose relevance to the case was weighed independently of the manner in which it was gathered. Hogan would have had a lawful excuse for delaying the test had he stubbornly insisted that he would not comply until he had consulted a lawyer, but he did not. The case would then have most likely followed the Brownridge decision, and the conviction would have been quashed. As it was, since the damaging evidence was already gathered, the Steeves interpretation applied.

> The common law rule of admissibility of illegally or improperly obtained evidence rests primarily on the relevance of that evidence subject only to the discretion of the trial Judge to exclude it on the ground of unfairness as that word was interpreted in this Court in *R. v. Wray* (1970) (*Hogan v. The Queen*, 1975: 70).

Consequently, the illegal act of the police in flouting the Bill of Rights in favour of the Criminal Code could have remedy, not in the exclusion of the evidence, but in a civil suit. Justice Laskin's dissent advocated the American practice of excluding such evidence, while Justice Pigeon's judgement strongly advised against it. Hogan's appeal was dismissed.

The Right to Counsel in Review

These cases indicate that the importance of the right to counsel is overshadowed by the importance of *knowing* and *exercising* this right. The right to retain legal counsel, according to Justice Laskin, also implies the right to a telephone call in order to exercise this right. Since they are charged with upholding the laws of Parliament, the police have a duty to facilitate such contact by, among other things, providing access to a telephone. Though Justice Laskin resisted enunciating how many calls should be allowed, the right of access is nonetheless affirmed in his judgement in Brownridge. However, in *R. V. Giesbrecht* (1980), allowance of only one call to consult with counsel where the accused required further and reasonable opportunity to communicate with his lawyer was held to be an abrogation of s.2c of the Bill of Rights. The right to counsel is also abrogated if the police refuse an accused access to a long-distance line to speak to his lawyer (*R. v. Hogan*, 1980). Lastly, the decision in *R. V. Gaff* (1980) has indicated that the right to retain counsel via telephone is abrogated if the police insist on monitoring the call by refusing to leave the room during the call.

The implications of abrogation of the right to counsel are case specific. Where the denial allows police to gather evidence in support of a criminal charge, the manner in which it is obtained is irrelevant to the admissibility of the evidence under the 1960 Bill of Rights: notably, the Bill failed to specify any penalty for those individuals who failed to uphold it. Injured parties were advised to seek civil damages. Only in cases like Brownridge, where the individual's attempt to exercise his right entails actions that can be construed by the police as themselves unlawful, or where exercise of such right provides a reasonable excuse for omitting some duty compelled by another law, does the abrogation of the right to counsel lead to the invalidation of a conviction. It is difficult to imagine situations, aside from those generated by the breathalyzer law, where such unusual conditions would hold. This is surely a liability of deriving most of our interpretions of our right to counsel from this narrow range of legislation. Since the offending parties in these cases are typically violating section 234 of the Criminal Code, large damage awards in civil proceedings are quite unlikely. This is because the evidence of illegal levels of alcohol in the bloodstream tends to vindicate the behaviour of the police—for they can surely have had no intent to harm the individual if they formed the impression he or she was impaired and needed to be taken off the road for reasons of safety. Consequently, successful civil suits against the police by aggrieved citizens for denial of right to counsel in breathalyzer cases are unheard of. Predictably this tends to neutralize the control of illegal police conduct and leaves the door open for abuse. An alternative criminal remedy has been suggested by civil libertarians and Supreme Court judges. Section 115 of the Criminal Code is a blanket law that provides a penalty for anyone who disregards any federal law but is not liable under a particular section of the Criminal Code. It reads:

Everyone who, *without lawful excuse*, contravenes an Act of Parliament of Canada by wilfully doing anything that it forbids or by wilfully omitting to do anything that it requires to be done is, unless some penalty or punishment is expressly provided by law, guilty of an indictable offense and is liable to imprisonment for two years. [emphasis added]

It is argued that since the 1960 Bill of Rights did not provide a penalty for contravention, and since the police were charged with upholding this Act of Parliament, the police might have been charged under S.115 for failure to observe the rights and liberties guaranteed by the Bill. While laying such a charge would be itself problematic, it is unclear whether the police in any of the cases examined here could be convicted. Police might argue that observance of the Criminal Code gives them "a lawful excuse" for failure to give a warning and that even if they failed to facilitate a suspect's access to counsel this would not be an *intentional* act to contravene the Bill of Rights. Consequently this does not appear to be a compelling remedy to "civil rights crimes" (Reasons, 1982), and it has never been successfully exercised in such cases (see Henshel, 1983: 12-21).

As noted in the previous chapter, police have faced prosecution under S. 115 for break, enter and theft at the APLQ. Glasbeek and Mandel (1979) point out that this section of the Criminal Code was used to jail labour leader Jean-Claude Parrot for what was essentially a labour relations offense. Consequently the force of this law seems to change depending on the criminal. Glasbeek and Mandel suggest that it is not very punitive when directed at policemen but is overpunitive when directed at people like Parrot.

Responses, Past and Future

The Canadian Civil Liberties Association instituted a programme to attempt to alleviate the tension caused by the duty of police to simultaneously uphold the Bill of Rights and the Criminal Code. In 1973, the Legal Aid committee set up a system by which persons arrested in Toronto between 5 p.m. and 8 a.m. could contact a lawyer for advice about their cases. The idea was to facilitate contact with a lawyer for people who would typically be too poor to have a family lawyer and who would require legal aid. Since an application for legal aid often takes weeks to process, individuals are usually without counsel during the most important part of the police investigation of their cases. A survey was conducted in 1974 to see how effective this "instant counsel" arrangement was. About three-quarters of those sampled had been questioned and, except for one person, none had spoken to a lawyer. Only about one-quarter were even aware of the evening duty counsel service — and even some of these were denied access to it by the police. About half of those sampled made statements to the police. In commenting on this situation, Alan Borovoy (1975: 119) noted:

> The impact of custodial confessions is such that in many of these cases, the eventual involvement of lawyers will be reduced to ritualistic significance. Faced with incriminating statements that are admissible as evidence, many lawyers advise their clients simply to plead guilty in court. Thus, the effective trial for such people is not the model envisioned by the Bill of Rights — a public hearing conducted, with the assistance of counsel, by an impartial judge. It is a private interrogation conducted, in the absence of counsel, by the very partial police.

The problem arises because the police feel under a stronger "allegiance" to the Criminal Code than to the Bill of Rights or the Charter of Rights and in the past have found it more expedient to seek incriminating statements first, and a lawyer for the accused afterwards. Borovoy (1975: 119) suggested that certain changes should be made in the law.

> First, I would recommend that the law be amended in order to provide that the police have an affirmative duty to advise people, as soon as practicable following arrest, of their rights to silence, to consult a lawyer, and to whatever legal aid is available in that jurisdiction. Second, that the police be under an obligation to make available, at the earliest practicable moment following arrest, an effective means of communication between the prisoner and a lawyer — at the very least, a telephone. Third, in the absence of some imminent and overwhelming peril, the police should be required by law to desist from all custodial interrogations, until and unless the arrested person has either consulted with counsel or has waived his right to do so.

With respect to the last point, Borovoy points out that in Scotland virtually all statements given as the result of custodial interrogation are inadmissible in court; nonetheless the crime clearance rate, that is, the measure of crimes solved by arrest, is similar to Canada's. On the other hand, it could be argued that such a practice overly inhibits police investigation and deprives the accused of the freedom to waive the right to silence. There is some merit in owning up to one's criminal acts. A more reasonable alternative would be a formal legal requirement making it the duty of the arresting officer to issue an unambiguous warning to the accused and to communicate a clear indication of the right to silence.

With respect to the second recommendation, we already enjoy the right to call a lawyer on the police department's telephone; but the problem is that the police need to be better informed about this. This would be facilitated if the law prescribed clear penalties for those who fail to facilitate the right to counsel.

Lastly, with respect to the first point, the police may not have had a duty to inform people of their right to counsel under the 1960 Bill of Rights. However, this is clearly indicated in the Charter of Rights and Freedoms passed by Parliament. "Everyone has the right on arrest or detention to retain and instruct counsel without delay and to be informed of that right." The same legislation also provides the courts with the power to order specific remedies for breach of Charter rights. Section 24(1) reads:

> Anyone whose rights or freedoms, as guaranteed by this Charter, have been infringed or denied may apply to a court of competent jurisdiction to obtain such remedy as the court considers appropriate and just in the circumstances.

In the case of breaches of civil rights, this remedy may not be any different from the situation under the 1960 Bill for no criminal court will impose a fine or jail term without the authority and accordance of the Criminal Code. In all probability, remedies would have to be by way of civil suit, which is, in terms of our current experience, a situation that has been less than satisfactory. Though a Charter of Rights and Freedoms must be greeted with optimism in any democratic society, only time will tell how willing the courts will be to give the provisions of the Charter a liberal or a narrow interpretation. We must not forget that the institution of slavery existed side by side with the American Declaration of Independence and the Bill of Rights for the better part of a century, despite the recognition of the principle that all men are created equal. Having the document is only the first step. Ensuring that it is acted upon, and how it is acted upon are more important matters.

Legal Rights Under the Charter of Rights and Freedoms

Life, liberty and security of person

7. Everyone has the right to life, liberty and security of the person and the right not to be deprived thereof except in accordance with the principles of fundamental justice.

Search and seizure

8. Everyone has the right to be secure against unreasonable search or seizure.

Detention or imprisonment

9. Everyone has the right not to be arbitrarily detained or imprisoned.

Arrest or detention

10. Everyone has the right on arrest or detention

(a) to be informed promptly of the reasons therefor;

(b) to retain and instruct counsel without delay and to be informed of that right; and

(c) to have the validity of the detention determined by way of habeas corpus and to be released if the detention is not lawful.

Proceedings in criminal and penal matters

11. Any person charged with an offence has the right

(a) to be informed without unreasonable delay of the specific offence;

(b) to be tried within a reasonable time;

(c) not to be compelled to be a witness in proceedings against that person in respect of the offence;

(d) to be presumed innocent until proven guilty according to law in a fair and public hearing by an independent and impartial tribunal;

(e) not to be denied reasonable bail without just cause;

(f) except in the case of an offence under military law tried before a military tribunal, to the benefit of trial by jury where the maximum punishment for the offence is imprisonment for five years or a more severe punishment;

(g) not to be found guilty on account of any act or omission unless, at the time of the act or omission, it constituted an offence under Canadian or international law or was criminal according to the general principles of law recognized by the community of nations;

(h) if finally acquitted of the offence, not to be tried for it again and, if finally found guilty and punished for the offence, not to be tried or punished for it again; and
(i) if found guilty of the offence and if the punishment for the offence has been varied between the time of commission and the time of sentencing, to the benefit of the lesser punishment.

Treatment or punishment

12. Everyone has the right not to be subjected to any cruel and unusual treatment or punishment.

Self-crimination

13. A witness who testifies in any proceedings has the right not to have any incriminating evidence so given used to incriminate that witness in any other proceedings, except in a prosecution for perjury or for the giving of contradictory evidence.

Interpreter

14. A party or witness in any proceedings who does not understand or speak the language in which the proceedings are conducted or who is deaf has the right to the assistance of an interpreter.

Guarantees under the Charter

Critics of the Charter point out its guarantee of rights and freedoms is very narrow. The first section states:

The Canadian Charter of Rights and Freedoms guarantees the rights and freedoms set out in it, subject only to such reasonable limits prescribed by law as can be demonstrably justified in a free and democratic society.

This means that the provisions can be suspended at the discretion of the Cabinet by virtue of, for example, a declaration of the War Measures Act. This was the device used to confiscate the wealth of Japanese Canadians during the Second World War. The same device was used to round up hundreds of suspected terrorists in Montreal cafés during the 1970 October crisis. While the government claimed evidence of an "armed insurrection" aimed at seizing the control of the state, no such evidence has ever been adduced. The rationale given for such secrecy about the sources of information was "national security." In other words, liberties can be suspended, and governments can avoid accountability by hiding the matter under the blanket of national security. The application of the Charter is limited in other ways. The Equality Rights provisions in Section 15 do not come into effect until 1985. Presumably, this will allow the society a chance to contemplate what it could be getting itself into. Lastly, Section 33(1) of the Charter allows any province to pass a law that "shall operate notwithstanding a provision included in section 2 or sections 7 to 15." In other words, any province can opt out of observing the fundamental freedoms provisions of section 2, as well as the legal rights and equality rights sections if it chooses to pass a law at variance with these provisions. Such a law "shall cease to have effect five years after it comes into force" (S. 33(3)). However, it may be reenacted. This suggests that our "fundamental" freedoms are not perceived by politicians as very transcendental or durable commodities, and must be revived or squashed by periodic legislation.

The most notable positive feature of the new Charter's enforcement section is that it leaves the door open for an American-style exclusionary rule. Section 24 reads:

Enforcement

(1) Anyone whose rights or freedoms, as guaranteed by this Charter, have been infringed or denied may apply to a court of competent jurisdiction to obtain such remedy as the court considers appropriate and just in the circumstances. Where, in proceedings under subsection (1), a court concludes that evidence was obtained in a manner that infringed or denied any rights or freedoms guaranteed by this Charter, the evidence shall be excluded if it is established that, having regard to all the circumstances, the admission of it in the proceedings would bring the administration of justice into disrepute.

Since it is for the trial judge to determine the admissibility of evidence, the course of Canadian justice and, specifically, the protection of civil rights from overzealous police and prosecutors is in the hands of a relatively conservative element in society: the judiciary. Early indications suggest that there are few things so morally repugnant that a trial judge would exclude them solely on the basis of the Charter. After all, it could be argued that the use of illegally obtained evidence reflected badly only on those who broke the law to get it — not on the entire administration of justice, including the judiciary. As well, the judiciary will be very reluctant to break with the paramount considerations of evidence in the English system of justice: whether the facts, however gathered, are relevant and whether statements or confessions are voluntary. We shall be very much greyer than we are today before we discover the significance and implications of this new legislation.

In his review of the experience of right to counsel under the 1960 Bill of Rights, Clayton Rice (1982) points out there was a reluctance on the part of the judiciary to make the Bill work. He cites cases in which persons who could not afford lawyers and could not qualify for legal aid were forced to go to trial undefended in extremely serious criminal cases. According to Rice (1982: 212), "during the last decade, the Bill never truly succeeded in favour of a person who really needed it."

The right to counsel is a lie. And the judicially created promise of a fair trial in Canada in the absence of the Bill's "guarantee" of the right to counsel at trial for an accused person is no less of a fiction. Yet we persist in our national belief that the contrary is true, knowing full well that it is not, and we do not seem to be ashamed about it . . . It is time that we seriously questioned whether we have not abandoned the right to be human to the care of the judiciary's interpretation of the Canadian Bill of Rights — a judiciary and a Bill which have failed us (1982: 212-213).

Whether the New Charter will experience the same results is an open question. However, one thing remains certain: while we may have changed the law, we have not changed the judiciary.

Summary

The common law has slowly evolved certain principles regarding the basic rights of individuals in criminal matters. The two chief principles are the right to remain silent and the presumption of innocence. In Canada there was no formal legislation outlining and guaranteeing civil rights until passage of the 1960 Bill of Rights by the Conservative government of John Diefenbaker. This was replaced by the 1982 Charter of Rights and Freedoms. The new Charter covers areas of fundamental freedoms (freedom of religion, thought, assembly and association), freedom to vote, to move within Canada, legal freedoms, equality, minority language rights and more. However, a review of the history of right-to-counsel cases suggests that our rights, under the 1960 Bill, were interpreted quite narrowly by the police and the courts. Legal counsel, so central in advising the accused of rights and obligations, has frequently been denied in criminal cases, and this denial as we have seen in our review of decided cases, has been virtually sanctioned by the higher courts and has resulted in convictions based on illegally obtained evidence. The new Charter allows the judiciary to ignore such evidence if it brings the system of justice into disrepute. While not fully endorsing the American model, the new legislation promises to provide some restraint against overzealous police forces who have been quick in the past to dispose of civil rights in the interests of crime control. In contrast to Britain, which has no automatic exclusionary rule for tainted evidence (aside from involuntary confessions), and in contrast to the US, which follows an automatic exclusionary rule, the Canadian Charter strikes a middle course. As for the future, the impact of the Charter will turn on the willingness of the judiciary and the legal profession generally to give it a liberal as opposed to a narrow interpretation.

FURTHER READINGS

Thomas R. Berger, *Fragile Freedoms: Human Rights and Dissent in Canada.* Toronto: Clarke, Irwin, 1982.

June Callwood, *Portrait of Canada.* Toronto: Doubleday, 1981.

Edgar Z. Friedenberg, *Deference to Authority: The Case of Canada.* White Plains, N.Y.: M.E. Sharpe, 1980.

Gerald L. Gall, *Civil Liberties in Canada Entering the 1980's.* Toronto: Butterworths, 1982.

John B. Laskin, Edward L. Greenspan and J. Bruce Dunlop (Editorial Board), *Canadian Charter of Rights Annotated.* Aurora: Canada Law Book, 1982.

A. Wayne MacKay, *The Canadian Charter of Rights: Law Practice Revolutionized.* Halifax: Faculty of Law, Dalhousie University, 1982.

Walter S. Tarnopolsky, *The Canadian Bill of Rights, Second Edition.* Toronto: McClelland and Stewart, 1975.

Walter S. Tarnopolsky (ed.), *Some Civil Liberties Issues of the Seventies.* Toronto: Carswell, 1975.

Walter S. Tarnopolsky and Gerald A. Beaudoin, *The Canadian Charter of Rights and Freedoms: Commentary.* Toronto: Carswell, 1982.

Regina v. Wray, Canadian Criminal Cases, New Series, 1970, Vol. 4, pp. 1-27.

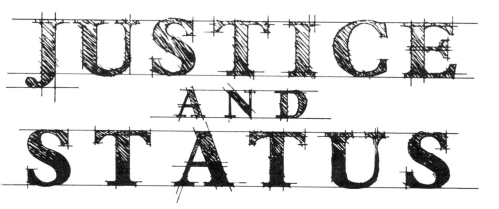

CHAPTER 5

Criminal Justice: A Crime Funnel or a Crime Net?

Introduction

For criminologists analyzing the system of justice in Canada, the primary phenomena are the structures of the justice process. These are the laws and law makers, the police who enforce laws, the courts which interpret them and the prisons which deal with their transgressors. The second major phenomenon is the transformation of criminal cohorts as they pass through these structures. A leading metaphor devised to describe this process is the crime funnel. The funnel is a series of steps or points in a flowchart in the development of criminal cases from the initial investigation and arrest to all the possible outcomes as the cases develop. In this chapter we will explore this conception of the system as a crime funnel and contrast it to an alternative approach that views justice as a crime net.

The Crime Funnel

Research has indicated that from one point to the next in the criminal justice process, the crime population is transformed in character and reduced in size. What is principally indicated by the metaphor of the funnel is the sense of loss. Cases are lost or terminated as the cohort is marched through the investigation, the prosecution, the trial, the sentence, until it at last arrives at the dungeon of corrections. The Criminal Law Review, for example, suggests that of all the break and enters committed in British Columbia and Ontario, only three-fifths are reported to the police, only one in ten are cleared by a criminal charge and only one in seventeen leads to a conviction. Of those convicted only about two-fifths receive jail sentences.

The result of this chain of decisions is that relatively few cases result in conviction and relatively few offenders are imprisoned in comparison with the total number of offenses committed, even for a relatively serious offense such as break and enter. (Chretien, 1982: 90)

The major points of loss have frequently been discussed by criminologists and have been cause for concern in the assessment of the actual volume of crime in the society. Clearly the volume of crime varies at the point at which it is measured. Only a portion of all crimes will be noticed by the public or the victim. Of these, only a portion will be reported to the police. Of these, only a portion will result in an arrest. Of these, only a portion will be prosecuted. And of these, only a portion will be convicted. Consequently, the size of a cohort dwindles the further along in the process it gets. We shall examine each of these points of loss as cases are funnelled through the system of justice.

Debate over the crime funnel has become ideologically charged since some commentators have interpreted the "loss" as evidence of the failure of justice. For example, Walter Berns (1979: 107) argues that for every 100 crimes, there are only 20 arrested persons, and only about nine convictions. This conclusion feeds public hysteria over crime inasmuch as it suggests that 80% of crimes go unresolved and unpunished. Such a conclusion results in calls for greater law and order. However, this conclusion is palpable nonsense. It presumes that each crime is committed by a separate criminal, that every report of a crime is valid and that there is no overlap or duplicity in crimes reported by the police. On each of these points, evidence suggests the contrary. Most criminals, especially serious career criminals, are responsible for more than one crime. Hence the arrest rate of individual criminals will be only a fraction of reported crimes. So too, many allegations reported to the police will prove, upon closer examination, to be unfounded. Lastly, criminal investigations may generate numerous overlapping charges that patently exaggerate or overstate the gravity of the case, and that in fact constitute alternative as opposed to accumulative indictments. These factors produce rates of convictions of individual culprits that are understandably smaller than the rates of crimes reported to the police. The "loss" here is more apparent than real. Consequently, we must examine each phase in the process to understand how the magnitude of crime is recognized and transformed.

Between Crime and Detection

Not all victims of crime realize they have been victimized. A wallet believed to be misplaced might have been stolen by a pickpocket, a flat tire deflated by a vandal, or a higher price artificially inflated by a corporation. Additionally, there may be no discrete and obvious victim of crime, as when a motorist runs a red light or speeds, or where a businessman evades taxes by claiming his wife as an employee, or a farmer fills a car with tractor fuel, avoiding the highway gas tax. While such transgressions occur on a wholesale basis and in numerous sectors of society, there is a great variability in the extent to which they are detected. While you may be unaware that a missing wallet has been stolen, you are unlikely to overlook the disappearance and/or death of a loved one. Consequently, the more serious and visible a crime, the more detectable it is. As a result, we probably have more reliable estimates of serious predatory crimes like murder, wounding, assault causing bodily harm, robbery and kidnapping than other sorts of crimes, such as computer fraud, stock fraud and tax evasion.

When we posit a universe of actual crimes, we usually have in mind clear-cut predatory acts like murder and robbery. However, the criminal quality of many kinds of behaviour is problematic, especially where the laws are not specific. This is the situation in cases of criminal negligence and reckless homicide. Was the reluctance of McDonald-Douglas to modify the engine carriage of the DC10 a criminal behaviour? This alternation might have prevented the worst accident in American aviation history. And was the Ford Motor Company criminally liable in their refusal to change the location of the explosion-prone gas tanks in the Pinto? Such a change would have saved hundreds of drivers from fiery deaths or lifetime disfigurements. Though convictions on criminal charges have not succeeded in either case, both companies have paid out hundreds of millions of dollars in civil damages. This was Ford's ''better idea.'' These cases show that aside from the instances of obvious predation, the concept of a ''universe of actual crime'' is a convenient fiction. The labelling of criminal behaviour and its detection are often intertwined. We usually miss this point because there is no disagreement about the criminality of illegal behaviours. We all agree murder is a crime. The clincher comes when we must determine whether instances of abortion, euthanasia, capital punishment, reckless driving involving death and the conduct of war can be construed as examples of murder. The lethal hazards of numerous workplaces and the occupational health and safety violations that claim tens of thousands of workers annually present an even more contentious situation (Reasons, Ross and Paterson, 1981). The boundaries of a universe of actual crime are inherently problematic, reflecting the politicality of the criminal law. Laws are decided through a political process and are no longer given at the burning bush. Consequently, they are conventional, and so the line between criminality and normality is often arbitrary.

Between Detection and Reportings

The vast majority of crimes the police learn about are brought to their attention by victims and witnesses. Except for a minority of activities involving the drug and morality squads, most police work is reactive. It is complaint initiated. Consequently, the public has an enormous discretionary power in deciding whether to invoke official police participation. Many conditions of resistance or reluctance have been discussed by criminologists.

For example, crimes may be viewed as too minor for official law enforcement. In one US study, it was discovered that only about one-quarter of all shoplifters caught by store detectives were turned over to the police for charges (Sutherland and Cressey, 1974: 27). Crime may involve victims who are otherwise on intimate terms with their attackers as in cases of wife-beating, incest and child abuse. Alternatively, the victims may be willing participants in illegal activities as in acts of homosexuality, pornography, underage drinking, use of illegal drugs, prostitution, gambling and other lifestyle offenses. Crimes may also go unreported because it is felt that the process of reporting and launching a charge may be itself aggravating. This situation is found among sexual assault victims who fear the continued and protracted degradation of reporting their stories to the police and the courts. Many merchants who are victims of robbery often lose more money because of time spent as witnesses in court away from the store than they do in the original robbery:

If I had to do it again, I wouldn't even have reported the robbery. . . Every time I go down to court, I close the store and lose work. They got $125 off me, I'd pay $125 to get out of it (Bartlett and Steele, 1973: 21).

Consequently, many witnesses to crime are reluctant to get involved and the official record of crime is affected accordingly.

Between Crimes Detected and Crimes Recorded by Police

Even if brought to the attention of the police, many crimes go unrecorded. In a study of police discretion in Boston, Chicago, and Washington, DC, Donald J. Black (1970) discovered that 35% of all crimes reported to the police and investigated by them went unrecorded. In other words, official occurrence reports were filled out in only 65% of the police-citizen contacts arising from an alleged crime. Black identified a series of variables that affected the decision to make an official record of the crime. These included the seriousness of the crime, the preference of the complainant for the arrest of the suspect, the degree of familiarity between the victim and suspect, and the amount of deference and respect shown to the police by the complainant.

Other studies indicate that, where a victim of a crime is unwilling to press charges, the police are reluctant to do so on their own because of the difficulty of getting the cooperation of the victim at trial. This situation occurs frequently in domestic disputes where an abused wife might be eager to have the police come to the home in order to control her husband but would be unwilling to offer the testimony needed to register a conviction against him later. Consequently, there is pressure to avoid instituting an official charge because of the low probability of a successful conviction. This affects the events that enter the official records of crime.

Other situations affect the volume of crimes processed by the police. The success of a police division is monitored periodically by examination of the clearance rates for various crimes. Complaints are assumed to be cleared or resolved by arresting a suspect and obtaining an admission of guilt. However, detectives will often clear the slate of outstanding cases by tagging them to a newly arrested suspect on the basis of a similar *modus operandi*, whether or not the suspect acknowledges involvement in these crimes. Alternatively, where they have unmanageable case loads and few leads, detectives will call up complainants and report their lack of progress, suggesting that the matter is unlikely to be resolved by further police work. If the complainant wishes to close the investigation, the case is also marked "solved" or "cleared by withdrawal of complaint." Again, the volume of crime is artificially modified by the pressure of circumstances in police work (Ericson, 1981: 110ff).

Between Arrest and Prosecution

Following arrest and the preparation of the case, the next step faced by the suspect is the trial process. However, there are several important forces that have the effect of reducing the number of crimes actually prosecuted. First of all, contrary to popular opinion, a person may be charged with two crimes arising from the same situation, though he or she may not be put in double jeopardy by being convicted of both charges. A person with more than 80 milligrams of alcohol per 100 millilitres of blood who is operating a motor vehicle may be charged with "over 80," as well as driving while impaired. However, the person cannot be convicted of both charges on the evidence of the breath tests (McLeod et al., 1981). Nonetheless, police often lay both charges and collect evidence of "over 80" as well as evidence of the signs of impairment. This redundancy of effort heightens the likelihood of conviction on either count. The police lay two charges where they are seeking one conviction because it may create a bargaining situation for them (Ericson, 1981; Ericson and Baranek, 1982).

A second situation affecting the transformation of cases is plea bargaining. Often with first time offenders, the Crown will reduce the number of charges against an accused to a single charge, or reduce a series of related charges to the most serious one, on the understanding that the accused will submit a plea of guilty. Consequently, the police in many jurisdictions tend to lay multiple charges on the understanding that there will be a conviction involving only one or two charges. This strategy is said to provide a great deal of latitude to the defense counsel and the Crown in reaching a pre-trial agreement about which charges to drop and which charges to plead guilty to, and, while it results in a conviction of most of those accused of crimes, it does so with only a minority of the charges actually laid. Indeed, some charges are referred to as kicker charges or insurance charges and are laid not with the intent of registering a conviction, but with the intent of giving the police maximum control over the development of the case (by, for example, making release on bail highly problematic). These situations, like the practice of clearing the slate of outstanding cases by tagging them to a recently arrested accused, make the presumption of an actual universe of crime very contentious.

Between Prosecution and Conviction

As we shall see in chapter seven, the great proportion of all crimes that come to the attention of the criminal division of the lower courts result in guilty pleas. Nonetheless, some individuals do plead not guilty and succeed in being cleared of the charges. In other words, not all people presumed to be guilty enough to be charged are found guilty in court. Systematic evidence of the conviction rate for various offenses tried in the USA shows it varies greatly. "In 2925 cities in 1975, 48 percent of the persons charged with murder were found guilty as compared to 33 percent of those charged with rape, 44 percent of those charged with aggravated assault, 36 percent of those charged with robbery, 27 percent of those charged with burglary, 44 percent of those charged with larceny [theft] and 20 percent of those charged with automobile theft" (Sutherland and Cressey, 1978: 31).

These statistics have interesting implications. Most criminologists base their impressions of trends in crime on official statistics, but these are based on occurrence reports and arrests by the police. Police records reflect the reasonable and probable grounds that individual officers have for believing that a crime has occurred. However cogent these might be at the time of arrest, we discover that, under conditions where evidence is controlled, 61% of those charged with murder are not found guilty of murder, 73% of suspected rapists are not found guilty, 80% of suspected robbers are not found guilty and 77% of suspected burglars are not found guilty. Consequently, many things that strike us at the outset as criminal cease to be so on closer inspection. If this is the case, then it is misleading to think of the crime funnel as a place of "loss." How can something be lost if it was not "owned" in the first place? It should also be noted that everyone charged who is not convicted of a crime is not necessarily acquitted. Some will face conviction on reduced charges or on a reduced number of charges. Some will have charges dismissed for lack of evidence and others will successfully contest the charges at trial. Connidis (1979) points out that for a sample of 105 murder charges in Ontario in 1972, 33 cases resulted in conviction to lesser charges, 26 were convicted of murder, 16 were acquitted, 12 were detained for insanity and the remainder otherwise disposed of. Nonetheless, the number of crimes as registered at the point of conviction is substantially reduced compared to the number of crimes at the point of charging. Criminologists might object that these remarks are unfair inasmuch as researchers can determine the crime rate through self-report studies and victimization studies. Such studies invariably indicate that the crime rate is much *higher* than official records indicate. However, one must suppose that the acquittal rate by the courts would also be much higher if these additional criminal cases identified by social scientists were actually adjudicated by the courts. With respect to the official records, the fact that the conviction rate varies so massively between murder (39%) and auto theft (17%) also indicates that the validity of police knowledge is not consistent across the board. On the whole, it would appear to be least sound on those offenses that are deemed less serious and that occur most frequently.

What are the implications of the changes in the criminal cohort as it progresses through the system? First of all, it is abundantly clear that it is misleading to represent the justice system as a kind of funnel or sieve that loses things. It is, on the contrary, a sequence of activities that transforms and packages the elements put through it. The system is subject to a number of sources of pressure. These include the common sense of justice, which motivates citizens to screen technical infractions from morally reprehensible acts; the observability and detectability of crimes that result in a stress on predatory infractions; the occupational and organizational constraints on the police and the prosecutor, which motivate their displays of success through clearance rates on especially obvious harmful infractions, as well as self-serving policies of overcharging and plea bargaining; and judicial pressure, in the form of rules of evidence that restructure, often artificially, the original events according to ideals of reliability, competence, consistency, community sentiment, common law precedent and credibility. Consequently, the image of a funnel through which batches of accused people are poured is highly misleading. Not only does it mystify the process of loss and transformation, it misdirects our attention to the institutional phases through which a case is processed, while indicating little about why cases such as those that flood our system are selected in the first place.

The Crime Net: An Alternative Perspective on the System of Justice

Rather than viewing the justice system as an organizational flow chart, or a record of the paths of average criminals injected into the body of justice, we should think of the system as a net thrown out to capture certain objects the way fish are caught. Just as the fisherman does not cast his net randomly, neither do the police. The size of the holes in the netting, the depth to which it is dropped and the places where it is dropped all affect the kind of fish taken, as well as the size of the catch. By analogy the "catch" of the police is a function of the style of policing. If all the police are put on patrol downtown, we should expect increased arrests for soliciting, jay walking, and double parking. The following item illustrates an extreme instance of selective policing.

HOMOSEXUALS, LAWYERS CLAIMING HARASSMENT
OVER BATHHOUSE RAIDS

The raid by about 150 Metropolitan Toronto policemen on four downtown bathhouses Thursday night constitutes harassment of homosexuals, some lawyers and homosexual spokesman charged yesterday.

As a result of the raids in which police with flashlights, crowbars and sledgehammers swept through the darkened hallways breaking down cubicle doors, more than 250 men have been charged as found-ins in common bawdy houses.

Twenty men have been charged with keeping a common bawdy house and 14 minor drug charges have been laid. . . .

Chief Ackroyd said that the type of charges laid by the officers are valid. He said that police must have had reasonable and probable grounds to believe that the bathhouses were being used for prostitution and indecent acts. He refused to elaborate on what constituted prostitution or indecent acts. Staff Inspector D.R. Banks, who led the investigation, said in an interview yesterday that indecent acts must involve more than two people and that it is up to the courts to decide the issue of indecency, based on community standards. . . .

However, a bill currently before Parliament, if passed, will allow such acts between any number of consenting adults as long as they take place in private.

"Do the police care what goes on inside of them? Do we really have to spend all that money for this kind of situation? Who cares? Who really cares except the morality squad? There are killers that haven't been caught in this city, why don't we concentrate on them?"

Mr. Manning said doors were broken in at the clubs, windows and glass smashed and paintings ripped off the walls. . . . (*Globe and Mail*, 7 February 1981)

Clearly on this raid the police were out fishing for a certain kind of offender. No one casually rounds up 290 homosexuals on a regular patrol. In fact, this was the greatest mass arrest in Canada since the invocation of the War Measures Act in 1970. It was revealed that the raids were initiated by the Metro Toronto Police Intelligence Squad, not the morality squad, and that they were initiated days before the squad's budget was to be reviewed. Perhaps coincidentally, Alan Fotheringham (1982: 93) notes, the raids occurred one week after the announcement of the Ontario provincial election. The idea that the raids were undertaken to serve an organizational police objective, and/or to evoke confidence in the conservative rural body politic, is revealed by the conviction rate. As of January, 1983, 251 men had successfully challenged the charge of being found-ins in a common bawdy house, 19 pleaded guilty, 18 were found guilty at trial and the remaining cases were not completed. In other words, the charges were unfounded in 87% of the arrests (Right to Privacy Committee, 1983: 6). This surely undermines public confidence in the fairness of justice and challenges the idea that the police were merely administering the laws.

The selective operation of the system is revealed in more prosaic occasions. For example, though all police forces are likely to divert juvenile suspects into informal social control situations, some forces are more forgiving than others. As noted in our discussion of police, James Wilson (1968b) found that the degree of professionalism of a police force affects the arrest rate of suspected juvenile offenders: the more professional the force, the higher the formal arrest rate. If mounted patrols are deployed in urban parks and ravines, arrests for underage drinking will be more probable. Similarly, the larger the commercial crime branch, the greater the number of investigations of commercial crime complaints.

The criminal justice system cannot detect all crimes for pragmatic as well as for moral reasons. Pragmatically, current criminal justice systems expend enormous sums of money on policing and could easily bankrupt the citizens they protect if allowed unchecked growth. Morally, the enforcement of every possible crime in every sector of society would turn society into an Orwellian police state. Consequently, the selective attention of the system of justice is unavoidable. Discretion as well as policies that interpret which sections of the Criminal Code require highest priority are inherent in the administration of the rules of justice.

If this is so, a major question must be whether this discretion in the administration of the law is directed at any particular sector of society. Who is bearing the brunt of justice? Many critical criminologists argue that the law is a mechanism for the control and suppression of the lower classes, the poor and the minority groups. This view tends to obfuscate the obvious liberal trends in the evolution of justice and tends to engender a cynicism about the nature of laws per se. In this chapter, an alternative hypothesis will be examined. Rather than arguing that the justice system is aimed at the suppression of these groups, we shall argue in agreement with Jeffrey Reiman (1979) that the system operates in a way that weeds out the rich, the middle class offenders, higher status occupational groups, the politically prominent and the well-educated. What this means is that those people who are arrested and go to jail are, by and large, quite guilty of their crimes, but they are not the only elements of society engaged in serious, harmful behaviour, nor are they the only elements of society to be engaged in serious criminal cases as a result of that behaviour. They are, nonetheless, overrepresented in the cohorts that receive the most punitive treatment by the criminal justice system. We shall develop the argument in four stages.

The Slant of the Laws

The way the laws are written focusses attention on interpersonal predatory behaviour and property offenses. The conduct of individuals in an organizational or occupational context is generally exempted from criminal law: recall from previous chapters the differences in the anti-opium laws directed at the Asiatic minority and the Proprietary Medicine Act directed at physicians. The same differences in penalties were reflected in the Comprehensive Drug Law (1970, USA) and the regulation of prescriptions. The 1970 law avoided any control of valium despite the widespread illicit and dangerous use of this legally manufactured drug. The 1980 Indiana criminal charges against the Ford Motor Company in the exploding Pinto affair designated Ford, not its executives, as responsible for criminal recklessness and reckless homocide. The point of all this is captured in the following news item.

CALGARY FIRM CHARGED IN MINE DEATHS

Calgary-based Belmoral Mines Ltd. has been charged with eight counts of manslaughter in connection with a cave-in last year at its Ferderber gold mine in Val d'Or, Que., which left eight miners dead.

Crown prosecutor Jean-Pierre Major said Friday the company is to respond to the charges next Thursday at a court arraignment in the northwestern Quebec mining town.

The decision to lay charges was based on transcripts of hearings last September by the commission of inquiry presided by provincial labor court judge René Beaudry.

Its report, released last week, concluded that the mine cave-in was foreseeable and accused the company of placing profits before safety.

Beaudry plans to submit a follow-up report within a month discussing the fruitless attempts to rescue the eight Belmoral victims, who were killed by a torrent of sediment released by the cave-in. Eighteen others escaped by running up a ventilation shaft. (*Calgary Herald*, 11 April 1981, p. 1)

When the case came to court in Calgary, the charges were almost immediately dismissed. This situation is not uncharacteristic. While executives and businessmen operate unsafe work situations, market dangerous products and poison the environment, no one has spent a day in jail for any resulting deaths. In 1974 in the USA there were approximately 100,000 occupationally induced deaths on the job and deaths from industrially induced disease, as well as 390,000 physical injuries. During this same period there were 20,600 murders and non-negligent manslaughters (Reiman, 1979: 75). Clearly, there is a far greater risk to life as a result of health and safety violations on the job than there is of dying at the hands of a gunman. However, none of these health and safety violations are construed as acts of murder because the law is wired to criminalize only individuals acting with the intent to kill. Our notion of culpability has become too narrow to control the massive harmfulness of industry-related killings. Businesses and corporations are rarely criminally liable for deaths on their premises or deaths caused by their products, and executives are never held personally responsible.

Jeffrey Reiman (1979: 65-74) points out in a similar vein that in the USA there are 15,000 deaths annually as a result of complications arising from unnecessary operations. Further, 60% to 90% of the annual 365,000 victims of cancer in the USA are killed by artificial carcinogens. He contrasts criminal murders with the far more pervasive picture of fatality caused by business-related behaviours.

TABLE 1
How Americans Are Murdered (Criminal)
Murder, Type of Weapon Used

Firearms	Knife or Other Cutting Instrument	Other Weapon: Club, Poison, etc.	Personal Weapon: Hands, Fists, etc.	Total
13,987	3,626	1,401	1,586	20,600

TABLE 2
How Americans Are Murdered (Other)
Murder, Type of Weapon Used

Occupational Hazard	Inadequate Emergency Medical Care	Knife or Other Cutting Instrument Including Scalpel	Firearms	Hypodermic or Prescription	Other Weapon: Club, Poison, etc.	Personal Weapon: Hands, Fists, etc.	Total
114,000	20,000	15,626	13,987	2,000	1,401	1,586	168,600

Source: Reiman, 1979: 75.

In none of the circumstances in Table 2 are middle- and upper-class doctors, executives or businessmen liable to criminal prosecution, despite the proven harmfulness of their business-related activities.

Law Enforcement and Social Class

In a study of juvenile delinquency, Aaron Cicourel (1968) showed that the common-sense belief among police officers that poverty is a cause of broken homes and that broken homes are the cause of delinquency has become a self-fulfilling prophecy. In his study he observed that children from broken homes were selected out for formal processing in the juvenile courts while middle-class offenders were diverted to psychiatric settings and other social welfare agencies for the same kind of infractions. The police believed this appropriate because they viewed the lower-class offenders as essentially incorrigible. The resources of middle- and upper-class families prevented their children from receiving formal processing. When these police practices yielded aggregate figures for arrests and conviction, this only confirmed the suspicions of the police that the majority of crimes occur at the bottom of the social ladder. However, in Cicourel's view, these statistics were more instructive as indicators of what the police, not the crooks, were doing. His view is corroborated by students of middle-class delinquency.

A number of studies support the idea that serious criminal behaviour is widespread among middle- and upper-class juveniles, although these individuals are rarely arrested. Some of the studies show that there are no significant differences between economic classes in the incidence of criminal behaviour (Erikson, 1973). Others conclude that, while lower-class individuals do commit more than their share of crimes, arrest records overstate their share and understate that of the middle and upper classes (Gold, 1966). Still other studies suggest that some forms of serious crime usually associated with lower-class youth show up more frequently among middle-class persons than among lower. For example, Empey and Erikson (1966) interviewed about 200 white males (age 15-17) drawn from different economic strata. They found that "virtually all respondents reported having committed not one, but a variety of different offenses." Although middle-class youngsters equaled 55% of the sample, they were involved in 67% of the instances of break and enter, 70% of the instances of property destruction, and 87% of all robberies admitted to by the adolescents in this self-report study.

Another study done by Williams and Gold (1972) was a nation-wide sample of 847 males and females between 13 and 16 years old. Of these, 88% admitted to at least one delinquent offense. One thing especially notable in this study was the finding that higher-status white boys were more seriously delinquent than lower-status white boys. The greater seriousness of the high-status boys' delinquency stemmed from their greater participation in theft, joy riding and assaults (versus truancy, smoking, disrespect toward teachers). Gold (1966) points out that the lower-class boys are overrepresented in the criminal records. He argues that if the criminal records accurately reflected behaviour we would expect to find low-status boys in a ratio of 1.5 to 1.0 to mid- and high-status boys, but we find a ratio of 5:1. The police are far more likely to seek non-court options for middle- and upper-class boys who are caught in crime. Hence, the net selectively picks out the poorer elements of society.

Similar results were reported in Terence Thornberry's 1973 study of 3,475 delinquent boys in Philadelphia. Among boys arrested for equally serious offenses who had similar police records, police were more likely to refer lower-class boys to juvenile court than higher-class boys and they were also more likely to be institutionalized in training schools than wealthier boys, who were more likely to get probation.

Ronald Goldfarb reports a 1966 study of the well-to-do suburb of Lafayette in Contra Costa County, California, which revealed great differences between the processing of juveniles in this suburb compared to the rest of California on a number of counts. For example, comparison of rates of release of juveniles without charges: 48.2% for California vs 80% for Lafayette; of those arrested and charged, 46.5% eventually went to Juvenile Court for all of California vs only 17.9% for LaFayette; of those eventually institutionalized by Juvenile Court, 5.3% for California vs 1.3% for Lafayette (cited in Reiman, 1979: 103).

There are a number of reasons for the class differences in addition to Cicourel's observation about the self-fulfilling prophecy of police folk beliefs. People who live in ghettos treat the street corner and the sidewalk as their own "turf." If any illegal acts like buying and smoking marihuana are committed there, they are more likely to be observed by the police. Obviously the middle- and upper-class delinquents who sniff cocaine in their backyards are out of the view of the law. Additionally, there are differences in lower- and upper-class victims of crimes. A lower-class victim might make greater demands on the police for arrest and punishment of a suspect where an upper-class complainant is more liable to seek informal and/or civil remedies for a harm. Lastly, the density of lower-class ghettos makes them greater targets for surveillance by law enforcement officials. In other words, though the crime rate in a lower-class area might not be unusually high, the high population density makes the absolute number of crimes greater. Hence, an eight-hour shift will net more criminals in the ghetto than in the suburbs. Administratively, this means a better deployment of police manpower.

The next two steps in the crime net are conviction and sentencing. Following the framework advanced by Reiman (1979), the propositions in these two areas are as follows. Criminal convictions do not reflect the only or the most dangerous elements of society or the most dangerous individuals arrested. Conviction is hinged on ability to hire a good lawyer. Status plays a role here as well. And sentencing after convictions does not reflect the degree of danger or harmfulness of the activity. That is, the most harmful acts are not the most severely punished. Corporate criminals are fined; the poor are jailed.

On Convictions

There is evidence to suggest that, if we compare rich and poor individuals accused of similar offenses and with similar prior police records, the poor defendant is more likely to be judged guilty than the wealthier defendant. In the adjudication process, the only matters that should count are whether the accused is guilty and whether the Crown can prove it beyond a reasonable doubt. Unfortunately, other factors can affect this process. Prior to the Bail Reform Act of 1971, it was often relatively difficult for arrested persons to get release on bail, especially if they were too poor to post the amount of bail set for their release. Property owners had an advantage. They could use their houses as surety or security for the purposes of getting bail. Therefore, since the poor tend to rent and save little, they were at a disadvantage and were deprived of the opportunity to gather facts in defense of their own cases. This situation has been corrected by the current bail law, which puts the onus on the Crown to show why bail should be denied.

Nonetheless, there is still a second source of inequity. Though the poor do have the right to legal aid defense (in Canada) and Public Defenders (in the USA), evidence suggests that these are not the most successful practitioners in the legal field and/or that legal aid cases are not handled with comparable time and care as private cases. For example, under the Ontario legal aid system, the lawyer is paid a fixed fee of approximately $250 per day for one court appearance and is required in Ontario to return 25% of that fee into the legal aid plan. We might calculate the earning as follows: $187.50 (75% of $250) per day × 5 days per week = $937.50 × 50 weeks = $46,875. From this the lawyer must pay for an office and a secretary, as well as investigators' fees and witness fees. Consequently, there is a great pressure on the lawyer to manage a high volume of cases that will take little time to complete. The result may be pressure from the lawyer on the defendant to be "reasonable and plead guilty." Therefore, a lawyer maximizes profitability of the day in court. Frequently we find that 75%-90% of convictions in the lower courts (which do most of the business) result from negotiated guilty pleas or plea bargains. Blumberg's 1969 study of 724 male felony defendants in the USA indicated that, in the majority of cases, it was the defense lawyer who initially introduced the idea of "copping a plea," and that the public defender and assigned counsel suggested pleading guilty earlier in the case preparation than the privately retained lawyers (p. 236). Privately retained counsel suggested the plea option in the initial interview in 35% of their cases vs public defenders in 49% and assigned counsel in 60%.

The kind of lawyer defending a case may make a difference in the sort of preparation the case gets. Public defenders and legal aid lawyers have little time for investigative preparation. Their success in court appears to reflect this. Blumberg reports significant differences in the success rates of different kinds of lawyers. Public defenders received dismissal of charges in 8% of cases, assigned lawyers in 6%, and privately retained counsel in 29% of cases. Also, as might be expected, the overall acquittal rate for privately retained counsel is considerably better. The same study shows that public defenders achieved either dismissal of charges or a finding of not guilty in 17% of felony indictments, versus 18% for assigned counsel, and 36% for privately retained lawyers.

This is not to say money will buy your freedom, but it will make sure that every safeguard is observed and that the prosecution establishes every single necessary fact and observes every procedural requirement in the case. It will also mean a greater utilization of investigation by the defense. In Canada, it will mean that there will be no delay of weeks while the accused's application for legal aid is processed.

Some relevant Canadian evidence was gathered by James Wilkins in a study of *Legal Aid in the Criminal Courts* (1975). He examined the question of whether the finding of the court varied with the type of defense lawyer.

TABLE 3
Finding of Court by Type of Counsel Retained

A. FOR ALL CHARGES

Type of Representation	Finding of Guilt	Finding of Not Guilty Dismissed or Withdrawn
No Lawyer	75.2%	24.8%
Legal Aid Lawyer	69%	31%
Privately Retained Lawyer	64.3%	35.7%
Duty Counsel	83.7%	16.3%

B. FOR THE MOST SERIOUS CHARGES ONLY

Type of Representation	Finding of Guilt	Finding of Not Guilty Dismissed or Withdrawn
No Lawyer	68.6%	31.4%
Legal Aid Lawyer	46.2%	53.8%
Privately Retained Lawyer	54.2%	45.8%
Duty Counsel	76.1%	23.9%

Source: Wilkins, 1975: 116 and 118.

This study was a one-day investigation of all the cases disposed of in a Toronto Provincial Court, Criminal Division (Old City Hall). These tables generally support the conclusions reported in American studies. Having a lawyer is better than not having one. However, to determine what difference the lawyer makes, one would have to control for the plea because if everyone pleaded guilty, how could the lawyer be effective? The next table sheds some light on this question. It deals with convictions, examining again the type of defense but controlling for whether or not the individual pleads guilty.

TABLE 4
Findings by the Court -
Success of Lawyer Controlling for Type of Plea Entered

Type of Representation	Plea	Finding of Court Guilty	Combination Guilty/ Non-guilty	Only Not Guilty Dismissed/ Withdrawn
1. Unrepresented	Guilty	86.0%	10.5%	3.5%
	Not G.	46.2%	15.4%	38.5%
2. Legal Aid Lawyer	Guilty	50.0%	47.2%	2.8%
	Not G.	37.9%	31.0%	31.0%
3. Privately Retained	Guilty	70.7%	25.3%	4.0%
	Not G.	36.7%	12.2%	51.0%
4. Duty Counsel	Guilty	68.0%	25.3%	6.7%
	Not G.	0	66.7%	33.3%

Source: Wilkins, 1975: 125.

Duty counsel service provided under the Ontario Legal Aid plan locates a lawyer in the court building who can be consulted by accused persons, and whose chief function is to facilitate applications for legal aid. In those rare cases where the lawyer thinks it appropriate, he or she may suggest submission of guilty pleas and often speaks on the accused's behalf before sentencing in such cases. However, the duty counsel will virtually never represent an accused in a trial as the public defender does in the USA. Less than 10% of the cases in the Wilkins study involved representation by duty counsel.

When reading Table 4, one should keep in mind that a large number of criminals are facing several simultaneous charges at trial. An individual may submit a plea of guilty to one or two and find that upon conviction the Crown withdraws or dismisses the other charges. This means that there are three possible outcomes: guilty on all counts not guilty on all counts and a combination of guilty and not guilty. With this in mind, what does the table suggest? First of all, if we compare the findings of guilty for persons without lawyers to persons with lawyers of any kind, we see that those without representation do much worse when pleading guilty. That is, most of them (86%) are convicted of everything. And when pleading not guilty, they do worse than those with either a legal aid lawyer (37.9%) or a private lawyer (36.7%). Secondly, if we compare the legal aid and the private lawyer, when pleading their clients not guilty, they experience findings of guilty at about the same rate. In other words, in both cases, 36% or 37% of their cases result in findings of guilty. Thirdly, if we follow up this same comparison and ask what percent of the cases of the private and the legal aid lawyers results in complete exoneration, we get a different picture. The private lawyer experiences complete exoneration in 51% of the cases when pleading not guilty, compared to 31% for the legal aid lawyer. The latter handles far more individuals with mixed dispositions. And lastly, when pleading guilty, the privately retained lawyer finds that more clients will be convicted of all charges (in 71% of cases) compared with the legal aid lawyer (who finds 50% of cases found only guilty). Obviously, the benefit of the privately retained lawyer is in not guilty pleas and in having charges withdrawn or dismissed.

The picture painted by the Canadian study is consistent with findings from the USA, though there is a difference in the success rates of private lawyers versus the public defender in the USA and the legal aid lawyer in Canada. The legal aid lawyer is not really the equivalent of the public defender. The American public defender is a separate occupational niche in USA courts, while in Canada a lawyer may be in court one day on a legal aid case, and the next on a privately retained case. Consequently in Canada, the differences arise not from the quality of the practitioner, but from the care the lawyer can afford to give to each case depending on the source (and hence amount) of compensation. This explains why the differences observed by Wilkins are not as dramatic as in the USA, but are nonetheless consistent with the American trends.

On Sentencing

So far we have examined three ways in which the justice system operates as a net: the slanting of laws, the administration of laws and the trial sequence. The fourth step in this process involves sentencing. We have numerous anecdotal accounts of the differences in sentencing according to one's social status (and hence the kind of lawyer one can afford). (Reiman, 1979: 115) cites a good example from the *New York Times* (September 27, 1972).

> Jack Greenberg took $15 from a post office; last May in Federal Court in Manhattan he drew six months in jail. Howard Lazell "misapplied" $150,000 from a bank, in the same month in the same courthouse he drew probation.

Mandel (1983a) explored a similar type of class bias running systematically throughout a series of Canadian cases involving middle and upper class offenders. His work traces how social history is used to justify keeping high status offenders out of jail. A good example of this is the case of *Regina v. A* (1976). *A* was a businessman who attacked and attempted to rape one of his female employees. She resisted vigorously and escaped. *A* was charged with attempted rape but was convicted of indecent assault. Throughout his brush with the law, *A*'s identity remained unpublished. Upon conviction he received a suspended sentence and was put on probation for three years. One provision of his probation order called for *A* to pay $1,000 compensation to the victim. The court provided the following justification:

Imprisonment would be of no assistance to the accused. It is likely it would ruin his one-man business. To him the conviction itself forms a substantial portion of the punishment . . . While the solution I propose to follow here cannot be adopted in all cases, because the offender is usually without funds, here the offender is a man of modest means. . . . I propose to make compensation of the victim part of the process of rehabilitation. After all it has long been recognized that restitution for wrong done is rehabilitation. (1976: 475-476)

The *New York Times* article and the case of *A* suggest that the poor get harsher sentences than the well-to-do. A study by Stuart Nagel (1970: 39) indicated that 27% of the indigent (those earning less than $2,000 per year) with no prior records were not recommended for probation vs 16% of the non-indigent, and that 23% of the indigent did not receive suspended sentences vs 15% of the non-indigent. The result is that the jails become the monopoly of the poor. In the USA, blacks make up 20% of the population; they constitute 25% of all the arrests, but they make up 40% of the prison population. In Canada, native peoples make up 10% of the inmates of federal prisons, and a disproportionate number of the provincial jail population.

TABLE 5
Incarceration of Indians in Provincial Jails

Province	Time Period	% of Population	% of Jail Populations
Alberta	1965-1972	5.5	23.4 - 30.8
Saskatchewan	1969-1970	12.7	48.9
Manitoba	1966-1971	12.0	39.4 - 50.9
British Columbia	various times	5.0	10 - 20

Source: Schmeiser, 1974: 1-11.

Mary Cameron's (1969) study of shoplifting provided similar results. She reported that there were great differences in both convictions as well as sentences for black versus white shoplifters. Judges found 16% of white woman not guilty, compared with 4% of black women. Also, only 4% of the white women convicted of shoplifting were sentenced to jail terms compared to 22% of black women. Of those sentenced to over 30 days in jail, only 10% of white versus 26% of black women received this stiffer form of sentence.

TABLE 6
Cameron Study of Shoplifting Convictions

Race	Convicted	Jailed	Jailed over 30 days
Black	96%	22%	26%
White	84%	4%	10%

Note: Figures control for value of merchandise stolen.
Source: Cameron, 1969: 188.

Another problem to consider in comparing the sentences of convicted people is that while the laws structure maximum sentences, classes differentially participate in different forms of harmful activities that have different maximum penalties. Executives sentenced in the famous Electric Equipment Price Fixing Conspiracy in the USA in the

1960s received 30 days in jail. This reflects the fact that white-collar workers are treated entirely differently from blue-collar workers in terms of sentencing. Reiman (1979) explored the differences in lower-class thefts and upper-class thefts in terms of the number of months convicted individuals received for each kind of crime. The following table compares the crimes of the poor and crimes of the affluent with respect to magnitude of penalty.

TABLE 7
Sentences for Different Classes of Crime

	Average Sentence (in months)	Average Time Until Parole (in months)
Crimes of the poor		
Robbery	133.3	51.2
Burglary	58.7	30.2
Larceny/theft	32.8	18.7
Crimes of the affluent		
Embezzlement	21.1	13.2
Fraud	27.2	14.3
Income tax evasion	12.8	9.7

Source: Federal Bureau of Prisons, Statistical Report, Fiscal Year 1973. Cited in Reiman, 1979: 119.

Mandel (1983a) cites similar figures for Canada that indicate that the average prison sentence for robbery is 38.9 months compared to 1.4 months for income tax evasion. This is only one kind of evidence that indicates that sentences for the poor tend to be greater than for the well-to-do. Another kind of evidence relates to variance between sentences based on type of representation (none vs duty counsel vs legal aid vs private counsel). The following figures lend some support to this position. Again we turn to Wilkins' study of Legal Aid in the Criminal Courts (1975).

TABLE 8
Sentencing by Representation

Type of Representation	Sentence		
	Jail	Fine or Jail	No Fine or Jail
Unrepresented	12.9%	53.5%	33.7%
Legal Aid	45.8%	25.0%	29.2%
Privately Retained	22.8%	65.2%	12.0%
Duty Counsel	33.8%	36.8%	29.4%

Source: Wilkins, 1975: 129.

Table 8 suggests three interesting findings. First, most self-represented convicted persons receive the option of fine or jail (54%). However, it must be assumed that these cases were not truly serious, for few judges will allow a defendent to face a grave criminal matter without benefit of counsel. This, of course, is not absolute, as our last chapter indicated. Sixty-five percent of privately retained lawyers' cases result in an option of a fine or jail time, compared to only 25% of the legal aid cases. Consequently, the legal aid lawyer sees far more of his clients ending up in jail compared with the privately retained lawyer. Lastly, the duty counsel seems to be about equally successful in all three alternatives, although duty counsel is midway between the private lawyer and the legal aid lawyer in keeping individuals out of jail. But again, as with self-represented persons, serious cases will normally not be defended by duty counsel.

However, type of representation is not the only relevant question. In a study of the differential sentencing of offenders in several US federal courts, Hagan, Nagel and Albonetti (1980) raised important points about the nature of white-collar crime prosecutions. They found that where prosecutors aggressively pursued white-collar criminals, this was associated with a lenient sentencing policy compared with the sentencing of common criminals. Hagan et al argued that this difference appears to have arisen because of the nature of much white-collar or business crime. Since there usually are no witnesses or immediate victims, prosecutors must persuade participants to inform on themselves and others, and do so by striking bargains for lenient sentences. As Hagan *et al* (1980: 819) note, "the sense is of a style of prosecution that gives preferential treatment to highly educated white-collar offenders. That this may be what is required to successfully prosecute important white-collar cases is an uncomfortable paradox that policy makers as well as theorists will do well to consider." The implication is that white-collar crime by the very way it is committed will either be underprosecuted or will continue to guarantee a sentencing advantage to white-collar crimes.

Summary

The slant of the laws, the selective enforcement of the Criminal Code, the differential conviction rates and differential sentencing rates, reflect not a simple production of outcomes based on a division of labour, but a systematic orientation in the system of justice to particular sectors of society and a studied blindness to other sectors. This is what the metaphor of the crime net tells us. By contrast, the crime funnel, in its methodological focus on the divisions of labour as points of loss, and its presumption of an actual universe of crime that underlies and motivates the system of justice, masks the more basic substantive issues of how the law selectively manufactures criminality and how the police selectively discover it. One strong advantage of the critical orientation of the net model is that it points up areas of change that must be explored to guarantee a more just system of law. While it cannot be denied that the textbook criminal is typically guilty of theft and/or predatory behaviour, the slavish reproduction of this particular imagery of what constitutes crime in the mass media dramas of cops and robbers, in the network news, in magazines, in the academic textbook market and in the images of justice as mere funnels of crime — all this stereotyping of crime as wilful predation, and the ritual scapegoating of its practitioners is gained by an enormous loss of vision and loss of control over possible social changes. We are blind to the destruction — not to mention the frequently illegal conduct — entailed in the ordinary conduct of business and government. Harmful business activities and their countless victims are chalked up indifferently to poor business practices because our sense of liability, causation and intention has failed to keep abreast of the technological changes in society and the harm these have brought with the modernization of production. This is what is overlooked by the funnel metaphor. Compared to this funnel vision, a more balanced perspective brings into scrutiny the *limitations* of our control system, especially involving upperworld crime. This is explored in our next chapter.

FURTHER READING

Abraham S. Blumerg, *Criminal Justice*, Revised Edition. New York: New Viewpoints, 1979.
Steven Box, "The social construction of official statistics on criminal deviance", Chapter 6 in *Deviance, Reality and Society*, Second Edition. London: Holt, Rinehart and Winston, 1981.
William J. Chambliss (ed.), *Crime and the Legal Process*. New York: McGraw-Hill, 1969.
William Chambliss and Robert Seidman, *Law Order and Power*, Second Edition. Reading, Mass.: Addison-Wesley, 1982.
William J. Chambliss (ed.), *Crime and the Legal Process*. New York: McGraw-Hill, 1969.
Richard V. Ericson and Patricia M. Baranek, *The Ordering of Justice: A Study of Accused Persons as Dependants in the Criminal Process*. Toronto: University of Toronto Press, 1982.
Jeffrey H. Reiman, *The Rich Get Richer and the Poor Get Prison*. New York: Wiley, 1979.
Ryerson Polytechnical Institute (ed.), *Readings in Sociology: A Critical Perspective*. Toronto: Concept Press, 1982.
Laureen Snider, "The criminal justice system", pp. 345-439 in Dennis Forcese and Stephen Richer (eds.), *Social Issues: Sociological Views of Canada*. Scarborough: Prentice-Hall, 1982.
Ian Taylor, *Law and Order: Arguments for Socialism*. London: Macmillan, 1981.
James L. Wilkins, *Legal Aid in the Criminal Courts*. Toronto: University of Toronto Press, 1975.

CHAPTER 6

Policing Deviance in Business

Introduction

We have seen that the system of justice appears to focus on low-status offenders. In this chapter we shall explore the reverse question: the extent to which high-status offenders manage to resist control by the criminal justice system. The problem is nicely illustrated by the recent publication of the Bertrand Inquiry. Bertrand was the chief invesigator for the Federal Combines Investigation Branch — a federal agency charged with enforcing the anti-combines legislation that makes monopolistic business practices unlawful. Bertrand's seven-volume report (1981) focussed on the questionable business practices of the large multinational oil and gas companies operating in Canada, which had resulted in massive price inflations to the Canadian consumer. The practices involved illegal efforts to control the refining, transportation and selling of petroleum products. Bertrand's investigation charged that Canadian subsidiaries of multinational companies paid too much for the imported oil bought from the mother companies and shipped to Canada for refining for the local market; that crude prices in Ontario were artificially enhanced; and that the major dealers systematically underpriced independent retailers of gasoline to squeeze them out of the market, even though this meant losses for the majors in the short run — and higher costs to consumers in the long run when the real competition was gone. Bertrand calculated the inflated costs to consumers between 1958 and 1973 as 12.1 billion dollars. This figure does not take inflation into account. Translating this figure into 1981 dollars reveals that inflated costs to Canadians amounted to $89.2 billion, or approximately $15,000 per family (Bertrand, 1981, Vol. 1: 18).

Under the Combines Investigation Act the government may prosecute offenders in a criminal court, or may publish the results of the investigation and hold hearings to communicate the problem to the public. Hopefully monopolistic business practices are discouraged by the public airing of the dirty laundry. Furthermore, the public inquiry route skirts all the legal issues would have to be established at a trial. Many critics of the Canadian anti-trust law argue that the current law borders on being unenforceable. This situation has been present since the law's inception. In their study of *Corporate Crime in Canada*, Goff and Reasons (1978) argue that the wording of the legislation is ambiguous, that the administration of the law has been ineffective from the beginning and that the rates and consequences of conviction have been trifling. We shall deal with these points in turn.

Ambiguous Legislation

The first anti-combines law was introduced to the Canadian Criminal Code in 1889 in a private member's bill sponsored by Clarke Wallace. Wallace was a Conservative MP who represented the interests of small-time businessmen, who feared the domination of the production and consumer markets by monopolistic businesses. The USA had witnessed the rise of massive monopolies in which single entrepreneurs owned entire industries, including coal mines, the steel plants and the railways connecting them. Monopolistic control is harmful in a capitalistic economy because it undermines competition and allows prices to rise out of control. As potential victims of monopolistic big businesses, Wallace's constituency wanted laws to prevent artificial market concentration. The bill made it illegal to (or to conspire to) limit facilities, restrain trade, fix prices or prevent competition. Initially the word "unlawfully" was inserted into the bill making it illegal to "unlawfully" limit facilities, restrain trade etc. This wording implied that it had been a crime at common law to do these things. This situation was only discovered in 1899 when the legislation was reviewed to tidy up some of the wording. According to Goff and Reasons (1978: 49) "unlawfully" was removed and the law became viable for the first time. However, it was not tested until charges were first laid in 1903, 14 years after the law was passed. In the meanwhile a Liberal government had come to power and passed a bill in 1897 to control combines. The Customs Tariffs Act allowed the federal government to reduce tariffs on imported goods. This non-criminal type of control worked to prevent mergers and combines by letting cheaper American imports force down Canadian prices, which had risen because of the lack of competition among merging Canadian businesses. However, Goff and Reasons report that from 1905 to 1910 196 Canadian firms were collapsed to 85, thanks to mergers. Apparently, neither the Anti-Combines Law nor the Custom Tariff Act had the desired effect. The current anti-combines law is a revision of the original 1889 legislation.

The legislation continues to be ambiguous thanks to the presence of terms like "unduly." Presumably, prices can be fixed by a group of competitors, but not unduly. This is the sort of lack of specificity that undermines the ability of the law to control the type of situation investigated by Bertrand and numerous investigators before him.

Administering the Laws

Goff and Reasons outline the absence of any consistent and efficient way of administering the anti-combines law. They find by contrast a number of strategies of varied importance. In 1889 the responsibility for policing mergers and price fixing went to the offices of the various provincial attorneys general, which is how the Criminal Code is administered. In 1903 there were several successful cases prosecuted in Ontario, but no specific agency existed with an explicit mandate to investigate complaints and take action. There was also substantial hesitancy in the provincial bureaucracy to police the business sector, especially since these people were in every other respect law-abiding citizens, and usually political party supporters as well.

In 1910 the new Combines Investigation Act provided for the creation of an ad hoc committee to investigate complaints from the public. This legislation provided for fines of up to $1000 per day in cases of failure to desist where the committee found that the combine was detrimental to consumers or other business competitors. Goff and Reasons report that no prosecutions were ever undertaken under this Act. In 1919, following the Winnipeg General Strike, a new act was passed. The Combines and Fair Prices Act was very effective in reviewing consumer prices. The three member board reviewed changes in consumer prices and rolled back numerous price increases. In 1921, however, the Judicial Committee of the Privy Council ruled that such actions were beyond the power of the Combines Committee.

In 1923 the 1910 Act was rejuvenated and a permanent secretary was appointed to receive complaints. The new act stiffened sentences for convictions, made it easier to investigate complaints, and significantly made it illegal to merely have conspired to form a combine (the 1910 Act made it illegal to persist after an illegal combine was identified). According to Goff and Reasons the Conservative election victory in 1931 reversed the thrust of this legislation. A similar rocky road has persisted until the present period.

Today the administration of the law remains ambiguous. As noted earlier, the law does not require that offenders be prosecuted in a criminal court. The Director of Investigations can merely publish the results of an investigation and allow the involved parties to respond under oath. No jury-type judgement is officially recorded. Presumably most people behind bars today would have relished the same type of opportunity.

Rates of Conviction

From 1889 to 1972, there were 158 investigative reports written, 136 of which were published (Goff and Reasons, 1978: 91). From these the government succeeded in obtaining convictions in 84 cases. There were 14 acquittals and 38 cases ended without any action, presumably because the government took a "wait and see" approach to the effects of mergers. This suggests that in 28% of cases, various governments have shown uncommon latitude to business crimes documented by reports from the civil service.

From 1960 to 1972 there were 3,572 business mergers in Canada. Only nine resulted in charges and three resulted in conviction (two resulted in orders of prohibition and one company was fined $40,000). This leads Goff and Reasons (1978: 103-104) to comment that "only .003% of the total number of mergers have been charged as violations of the combines law, and only .0005% of the mergers in this same time period have been successfully convicted." The harm of mergers is that they undermine competition and create monopolistic market conditions and, through centralization, eliminate jobs. Cy Gonick (1975: 22) suggests that "the overall cost of monopoly and shared monopoly in terms of lost production is somewhere between $48 billion and $60 billion annually [in the US]. In Canada, lost output due to the same cause would be in the order of $4.5 to $6 billion dollars.''

Laureen Snider (1978) studied the application of different forms of federal legislation used to control corporations and businesses—including the Weights and Measures Act, Food and Drug Act and Hazardous Products Act. She reported a skyrocketing number of inquiries from 1966 to 1974, associated with a shrinking percentage of convictions. For example in 1964, 15 files were opened to investigate charges of misleading advertising and four charges were laid. In 1974, 4387 files were opened and only 110 charges laid. Consequently in ten years the number of complaints increased 300-fold while the number of companies taken to court dropped from about 25% to 2.5%. In addition, the usual fines given offenders under these regulatory acts are little more than a tariff. Snider reports that in the 1970s the average fine was well under $1000. Like Goff and Reasons, Snider reports ineffectiveness in the use of the anti-combines law.

Business Negligence as Deviance

Aside from harms that are specifically financial in character, criminologists have identified other areas of corporate deviance that are rarely viewed as criminal matters. These include the maintenance of unhealthy working conditions, the marketing of dangerous products and the pollution of the environment by corporations and businesses. For example, in the notorious American case of *Silkwood vs Kerr-McGee*, it was established that the Kerr-McGee plutonium plant, which manufactured fuel rods for nuclear reactors, maintained an extremely sloppy and dangerous workplace. Even though plutonium is one of the most toxic substances known to man, most of the workers were given only hours of safety instructions and some were given none at all. In fact, there was no attempt in the health and safety handbook to outline the link between radioactive materials and cancer. Furthermore it was established that the handbook was plagiarized from a 1959 scientific article and that it selectively omitted reference to the long-term and short-term health hazards associated with work-site radiation discussed in the original article. In addition, the chief designer of the facility admitted that he had never taken a course in radiation physics, despite the fact that the chief design problem was maintaining effective barriers between the workers and the deadly radioactive materials they were required to work with. As for the inspection of the plant facilities by external government agents, evidence suggested that the company was frequently given advance notice of "unannounced" inspections. In terms of the technical staff, the evidence indicated that the plant employed a number of welders, though none of them were certified. Predictably, there were numerous leaks of plutonium-contaminated water outside and inside the plant. In one instance a leakage of contaminants into the nearby river caused a fish kill, which was covered up by having the employees bury the dead fish. On the inside, spills of contaminants were "neutralized" by sealing the area with paint, which proceeded with time to peel off the cinder block walls. Lastly, the health physics director in the plant was shown to have no training in health physics but rather a degree in poultry science (Rashke, 1981: 326-373). The evidence suggested a reckless disregard for worker and public safety and a company reliance on the complacency of uninformed and underskilled workers.

Karen Silkwood was disturbed by the situation of worker safety and was determined to do something about it. Unfortunately, she was killed in a car accident on her way to meet a *New York Times* reporter and a union representative purportedly to show them evidence that the company was falsifying its records regarding worker contamination. Employees from Kerr-McGee searched the wreckage and the documents disappeared. These facts were established in a lawsuit brought against the company by Silkwood's estate. The suit did not involve her death but substantial damages were paid to the estate for the plutonium poisoning of Silkwood, a condition that was discovered shortly before she was run off the road and killed in November of 1974.

The safety questions raised in the contamination of Karen Silkwood are far from being isolated or exceptional in the nuclear industry. Notably, questions of worker training and worker and public safety were raised in the aftermath of the near meltdown of the nuclear core at the Metropolitan Edison Three Mile Island power plant. The major risk of nuclear power plants is not that they can explode like atomic bombs, but that a meltdown of the radioactive core materials can produce a vaporization of the coolant, which might in turn rupture the containment building and emit the toxic fissionable materials into the environment. It is not clear that a loss-of-coolant meltdown with a release of toxic substances would be any less disastrous than an actual nuclear explosion. Ford and Kendall relate that "a large reactor . . . will contain about two tons of radioactive material mixed with about 100 tons of slightly enriched uranium oxide. For comparison the Hiroshima atomic bomb produced about two pounds of similar material" (1975: 72-73). The potential for large-scale contamination of both workers and the public is real. The Presidential Committee of Inquiry into the Three Mile Island accident reported that the people operating the control room of the plant in March 1979 did not understand the dynamics of the reactor cooling system, and that there were serious deficiencies in their training (Torrey, 1979). Presumably Metropolitan Edison found it more expedient to operate with a cheaper, uninformed labour force than well-paid and highly skilled personnel. One of the advantages of this choice is that it tends to insure a low level of safety consciousness among the workers, and a minimum of expenditures on health and safety equipment for the companies.

The same question of untrained operators arose in the Ocean Ranger disaster. The Ocean Ranger was a semi-submersible oil rig, the largest of its kind, which sank in a storm off Newfoundland in February of 1982. All 84 workers were lost at sea. The various inquiries that emerged in the aftermath identified a series of shortcomings with the rig and its operators. A porthole in the control room was under-designed and smashed during the storm allowing seawater to enter and short circuit the automatic ballast controls. The controls could be worked manually but the operators were probably not instructed in how to work them.

The previous skipper of the Ocean Ranger had quit and left the job over safety questions before the rig went down. When there was a decision to abandon the rig, the workers could only launch some of the lifeboats since these were designed to release only when the vessel was level. To make matters worse, it was also established that the drillers had refused to allot the required time to safety drills (National Transportation Safety Board, 1983). Notably, the labour force in offshore drilling is not unionized. In this case, as at Three Mile Island, massive capital was expended on equipment that was then manned by inadequately trained personnel with little regard for the question of worker safety.

Workers cannot be entirely blamed for their naiveté. In the areas of radioactive handling there have been numerous cases in which both industry and government have suppressed or distorted the evidence of hazards from radiation and dangerous chemicals (see Schurgin and Hollocher, 1975). The Utah Department of Public Health together with the Atomic Energy Commission documented changes in the cancer rates in towns downwind of the experimental nuclear blasts in Nevada. This information was suppressed until released under a freedom of information action by Paul Jacobs (1979). In addition, when researchers working on grants from the defunct Atomic Energy Commission in the US raised questions about the harmfulness of low-level radiation, they found that their funds were cut and the research was subject to discrediting by other industry scientists. This was the case with both John Gofman (Rashke, 1981: 332) and Dr. Thomas S. Mancuso (Jacobs, 1979). Mancuso (1979) studied the incidence of cancer among atomic workers, looking not just at people who remained in the atomic industry for life, but at the health of people who had moved to other jobs. He found an unusually high rate of cancer. Mancuso's work was rejected by the atomic industry and his federal research funding was cut.

Ernest Sternglass, a professor of radiation physics at the Pittsburg University School of Medicine, is another noted critic of the nuclear industry. His focus is not workers per se but the public at large. While the President's Commission concluded that the amount of radiation released during the accident at Three Mile Island was negligible and would have no measurable impact on the cancer rates, Sternglass suggests this was totally inaccurate. Sternglass argues that information given to the US Secretary of Health by his own staff was based solely on a measure of external radiation. This indicated that residents who lived within eight kilometres of the reactor received only 80 millirems of radiation exposure while the average citizen in the same area normally received about 100 millirems per year from natural background sources. Sternglass argues that because radiation badges minimize the measure of radiation they were misused at Three Mile Island as well as in the US army's experimental test blasts in the 1950s. According to Sternglass, the radiation badges fail to register the concentration of radioactive particles in the internal organs. For example, the fetal thyroid gland could have a concentration of radioactive particles 100 times higher than what the external badge measured.

Sternglass suggests that the economics of nuclear power and the prospect of exporting nuclear technology created pressure on the US government to control information unfavourable to the growth of the industry. Sternglass further suggests that the Secretary of Health was deliberately misinformed by his staff "because they thought it was in the best national interest to do so" (Torrey, 1980: 197).

Sternglass bases his case for harm in anomalies in the infant mortality rates for Pennsylvania and nearby states reported in the US *Monthly Vital Statistics*. He discovered that infant deaths rose dramatically following the accident, and that they occurred most frequently downwind of the reactor. The Three Mile Island accident occurred on March 28, 1979. During the summer of 1979 infant mortality in Pennsylvania increased by 92%, returning to normal levels in September; there were 240 more infant deaths in Pennsylvania than normal. And in Harrisburg, the city closest to the reactor, the infant mortality rate shot up 600% during the summer of 1979 (Torrey, 1980). In Kingston, Ontario, which was downwind of the accident, the General Hospital registered a doubling of the infant mortality rates in the three months after the accident (Pawlick, 1980: 35).

Sternglass argues the volumes of radioactive iodine 131 released into the air at the accident would have gone into the soil and through the grass to the cattle to the mother in cow's milk and across the placental barrier to the fetus. The radioactive iodine would be concentrated in the fetal thyroid gland, causing undersized and aborted babies (Pawlick, 1980). Consequently, the internal harm caused by the uptake of radioactive particles is much more dangerous than exposure to radiation from external particles.

While the Canadian public is familiar with the Three Mile Island accident, few Canadians are aware of the radioactive gas emissions that escaped from two nuclear reactors in New York State across the lake from Kingston, Ontario. Changes in infant mortality rates in Frontenac County (where Kingston is located) reflect these emissions. An examination of health vital statistics published by the province of Ontario shows that the infant death rate (by geographical occurrence) per thousand live births for the county, which had been falling steadily from a high of 27.74 in 1968 to a low of 19.36 per thousand in 1974, suddenly shot up again to 26.41 per thousand in 1975. It then fell even more sharply to 13.91 deaths per thousand live births in 1976. . . . . These figures correspond with a rise in emissions of noble gases at the Nine Mile Point reactor from a total of 558 kilocuries in 1974 to 1,300 kilocuries in 1975 followed by a drop to 176 kilocuries in 1976 (Pawlick and Matthews, 1980: 40-41).

Despite these observations nuclear proponents cling to the claim that nuclear power is safe and that exposure to low-level doses of radiation is harmless. This optimistic outlook seems grossly incompatible with a once-secret report commissioned by the US Atomic Energy Commission in 1956 at Brookhaven Labs on Long Island. The Brookhaven Report estimated the damages from a runaway incident in which 50% of the core's radiation was presumed to escape into the atmosphere. The report predicted that such an incident would cause 3,400 deaths, 43,000 injuries, and the contamination of land the size of Maryland with a probable direct loss of property on the order of $7 billion (in 1957 dollars). People would be killed up to a distance of 15 miles and injured up to 45 miles away. The report dealt with the 500 megawatt reactors planned at that time, not the 3,500 plus megawatt reactors of today. In 1964-65 the AEC updated the estimates for larger reactors. The new report estimated that a worst case accident would kill 45,000 people, injure 100,000 more, do $17 billion (1965 dollars) in property damage and contaminate land downwind an area the size of Pennsylvania (Gyorgy, 1979: 111-112). In this revised scenario the radioactive fallout would be lethal up to 65 miles and harmful up to 400 miles away (Ford and Kendall, 1975: 80). Both Atomic Energy Commission reports were suppressed until brought to light under the threat of a freedom of information suit in 1973. The Atomic Energy Commission obviously thought the best interests of the nuclear industry would be served by keeping the public in the dark about the real risks of nuclear technology.

One of the issues raised in discussing the harmfulness or dangerousness of nuclear plants is that because these are on the frontier of technology it will take decades to accurately assess the risks to workers and the public. Presumably we will only be able to determine the damage in 20 or 25 years when atomic workers experience unnaturally high rates of lung cancer (and when the plants will have coincidentally lived out most of their projected life cycles). However, evidence suggests that it is not necessarily the unknowns in the technology that lead to the harm (Carson, 1982). For example, in the coal mining, cotton milling and asbestos industries workers reported occupationally specific lung diseases long before the corporations and businesses were willing to officially acknowledge them. Companies typically denied that diseases like black lung, brown lung or asbestosis were caused by the work site.

Ermann and Lundman (1982) outlined this situation in the context of the asbestos industry. As late as the 1960s, levels of airborne asbestos fibres were extremely high in the work sites and in the towns downwind of the asbestos mine tailings. This is deplorable since asbestos fibres that lodge themselves in soft lung tissues are carcinogenic.

The toxicity of asbestos is measured in the number of fibres per cubic centimetre of air. In 1976 the US standard was dropped from five fibres per cc of air to two. Nonetheless, in the 1960s and early 1970s, the usual levels in the Johns-Manville and Corningware mills were far in excess of this. Indeed about 85% of all work sites exceeded this level. Ermann and Lundman reported that workers frequently were faced with conditions where "the air was so thick with asbestos dust in some places you couldn't see" (p. 64). Respirators proved useless as their filters became clogged with asbestos.

In the Eastern Townships of Quebec in February of 1949 the asbestos workers went out on a wildcat strike to protest a number of issues in their collective agreement with the Johns-Manville asbestos company, chief among them being the question of unhealthy working conditions (Trudeau, 1956: 183). The dictatorial provincial government of Duplessis ordered 100 members of the Quebec Provincial Police into the town of Asbestos to harass the strikers and protect the company. The police set up their command post in the company's social club. In May when a mass of strike breakers descended on the Johns-Manville plant to take over jobs of striking workers, they were turned away by a mob.

> In retaliation, a gang of provincial police burst into the town of Asbestos and beat up union leaders, invaded a church where some workers were gathered and beat them up, arrested 125 townspeople on various charges, took them back to the company headquarters and beat them up too. (Stewart, 1977: 85)

Asbestos has been an important mining and milling industry in Canada and the US throughout the twentieth century. What evidence is there that asbestos producers were aware of the harmfulness of their products, and the dangers involved in both the work sites and town sites where the mining and processing took place? Ermann and Lundman (1982) show that as a result of civil actions for damages against Johns-Manville, approximately 150 pages of secret corporate memos and documents have thrown light on the knowledge and culpability of the company. The documents include evidence that company executives suppressed information of health damage from asbestos, that industry research tests at Saranac Lake, New York, which provided evidence of health defects were barred from publication by the asbestos companies, that companies made private settlements with individual injured workers while denying publically any deleterious effect from asbestos and that, as late as the 1970s, evidence of early signs of asbestos-related diseases in company health records was not revealed to workers (Ermann and Lundman, 1982: 68-69).

These documents indicate that the major producers of asbestos products were not only aware of the dangers of asbestos dust, but that they actively suppressed this information. This policy effectively guaranteed worker illness just as surely as if the company had poisoned the local drinking water.

To return to our earlier discussion of the risks of nuclear power we can safely say that if the experience in the asbestos industry is any guide, the problem is not a problem created by the operation of a new technology. Presumably, if this were so, the industry would dramatically retool to minimize or eliminate the danger, even if this meant looking for less exotic ways of boiling water to turn electrical turbines. What seems to be involved instead is that the mode of production becomes so capitalized in a particular work arrangement that the industries, both old and new, would sooner suppress the relevant evidence of harmfulness rather than invest in alternative, safer methods of production. This is the classical Faustian bargain with the Devil: a number of lives are exchanged for a certain rate of return on an investment. In the same vein, the Ford Motor Company rationally calculated that it was better to lose $49.5 million in death and injury claims in the exploding Pinto scandal rather than retool the assembly line to make a safer car at the cost of $137 million (Reasons, 1982: 165; Swigert and Farrell, 1980-81).

Pollution as Deviance

Besides creating health risks to workers and members of the public generally, some business activities are harmful inasmuch as they damage the environment. The release of toxic by-products of industrial processes into the common air and waterways illustrates this problem, as do the respiratory diseases that have been associated with industrialization throughout the 19th and 20th centuries. For instance, the infamous London smog of 1952, aggravated by a weather inversion, claimed some 4,000 lives. Clearly it would be extremely difficult for any victim who managed to survive such a tragedy to seek compensation. The sources of the pollutants in such events include every automobile and chimney, and such events are episodic. Also, there would be no evidence of intent to harm or knowledge of harm among the millions of drivers and home owners. However, the culpability is easier to assign when the toxic emissions are significant, chronic, traceable and clearly harmful. This is evident in such cases as the sulphur dioxide (SO_2) emissions from the nickel-smelting operations in Sudbury, Ontario and the mercury poisoning of the river and lake systems downstream from the Northern Ontario Dryden pulp and paper mills.

Sulphur Dioxide Poisoning

For the last century, successive nickel companies have mined nickel ore from beneath the Sudbury basin and separated it from the rock by cooking it at high temperatures. This was done initially by roasting the ore in open pits between layers of unsplit logs. By 1900 there were 80 such operations driving off toxic SO_2 gas into the Sudbury basin (Weller, 1980: 30). The principle behind the smelting process has not changed very drastically to this date. In the 1960s Inco was releasing on the order of 5,000 tons of sulphur dioxide *per day* from its Sudbury operation. Inco is recognized as the single largest source of SO_2 pollution in North America (Howard and Perley, 1980; Irwin, 1981; Swift, 1977). The harm of SO_2 emission is not simply that it smells foul and collects as smoke in the valleys, but that the gaseous SO_2 combines with water vapour to produce a corrosive acid, which produces acid-rich precipitation. In the Sudbury basin, the acidic smoke killed most of the vegetation decades ago, with the result that the soil has been virtually washed away, giving Sudbury its notorious "moon-scape" look. Farming and gardening ended over 50 years ago. The destruction of the physical environment will persist for centuries after Inco has closed. In addition to denuding the Sudbury basin, acid precipitation builds up as snow during the winter and accumulates in high concentration in rivers and lakes during the spring run-off. This "acid shock" can raise the acidity of the water ten-fold in the space of several days, killing off microscopic animals and vegetation as well as fish. According to the Ontario Ministry of the Environment, 140 lakes have already been declared "dead," and 48,000 of the province's 180,000 lakes will probably become barren in the next 20 years (see Weller, 1980: 85; Irwin, 1981: 27). The effect on the tourist and sport fishing industries is obvious. In addition, the elimination of waterlife seriously depresses the value of recreational properties in northern Ontario and Quebec. Besides damaging soils and wildlife, acid precipitation causes damages to buildings, monuments and automobiles by accelerating the erosion of concrete and the corrosion of metals. The forests and agricultural crops likewise face deterioration and lower productivity with increased acidification by rain (Howard and Perley, 1980: 104-5). Lastly, the Standing Committee on Resource Development in Ontario estimated health costs to Ontarians from acid rain to be about $80 million per year (see Weller, 1980: 25).

Of course, not all this damage can be traced to Inco. In fact, a Crown corporation, Ontario Hydro, places several coal-fed electrical power plants in the list of Canada's worst ten SO_2 pollutors. In addition, as much as half of central Canada's pollution is exported from the US by winds from Ohio, Kentucky and Pennsylvania. Nonetheless, in a study for the federal Department of the Environment, economists Carter and McCauley estimated that in 1974 damages to the environment from Inco alone were $465 million (see Weller, 1980: 35). Where proponents of nuclear power argue that the technology possesses justifiable risks because it is new, "at the frontiers of technology," the nickel smelters claim the opposite: the damage to the environment is inevitable because the technology is so old and the costs of extracting pollutants are prohibitive. The Inco case is useful because it illustrates the nature of the social control mobilized by government to police this type of environmental dumping.

Following growing public awareness of questions of environmental safety in the 1960s, the Ontario government in 1970 issued a Ministerial Control Order to Inco calling for successive reductions in SO_2 emissions. It required that the 1970 level of 5,200 tons per day be reduced to 4,400 tons by 1974, and further reduced to 3,600 tons by 1976 and finally reduced to 750 tons by 1978. The Order also required that Inco build a "superstack" to improve the local air quality in Sudbury. However, the company's annual report in 1969 had already included plans for the 1250-foot chimney, leading critics to infer that the government control order was in part dictated by the company's own plans. At 1,250 feet, Inco's superstack was the tallest chimney in the world. It was completed in 1972 and resulted in an enormous improvement in local air quality. Nonetheless the height of the chimney created damage to the environment at much greater distances as wind carried the smoke for hundreds of miles. During the 1970s, as the final date for emission reductions approached, it was obvious that Inco would not meet the deadline and was unprepared to install the required pollution abatement equipment. The company claimed the equipment was not economically feasible. Nonetheless, when the company had enjoyed great profitability it found itself solvent enough to invest massive capital elsewhere. In 1971 Inco showed profits of $94 million and had accumulated deferred taxes of $238 million (a sort of interest-free loan from Ottawa). In 1974, this profitability allowed Inco to acquire the E.S.B. Ltd. battery company in the US at a cost of $234 million. Additionally, Inco invested hundreds of millions of dollars in a nickel plant in Guatemala. Both investments later failed. When times were good Inco invested elsewhere, while in times of recession, pollution abatement was uneconomical at home.

Meanwhile, the 1978 deadline for a 750-ton limit on emissions approached without any hope of compliance. Inco and the Ontario Ministry of the Environment negotiated a new control order by which emissions would be limited to 3,600 tons daily. Later in 1980, the Ontario Minister of the Environment issued an unappealable Order-in-Council, which required daily limits on SO_2 emissions to be put at 2,500 tons by 1980 and at 1,950 tons by 1983. Throughout, Inco has maintained that the pollution abatement price tag of $300-$500 million has been altogether too expensive. Simultaneously, an internal

Inco engineering report indicated that at a cost of $300 million Inco could feasibly reduce pollution with existing technology to under 1500 tons per day. And even if the bill ran to $600 million, Floyd Laughren, who represents the Nickel Belt riding in the Ontario Legislature, estimates that the tax incentives would reduce the direct costs to Inco to some $270 million and would increase the productivity and profitability of the Sudbury operation, which is already the most efficient nickel producer in the world. Laughren speculates that the reason for Inco's reluctance to upgrade its Sudbury facilities in the face of its massive expenditures elsewhere can only be explained by Inco's expectation that the Ontario government will step in and finance the entire smelter upgrading program, and will do so in the name of environmental rescue (cf. Savan, 1983: 31). The showdown between Inco and the Ministry of the Environment has yet to come. However, if Canadians are to convince Americans about the seriousness of the acid rain problem originating south of the border, an effective and continuing policing of Inco will be inevitable.

Mercury Poisoning

In 1973 a Japanese court in Minamata awarded families of several dozen victims of mercury poisoning $3.2 million in damages for physical and mental abnormalities caused by eating seafood contaminated with mercury compounds. The Chisso petrochemical plant in Minamata had been discharging mercury pollutants into Minamata Bay for decades. During this period, the company had consistently ignored complaints concerning health hazards, birth defects, deformities, blindness, nerve damage and premature aging associated with the industrial pollutants. Following the 1973 court decision, Chisso faced a further $80 million in settlements with other victims (Hutchison and Wallace, 1977: 118).

Notably, the Japanese court made a finding of negligence despite the company's adherence to pollution guidelines (Hutchinson and Wallace, 1977: 118). Meanwhile Reed paper in its Dryden, Ontario mill was discharging mercury compounds into the sport fishing English-Wabigoon River system. By 1970 approximately 20,000 pounds of mercury had been dumped at Dryden. This process continued until 1975. During 1972-74, 4,685 pounds of mercury were discharged (Harding, 1976:19). Additionally there were large releases of mercury vapour into the atmosphere. Measures of mercury in the river bed below the Dryden mill and levels of mercury in the fish rivalled the readings taken at Minamata. Japanese and Swedish studies confirmed the health hazards of industrial mercury processes.

In 1970 Lake St. Clair was closed to commercial fishing because of mercury contamination from the Dow Chemical plant in Sarnia. A 1972 Ontario Ministry of the Environment report documented the health risks of mercury in the food chain but this report was suppressed for three years. Japanese doctors invited to the Grassy Narrows and White Dog Indian villages documented 20 or 30 cases of Minamata disease among the Indians downstream from Dryden. Notably the Ontario government had sent warnings to the white lodge owners in the area advising them to avoid eating the fish while it failed to send the same message to the Indian villages, claiming that there was no evidence of disease among the natives (Harding, 1976: 17,22). The Ontario government prosecuted Dow in Sarnia for its pollution of Lake St. Clair but no action was taken at Dryden. In 1975 the Reed Paper Company changed its operation to a non-mercury system. George Kerr, the previous Minister of the Environment, had claimed the river system would clean itself out in 12 weeks; it will probably take 50 to 100 years before the mercury sediment is finally flushed out.

In the meantime there has not been a single successful action for damages caused by the Reed Paper Company by either the natives, the government or the private lodge operators. The operators were forced to walk away from their fishing lodges as the summer tourist trade dwindled. The natives were relocated at cost to the taxpayer to new locations and given freezers and frozen fish supplies. Reed paper and the Ontario government have gone on to negotiate a deal giving Reed Paper cutting rights on a further 19,000 square miles of Northern Ontario black spruce forests (Troyer, 1977: 217).

Again the picture that emerges is bleak. The Reed Paper Company continued to dump mercury into the water system for five years after the health risks were acknowledged and after the Ontario government ordered curtailment of mercury dumping (Troyer, 1977: 98-111). Yet instead of any finding of culpability against Reed Paper, and instead of a dredging order to clean out the river system, the government closed the river to fishing. This is like advising the potential victims of crime to stay indoors while the culprit is allowed the freedom of the streets. As in the case of SO_2 pollution, the absence of any meaningful policing of pollution effectively creates incentives to continue polluting and allows the companies to transfer the real costs of production to the public section.

Billing the Public Sector

One of the astonishing aspects of corporate harm is the ease with which companies have been able to pass the costs of their activities to the general public. In the mid-1970s there emerged a widespread militancy about the carcinogenic effects of asbestos dust. When Johns-Manville was confronted with the prospect of thousands of damage suits from injured workers, the company declared it would go bankrupt if required to make settlements.

In 1977 a bill was introduced to the US Congress, The Asbestos Health Hazards Compensation Act. The bill would compensate victims of asbestos by using corporate, union, tobacco industry and government funds; in fact, the bill called for the government, that is the taxpayer, to cover half the costs in all settlements (Ermann and Lundman, 1982: 75-76). All other forms of compensation, including individual damage suits would be prohibited, and there would be no allowance for punitive damages. The effect of this law will be to neutralize the corporate liability and shift the costs of maintaining a dangerous work site from the companies to the public.

Not surprisingly, a parallel situation exists in the US and Canadian nuclear industries. Throughout the age of nuclear power, insurance companies have been exceedingly reluctant to underwrite electrical utilities to cover possible public damages from nuclear reactor accidents. The most recent estimate of financial liability to a utility company in the event of a worst case nuclear reactor accident is about $40.5 billion (Gyorgy, 1979: 179). This would require annual insurance premiums on the order of $23.5 million per reactor facility *if* the insurance industry were interested in underwriting the risks. This figure equals the annual operating and maintenance budget of most nuclear reactors. If the nuclear industry had to rely on its insurability it would never have been commercially viable, for even after pressure from a Joint Committee of the US Congress, insurance conglomerates had no confidence in the safety of the nuclear power industry.

In fact most insurance companies exclude coverage on home ownership policies for nuclear contamination. The Joint Committee on Atomic Energy reported that "the problem of possible liability in connection with the operation of reactors is a major deterrent to further industrial participation in the program . . . the problem of liability has become a major roadblock" (in Novick, 1969: 69ff). The solution to this impasse was to limit the liability of utility companies by a simple act of Congress. The Price-Anderson Indemnity Act limited the liability of a company to $500 million in the event of a single major reactor accident. In addition the utilities were required to obtain whatever other insurance they could. This has usually been well under $100 million. By the terms of the Price-Anderson Act the US public had their liability collectively limited to under $600 million (though estimates of damage run to over $40 billion), while acting at the same time as the insurer on behalf of the nuclear industry (Novick, 1969: 62-89; Gofman and Tamplin, 1979: 157-159). The Canadian law works in a similar fashion. Under the Nuclear Liability Act, which was proclaimed in 1976, licencees such as Ontario Hydro are required to carry $75 million insurance, but are covered by a provision of the Act by which the federal government will bail out the company in the event of any incident whose costs exceed the limits of the insurance. This provision has raised eyebrows in the light of the massive spills of contaminated water both inside and outside the nuclear facilities at Pickering, Ontario in 1983.

There is a similar limitation of company liability in cases of work-related illness and injury. This is part of the Workers' Compensation legislation. Toward the end of the First World War the federal government created a system of insurance for injured workers that was to be supported by payments from industry and government. Notably, the legislation deprived the worker of the right to sue an employer directly for damages received at the work place in the normal course of employment; alternatively, the worker was required to make claims to the Workers' Compensation Board, which would be limited to the actual losses resulting from injury and which precluded the possibility of punitive damages. At the time the legislation was a blessing for the labouring classes because few if any injured workers could afford the services of lawyers to seek settlements from employers who created and maintained dangerous work places. However, with the present bureaucratic administration of claims and the quota limits on the number of claims to be processed, workers have experienced a reluctance by Workers' Compensation Boards to certify claims as work-related, and a persistent effort to minimize the assessment of damages. There has also been a reluctance to certify long-term worker health problems as compensable; only in 1982 did the Workers' Compensation Board agree to compensate atomic workers who had contracted cancer after years of exposure to low-level radiation at the experimental Chalk River nuclear facility. The 1982 decision was truly a landmark but like the situations in the US involving nuclear energy risks and asbestosis, the existence of the Workers' Compensation Board only acts to shift the costs and liability for damage to worker health from the employers producing the damage to the government, workers and taxpayers. This effectively removes any general or specific deterrent effect that might come from successful private law suits against corporations or companies.

The situation regarding the policing of pollution is even more complicated. First of all, the Federal Clean Air Act, which sets standards of air quality, is only advisory legislation that has no legal effect unless incorporated into provincial laws (Irwin, 1981: 80). Where incorporated into provincial laws there is a reluctance to police industries vigorously and to seek court judgements against such companies. In most jurisdictions there seems to be a belief that a *threat* to prosecute violations of air standards is coercion enough and that orders to desist violating standards are adequate control. For example, in 1974 the Sudbury Environmental Law Association successfully brought charges against Inco in a case where the Ministry of the Environment had decided not to prosecute after the unlawful emissions were terminated. Nonetheless, the emissions were so dense that they made driving impossible in the immediate area of the nickel refinery. Inco was fined $1,500. In another 1974 incident, Inco was convicted for exceeding the lawful SO_2 emissions level from an iron-ore recovery plant by almost 90%. The Provincial Court judge who ruled against Inco characterized the emission as a quasi-criminal act (Savan, 1983: 25). Nonetheless, the fine was $2,500 in a year when Inco showed profits of nearly $300 million. At Falconbridge Nickel Mines, another producer in the Sudbury basin, there were such concentrated levels of SO_2 that air in the nearby hamlets became unbreathable. The Ontario Department of the Environment put air monitors in the hamlet of Happy Valley; they registered a maximum acceptable limit of SO_2 concentration with an index marking of 32. In 1972 and 1973 the monitor registered peaks of 141 and 94 respectively (Weller, 1980: 64). Rather than require the company to cut back production to meet the environmental air quality standards, the government decided to relocate the hamlet away from the pollution source! This decision was consistent with the latitude historically given to the nickel producers at the expense of the general public. For example, the Ontario Industrial Mining Lands Compensation Act of 1918 allowed the nickel producers to establish smoke easements on local properties that prevented future landowners from suing for damage from SO_2 pollution. Also, the 1921 Damages by Fumes Arbitration Act required property owners who suffered damages from smelting fumes to register complaints within seven days of the damage and precluded other methods of seeking compensation from the offending companies. As though this were not enough, the Ontario government in 1916 had declared 12 Sudbury area townships unfit for agricultural settlement, thereby undermining the ability of individual farmers to claim agricultural losses (Weller, 1980: 32). The impact of these actions was effectively to shift the costs of pollution from the private producers to the public.

Mercury contamination has not been policed any better. Just as the residents of Happy Valley were relocated at public expense away from the SO_2 air dumps, the natives of the Grassy Narrows and White Dog Reserves were resettled away from the mercury polluted waters at public expense. They were barred from fishing and were provided with freezers and frozen fish. Predictably this aggravated the unemployment problem and fostered greater dependence on government handouts. As for actions against the water polluters, an unpublished 1976 Ontario Ministry of the Environment summarized the situation:

> Between 1968 and the present, only twelve convictions under the Ontario Water Resources Act and five convictions under the Environmental Protection Act have been obtained against pulp and paper companies. The fines for water pollution averaged $812 per conviction; for air $1,400 per conviction. Fines of this magnitude provide the companies with virtually no economic incentive to incur the much greater costs for pollution control. This is especially the case in the pulp and paper industry since there have been no convictions for water pollution by these mills since 1971, and only two for air pollution, both in 1974.

> Continuing the present policy approach is, therefore, unlikely to achieve the Ministry's abatement objectives over the next ten years. Furthermore, it is inequitable in that some mills have spent large sums of money on pollution

abatement while those who still pollute excessively have not been penalized. This situation will not be remedied by an even greater share of the costs of pollution control being shifted to the Government as has been proposed by representatives of the pulp and paper industry. The primary deficiency lies in the lack of an adequate penalty to induce companies to abate their pollution to the desired levels (in Troyer, 1977: 223).

Jim Harding reports that one proposal to deal with mercury pollution at Dryden would have got both the Reed Paper Company and the Ontario government off the hook by turning the English-Wabigoon River system into a national park. This proposal "is a further attempt to avoid making the polluter legally and financially responsible for its damage. A federal park would allow compensation to be paid to tourist camp owners and, secondarily, native fishermen without the Ontario government losing face or money after making high investments in the affected tourist area (Minaki Lodge, etc.) since the contamination began" (Harding, 1976: 23).

This is surely one of the most imaginative ways for business to free itself from the costs of production. Fortunately, there has been little interest expressed in this option. Unfortunately, the condition of the English-Wabigoon River system remains deplorable. Even after the mercury bleaching process was removed from the pulp and paper mill, the Reed Paper company has continued to dump tens of tons of organic pulp wastes into the system daily without liability (Troyer, 1977: 221).

Controlling Business Deviance

In their book *Corporate Deviance* (1982) Ermann and Lundman describe two types of social responses to harmful corporate activities: penetrating versus non-penetrating controls. As it turns out, most controls placed on businesses lack the design features required to halt the harmful practices. The non-penetrating controls consist of three main things.

1. Beneficiary-Choice Systems. This "free market" position argues that if people do not like the way a corporation or company is handling itself, then they can respond by boycotting the goods and services provided by it. This will provide a benefit to the company's rivals and so the drop in market share will penalize the deviant corporation. Ermann and Lundman argue that this system of control is questionable for several reasons. First, where it assumes that there is a choice in the marketplace between different companies, we frequently find that there is massive concentration within industries that severely restricts choice of opportunity. Second, this concentration tends to undermine competition between industries and tends to standardize the safety questions, product features and pollution practices across different companies. Third, the concentration in the industries militates against the opportunities for new companies in the existing markets; this was the experience of the independents who failed to hold their market share in the retail gasoline business. These points emphasize that for the beneficiary-choice method to work, the customers or beneficiaries must be able to *exercise* a choice. Yet what choice has the consumer when all the airlines fly jets made with substandard seat fibres that cause poisonous fumes if ignited? This was the cause of substantial loss of life in the Air Canada flight that was forced to land in Cincinnati in the summer of 1983. Without the choice, there is no control. Lastly, the beneficiary-choice method assumes that the resources flowing to the company are controlled exclusively by normal market forces. However we see that governments repeatedly step in to indemnify companies against capital losses resulting from harmful conduct. Consequently, this conservative form of control has little impact.

2. Control through Negative Publicity. As Ermann and Lundman argue, the ability of bad press to deter corporate deviance is questionable. They cite the practice by which under US law those convicted of false advertising were required to publish corrections. Such companies usually avoid printing corrections in the same magazines as their original misleading ads. Consequently, the detriment to the company is minimized. Also, the practice in Canada of publishing the results of anti-combines investigations and the holding of public hearings allow the companies involved to use the hearings as a public relations forum in a way that would be impossible in a criminal court. Since no finding is ever registered in the way that a criminal jury makes a clear decision, the parties can turn the hearings into a battle of expert opinion and so can avoid the clear stigma that could result if the hearings were actually a criminal trial.

3. Fines as Controls. One school of thought in criminology holds that society effectively criminalizes or decriminalizes an act to the extent that it controls the act severely. Severe control, which in this case means the fines are substantial, demonstrates the society's rejection of the behaviour. Small fines indicate the opposite. In fact, the small fine paid to the state is almost identical to a permit fee or tariff to be paid in order to allow business the opportunity to continue its behaviour (Kennedy, 1976). In weighting the severity of a fine, Ermann and Lundman argue that there must be some consideration of the company's ability to deflect the fine against its gross revenues and equity. If examined in this way, the typical fines received by companies as a result of the common infractions of the federal anti-combines laws and regulatory laws are miniscule. Fines of several hundred dollars to companies with gross assets in the hundreds of millions of dollars are trifling. Ermann and Lundman looked at the fines paid by the manufacturing companies in the 1961 electrical equipment price rigging scandal and the 1976 folding carton price rigging scandal. If we calculate the size of the fine as a proportion of the gross company revenues, and determine what a comparable proportion would be for an individual earning $15,000, we discover that the fines have a relative value of twenty cents to twelve dollars, depending on the size of the company. Just as a twenty cent/twelve dollar fine is trifling to an individual earning $15,000 per year, so too is a $50,000 fine to a company worth $500,000,000. Ermann and Lundman report that civil damage suits recovered marginally more, but still only payments on the order of $50-$150 using the $15,000 wage scale. We find direct parallels to fines paid under Canadian pollution laws. In 1974 Inco, with profits of $300 million, was fined two or three thousand dollars. In 1970 Domtar, with a net profit of $17 million, was fined $1,000 for pollution violations (Troyer, 1977: 120).

In contrast to these non-penetrating controls, three sets of controls with more teeth are discussed by Ermann and Lundman.

1. Controlling Corporations through Charters. While corporations are currently provincially registered, it is recommended that they be brought under central federal charters to allow imposition of controls on the ways corporations operate. The benefit of this system is that it would prevent the relocation of company headquarters to provinces with few or lax restrictions. In the USA, a disportionate number of corporations have located their head offices in Delaware because of the loose state controls that exist there. In addition part of the federal chartering system would require some external representation on the board of directors to insure that any corporate practice that was harmful to the owners, the workers, the customers, the public or the government would be made accountable to the government or to an ombudsman, and so would be challenged. The utility of this type of control is obviously dubious in cases of transnational corporations, which can move headquarters from one country to another.

2. Protecting the Whistleblowers. Ermannn and Lundman point out that many companies as well as government employees who have leaked information of corporate deviance to the public have been fired and/or blackballed in an industry. Just as the police give special protection to crime informants (who are often themselves criminals), so too should special protection or consideration be given to corporate crime informants.

3. Penalizing Individuals. The last protection or control is to develop and impose individual penalties on the actual personnel who manage and/or own the companies in question. Instead of naming the corporation in cases of company deviance, if the individual Ford executives risked going to jail for manslaughter or if the Inco managers risked going to jail for wilful damage to property, this would create major individual incentives to ensure a minimum of deviance. Similarly if the fines were paid by the executives out of their salaries and not deflected to tax deductible budget items, businessmen in positions of authority would be much more personally accountable and their companies would operate much more safely. By targeting individual managers and owners, Ermann and Lundman suggest that the increased personal liability would affect whole organizations and would eliminate the legal fiction that corporations and not their principals are accountable.

Legal Issues in Personal Accountability: Applying Criminal Sanctions to Business

When we examine the list of six controls it is clear that we already have in place mechanisms to fine corporations, mechanisms of airing bad publicity as well as beneficiary choice. In other words, of those things that are felt to be least effective in checking corporate harms, we have plenty. We do not have special safeguards for whistleblowers or revisions of the terms of reference for corporations, nor are we likely to find much political support for such measures. We do however have a criminal code. To what extent can the criminal code be brought to bear to control the types of deviance described in this chapter? As we shall see, a number of the elements of criminal behaviour that were discussed in an earlier chapter fit business deviance only obliquely. Three issues are especially important.

1. Mens Rea. To be held accountable for a crime, an individual must have the guilty mind, and must intend to produce the harm. Alternatively, the person must be so careless in his or her conduct that the harm resulted from that negligence and the total absence of due care and concern. The issue of intention is quite unproblematic in cases of bid-rigging and conspiracy to fix prices, and governments have been relatively successful in responding to these types of corporate crimes. However, the operation of an unsafe worksite, the creation of unsafe products or wilful damage to the environment through pollution are not usually done purposefully, nor as ends in themselves. Usually, the criminal liability develops where companies fail to take action to prevent or lessen a harm once they have gained knowledge of its existence. Recall *Fagan v Commission of Metropolitan Police*. The crime occurred when the driver refused to move his car off the policeman's foot, thereby turning a coincidence into a wilful act. Likewise when a corporation learns that an industrial emission is starting to cause health problems down-wind from the plant and, rather than investigating the situation and containing the noxious substance, the corporation decides to deny the problem and ignore the harm thereby inflicted, this smacks of negligence and recklessness. Negligence would apply if the corporate agents failed to show the type of care and consideration expected in similar circumstances. Recklessness would apply if the agents could foresee the likeli-hood of harmful consequences and unreasonably gambled that such consequences just would not happen. In both cases, evidence of negligence or recklessness would create grounds for inferring the required mental element, the *mens rea*, even though there would be no fully formed "wicked" intention. Nonetheless, it is much harder to estab-lish the *mens rea* in these grey areas.

2. *Causality.* Criminal law recognizes that there must be intent to harm as well as an actual effect of harmfulness. But the relationship must be causal, not coincidental. You can plan to murder your wife on Monday and accidentally run her over with your car on Wednesday, but there is no crime unless the intent and the harmful act are causally linked. This applies to some of the corporate deviance cases in several ways. For example, while we might agree that a worksite showed evidence of radiation leakage, leakage that the owners were aware of but about which they did nothing, and while we might show experimentally that low-level radiation causes cancer in rats, the question of what it produces causally in people exposed to recklessly radioactive worksites may be difficult to establish. This is especially problematic when the carcinogen may take 20 years or more to produce its malignant tumours. The relationship is further compounded by the fact that not everyone exposed to workplace carcinogens gets cancer, and not every-one who gets cancer was exposed to workplace carcinogens. In such a situation the company would be entitled to argue, just as cigarette companies in the aftermath of warning about hazards from smoking, that there is no *causal* relationship between main-taining a needlessly dangerous worksite, and the harms experienced later by workers, customers or the public. In other words, even if it were shown that corporate agents were negligent or reckless, the causal effects of this might be open to interpretation.

The test in criminal courts is "beyond a reasonable doubt"; in other words there can be no reasonable doubt that worker X developed cancer thanks to the company's unsafe workplace. This is an extremely stringent test, especially since health problems can easily originate from other causes. Furthermore there may be interaction effects as when smoking makes the worker more susceptible to industrial illnesses. In contrast to the criminal court test, the civil courts rely on a test called "the balance of probabilities," which is the overall likelihood that the harm came from reckless corporate behaviour. This difference in tests would suggest that the assessment of individual guilt and re-sponsibility would be easier to establish in the civil courts in a private suit for damages as opposed to the criminal court in a formal criminal charge. However, as established earlier, such a suit would generally be unavailable to a worker other than through Workers'

Compensation. Workers' Compensation never assesses the kind of individual culpability of the agent responsible, except perhaps to blame the worker for his or her own misfortune.

Causality is also problematic in some cases of environmental pollution. A resort owner might see acid rain wipe away the value of his summer fishing lodge. He might also establish a reckless and even unlawful level of sulphur dioxide emissions from an industrial belt. But in which of two dozen companies can the owner begin to look for the offending party? And perhaps having cornered the management of the biggest offender, to what extent is the relationship between their careless polluting responsible for his loss of resort business, as opposed to a quirk of the weather which brought down all the pollutants in that area? In cases like this the causal chain becomes remote, and hence individual culpability becomes harder to establish.

3. Mistake of Fact. In light of the questions raised by causality and the inherently indirect links between corporate behaviour and harm, corporate managers brought before criminal courts to answer criminal charges could well offer the excuse of mistake of fact. This excuse was discussed in the context of the *Pappajohn* rape case. In that case the defendant offered the excuse that despite the woman's protestations, he formed the impression that she was consenting to sexual intercourse. The Supreme Court did not attach any weight to his use of this excuse in this particular case but did affirm that if the defendant honestly held the belief that consent was given, this could have stood as a lawful excuse. Transposing this logic to the corporate world, managers could argue that they acted the way they did, despite the better advice from scores of experts and despite numerous complaints from workers, customers and the public, on the mistaken belief that operating the facility in the way they did was quite harmless. Even though objectively their behaviour may have been harmful, if they sincerely believed it to be lawful and safe, they are entitled to be given the benefit of the doubt by the jury. What this suggests is that in those cases where there is no direct intent to do harm (which covers most of the illustrations discussed in this chapter), and where there is even the slightest controversy about the link between the corporation's conduct and the harm resulting, the mistake of fact defense will make criminal convictions highly unlikely, especially where the defendants tell the jury they honestly thought they were doing the right thing.

Ermann and Lundmann cite the targeting of specific managers and owners for criminal sanctions as one of the most relevant of the penetrating controls. However, our re-examination of some of the elements of criminal behaviour suggests that such controls are marked by their own weaknesses, weaknesses that arise from the safeguards against false convictions in non-business crimes. In other words, the safeguards that militate against wrongful conviction of working class criminals are probably more effective in preventing the convictions of corporate criminals. This surely must dampen optimism about the effectiveness of Ermann and Lundman's penetrating controls. In his study of "the corporate advantage," John Hagan (1982: 1016) argued that "the modern criminal justice system better serves corporate than individual interests. . . . Criminal justice agencies originally thought to have emerged for the purpose of protecting individuals against individuals today are devoting a substantial share of their resources to the protection of large affluent corporate actions." Clearly this takes the form not only of insuring the culpability of individuals who hurt corporations, but, more importantly, of minimizing the culpability of corporations who hurt individuals.

Is the Law Wired for Corporate Crime?

In the previous chapter we outlined a conception of the justice system as a highly selective crime net that appears to differentially deflect attention away from high-status offenders. It was argued that current laws fail to criminalize many of the harmful behaviours of high-status offenders, leaving them to regulatory and administrative laws and devices. This observation has been borne out by the current examination of business and corporate deviance and is especially reinforced by the narrowness of our legal concepts like *mens rea* and causality and their impotence in the face of corporate harm. The class biases in the application of laws were likewise reinforced in this chapter in our estimation of the weakness of sanctions directed at corporate business offenders. It has not escaped our attention that the law does provide judges with enormous latitude in punishing offenders. For example, the maximum penalty under Section 32(1) of the Anti-Combines Act is five years imprisonment and/or a one million dollar fine. However, as argued earlier, substantial fines are rarely given. The most sensational corporate crime trial in Canada to date did involve substantial fines as well as jail terms. This was the case of *Regina v. McNamara et al.* This involved a case of "rigging" the bids for government contracts on dredging and construction works. Section 32.2 of the Anti-Combines Act makes it illegal to rig bids and provides for substantial penalties for offenders. "Everyone who is a party to bid-rigging is guilty of an indictable offence and is liable on conviction to a fine in the discretion of the court or to imprisonment for five years or to both."

In the McNamara case, the McNamara Construction Company, Pitt Engineering and a number of dredging companies controlled bids on jobs to dredge habours in Hamilton and elsewhere in central Canada. One would have thought that since the *actus reus* of the case was fixing bids that charges under Section 32(2) would have been laid. However, the Crown charged McNamara and company under Section 338 of the Criminal Code, which makes it illegal to defraud. Notably, the maximum jail penalty under Section 338(1) is a jail penalty of two years, not the five year maximum under a charge of bid rigging. Even before the trial started, the accused appeared to have been given the benefit of a less severe charge. The evidence indicated that the accused had inflated costs to government and public agencies by several million dollars as a result of a conspiracy by which a number of companies would agree to artificially inflate their closed bids for dredging contracts with the expectation that the lowest bidder would receive the job. In return, the successful lowest bidder would pay compensation to the others by direct cash payments or by paying false invoices from these companies for performance of non-existent services. These fraudulent practices extended over a minimum of five years and possibly fourteen years, and involved nine corporations and eleven corporate executives. This resulted in the longest criminal trial in Canadian history and involved many of the leading figures of the dredging business. Initially, five persons and eight corporations were found guilty of conspiracy to defraud but following a bout of appeals, this figure was reduced to two executive convictions — Harold McNamara of McNamara Corporation and Sydney Cooper of Pitt Engineering — and seven corporations. Mr. McNamara received a jail term of five years while Mr. Cooper received three years.

Ermann and Lundman, among others, have stressed the utility of jail as possibly the most important existing method of deterrence for corporate deviance. In the *McNamara* case, we ought to be optimistic about the outcome. Here justice appears to have moved beyond mere bad publicity and corporate fines; beyond the non-penetrating controls; beyond the slanting of the laws that typically legitimate corporate business, production and marketing practices; beyond the selective administration of the law though only partially since the accused faced the less serious section 338(1) of the Criminal Code as opposed to section 32(2) of the Anti-Combines Act. In the end, the crooks received penitentiary sentences and ended up behind bars.

In his analysis of the *McNamara et al* case, Michael Mandel (1983a) points out that McNamara and Cooper ended up free on the streets in ten months and six months respectively. Both were given 24 hour releases on day parole to return to their homes and families after serving one-sixth of their sentences. Normally, day parole is selectively approved to provide inmates with access to community resources and programs, to "test" for the inmates' readiness for full parole and to help reintegrate the convict into civil society. While full parole is available after one-third of the sentence has been served, day parole is available at the one-sixth point. The Solicitor General's *Study of Conditional Release* (Working Group, 1981: 6) suggests that "it takes about five months for a day parole application to reach a decision." This would lead one to believe that rather speedy consideration must have been given to Mr. Cooper, who was released after six months. In addition, as Mandel points out, the day parole of McNamara and Cooper amounted to full parole.

In other words, the National Parole Board effectively cut the sentences in half by granting these particular criminals the widest possible interpretation of the parole regulations. In a letter to the *Globe and Mail* (May 11, 1982), the chairman of the National Parole Board, William Outerbridge, responded to criticism that these actions smacked of political favouritism to Liberal Party supporters. He said in part that "the opprobrium attached to Mr. Cooper and Mr. McNamara during their trial and incarceration is the greatest deterrence to this type of non-violent crime." However, the original trial judge had based his sentence in part on the need to deter other corporate criminals from similar acts. Obviously, in Canada the National Parole Board is allowed to second guess the trial sentence and to substitute its own view, at least with high-status offenders. In point of fact, the diminution of this sentence is more liable to neutralize the general deterrence of business crimes. Further, the idea that "opprobrium" is punishment enough in the case of high-status offenders is certainly questionable. If taken seriously every non-violent property offender in Canada should be allowed to plead that the bad publicity during the trial is suffcent retribution to deter similar crimes. Surely this would be equality before the law. However, we have reason to believe that bad publicity or "opprobrium" alone is not sufficient. In this case it would seem to be a device to grant uncommon consideration to those of high-status who have inadvertently slipped by the safety devices have been put in place to weed out the high-status and higher-class offenders. The lesson to be drawn from this most important corporate crime case is that even the most penetrating of Ermann and Lundman's penetrating controls is of doubtful utility in controlling Canadian corporate criminals.

Summary

In this chapter we have examined a range of harms that arise as a result of or in the normal course of business. Some of these are covered by penal law, law that provides for individual punishment and incarceration. As noted in our discussion of the anti-combines law at the beginning of this chapter, and in our review of the *McNamara et al* case, the success of these laws in protecting the public from harms is marginal. In addition to activities covered by penal law, we have reviewed a series of situations beyond the scope of the criminal law that nonetheless involve substantial physical hazards to workers, customers and members of the public. Regulatory and administrative laws have had little effect in curbing the creation of dangerous worksites, and in the pollution of the environment. In addition, when the dangers of business practices are acknowledged, the cost of redressing them is frequently transferred to the public sector. In attempting to revise the criminal law to make it an effective control of such practices, a number of legal problems arise that tend to neutralize the force of this avenue of social control. Obviously the policing of business harms is an area that requires major new initiatives in public policy and major changes in our understanding of the liability of harmful business conduct.

FURTHER READING

Robert J. Bertrand, *The State of Competition in the Canadian Petroleum Industry*, Seven Volumes. Ottawa: Supply and Services, 1981.

Marshall B. Clinard and Peter C. Yeager, *Corporate Crime*. New York: Free Press, 1980.

M. David Ermann and Richard J. Lundman, *Corporate Deviance*. New York: Holt, Rinehart and Winston, 1982.

Gilbert Geis and Robert F. Meier, *White Collar Crime*, Revised Edition. New York: Free Press, 1977.

Colin Goff and Charles E. Reasons, *Corporate Crime in Canada*. Scarborough: Prentice-Hall, 1978.

Ross Howard and Michael Perley, *Acid Rain: The North American Forecast*. Toronto: Anansi, 1980.

Paul McKay, *Electric Empire: The Inside Story of Ontario Hydro*. Foreword by Ralph Nader. Toronto: Between the Lines, 1983.

Frank Pearce, *Crimes of the Powerful*, Foreword by Jock Young. London: Pluto Press, 1976.

Richard Rashke, *The Killing of Karen Silkwood*. Harmondsworth: Penguin, 1981.

C.E. Reasons, L.L. Ross and C. Paterson, *Assault on the Worker: Occupational Health and Safety in Canada*. Foreword by Robert Sass. Toronto: Butterworth, 1981.

Warner Troyer, *No Safe Place*. Toronto: Clarke, Irwin, 1977.

COURTS

CHAPTER 7

Criminal Justice in the Lower Court

Plea Bargaining in Lower-Court Justice

Of all the charges laid by police in criminal matters, only a small fraction ever go to a higher court to be tried by a judge and jury. The vast majority are disposed of in the lower courts by a magistrate. This does not indicate that all lower-court cases are only minor infractions. Though there are some exceptions, the accused when charged with an indictable offense generally has the option of having the case heard in a lower court before a magistrate, in a higher court before a judge or in a higher court with judge and jury. Some of the exceptions involve cases under Section 483 of the Criminal Code, where the lower-court magistrate has absolute jurisdiction over the case (theft and/or possession of stolen property under $200, gambling offenses) as well as cases under Section 427 (treason, sedition, piracy, murder, etc.), which must be heard in a superior court. Also, except for Alberta, the Attorney General under Section 498 may order a trial by jury. A distinctive feature of the higher-court option is that it frequently entails a preliminary hearing. Often the defense will exercise its right to go to higher court in order to obtain discovery of the prosecution's facts and witnesses and may re-elect before trial with the written consent of the Attorney General under Sections 491 and 492 to go back to the lower court, usually with the intention of entering a guilty plea. This latitude allows the defense a small measure of control over which judge will hear the case and/or pass sentence, and is sometimes characterized as "judge-shopping." However, it is only allowable with the consent of the Attorney General. Furthermore, it does not guarantee that the defense will get the desired judge, but may allow some control in avoiding a particularly punitive or unsympathetic one (Radway, 1979).

In this chapter we will examine the nature of justice as it is experienced in the lower courts. Central here is the phenomenon of "plea bargaining" and the ethical and practical matters that accompany this subject. After outlining some of the ethical and theoretical questions, we will turn our attention to some research materials that shed more light on the process of informal case agreements in the lower courts.

The lower courts handle the vast majority of criminal cases, but experience very few trials. Though estimates vary from jurisdiction to jurisdiction, it is argued in the USA that no more than 5% or 10% of lower court cases involve trials contesting the charges. Consequently it is frequently estimated that as much as 90% or 95% of lower court criminal matters are disposed of via guilty pleas and that the majority of these are "negotiated guilty pleas" (Newman, 1956). In Canada, however, the figures appear to be much lower. Ericson and Baranek reported that about 70% of their sample of accused entered guilty pleas to at least some of their charges (1982: 156-157). Figures from earlier studies in Toronto and Montreal show even smaller percentages, in the 50% and 60% ranges (Ericson and Baranek, 1982: 248-249). Ferguson and Roberts (1974) similarly argue that the estimates of negotiated guilty pleas overstate the situation.

The negotiated guilty plea or "plea bargaining" involves a process of informal consultation between the defense and prosecuting attorneys to arrive at a mutually agreeable case outcome without a formal trial. Donald J. Newman argues that an accused may be persuaded to submit a plea of guilty to a crime in return for some concession or consideration from the prosecutor (1956; 1966). For example, the prosecutor may reduce the charge from a serious offense to a less serious one (i.e., robbery to theft). Alternatively, the prosecutor may reduce a batch of charges to one or two of the most serious. Or, where an accused faces several charges for the same offense, there may be a reduction in the number of counts actually prosecuted.

Plea discussions often touch on the area of sentencing. Though in most jurisdictions the onus of deciding the size of the penalty faced by an accused is the prerogative of the judge, the opinions of the lawyers from each side in the case are nonetheless considered. Some informal pre-trial discussions are directed toward extracting from the prosecutor a promise not to make recommendations for a severe sentence or to seek as light a sentence as possible from the judge in exchange for a guilty plea from the defendant. Most criminologists argue that the motive for the defendant, no matter what he or she might have originally done, is to get away with the smallest penalty and/or the least serious police record possible; in other words, the accused is rewarded for cooperation by facing a less severe penalty — hence the bargain imagery (Klein, 1976b).

Two related explanations are given as motivation for the affected parties. The first is the expediency argument: if everyone facing criminal charges elected to have his or her case heard at a trial, the already crowded court calendar would face mayhem. Delays would be interminable. Consequently an inducement has developed to persuade accused persons to cooperate with the system and save everyone the time and bother of a trial (Lummus, 1937: 46; Grosman, 1969).

However, research by Milton Heumann (1978) suggests that the trial rates in the jurisdiction he studied remained the same in spite of significant fluctuations in the number of cases. If expediency were the decisive thing, presumably we would find more trials when the courts were less busy and vice versa, but this was not what Heumann found. Other studies show that where plea bargaining has been banned, there is no swelling of the court calendar by accused persons demanding full trials (Reid, 1979: 288-289). What the expediency model ignores is that if one elects a trial, one has to make a defense against the charge, something difficult to do if the evidence is clear cut and everyone involved, including the accused, is convinced of his or her guilt. Perhaps the only exception to this that occurs regularly involves the Canadian breathalizer law. Defense counsel sometimes will go to trial without an excuse on the "over 80" charge (having over 80 milligrams of alcohol per 100 millilitres of blood) on the hope that the Crown and/or the police will bungle the production of the certificate evidence and fail to convict for technical evidential reasons in what is otherwise an open-and-shut case. But this situation is atypical and turns on the intricacies of the evidence required under Section 237.

Patterns of Charging

A second related argument has to do with overcharging by the police. This argument holds that for any given criminal behaviour the police lay as many charges as possible in order to register a conviction on at least one of them. The rationale is to convict the offender but to do this with whatever charge will work. Research by Ericson (1981, 1982) and Helder (1979) throw some light on this.

In a study of discretionary justice conducted at the Centre of Criminology in Toronto, 100 criminal incidents were identified in a "ride along" study of police patrols and pursued through the courts to their final disposition. The initial 100 incidents involved 131 suspects, and 292 charges were initially laid. In subsequent weeks 81 further charges were laid as a result of further investigation, as well as a result of infractions against the system of justice (such as assault of arresting officer, resisting arrest and violation of the terms of bail and release orders). Consequently, the 131 accused faced 373 charges (Helder, 1979: 34). Most faced more than one charge (one individual faced 21). When the matters finally went to trial, 37.5% of all charges were dropped by the Crown. This affected over half the individuals charged. The question is, in view of the large number of charges dropped, how many accused were subsequently convicted?

TABLE 1
Disposition of the Accused
(n = 131)

a. guilty plea to at least 1 charge	72.1%
b. found guilty at trial of at least 1 charge	9.9%
c. found not guilty of anything	5.3%
d. all charges against the individual withdrawn	11.5%
e. outcome unknown	2.3%

The dispositions indicate that the great majority of the accused were found guilty of something either by plea or by trial. However, the guilt was established with only a portion of the charges laid. Only 209 out of the 373 charges were required to register a conviction.

To characterize this situation as overcharging is somewhat misleading. The police are not making up facts to warrant extra charges. However, it could be argued that they may be acting technically in their charging behaviour. By not pre-sorting the cases, they are in effect pressing most of the possible charges. They do this for several reasons. According to Ericson and associates, this practice produces negotiable cases and provides both defense counsel and the Crown with various matters for the lawyers to consolidate. Also, as we have seen earlier, this practice gives the police a greater control over the case outcomes both in the short as well as the long run.

Helder (1979: 49ff) illustrates this last point in the case of a 15-year-old boy who had a 22-year-old lover who was also a male. The mother of the juvenile called the police when she learned of the relationship. Detectives laid a charge of buggery. When they questioned the 15-year-old about corroborating details that might clinch the case for them, the boy mentioned the presence of a marihuana plant in the accused's apartment. The detectives obtained a search warrant to look for the plant, but also so they could discover any items of bondage. They never laid a narcotics charge. This would have involved the RCMP, and they would have lost control of the case. As a result of their finds in the apartment, details of the juvenile's story were borne out, and the detectives laid two further charges, which they referred to as insurance charges: contributing to juvenile delinquency and indecent assault. The final plea in the case was a guilty plea to buggery. While they did not expect conviction on the insurance charges, their existence more or less convinced the accused's lawyer that the best option was to seek a plea to the first charge, and seek withdrawal of the other two since they all stemmed from the same situation. It would be very unlikely that there could be convictions on the insurance charges over and above the initial charge. Nonetheless, they provide alternative counts if a trial on the first charge failed.

In another case from the Centre of Criminology study, a man had been convicted of two weapons charges following an incident in which he had taken his girlfriend to a field and shot off several rounds of ammunition to frighten her; apparently she was having an affair with another man. He was charged with illegal possession of a weapon, and unlawfully discharging a firearm. A kidnapping charge was dropped because the couple had shared a common-law relationship. Following his conviction on the weapons offenses, he was alleged to have telephoned this woman and threatened her life. His new girlfriend was present during the call at his end of the line; she indicated this did not happen. The new boyfriend of the first woman at the other end of the line overheard her part of the conversation, but could not hear what was being said to her. Following the call, the woman contacted detectives who proceeded to arrest the man once more. According to the researchers the police were aggressive with the man when they arrested him. In addition to a charge of Section 331, threatening life over the phone, his protests won him two further charges: assaulting a police officer, and resisting arrest. The researcher with the police indicated that the detectives wanted these two further charges as kicker charges or insurance charges, which would have the effect of making the accused look like a violent and dangerous individual. For this reason, it was successfully argued during his bail hearing that he should be denied bail. He spent the two weeks in the jail cells until his court date came up. At that point all charges were dropped. However, the detectives had managed to achieve what they wanted: to get the man away from his former girlfriend until the interpersonal tension had cooled off.

This case is interesting inasmuch as it contributes to the perceived blooming of charges, and their eventual withdrawal in court. This is not evidence that the police are laying charges for which there were no factual bases. On the contrary, from an occupational perspective for the police this is an artful use of the law to control breaches of the peace even if this is undertaken without the intent to carry all the cases forward to trial. And even when the police are seeking a conviction against a specific individual the proliferation of charges that some accused persons face is not born necessarily of police maliciousness. In such cases police are typically not looking for a conviction on every charge laid even though where there is no real redundancy, this may be possible.

The proliferation serves to signal all the relevant court personnel that the individual badly needs dealing with. Even for the defense counsel, who might be sceptical of the police, the proliferation of charges creates the distinct impression that the client though probably not guilty of everything must surely be guilty of something. For the police, this practice of what Helder (1979) calls *saturation charging* tends to ensure that the majority of arrested individuals are controlled even though this might be achieved at the expense of dropping some, if not most, individual charges. For them, the important focus is the individual criminal, not the individual charge or case. This type of occupational adaptation helps to increase police control over outcomes in the legal and court environment. However, for the lawyers in this process, it makes case negotiation imperative, which in turn takes their work into the informal environment of pretrial discussions.

Another important matter here is that the case law with respect to double jeopardy puts a limit, however ambiguous, on the duplication of charges arising from the same fact situation. Consequently, charges of resisting arrest and assaulting a police officer would probably be viewed as *alternative* methods of proceeding for the prosecutor. Though frequently such redundant convictions are allowed to proceed in spite of the double jeopardy that results, this is usually because it is standard practice for judges to make the sentences on related matters concurrent, not consecutive. This lessens the effect of redundancy in charges. Justice Laskin of the Supreme Court of Canada noted this in *Kienapple v. the Queen* (1974: 539):

> Although there have been cases where multiple convictions were registered, when in substance only one "crime" has been committed, refusal to interfere on appeal was justified because only one sentence was imposed. . . . the better practice is to avoid multiple convictions.

While it may be in the interest of justice to avoid multiple charging, it appears to be in the interest of the police to generate as many charges as possible to attempt to guarantee conviction for something. We shall return to *Kienapple* later.

Evaluative Questions

The fact that most criminal matters in our society are effectively resolved through informal discussions conducted out of court in the absence of the judge, the victim and the accused and without the benefit of formal rules, has led to a number of evaluative criticisms of plea negotiation (Ferguson and Roberts, 1974: 550ff).

First, critics argue that the informality of these discussions is a travesty of justice, because it ignores the rule of law and due process. Cases for which there exist factual bases are discarded in a secretive and hence unaccountable fashion as a result of the subjective decisions of individual prosecutors. Part and parcel of this criticism is the claim that informal negotiations abrogate one of the most basic premises of English justice — *the adversarial process*. Unlike criminal law in many European countries, which is based on the *inquisitorial method*, the common law tradition is based on the concept of a contest between two equal parties governed by stringent rules of evidence and procedure. This is negated when the defense counsel informally strikes a deal with the prosecutor behind closed doors. The most obvious cost to be paid by such an arrangement, according to Abraham Blumberg (1969) is that innocent accused are stampeded by the conspiracy of lawyers to admit guilt to crimes they did not commit. The alleged threat that the prosecutor will be punitive should the accused act taciturn and fail to cooperate is cited as the reason for submission to false charges. In fact, Blumberg characterizes the role of the defense counsel as a kind of confidence man who swindles the client by making deals with prosecutors that serve the interests of both professionals at the expense of the client. Though undoubtedly this can happen, there is no reason to believe that it occurs in any systematic way.

Another line of criticism of plea bargaining has to do with the damage it does to the image of justice. A frequently cited rubric of the organization of the legal system is that not only must justice be done, it must be *seen* to be done. In other words, not only must the law operate fairly and impartially, but it must have the confidence of society that this is so. Consequently, it is argued that the practice of plea bargaining generates disregard for the law and hence tends to bring the system of justice into disrepute. If the public feels that judicial decisions are arrived at in the same way that one haggles over the price of a car, justice loses its special status or respect as a force over and above the normal course of affairs. One implication of this, it is argued, is that with the loss of respect for justice among accused persons, plea bargaining tends to undermine the rehabilitation of offenders. As with most of the evaluative claims about this process, there is no systematic evidence to support this. Similarly it is claimed that the informality of plea bargaining ensures inconsistency in the manner of case disposition and greater inconsistencies or differentials between the sentences of those who do and those who do not engage in it. Again, this claim is unsupported. One might argue on the contrary that the inconsistencies in sentence are already so gross as to be only mildly liable to any further compounding (Hogarth, 1971). This latter point, even if true, is subject to an alternative explanation. It is an accepted premise of sentencing that the submission of a guilty plea is evidence of remorse and hence is the first step to rehabilitation. Consequently, there is sound judicial reasoning behind any differentials in the sentencing of those who plead guilty versus those who are found guilty having pleaded not guilty. This applies whether there has been a negotiated plea or not (see *R. v. Johnston and Tremayne*, 1970; *R. v. Shanower*, 1972).

A Descriptive Approach to Plea Bargaining

It is paradoxical that in the face of these serious evaluative charges about plea discussion, there has been very little direct research of this phenomenon. For instance, Hartnagel and Wynne studied plea bargaining by examining prosecution files for evidence of changes in charging where there was also "physical evidence," such as letters requesting reductions that the defense had sought (1975: 45-46). The problem with this approach is that it chalks up any and all inherent weaknesses in the evidence, incorrect or duplicitous charges, or other problems to plea bargaining.

James L. Wilkins (1979; Forthcoming) studied pre-court interaction by taping and analyzing conversations between Crown prosecutors and defense lawyers in order to determine how specific cases were negotiated, what types of arguments were effective and what sorts of circumstances were relevant. Wilkins also focussed on the organizational context of case dispositions. Case discussions typically take place in the office of the prosecutor in the lower courts prior to the commencement of the court at ten a.m. However, they may continue during the recesses and the lunch hour. In the lower courts it is not unusual for a prosecutor to have 30 or even 40 items on the daily court list or docket. These items will include cases set for sentencing, as well as for trial. For a variety of reasons, most cases set for trial are not heard; the case may be remanded or postponed, charges may be withdrawn, and/or guilty pleas may be entered. The prosecutor must review the materials associated with each of the items on the docket. This entails reviewing packages containing prior conviction records, occurrence reports, the formal information or charge sheet, evidence sheets, statements, confessions, bail records, pre-sentence reports, psychiatric letters and the like. Usually, the prosecutor will read the relevant evidence sheets and will discuss the evidence with the policemen and witnesses involved, the victim (if necessary) and other court personnel. The office is frequently pandemonic as policemen, court officers, witnesses and lawyers shuffle in and out with their own business on each of the many cases. Matters frequently get more frantic when an evidence package gets lost in the shuffle from the police department on its way to the court, or when key witnesses go missing or go for coffee at the last minute, or cases get shunted off to different courts in the same courthouse as schedules free up. It is in this context that the prosecutor tries to learn the relevant elements of the case that he or she has typically not seen before, and that the charges, the evidence and the witnesses are disputed and discounted in the defense counsel's bid to have the cases disposed of advantageously.

A Case Illustration of Charge Negotiation

In order to illustrate the kinds of things that control case discussions, we shall focus on a single representative case from the Wilkins' study (see Brannigan and Levy, 1983). The case is typical of the sort of *normal* crimes heard in the lower courts (Sudnow, 1965). The defendants are three young men, who each face several charges arising from an episode of theft. Only one has a criminal record, though not a serious one. Once apprehended, the young men were cooperative with the police and helped to recover the stolen goods and/or make restitution. The charges arose from an evening when "the boys" decided to have some fun by driving around in a van and raiding garages. They broke into another vehicle and stole a chest of mechanic's tools, a car aerial and two other minor items. They were caught by the owner. Since the tools were worth over $200, they each faced four criminal charges: three counts of theft under and one count of theft over. The police searched their van and discovered a gasoline credit card that was not owned by any of the boys. It had apparently been lost by or stolen from another person, and two of the boys had used it on different occasions to fill up their cars. One had charged about $12, the other about $120. Based on four forged gas receipts the first boy faced one count of Section 301.1, the second faced three counts of 301.1. This section deals with credit card offenses. Consequently, the docket showed three individuals facing a total of 16 charges. However, the final disposition involved guilty pleas to only four charges. Most criminologists would chalk up this "loss" of cases to plea bargaining on the premise that the accused agreed to "go along" with the prosecution and plead guilty in exchange for a promise to "go easy" on them. However, an examination of the transcript shows the situation to be more complex than this. Though we cannot explore every detail of the twenty-five minute exchange here, suffice it to say that a number of key features emerge that are typically ignored in the majority of studies of plea bargaining. They include the following:

1. Expediency vs Case Strength. When it is argued that plea bargaining is motivated by simple expediency, one infers that the lawyers are motivated by their own self-interest — specifically their sole objective is to minimize time spent and effort expended. However, the plea discussions analyzed in the Wilkins study revealed a preoccupation with what actually happened in the crime and the relevance or accuracy of the charges that resulted. In other words, there is a concern for the adequacy of the matching between the events as they transpired and the charges that resulted. Generally, there is no outright denial of guilt, but a discussion of *how* guilty the party is. These conversations reveal that the counsel are exchanging legal arguments and that they are posturing with one another on the basis of perceived strengths or advantages they find in their cases. There is little evidence here of Blumberg's confidence men motivated solely by expediency. The excerpts here are taken from a conversation held during a morning recess on the day set for trial. It involves three defense counsel, the Crown prosecutor and various police officers involved in the case.

CROWN: O.K. Counsel, do I take your position on the thefts that you feel that your man is totally not guilty on it?
DEFENSE COUNSEL 2: No. No. I don't think that he's totally guilty, but I don't think he's guilty of any indictable offense. I think on the summary offense, he's probably guilty.

(Tape 115, p. 3)

Theft under $200 is called a hybrid offense; the Crown can elect to proceed with the case as either a summary conviction offense, or an indictable offense. Penalty for any summary conviction is limited to a maximum fine of $500 and/or a jail term of six months. For Defense Counsel 2, the distinction is a legal one, not an expedient one. He argues that his client did not really know what was going on, and though he might have accompanied his two friends, he did not have the guilty mind, and so should be allowed to plead to a less serious summary conviction charge. The Crown checks this version of events with the police, who disagree. However, it is also pointed out that the statement that was supposedly given by this individual was only a "verbal" statement and nothing was written down and signed. The Crown counters defense counsel's position by pointing out that under Section 21 the accused is still liable to the same penalty as the others by virtue of being party to the offense - particularly the "theft over," which involved the tool case that required everyone's strength to carry away. One of the police officers present for the discussion amplified the untenability of the lawyer's position.

POLICE OFFICER: What would you say if this was your tool case he was carrying down your driveway? Was he stealing it or is he just assisting his friend to carry it?
DEFENSE COUNSEL 2: He's assisting his friend to carry it.
POLICE OFFICER: Oh yeah — you'd say, "Stop, you bloody thief." [laughter]
CROWN: I, I mean I'm prepared to go to trial on that. Amply prepared to go to trial on that. I don't think, on the party offense, if nothing else, Section 21, I think I've got your man to rights.

(p.7)

Several points are suggested by this last exchange. First of all, the case discussion can fail. The Crown is not prepared to make any concession asked for just for the sake of expediency. Obviously, any concession he might consider must have some basis in the nature of the case, the facts or special circumstances and has to be reasonable. If the defense counsel cannot identify anything relevant as grounds for some consideration, the Crown has no impediments in going to trial. In other words, if he is not able to dispute the case informally, the defense counsel is not likely to have a leg to stand on in a real trial. On the other hand if he has an extremely strong case that challenges the police account, he is liable to succeed in getting the charges dropped outright. Usually, the true situation is somewhere in between. This is illustrated during the discussion of the credit card cases. The client of Defense Counsel 2 had used someone's credit card once to buy gas. Section 301.1 makes it an offense for anyone to use a credit card knowing that it had been obtained as a result of committing an indictable offense. Defense Counsel 2 argues that the 301.1 charge should be dropped against his client since, though he may have used it, he did not know the card was stolen, that it was merely passed to him by his friend.

DEFENSE COUNSEL 2: I really question whether you have a very solid case on the credit card though.

CROWN: On the credit card? Oh, you mean whether or not he knew it was stolen? I think, I think even the fact that, that he was involved with it in criminal activities with these guys before.

DEFENSE COUNSEL 2: Yes. What I'm pointing out is that the Crown would have to prove that true, he in fact knew that.

CROWN: Yes, that he had the guilty mind. I agree. Now I think what we have to do is go on, as far as I can see, I haven't got Mick here, so as far as I can see, we have to go on circumstantial evidence.

CROWN: What's Oak's involvement in the . . . the credit card?

DETECTIVE MICK: O.K. Ah. . .

CROWN: And how do we establish his guilty mind?

DETECTIVE MICK: Statements [laughs] admissions.

CROWN: He's, he's got the one statement to say that he got it from somebody and that that was in somebody else's name.

DEFENSE COUNSEL 2: All he said I think was that . . . he got it off Kevin Murray and used it once.

(pp.9-10)

In the previous challenge to the Crown's case, the *mens rea* defense was outflanked by Section 21. In this case, the Crown realizes that the accused's knowledge could be a live issue and reluctantly agrees to drop the charge.

DEFENSE COUNSEL 2: The arrangement which we were making was a plea of guilty to the over [i.e., theft over $200].

CROWN: Yes, combining, combining in all the items.

DEFENSE COUNSEL 2: In view of the fact that the guy has no previous record, and also possibly may not have another one.

CROWN: Yes.

DEFENSE COUNSEL 2: . . . then, you know, I'm suggesting just that one offense. [Pause] A guilty plea for that. [Long Pause]

CROWN: Used it once? Alright, what about, how are we going to arrange his paying back?

DEFENSE COUNSEL 2: Well I, I can only assure you that it will be paid back, . . . I know that the father or the son will pay, because the son works as well as going to school but . . . when the 12 dollars is sent off . . . which card was it?

DEFENSE COUNSEL 2: [Inaudible] already paid.
CROWN: Alright. Alright. Give 12 dollars to Detective Mick today.
DETECTIVE MICK: That's probably the best way around this.
DEFENSE COUNSEL 2: Sure, yeh, that's fine.
DEFENSE COUNSEL 3: Detective Mick can go out and buy a drink.
CROWN: And Detective Mick will make sure it gets back.

(pp. 13-14)

Here the matter is resolved after the lawyer takes some cash from his wallet and pays $12 to the detective in order to ensure that restitution gets to the offended party. Cash changes hands right in the office and the matter is closed. Despite its informality, this manner of disposing of the case does meet one legal objective, that of restitution, without risking the unpredictable outcome of a trial. What must be kept in mind is that if the Crown did insist on proceeding to trial and the case failed, any question of restitution would become irrelevant. Presumably a trial on this matter would have to turn on the doctrine of evidence called similar facts. Oak's guilt would be inferred from the fact that he had been involved as the Crown says "in criminal activities with these guys before" presumably involving the credit card. Oak's statement that he got the card from somebody and that it was in somebody else's name is probably not strong enough to support the similar facts argument alluded to in the Crown's reference to "circumstantial evidence." Oak's lawyer arranges to pay for the losses under conditions where this could probably not be compelled as a result of a trial because of the weakness of the evidence needed. In turn, the charge is dropped.

Aside from the discussion over *mens rea*, legal questions, legal reasoning and legal considerations are witnessed throughout. Murray's lawyer, Defense Counsel 3, points out that s. 301.1 is, like theft under $200, a hybrid offense and so the Crown has an option as to how he plans to prosecute. The immediate question for the Crown is whether there is a previous criminal record. The defense counsel then tries to point out that though there is a record it is quite minor. Similar discussions range over the questions of pre-sentence reports, recommendations for conditional discharge sentences, and the importance of restitution. Throughout the respective counsel are preoccupied with legal matters, not simple expediency. Also, despite its informality, the procedure is nonetheless adversarial. The case discussion is full of arguments and counterarguments that get to the heart of what could be argued in a trial if this were undertaken. Frequently these negotiations break down, resulting in no change in the charges if one of the adversaries is not content with the progress of the discussions. What these discussions allow to be aired are the respective positions about how strong the various cases are. One of the major sources for charge reduction is the successful identification of weaknesses in the prosecution cases prior to the actual court appearance. This is expedient in the good sense: it expedites justice by sharpening the mutual awareness of live issues and sorting out weak cases. Grosman makes a similar argument about the relevance of weaknesses in the Crown's case (1969: 59-60) as do Utz (1978) and Mather (1979) in American studies.

2. *Matching Facts and Laws.* One of the unavoidable aspects of criminal cases is that the key counsel involved in the case have to reconstruct the original events on the basis of incomplete knowledge. Their version of the event is put together from what the accused confess to the police, what they reveal to the lawyers, what witnesses remember, what police write into their notebooks and reports, and the like. These accounts

frequently vary in substantial ways. Under such circumstances common-sense abstractions often come into play in the case discussions. These abstractions are ad hoc but are nonetheless important in deciding the fit between the charges and the original facts. In the current case, the three young men each faced three counts of theft under and one of theft over. Because of the way he imagines the event actually happened, the Crown is amenable to collapsing the theft charges:

CROWN: I take the position that as far as I can see that this was really all happening in one night and they were joyriding around and they decided to steal a bunch of stuff, eh?

DEFENSE COUNSEL 2: When I was speaking to Officer Jackson about it . . . he had something confused. He thought in the first place that there was three vans involved in the incident (Crown: Yeah) actually being used by each of the individuals accused (Crown: Yeah) to pick up this stuff (Crown: Yeah). There wasn't, there was only one van.

CROWN: And there were all three of them in the one van.

(p.3)

* * * * * * * * *

CROWN: Now Doug (Defense Counsel 3), you were earlier speaking to me about a plea to ah, to the three unders and forgetting the over (Defense Counsel 3: Yeah). How does, how does lumping them altogether in the theft in one count of theft over since it was one night, rest with you?

(p.5)

The third defense counsel asks for consideration in the credit card cases on the same basis. Rather than talking about one night/one van/one theft, the defense lawyer raises another kind of integrity that unites (and hence collapses) the three credit card charges.

DEFENSE COUNSEL 3: . . . I indicated that because the three cards came all from the same wallet (Crown: Yes) and because they were all in the same name (Crown: Yes) that I would be willing to plead him to one count rather than three counts . . . of the possession of stolen credit cards . . .

(p.5)

Later the Crown explains to Defense Counsel 2 the reduction he thinks is reasonable in the theft cases.

CROWN: I'm considering . . . on Doug's . . . and it's subject to a conversation I'm going to have with the officers, but I'm pretty sure that sounds reasonable to me that one count of theft over, all lumped together because it was one night, that seems very reasonable to me . . .

(p.7)

The Crown subsequently explains the nature of the deal to the detective involved in the thefts and the credit card cases.

CROWN: The guy that's . . . primarily involved with the credit card, is really Doug's client and . . . Doug's already indicated that we're gonna lump, since . . . all three cards were from one wallet . . . and he used them on separate occasions, but it was an involvement really of just one (Det: transaction) transaction, I'm prepared to have him plead to the one with all the facts read in.

(p.10)

As Defense Counsel 2 observes in an aside, really the cards were obtained at another place at another time, and were used at several separate times during a period of months. These facts are selectively ignored in favour of the ad hoc version of events exchanged back and forth between the lawyers, even though it is clear that the credit card crimes involved a more complex series of events. After an interruption, the Crown restates the arrangement under discussion.

CROWN: . . . what's being proposed by Doug March, which sounds reasonable to me is that we have on the thefts, we have three thefts under and one theft over (Det.: right) all on one night (Det.: right), and proposing a plea to, theft over, combining one count of theft over, combining them. All the cards come from one wallet (Det.: Yeah), ah so it was really one *transaction*, even though he used it on several occasions over time (Det.: right) that there be a plea ah . . . to one count of the [Sec.301.1] and with all the facts read in, and that sounds reasonable to me.

(p.11)

After the informal discussions had ended, the Crown explained the rationale for his decisions to one of the researchers.

CROWN: I guess you've been around long enough to know why we were able to consolidate . . . all the separate counts into one. What the officers did is that, like, when they seized the items to begin with as their usual practice is they charged for each separate item. [Crown taps desk on each word] and ah . . . I think it's appropriate to proceed either way . . . lumping them altogether into one, which is what technically is going to happen. . . . Just to keep the informations straight, what I'm going to do is withdraw the three counts when I'm reading in the facts of all the informations, so that it will be the same thing as if he was charged with one count of theft over involving dot, dot, dot, dot, dot, dot all of the other ones, so that'll be the effect. And since it happened on one night, within an hour and a half, I think it's appropriate that . . . it be dealt with as one information for which they are prepared to plead guilty, and the advantage to them is that it appears on their record, one count of theft over instead of three theft under, and one theft over. In future sentencing I think that that affects them. It won't affect what happens today. On the uttering I'm not so happy. Hm. I think ah . . . but I think it's reasonable with three cards, from one wallet, one transaction, one involvement all in the same name, three credit cards in the same, in the same name, only different companies.

Hence the docket, which initially contained sixteen charges involving three individuals, was resolved with four guilty pleas. Each of the young men pleaded guilty to theft over, and one faced an additional conviction of Section 301.1. As the Crown noted, convictions on these items "won't affect what happens today" in the sense that none of them will face any kind of jail term. However, the existence of the record for theft over will put them in a bad light should they ever be returned to court on a future matter. This touches a central issue: since nothing is really given away, it would seem to be stretching things to characterize this as bargaining. And even if there had been a question of jail terms, as noted earlier, it is standard practice in Canada that sentences on related convictions run concurrently. This would have the effect of neutralizing multiple convictions that arise out of the same set of circumstances.

3. Bargaining or Consolidation? As one can gather from the Crown's remarks, reductions in the number and/or type of charges does not necessarily have major implications for sentencing, at least not on the initial charges. This is more or less guaranteed by the practice of "reading the facts in." Even if one pleads guilty, the practice is to have a description of the criminal circumstances read into the record, chiefly to aid the judge in arriving at a suitable sentence. Hence if an armed robbery is reduced to a case of theft, the mention of the weapon will not be lost on the judge. In the current case, though only one theft charge is actually taken to court, the facts of all the items stolen are given before the judge. Presumably, these facts are considered in sentencing. This also leads one to believe that nothing is really given away in plea bargaining.

With respect to sentence, several things must be kept in mind. Most first offenders rarely face any period of incarceration. In fact, the figure for offenders of all types, combining property, violent personal and sexual offenses was about 17% in 1972 (Law Reform Commission of Canada, 1976b: 76). Consequently, unless violence is involved, the chances are slight that an offender will face the most feared consequence of a criminal conviction, jail time. Also, in those very serious cases that are likely to result in jail sentences, there is very little incentive for the Crown to consolidate charges. After all, why should the prosecutor consolidate someone's charges when it appears by virtue of the gravity of the first charges that the individual is a long-term risk to the system? What is the point of trying to minimize the criminal record of an accused who appears from the start to be a lost cause? Nonetheless, there are circumstances in which the doctrine of double jeopardy would compel the prosecutor to treat the various charges laid as alternatives, only one of which could apply.

The implication of these points is that, if the consolidations described in this case are typical, it does not really make much difference whether the charges on a first offense are consolidated or not, especially when the facts are read in. In discussing the specific reductions that had been arranged, the Crown did not seem to think that the arrangement would affect the sentence.

CROWN: . . . I'm not particularly happy about that uttering [i.e., about dropping the charge of S. 301.1] but in, in light of all of the circumstances . . . that's appropriate (P.O.: Yeah). I think he's going to get, he would have gotten a conditional discharge, I think on that anyways.
POLICE OFFICER: So ah . . . it's six of one, half a dozen of the other.
CROWN: Precisely.

(p.15)

4. Informal Consolidation: Overcoming Mutual Binds. The opportunity to enter off-the-record discussions with the other counsel allows each counsel to explore areas that might not be accessible otherwise. For the defense, there is a chance to challenge the Crown on criminal matters for which the police have *already* obtained evidence including inculpatory statements made by their clients. Few if any studies of plea bargaining even refer to this fact. When the Crown reminds the defense counsel of some signed statements, the counsel replies humorously that "the officer had a gun to his head when he signed that" (p.5), and the negotiation carries on. On the prosecutor's side, the situation is more mixed. As noted above, in the case of the accused who faced the single 301.1 charge, restitution was arranged *without* a conviction. The transcript indicates at several points that the Crown is less than totally pleased with the withdrawal of this charge. In the account of his actions he offers to the researcher after the consolidation has proceeded, he seems to suggest that the decision was simply expedience. But a crucial question about the *source* of testimony comes out. Talking about the second accused he said:

CROWN: On this other guy, . . . the only thing I can say about that; it was convenience. It's something I don't usually do, but with this kind of tied up matter and confusion and everything else, I felt that that was the appropriate thing to do. Rather than call these two guys against him and . . . I think that might have been proper.

(p.16)

★ ★ ★ ★ ★ ★ ★ ★

CROWN: . . . But anyway, on the final uttering, I, I think that was just straight convenience and ah . . . we should have [prosecuted], we had him on all counts, we should have gone. I needed these two guys to . . . give evidence against him or at least this one guy to give evidence against him. So that I'm put in a position of saying . . . "You plead guilty to something better — if you turn state's evidence" and I'm not that happy with that. I'd rather let a little, little possession for 12 bucks and restitution go by the by than get into that nonsense . . .

(p.17)

The "convenience" that the Crown alludes to is quite a complex procedural matter. The Crown would have had to have set up separate trials because as things stood the three individuals were co-accused on the same indictment and none could be compelled to testify at trial even if the Crown only wanted one accused to implicate, not himself, but the other. Separate trials would have tied up enormous court and police resources for a relatively minor matter. The outcome negotiated in this case is not "simple expediency," but the deployment of finite resources with some sense of priority. Also, if the Crown wanted to pursue this arrangement, it would have produced an inversion of justice because it would require that in order to convict the second offender of the $12 offense, a greater inducement would have to be given to the third offender who had taken $120. Since the latter's three charges were already reduced to one, presumably the Crown would be put in the absurd position of dropping all charges against the more serious offender in order to induce the vital testimony needed for conviction of the less serious offender. In view of this unreasonable outcome, his decision is again certainly not based on simple convenience, but a sense of proportion.

The Legal Context of Multiple Charges

The last point to be examined involves some larger legal considerations that provide a framework for understanding the charge changes. Where a number of charges arise out of the same fact situation, it is possible that the accused may face multiple convictions and punishments for the same act. This is at variance with the common-law principle that an accused cannot be punished twice for the same offense. The matter arises not only where there are multiple charges of the same infractions but also where different

JUSTICE IN THE LOWER COURT 149

charges are derived from the same act. In the case of *R. v. Quon* (1949), the defendant was found guilty of armed robbery as well as unlawful possession of a firearm during the commission of a crime. The second charge was quashed on appeal because it was held that it was not actually an independent crime, but was an essential part of the first offense. The principal here is *transit in rem judicatam*, that is, the first conviction shall be a bar to all further proceedings for the same offense. In such cases the plea an accused would enter is called *res judicata* and is wider than the special plea of autrefois convict (i.e., convicted of the crime on a previous occasion). *Res judicata* also applied in the case of *R. v. Siggins* (1960) who was charged with theft as well as unlawful possession of the stolen goods. Since the possession is implied in the act of theft, the former conviction was quashed. Similar appeals have been upheld in the case of a charge of gross indecency that was added to a charge of buggery, and a conspiracy to defraud which was added to conspiracy to steal. The most recent case to clarify this principle is *Kienapple v. The Queen* (1974). Kienapple was charged and convicted of rape as well as unlawful sexual intercourse with an underage girl. In a narrow five-to-four decision, the Supreme Court of Canada quashed the second conviction, reasoning that while the second offense is not necessarily included in rape, there was nonetheless substantial overlap because the sexual intercourse involved a girl under 14 years without her consent. Lack of consent is an essential element of rape. However, had she consented the age factor would still have made the act a crime but it would be unlawful intercourse, as opposed to rape.

The court reasoned that "when both charges have been laid, they must be treated as alternative counts, and if an accused is convicted of rape he cannot also be convicted of unlawful sexual intercourse" (*Kienapple v. The Queen*, 1974: 524). The dissenting opinion argued that the defense of *res judicata* applied only to multiple proceedings for the same crime, but that it does not forbid a second prosecution for the same conduct where this conduct may consist of separate crimes. This was not the view of the majority. In the words of Mr. Justice Laskin "the relevant inquiry so far as *res judicata* is concerned is whether the same cause or matter (rather than the same offense) is comprehended by two or more offenses" (p. 750).

Nonetheless the application of the Kienapple doctrine is frequently quite ambiguous. Typically the police will lay whatever charges seem appropriate, leaving the question of double jeopardy for the lawyers to sort out. This affects plea discussions quite directly. Though the police in the current case laid separate charges for each of the stolen items worth less than $200, as well as one count of theft over $200, it could have been open to the defense to raise the Kienapple doctrine if there had been a conviction of theft over followed by an arraignment for the theft unders. It could be argued following *res judicata*, that the theft unders were covered by the first conviction. After all, if a wallet is stolen we do not expect the officer to lay a charge of theft under for each $20 bill taken but rather that the total value of the money will determine whether the charge is theft over or theft under. Consequently, the Kienapple doctrine provides a legal mandate to inspect the charges for possible redundancy and to seek the cancellation of some charges if such redundancy is detected. In the current case, though Kienapple may have been on everyone's mind, it is not referred to explicitly, and so while relevant in law it may have had little detectable consequence for the outcome.

A second legal issue appears to have been involved and was invoked rather more directly. Section 510.1 of the Criminal Code indicates that "each count in an indictment shall in general apply to a single transaction . . ." As noted earlier, the Crown recurrently characterizes the credit card offenses as well as the thefts as single transactions.

The courts have tended to give the notion of transaction a fairly wide interpretation and seem to recognize that the Crown has a considerable discretion to treat each identifiable component of a series of events as a transaction or the series itself as a transaction. For example, in the 1964 case of *R. v. Zamal et al*, five accused who had successively raped the same victim faced a joint charge of one count of rape. In the 1970 case of *R. v. Taylor*, though three separate incidents were involved over a six-month period, the accused's acts of gross indecency were deemed to constitute one transaction. Similarly other cases have held that a series of dissimilar but related acts may be charged as one continuing offense whether this includes importing, trafficking and exporting narcotics, or a string of fraudulent medical treatment claims (see Greenspan, 1981: s. 510.1). In the case study examined here, the Crown chose to treat the series of events as one transaction. However, if the Crown had pursued the other extreme and fragmented the series very finely, it would have been open to argument as to whether the various discrete actions, though they transpired at different times, were really part of the same chain of events — and in fact constituted the same crime. In this case, the Kienapple situation would come into play and the Crown would be barred from pursuing multiple convictions. This appears to account for the Crown's insistence on the singularity of the transaction despite the illegal use of the stolen card at several different points in time. In other words, the disposition negotiated here is determined in large measure by specific provision of the Criminal Code (Section 510.1), as well as by recent case law (*Kienapple v. The Queen*), and principles of common law justice (the defense of *res judicata*).

Clearly the relevance of such factors has been underestimated in studies of plea bargaining. This is distressing when we consider that one of the most prevalent areas of criminal behaviour, drinking and driving offenses, routinely results in negotiated outcomes pertinent to Kienapple. Specifically, in most Canadian jurisdictions, drivers who appear to be intoxicated are usually compelled to take a breathalyzer test and face charges for both impaired driving and "over 80." The penalties for both are identical. However, conviction on both is disallowed under the Kienapple doctrine (McLeod et al, 1981: 229-230). Impaired and "over 80" must be considered as alternative charges for court proceeding. Consequently, though bureaucratic factors may lead the police to lay charges on both items, very specific legal principles provide a framework in which the reduction of charges is inevitable. Though this reasoning is most evident in situations like impaired and "over 80," it is a pertinent consideration in any case where a proliferation of charges results from the same criminal cause or matter. Since charge reduction is inevitable in cases like these, this again suggests that informal case discussion is mischaracterized as bargaining.

Risk in Negotiated Dispositions: Broken Promises Regarding Sentence

Aside from the questions of how the legal and bureaucratic structures control the course of case dispositions, no examination of this matter is complete without some reference to the liability engendered by informal agreements with the prosecutor. By virtue of the fact that these informal agreements occur off the record, there is a question as to how binding any agreement is. In *R. v. Agozzino* (1970) the prosecutor appears to have agreed not to seek a jail term for an accused who agreed to plead guilty to a charge of possession of counterfeit money. The accused was merely fined by a judge, who indicated at the time of sentencing that he would have imposed a jail term had the prosecutor not called for a fine. The Crown's office subsequently appealed the sentence on the ground that it was too lenient. However, the Ontario Court of Appeal denied the appeal. Likewise the Ontario Court of Appeal restored the agreement made in R. v. Brown (1972), in which the prosecutor urged consecutive sentences on partially related convictions where the understanding had been that concurrent sentences would be sought.

However, the judiciary's attitude to such informal sentencing agreements has not always been consistent. Ferguson and Roberts (1974: 501) discuss several cases in the Quebec Court of Appeal in which sentences that were appealed for being too lenient were increased by the higher court, thereby allowing the prosecutor to renege on earlier agreements. The inconsistency of the appeal courts in these situations puts a grave liability on the defense and allows the Crown an enormous, potentially abusive latitude in the prosecutorial discretion. Though there are a number of things to recommend informal case disposition in the lower courts, the breaking of sentencing agreements needs to be treated more consistently by the judiciary, and individuals must be given better protection from the undue exercise by the Crown of its power to prosecute.

Summary

Informal case disposition appears to be crucial in the administration of lower court justice. The practice of plea negotiation or plea bargaining has been explained as an expedient solution arising from organizational pressures in the police department and in the courts. The materials presented here offer an alternative account. Plea negotiation is structured by a number of considerations, some of them strictly legal. First of all, charges may be reduced or dropped because of problems with the evidence and the unlikelihood of conviction. Secondly, charges may be changed or dropped to try to get a more accurate match between the original behaviour and the criminal code category corresponding to it. Third, charges may be changed or dropped because of their inherent redundancy or because convictions on related charges will be redundant at the point of sentencing. Lastly, charges may be changed or dropped because of the inherent difficulty of compelling co-accused to testify against one another. The authority for amalgamating related charges under one indictment is given by s. 510.1 and the wide sense of what constitutes a transaction. The authority which prevents multiple convictions aising from the same cause or matter is the *Kienapple* doctrine, according to which the multiple changes must be treated as alternatives.

Doreen McBarnet has demonstrated the utility in tracing organizational factors to their legal underpinnings in the context of arrest and conviction (1981). The legal framework is likewise important in understanding the operation of case negotiations. It suggests that this area of justice, which usually is explained solely in terms of organizational expediency, can be understood in terms of jurisprudence. This account suggests that statutes and common-law principles give lawyers a mandate over and above organizational factors to approach the Crown to seek changes in an indictment. Nonetheless, legal factors do not *overdetermine* case discussions. They provide the legal tools and resources that allow lawyers to argue their cases to best advantage and to do so both at and prior to court appearances.

Lastly, if this assessment of the parameters that come into play in out-of-court case discussions is correct, the many ethical objections that have been raised with the imagery of bargain justice are probably overstated and based typically on a misunderstanding of what such discussions consist of. Given the looseness of fit between police charging behaviour and the limitations of what convictions might be permissible, the consultation between counsel is not only unavoidable but desirable. Like discovery in private cases, it helps both sides in the case know what things will be at issue in the trial and how to prepare for it. Also, such discussions help establish independently of the police perception of the reasonable and probable grounds for arrest and independently of a preliminary inquiry whether a trial is warranted at all, and if warranted, whether warranted on all charges.

FURTHER READING

Pat Carlen, *Magistrate's Justice*. London: Martin Robertson, 1976.

Brian Grosman, *The Prosecutor*. Toronto: University of Toronto Press, 1969.

Milton Heumann, *Plea Bargaining: The Experience of Prosecutors, Judges and Defense Attorneys*. Chicago: University of Chicago Press, 1978.

John F. Klein, *Let's Make a Deal*. Lexington: Lexington Books, 1976.

Lynn Mather, *Plea Bargaining or Trial? The Process of Criminal Case Disposition*. Lexington: Lexington Books, 1979.

Doreen McBarnet, *Conviction: Law, the State and the Construction of Justice*. London: Macmillan, 1981.

Donald J. Newman, *Conviction: The Determination of Guilt or Innocence Without Trial*. Boston: Little, Brown, 1966.

J. Skolnick, *Justice Without Trial*. New York: Wiley, 1966.

P. Utz, *Settling the Facts: Discretion and Negotiation in the Criminal Courts*. Lexington: Lexington Books, 1978.

James L. Wilkins, *Ducus in a Row: The Practice of Prosecution*, forthcoming.

CHAPTER 8

The Higher Courts: A Study of R. v. Demeter

Introduction

In Canada, trial by jury is an option generally open to most offenders who face charges that could result in imprisonment for five years or more. Nonetheless, criminal jury trials do not occur frequently in the justice system. John Hagan (1977: 159) estimates that there are fewer than 2,000 per year in Canada. Griffiths, Klein, and Verdun-Jones (1980: 146) report that only 2.3% of criminal cases in British Columbia proceed to the higher courts at all and suggest that most higher-court cases are heard by a judge alone. This trend is typical and is corroborated by research elsewhere (MacKaay, 1976: 33). If we examine the Canadian statistics of those persons convicted of indictable offenses, we find only a fraction elected a jury trial. The following table is based on the report from Statistics Canada, *Statistics of Criminal and Other Offenses for 1972* (Friedland, 1978: 16).

TABLE 1
Numerical Distribution of Persons Convicted by Type of Trial:
Indictable Offenses, Total, 1972
(excluding Alberta and Quebec)

Judge and Jury	Judge without Jury	Magistrate's Jurisdiction with Consent*	Magistrate's Absolute Jurisdiction	Total
820	1678	22,385	20,731	45,614

*Trial at the election of the accused before a magistrate in the lower court, criminal division.

Table 1 shows the number of persons actually convicted, not the number of persons simply appearing in the various courts. However, the trends suggested here are consistent with other reports about the infrequency of jury trials.

In this chapter we explore some of the dimensions of the higher-court trial experience, as well as some of the problems raised by jury trials. The strategy will be to examine a particular trial, a famous Canadian murder case, and to view it in some depth in order to understand both the procedural wrangles that control the development of the trial, as well as the elusive factual determinations that the trial is aimed at establishing.

Despite its infrequency, the criminal jury trial is held by many to be the epitome or quintessence of the common-law system of justice. It is accusatorial and adversarial. That is, the trial is a forum in which a defendant is accused or indicted for a contravention of the criminal law and in which the merits of the accusation are decided in a factual way, within careful evidential rules by two opposing advocates representing the accused and the Crown and decided by a jury of one's peers. Because relatively few matters are decided in this fashion, some students of jurisprudence equate this with the demise of the adversarial system, assuming that the lack of trials is a direct function of plea bargaining (Law Reform Commission of Canada, 1974-75: 14; Verdun-Jones and Cousineau, 1982). A simpler interpretation would be that the cases are examined at several different levels, the weaker cases generally being sorted out before trial. Hence, most accused submit pleas of guilty, and think of themselves as guilty because under the current laws the majority are guilty. Nonetheless, what is distinctive about our system is that the adversarial forum allows an opportunity to contest that guilt, however few choose to do so.

Problems and Issues

This is not to say that the current situation could not be improved. Indeed, the criminal trial is marked by a number of problems and issues, three of which are outstanding. First, the use of a jury of 12 largely middle-aged and middle-class strangers to decide complex questions of fact and to digest instructions regarding the law is problematic. The problem is put rather strikingly by Oppenheimer (1937: 142):

> We commonly strive to assemble twelve persons collossally ignorant of all practical matters, fill their vacuous heads with law which they cannot comprehend, obfuscate their seldom intellects with testimony which they are incompetent to analyse or unable to remember, permit partisan lawyers to bewilder them with their meaningless sophistry, then lock them up until the most obstinate of their number coerce the others into submission or drive them into open revolt.

Ely Devons' British report indicates that instructions to jurors are routinely discarded and that the juries' decisions are frequently determined by what jurors feel the punishment might be, and whether the defendant deserves such treatment (1965: 561-570). This subjective element has been confirmed in Rita Simon's studies of simulated jury decisions in the US (1965). The same subjective process is revealed in cases such as *R. v. Morgentaler*, where a Montreal jury acquitted the accused of abortion charges only to see the decision reversed by the Quebec Court of Appeal and a jail term imposed. Presumably, the jury disregarded the laws of Canada and the evidence of the case in favour of their own sympathy for the accused (Pelrine, 1975).

A second problematic area involves the discretionary powers of the Crown prosecutor. The Crown has almost unchecked power to proceed by indictment or summary conviction on hybrid offenses, to withdraw charges or stay (i.e., suspend) proceedings, to control pretrial disclosure, and to negotiate charges and sentences. These decisions are, for the most part, outside the scrutiny of the court. A telling illustration of this latitude is reported in *R. v. Beaudry* (1967), where the trial judge instructed the jury to return a verdict of not guilty. Rather than lose the case, the Crown immediately stayed the prosecution and entered a new charge against the accused on which he was subsequently convicted. The power to stay, which allows the Crown to suspend proceedings for up to a period of one year, was upheld. However, the Court itself can stay a prosecution by declining "to hear a case which would bring the administration of justice into disrepute or make a sham of it" (see Greenspan, 1979: 451). In *R. v. Weightman and Cunningham* (1977), the prosecutor withdrew a charge and laid a related one when his request for an adjournment was refused. The Court refused to hear the new charge because the behaviour of the prosecutor involved an abuse of process arising from his disregard and arbitrary circumvention of the Court's ruling. This is one of the few cases where the right to withdraw charges (as opposed to stay proceedings) has been checked by considerations of abuse of process. However, the right of the Court (i.e., the judge) to stay criminal proceedings is quite weak and can be exercised only in the most exceptional circumstances.

A third problematic area in the higher courts concerns access to counsel. As we have seen, though legal aid or "judicare" services are available across Canada, these services are employed almost exclusively in the lower courts by defendants pleading guilty. Legal aid services are reluctant to support a matter on appeal, especially appeals to the Supreme Court of Canada, which often incur fees in excess of $10,000. This creates the possibility of a class bias in the area of appeals. Other problems occur in both the higher and lower courts and include such things as disparities in sentences, court delay, witness recollection, perjury and fabrication of evidence, and subjective assessments of credibility. Rather than dwell on each of these questions in a general way, we shall explore a particular case in detail to illustrate how some of these issues arise in real life. This approach is also useful to show how a criminal case is transformed over the duration of the trial and in the appeal courts. Before describing the case, a brief overview of the process is in order.

Procedures

The options of the accused as to how he wishes to have his case heard were outlined in the last chapter. Where the accused elects trial by judge and jury, the jury sits as "the trier of facts" and must weigh the testimony of witnesses and the other evidence to determine whether there is a reasonable doubt about the accused's alleged criminal behaviour. The role of the judge is to decide questions of law, involving such matters as the admissibility of evidence, as well as instructions to the jury about the points of law that pertain to their deliberations. The judge is also responsible for seeing that procedural laws governing the transaction are observed.

Once the accused has appeared in the lower court to set a date for trial and if he has elected to appear in higher court, a preliminary inquiry may be held before a lower-court magistrate. Though many defense counsel treat the preliminary inquiry as a method for discovery of or access to the Crown's case, in fact the Crown rarely develops its entire case in the preliminary (Law Reform Commission of Canada, 1974). Even though witnesses are sworn, examined and cross-examined, the point of this judicial inquiry is to allow the magistrate to determine if there is sufficient evidence to commit the accused for trial in the higher court. MacKaay (1976) reports that in Montreal, only a small fraction of cases result in dismissal. This appears to be true across Canada. Not surprisingly, the preliminary inquiry is not always held. In fact, in his study, MacKaay found that it was held only in a minority of cases, the defense preferring to proceed directly to trial. On the other hand, Section 507.3 of the Criminal Code gives the Crown the power to circumvent the preliminary by indicting the accused directly, either before the preliminary begins or ends. In fact, the Crown may take the accused to trial even if the provincial court judge or magistrate has found that the evidence for the charge in question is insufficient (Griffiths, Klein and Verdun-Jones, 1980: 139). In such cases, the written consent of the trial judge or the Attorney-General is required.

In Nova Scotia, indictments in higher court are arranged uniquely. A grand jury composed of citizens is presented with evidence in order to determine whether there are sufficient grounds for trial or not. Consequently, rather than returning a verdict of guilty or not guilty as at a trial, the Nova Scotia grand jury returns a "true bill" or "no bill" decision. A true bill, or well-founded indictment, proceeds to trial. In the other provinces, the indictment against the accused is not made by a grand jury decision but by the Attorney General (or a representative) in an indictment form (see Form 4 in the Criminal Code, Part XXV). The indictment differs from an information sworn before a justice of the peace. The information states that the informant, usually a policeman, has reasonable and probable grounds to believe that some person has committed a crime. In the magistrate's court, a trial can proceed on the basis of an information. In the higher courts, an indictment is used. The indictment in the 19th century had to be extremely accurate, very detailed and flawless in the description of the criminal behaviour. This practice was followed because it was felt that an erroneous or unclear indictment would render the guilt of the accused uncertain (Salhany, 1978: 139). Criminal charges were frequently nullified because of flaws in the indictments. Today, the indictment can be written in popular language and needs to be only as detailed as necessary to give the accused reasonable information about which act is to be proved against him (murder, theft, arson, etc.) as well as the transaction by which the act took place. Names of witnesses appear on the reverse side of the indictment.

At the trial proper, the proceedings typically begin with opening statements from each side, outlining the positions which they will pursue during trial. These positions are referred to as the theories of the defense and the prosecution. Following this, the examination in chief is conducted by the Crown Attorney. The Crown presents the state's case against the defendant, focussing on the elements of the offense, proof that the accused was involved, and whether he or she had the "guilty mind" in the actions. The step-by-step production of evidence in the stand is monitored by the judge and the defense counsel who make sure that what is being given in evidence is allowable under the various rules of evidence. What is admissible is subject to rules regarding hearsay, opinion witnessing, assessments of credibility, and so on. The defense counsel has the right to cross-examine the Crown witnesses on matters brought out by the Crown. Typically, it is the defense's objective to bring the credibility of the witness into question, to raise contrary interpretations to the same observations, or to establish some doubt in the witness's mind about what was seen or known. Following the last Crown witness, the defense counsel will often file a motion for dismissal of the case if the evidence is weak and/or of doubtful admissibility. This is less frequent in Canada than in the USA because of the Canadian system of pre-viewing the case in the preliminary hearing.

In many trials, there are no defense witnesses; the defense's case rests on impugning the theory and evidence of the Crown. In some cases, even the accused will be reluctant to take the stand, especially if the evidence against the accused is purely circumstantial, or because the accused's personality, previous criminal record, or reputation may draw an unfavourable reaction from the jury. The right to remain silent is fundamental in our system of justice. On the other hand, if you are falsely accused it makes sense to take the stand and shout at the top of your lungs that you are innocent. Contrary to the popular view, which holds that the jury cannot draw an inference from the reluctance of an accused to take the stand, the jury is quite within its rights to draw any inference from this that it feels sound. After all, if you are trying to escape from a well-founded accusation, this will probably require that you perjure yourself on the stand, an action that may be detected by the jury. It is this fear of detection that motivates the guilty to avoid the witness box. However, even the innocent defendant is subject to cross-examination by the Crown, and there is a legitimate fear that the Crown will put the defendant in an unfavourable light, however ill-founded the charges.

Much of the defense counsel thinking is designed to raise reasonable doubts about the force of the Crown's case, and hence reasonable doubts about the guilt of the accused. In the case to be examined, this is done by citing a cavalcade of other individuals who could possibly have committed the deed.

Once the defense has rested its case and the cross-examination and re-examinations are complete, the counsels make their closing arguments. These summations are designed to re-state the theories of the respective parties, but this time, the theories are embellished with facts, recollections of witness behaviours, and physical evidence. The summations are useful because they allow the respective counsel to gloss the thousands of utterances and exhibits, and to digest them for the consideration of the triers of fact. If the defense has not introduced its own witnesses, the Crown addresses the jury first, leaving the last word for the defense. However, if the defense has introduced witnesses, the Crown will address the jury last.

Once the prosecution and defense have finished their summations, a judgement of guilt or innocence must be delivered by the jury. The judge will instruct the jury about the points of law they must consider, the options they face in light of conviction (i.e., they may not find evidence of murder, but perhaps manslaughter). In some cases, a judge may instruct the jury that the evidence cannot support a conviction and may direct an acquittal. Let us turn now to a case that will reveal these stages and some of the problems raised by them. It warrants repeating that the value of examining a particular case in detail is that it illustrates how the legal framework transforms and selectively reconstructs the events of the case under rules of procedure and evidence. These rules and principles are designed to prevent reliance on tainted information and unfair procedural manoeuvres. They are artificial conventions and they limit the kinds of information put to the jury and so influence the jury's conclusion about guilt beyond a reasonable doubt. The presentation of the facts of this case and our review of the progress of the trial will allow the reader to take the place of the juror in trying to determine guilt or innocence, as well as allow the reader to comment on the fairness of the procedures independently of the question of guilt or innocence. The case chosen is the famous murder trial of *Regina vs Demeter*.

Regina v. Demeter

On July 18, 1973 Christine Demeter, age 33, a model and homemaker, and wife of Peter Demeter, was found dead in the garage of their fashionable home in Mississauga, Ontario. The condition of the body led the police to form the impression that her death was a homicide. She had been struck repeatedly over the head with a blunt instrument and pieces of brain tissue, hair and blood were splashed over the floor of the garage. Though there was no sign of sexual assault, the body showed other evidence indicating serious bruises on the legs as well as damage to the hand consistent with attempts to ward off blows. The bottom of the door of the family Cadillac was splattered with blood, suggesting that she had been hit repeatedly over the head after falling to the concrete. Despite a suggestion from her husband, suicide was ruled out almost immediately. At the time of the homicide, Mrs. Demeter and her daughter were at home alone. Mr. Demeter had taken some visiting relatives shopping for the evening. There was no evidence of forcible entry into the garage, though no fingerprints were taken from the back door. Within a month of the crime, Peter Demeter was arrested. Circumstances had quickly put the police on the trail of the husband. Demeter had a strong motive for wishing his wife dead: he was the beneficiary of a one-million-dollar insurance policy on her life. Judging from the extramarital affairs both had pursued, the marriage was rocky; in particular, Demeter had an intimate and longstanding relationship with another woman, which his wife discovered in the summer of 1973.

The police were also suspicious of Demeter from the start because he did not show the usual signs of emotional trauma, confusion, anger or rage that are associated with the sudden or unnatural death of a spouse. A day after the murder, Demeter retained a lawyer, paying him a retainer of $15,000. Within 24 hours of the murder, police had planted an electronic bug on the Demeter phone. Lastly, and most importantly, two days following the murder, the police received information from a former girlfriend of Demeter's close friend, Csaba Szilagyi, who reported that Demeter had offered his friend a substantial sum of money to help him get rid of his wife. Within hours of receiving this information, Szilagyi was interviewed and revealed that Demeter had frequently, over a period of years, suggested plots to dispose of Christine in a way that would look accidental. Szilagyi apparently agreed to cooperate in making recordings of conversations with Demeter with a secret body pack to try to establish Demeter's knowledge of the murder.

As a result of these conversations and the growing web of circumstantial evidence, Demeter was charged on August 17th with non-capital murder. The election of non-capital rather than capital murder was a discretionary power of the Attorney General of Canada exercised through the prosecuting Crown Attorney. Capital murder was punishable by capital punishment. Generally, the only murder cases punishable by death were those in which a policeman, prison guard, or similar person was killed in the course of duty. However, after about 1960, successive federal Cabinets effectively vetoed capital sentences, changing them to life imprisonment. In 1976, Parliament passed new laws abolishing the death penalty. Murder is now classified as either first-degree or second degree. First degree is murder that is "planned and deliberate." Conviction rests on proof of the planning of the act as well as the deliberate commission of the act. The murder must be considered and not impulsive. There are exceptions to the criteria for first-degree murder. If the victim is an on-duty policeman or prison guard, the act is considered first degree, whether spontaneous or deliberate. The same applies if murder is committed in the course of hijacking, kidnapping, sexual assault or indecent assault. All murder that is not first degree is second degree. The difference in terms of sentence is important. Though both are punishable by life imprisonment, a person convicted of first-degree murder cannot be considered for parole until 25 years of sentence have been served. Conviction for second-degree murder requires the serving of 10 years of sentence before eligibility for parole. Even so, release on parole is not automatic.

The indictment brought against Demeter did not state that he actually held the murder instrument himself. The actual murder was committed by persons unknown (Jonas and Amiel, 1977: 70). The particulars of the indictment read, "Such murder was committed by the said Peter Demeter by having a person or persons unknown kill the said Christine Demeter." In the Demeter case it was crucial to indicate in the indictment that Demeter himself did not wield the murder weapon, but had arranged the murder through another agent. Consequently, his absence at the time of death would be unproblematic. Demeter was held for several days and released on bail to await his court appearance. After the preliminary inquiry, which began on January 28 and concluded on March 8, 1974, Demeter's case was put over for trial.

The trial itself was heard in London, Ontario, as a result of the defense team's request for a change of venue or location. This motion was based on the wide publicity that had been given the case at the time of the murder, as well as during the preliminary inquiry, and the resulting improbability of finding neutral jurors in Mississauga. Jonas and Amiel (1977: 167-170) suggest that the most natural relocation would have been from Mississauga to Toronto, and that the move to London, a relatively conservative, white, Anglo-Saxon community, and a centre for the life insurance industry, favoured the prosecution. Presumably, the ethnic diversity of Toronto and the more urbane lifestyles found there would have tended, other things being equal, to produce a jury relatively sympathetic to the accused. While this is debatable, there nonetheless is some evidence that inequality in the process of jury selection in Canada tends to favour the prosecutor.

Before a prospective juror is sworn in, the defense can have him or her dismissed without giving any reason. The number of these challenges is limited by the seriousness of the case. In this case, the defense could challenge 12 such prospective jurors without giving cause. The Crown could challenge only four, but could "stand aside" up to 48 others until the entire pool assembled by the sheriff was exhausted. However, any number of jurors may be challenged by either side if cause is shown. The chief cause for dismissal of a prospective juror is the lack of impartiality toward the case. Further, the entire array of prospective jurors may be challenged by either side if there is evidence of partiality, fraud, or misconduct on the part of the sheriff who assembled the array. In the Demeter case, a noted demographer from the University of Western Ontario offered evidence for the defense that the array inaccurately reflected the composition of the county where the trial was held, but this was dismissed by the trial judge.

The Theories of the Case

The trial of Peter Demeter did not commence until September 23, 1974, some 14 months after the murder. At the beginning of the trial, the chief evidence against Demeter had changed little from what the police had gathered in the first days following the crime. It consisted of the testimony of Demeter's former close friend, Csaba Szilagyi, which was supplemented by transcripts of Demeter's taped conversations with Szilagyi and others. In addition, there was evidence that Demeter had isolated his wife to set her up for the crime. On the evening in question when he packed his visiting relatives into the car to go shopping, he insisted on taking the family dog. He advised the gardener to stay away from the property that evening. Furthermore, while at the shopping plaza, he telephoned Christine, presumably to have her go into the garage for something, and waved away one of the relatives who approached while he was on the phone. As the appeal court observed, "The theory of the Crown was that the appellant had conspired with one Stark or with some unknown person to have Mrs. Demeter killed in such a way as her death would appear accidental and that same person, perhaps one Oleynik, did the killing in furtherance of one or the other of such conspiracies."

Frank Stark was a small-time contractor and ex-legionnaire who appears to have been contacted by Demeter several times in the spring of 1973. Oleynik, who had worked as a labourer for Stark, was reported to have received a large sum of money around the time of the murder and had departed shortly thereafter for a trip to his native Hungary. Oleynik was later to die of a brain hemorrhage in police custody in Hungary in 1975 after revealing his involvement in a plot, which transpired two days before the murder, that required him to meet Christine at an address on Dawes Road and to kill her, making the death appear accidental. Since he knew she would be bringing a large sum of money wrapped in architectural drawings, he claimed that he planned not to kill her but only to steal the money. His wife also related that he had received a large sum of money in May or June of 1973 and that it had been wrapped in architectural plans, which were later shown to have been drawn for one of Demeter's building projects. After Oleynik left the country, Stark had visited Mrs. Oleynik looking for her husband and indicated that the latter had bilked Stark out of some money. The inference was that Stark had been contacted by Demeter to kill Demeter's wife for a sum of money, had arranged to have Oleynik do the job, and had been double crossed by the latter.

When he was first picked up by the police in October, 1974, Stark was arrested for his complicity in the murder of Mrs. Demeter. However, when he was presented at the trial to give evidence for the Crown on October 31st, his name was added to the back of the indictment as a witness, not to the front as a co-accused. Jonas and Amiel suggest that he was persuaded to testify against Demeter rather than face charges of conspiracy for the plot to murder that was aborted in the Dawes Road incident (1977: 212-219).

The Crown's theory was amplified by the testimony from a known police informer, Julius Virag, who indicated that Oleynik had been at the Woodbine Racetrack on the day of the murder, gambling large sums of money. The day after the murder Virag found him in a pub, lamenting his role in the killing. Virag's testimony was subsequently discredited. Nonetheless, the theory of the Crown was not hard and fast as to who the actual killers were. Stark's and Oleynik's connections with Demeter made Szilagyi's allegations more concrete. Where Szilagyi had provided evidence that Demeter speculated about murder plots, Stark and Oleynik showed that at least one plot had been hatched two days before the actual murder and that money had changed hands over this. However, the Crown ultimately left the question open as to who carried out the murder, though according to the Crown theory, the husband, Peter Demeter was the initator and benefactor of the act. His motives were that "he was the beneficiary named for the $1,000,000 proceeds of life insurance on her life and that it could be inferred he desired to free himself to live with his mistress" (*R. v. Demeter*, 1976: 425). All the evidence of conspiracy to murder and the exotic planning involving underworld hoods was consistent with the planning of plots reported by Szilagyi.

Szilagyi testified about several separate plots dating back for a period of five years. Apparently, Demeter would describe a scenario and ask Szilagyi to comment on its feasibility. Their conversations included plans 1) to throw Christine off the top landing of one of Demeter's unfinished three-storey houses; 2) to throw her down the basement stairs at the Dawes Road house and finish her off with a blow to the head; 3) to hit her over the head and drag her onto the nearby highway at night to be run over by the traffic; 4) to blow her up in the garage with a gasoline fire; 5) to cut the brake lines in her car; 6) to electrocute her in the swimming pool with a short circuit; and 7) to fake a robbery at the house to disguise the shooting of Christine (Jonas and Amiel, 1977: 151-152). On the morning of July 16, the date of the aborted Dawes Road incident, Demeter called Szilagyi to ask him to make sure that Szilagyi's girlfriend did not accompany Mrs. Demeter that day. Szilagyi refused and later in the day was rebuked in a phone call by Demeter, who is alleged to have asked Szilagyi what satisfaction he would "derive from the fact that he [Demeter] had just lost $10,000 and that he had received a phone call from a certain man who had told him that the deal was for one and not two" (Jonas and Amiel, 1977: 152). Presumably, when both Mrs. Demeter and Szilagyi's girlfriend appeared, the killer got cold feet. The various plots were partially corroborated by Szilagyi's tape conversations; and the sum of money paid out in the spring or summer of 1973 was corroborated by other witnesses. As the appeal court observed, "the massive evidence of conspiracies could have been contradicted only by the appellant [Demeter] and he did not testify" (p. 425).

One of the major problems of the defense was a lack of focus on any particular theory of the case. The senior counsel for the defense, Joseph Pomerant, did not disclose the theory of the defense with any clarity and even declined the Judge's invitation to tell him what the theory was. The junior counsel, Edward Greenspan, who represented Demeter on appeal, was closely questioned by the Court and suggested six defense theories, which were reported in the record of the Ontario Court of Appeal. As the record shows, the position of the defense shifted ground between theories of Mrs. Demeter's counter plots involving Oleynik, Stark, Eper and/or Szilagyi and allegations that Williams, the Streetsville murderer, may have been involved. While every variation of the Crown theory pointed to Demeter, every defense theory of necessity had to lay the blame at someone else's door. The theories consisted of the following:

(1) That the evidence was equally consistent with plots by the appellant that did not have a successful culmination. If the jury accepted the evidence of a plot by the appellant resulting in the abortive action of July 16th, it would have to regard the murder happening two days later and unconnected with the appellant as a simple matter of extraordinary coincidence, or be left in a reasonable doubt in that regard.

(2) That one Henry Williams or some other person unknown murdered the deceased in the course of an actual or attempted sexual assault. No evidence was offered in support of that theory. The Crown called Williams who admitted, under the protection of the Canada Evidence Act, R.S.O. 1970 c. E-10, to two sexual assaults followed by murder and one sexual assault followed by attempted murder all occurring, in a large sense, in the area of the appellant's home. Williams denied killing the deceased, and he and his wife testified to an alibi for the night of July 18, 1973. The expert testimony was inconsistent with any recent sexual intercourse by the deceased.

(3) That the murder was committed by Stark or Oleynik or by some unknown person procured by Stark or Szilagyi at the instigation of the deceased to cause the death of her husband. The motive was said to be a quarrel over such a

plot or an unsuccessful blackmail attempt. The evidence offered to support such a theory was that of Stark, a witness for the Crown. Stark said that in 1972 Mrs. Demeter offered him $3,000 for providing a rifle and an alibi for Szilagyi. Stark did not accept the offer. According to one Dinardo, Szilagyi was known to one Eper mentioned in (5) following. The only evidence of a connection between the deceased and Oleynik was the entry in her diary of the name "Jim Or," an alias used by Oleynik. In addition, the witness Viveca Esso testified that on July 17, 1973, the deceased said to her jokingly: "How would it be if I knocked Peter off and I would get a lot of money." The policies of life insurance for $1,000,000 were also on the appellant's life with the wife named as beneficiary in the event of his death. This was advanced as a motive for the deceased wanting to have her husband killed, along with evidence from which it could be inferred that she was unhappy in her marriage. No evidence supported the suggested motives of blackmail or a quarrel over a plot resulting in Stark or Oleynik or the other unknown alleged conspirators with the deceased killing her instead of the appellant.

(4) That the evidence of Stark of the appellant's conspiracy with him was a fabrication designed to shield Stark's participation (a) in a plot to kill the appellant, or (b) in a blackmail attempt by Stark or Oleynik resulting in the killing of Mrs. Demeter. No evidence was proffered to support this defence, which depended on the lack of credibility of Szilagyi and of Stark and his corroborating witnesses.

(5) That one Eper, a dangerous man and said to be unconnected with the appellant, was the killer. Eper was deceased at the time of trial. The motives were said to be the same as mentioned in (3). A convict named Dinardo with a long criminal record, and a dangerous and dishonest man by his own admission, gave evidence which, if believed, would lead very strongly to the inference that Eper was the killer. He also gave evidence that in July 1973, Eper was present and a party to an attempt by Mrs. Demeter to have Dinardo kill the appellant, from which it might be inferred that Eper himself would likely agree to do so. He said Szilagyi was present at his rendezvous with Eper, which led to the meeting with Mrs. Demeter where she made her offer to him, although Szilagyi did not accompany them to that meeting. There was no admissible evidence of the suggested motives of a quarrel or blackmail for Eper killing the deceased instead of the appellant. The trial Judge, without using such adjectives, quite properly, pointed out the highly improbable features of Dinardo's evidence that Eper was the killer. However, he also charged the jury, as was conceded by the Crown at trial, that if Dinardo's evidence that Eper was the killer raised a reasonable doubt in their minds, they should acquit the accused. That must have been on the assumption that Eper was unconnected with the appellant. However, there was evidence that a piece of paper was found in the place where Eper lived bearing the name of the appellant and the name of Deputy Chief Teggart, the officer in charge of the investigation of the crime. The appellant argues that it establishes a connection between Eper and the deceased but we think it equally establishes a connection between Eper and the appellant so that in this respect at least the charge to the jury was favourable to the appellant.

(6) That Szilagyi was an incredible witness and an unsavoury character. The jury asked to have and to read themselves Szilagyi's translation of his recorded conversations with the appellant and to have read his testimony (a) re plots using a third party, (b) re Gigi's meeting with Christine on the Monday and Tuesday

preceding her death (i.e., re the plot of July 16th, Gigi being a woman with whom Szilagyi was then living and a former employee of the Demeters). This was done except that the trial Judge read to the jury Szilagyi's translation rather than giving it to them to read themselves. The cross-examination of Szilagyi did not shake his testimony in any respect (*R. v. Demeter*, 1976:426-428).

The theory involving Eper was introduced by the defense witness, Joe Dinardo. He reported that his long-time friend and partner in crime had come to Dinardo's apartment in mid-July spattered with blood. Eper claimed that he went to see Mrs. Demeter to get some money, an argument broke out, and he "barred" her. Eper was later killed in a shootout with police. Though it corroborated the position of the defense, Dinardo's report of Eper's confession was excluded because it was hearsay. Hearsay occurs when a witness under oath reports as evidence what other people have said. Since it can be notoriously unreliable, hearsay is usually excluded. One exception to the hearsay rule that arose in this case involves statements made by someone against his own financial or pecuniary interests. These are usually deathbed admissions of unpaid debts or obligations and may be reported in court contrary to the usual exclusionary rule. In this case, Eper's alleged confession was primarily against his own penal interests — that is, his statements could have led to his imprisonment. However, the idea of penal risk was thought to be farfetched in these circumstances and the entire alleged confession was felt by the judge to be "highly improbable." Specifically, Dinardo admitted that he would never have reported the confession if Eper had been alive, and so Eper was really not saying anything that would put him at risk. Further, Eper had already been sentenced to life imprisonment and was only on the streets because he had escaped from custody. Had he been re-arrested, it is unclear whether he would have been any more liable to penalties. Consequently, it was reasoned that there should be no exception to the hearsay rule. The exclusion of this evidence was later supported by a Supreme Court of Canada decision (*Demeter v. The Queen*, 1977).

Dinardo was the last defense witness, and the Crown introduced a rebuttal to his testimony. A jail guard at the Guelph Jail in which Dinardo was incarcerated gave evidence which suggested that Dinardo's lawyer had brought a copy of a newspaper covering the Demeter story to the jail and had discussed the contents with Dinardo. In other words, it was implied that Dinardo's evidence had been coached. The only problem with this was that Dinardo's counsel was the prominent Ontario lawyer, Arthur Maloney, Q.C., who had also been an Ombudsman for the Ontario government and whose reputation was and remains impeccable.

Peter Demeter elected not to take the stand. Jonas and Amiel suggest that Demeter rarely managed to keep out of trouble when he spoke to anyone, so his decision had the merit of preventing him from further incriminating himself (1977: 293). However, the cost of the decision was obvious: Demeter had to forego the opportunity of refuting Szilagyi's allegations and the meaning of his taped utterances.

The judge's charge to the jury was given on December 3, 1974. It involved a massive sifting of the evidence and clarification of relevant points of law. The defense counsel objected strenuously that only five of the 225 minutes of instructions to the jury were spent on the positions of the defense. Greenspan requested that the entire charge to the jury be revised. The jury was recalled and the judge clarified some possible errors in his earlier remarks. He should not have said that Dinardo's statement about the colour of Mrs. Demeter's hair discredited him, or that Szilagyi went to the police voluntarily with information, or that Dinardo sent for lawyer Maloney. He added information missing from the initial charge refreshing the memory of jurors regarding Mrs. Demeter's extra-marital affair, as well as pointing out errors of fact discovered in prosecution witnesses. He also relayed that the defense had asked him to relate to the jury that, in the opinion of the defense, Eper had been the killer. The next day the jury indicated that they desired to have some evidence read back to them, most especially, the transcripts of the tape recordings involving Demeter. These were re-read by the judge. After three hours of deliberation, Demeter was found guilty as charged. As indicated earlier, the life sentence was automatic, though non-capital murder allows eligibility for parole after ten years imprisonment.

The Appeals

Edward Greenspan filed an appeal to the Ontario Court of Appeal stating 23 separate errors made at the trial court that, if taken seriously, required a new trial. The appeal courts do not re-try cases, or at least they should not. The purpose of the appeal court is to determine if, as a consequence of an error, whether this involved an issue of law or a question of fact or a mixture of both, there resulted a miscarriage of justice. The implication is that, even if errors are detected, these do not require the court to act automatically; the court must only act if such errors created a miscarriage of justice. If an appeal fails at the provincial level, it is possible to appeal this to the Supreme Court of Canada, but only with respect to errors involving questions of law.

Of the 23 grounds presented by Demeter's defense at the Ontario Court of Appeal, the Court found nine serious enough to require a response from the Crown. Demeter's conviction was nonetheless unanimously upheld by the five judges. By the time they had finished deliberating, Demeter had already spent more than a year in the penitentiary at Millhaven. The following discussion is limited to the first five grounds for appeal. Though incomplete, the discussions sample the posture of the Court towards irregularities and possible errors at the earlier trial. The grounds for appeal included the following:

1. Did the trial Judge make an error in failing to direct the jury's attention to certain evidence tending to weaken the case for the Crown or strengthen the theory of the defence and so misdirect in his charge to the jury? In reply the Court offered the following assessment:

> With the exception of the theory that E had been the killer, the theories of the defence, which were only presented with any clarity for the first time on the appeal, were unsupported by the evidence. Of the pieces of evidence which the accused argued should have been presented to the jury by the trial Judge in his charge, many went simply to the credibility of the Crown's witnesses and none could be said to be of such importance that their omission constituted misdirection. As to the defence theory that, based on D's evidence, E was the killer, the jury were clearly charged, and it was in fact conceded by the Crown, that if they had a reasonable doubt in regard to D's evidence they must acquit the accused. Although there may have been deficiencies in the Judge's charge regarding D's testimony, D was one of the last witnesses to be heard and accordingly his evidence would be fresh in the jury's mind. The trail Judge re-charged the jury on all matters that were objected to and in the circumstances there was no non-direction amounting to misdirection. Even if there was misdirection there was no resultant substantial wrong or miscarriage of justice having regard to the evidence as to prior plots, the accused's own statements as recorded on tape

which were virtually admissions of guilt, the failure of the accused to testify, the improbable features of D's testimony and the extraordinary coincidence that would be involved in accepting that the accused was unconnected with the death following the abortive attempt 10 days earlier (*R. v. Demeter*, 1976: 417-418).

2. Did the trial Judge mistakenly exclude the alleged confessions of Eper? and

3. Did the Judge mistakenly exclude Eper's admission to an involvement in a plan to kill Demeter on behalf of his wife?

As noted earlier, Eper's confession was hearsay and was not given in a way that any exception to the hearsay rule would apply. The Appeal Court also concluded with regard to this item that, even if an error had been made, it would have been inconsequential. "In any event there was no substantial wrong or miscarriage of justice occasioned by its exclusion at trial, since there was other admitted evidence forming a basis for the jury to speculate as to E's motive, including the motive suggested" (*R. v. Demeter*, 1976: 419). Consequently, though Eper's alleged confession was excluded, the jury was still given grounds to speculate on Eper's involvement, including a direct statement from the defense to the jury via the judge's revised charge. As to the alleged plan by Mrs. Demeter to have Eper kill her husband, not only did it too constitute hearsay, but it was unsupported by other evidence and required pure speculation to explain how the person who procured the murderer ended up being killed by him.

4. At several points throughout the trial, the defense filed motions to have a mistrial declared. The denial of three such motions provided the basis for the fourth appeal. First, it was argued that when evidence of Stark's conspiracy with Demeter was adduced, this constituted so basic a change in the theory of the Crown as to require a postponement in the proceedings in order to guarantee a fair trial. Denial of the request for a postponement precluded the possibility of a fair hearing, according to the defense. Second, when the news media reported the defense requests to sequester the jury (i.e., to isolate the jury together), and reported the judge's revocation of Demeter's release order, contrary to the Criminal Code, this so biased the jurors as to provide grounds for a mistrial. Last, when the judge refused the defense's request to take a commission of inquiry to Hungary to get evidence from Oleynik, this also constituted grounds for a mistrial.

In each case, the appeal court upheld the earlier trial judge's decisions. With respect to the first point, the Court pointed out that the evidence of Stark did not alter the theory of the Crown, but only embellished the factual basis of the Crown position by indicating a conspiracy between Stark and Demeter, and by identifying Oleynik as the killer. Though Oleynik became wanted for murder, given the vague nature of the indictment, this did not affect Demeter's defense. The Court pointed out that the defense was given 11 clear days notice of Stark's testimony, and five days regarding other new testimony, along with a summary of the evidence, thus allowing time to prepare a cross-examination. Consequently, there were no grounds to argue that a full reply and a fair trial were denied. Quoting from *R. v. Caccamo*, the Court also pointed out that, if there had been any limitation to Demeter's full defense, it was at least partially self-induced. In *R. v. Caccamo* Judge de Grandpré said:

I might add that in reaching a conclusion as to whether or not a miscarriage of justice exists, the Courts are entitled to take into account the fact that the accused did not testify, which is the situation in the case at bar. (Quoted in *R. v. Demeter*, 1976: 447.)

In choosing not to testify, Demeter imposed on his own defense a restricted ability to make a full response to the charge and the Crown evidence offered in support of it. Since this was his own choice, he had no grounds to claim that the courts had denied him a fair hearing.

Regarding the second matter, the Court agreed that media publication of testimony taken in a *voir dire* (in the absence of a jury) was a deplorable act, especially where that jury could separate at night and effectively hear on the radio and television what was excluded from them in court. With the introduction of Stark's testimony, the prosecution effectively petitioned to have Demeter taken into custody. The news of the revocation of Demeter's bail order and the defense requests for sequestration were subsequently broadcast in London. The judge, following repeated defense requests, finally ordered the jury to be sequestered. The defense argued that such news tended to convince the jury that Demeter had to be guilty and that the judge's order for sequestration was made after the damage was done. Though the Court agreed that such media publications were regrettable, the harm actually done to Demeter's case was thought doubtful.

> The publication of information with respect to the application to revoke the order admitting the appellant to bail and the subsequent revocation of that order is to be deplored and it is regrettable that the law officers of the Crown did not promptly take appropriate measures against the offending parties. The violation of the provisions of s. 576.1 of the *Code*, however, does not warrant an appellate Court setting aside the verdict of the jury unless the violation has resulted in a miscarriage of justice, nor in interfering with the discretion of the trial Judge in refusing to declare a mistrial under s. 576 (4) unless he has acted on a wrong principle (*R. v. Demeter*, 1976: 448).

Since the defense could adduce no evidence that a bias had actually been created against the accused, the Appeal Court could find no grounds for determining that a mistrial should have been declared, despite the acknowledgement that publication of *voir dire* testimony was totally illegal.

The third area where the question of mistrial was raised concerned the judge's refusal of a defense request to order a commission to take evidence from Oleynik in Hungary. The defense argued that it was necessary for Demeter's defense that all the facts be explored. Since no one knew whether the Hungarian authorities would cooperate, whether Oleynik would give any evidence, or even whether he would have anything admissible to say, the trial judge, it was ruled, rightly denied the motion for such a commission. The matter was further complicated following Stark's testimony when it became clear that Oleynik would be charged with murder: like Demeter, he could not be compelled to give evidence against himself. By the time these matters went to appeal, Oleynik had already died.

5. The fifth area of appeal went largely the way of the others. The Appeal Court acknowledged that an error had been made, but nothing so serious as to require an order for a new trial. The fifth ground for appeal concerned the evidence of the police informer, Julius Virag (dubbed "Tom Smith"). He had testified to seeing Oleynik spending large sums of money at the Woodbine Race Track on the day of the murder, and to seeing him emotionally upset the following afternoon. This evidence contradicted testimony of others close to Oleynik who claimed he left the country in the spring and was not seen again until the fall. Tom Smith's evidence was important in leading the jury to believe that Oleynik not only bilked Demeter out of a payoff, but actually did the killing. The grounds for the appeal here concerned new evidence unavailable to the defense at

the time of trial. An officer from the Ontario Jockey Club submitted a sworn statement that, on the day of the murder, the day Oleynik was supposed to be gambling his ill-gotten loot, the Woodbine Race Track was closed! Obviously Smith's testimony was highly suspicious and would probably have been discredited if this information had been brought out at trial. It would have brought into question Oleynik's role and his relationship to Stark and Demeter. Nonetheless, the looseness of the indictment made it possible to bracket the question of Oleynik's role without exonerating Demeter.

> The maximum effect that the destruction of "Smith's" evidence could have is the elimination of Oleynik as the killer of the deceased. The elimination of Oleynik as the killer does not effect the strength of the evidence against the appellant of a continuing design on his part to bring about the death of his wife (R. v. Demeter, 1976: 455).

Despite the fact that the new evidence was credible and was unknown at the time of trial, in the opinion of the Court of Appeal it probably would not have affected the verdict of the jury, and no new trial was required. In arriving at this conclusion, the Court relied extensively on the transcripts of conversations involving Demeter.

> Certain of these conversations, left unexplained, amounted to virtual admissions of guilt, the underlying theme running throughout them being that, though the accused may not have known the actual killer, he was clearly connected with her death (R. v. Demeter, 1976: 422).

The problem with this position is that, during the trial, the tapes were allowed to be entered only as evidence supporting the direct testimony of Szilagyi. In the decision prepared by the trial Judge, His Honour Judge Grant of the Ontario High Court of Justice indicated that:

> in the present case the Crown witness Szilagyi was a party to all the body packs and the telephone recording of August 19, 1973, and the communications thereon were between the accused and himself. His relation thereof was the primary evidence of the words used. In those cases the recordings are only confirmation of the evidence . . . and were used by him as an *aide memoire* in giving his testimony (R. v. Demeter, 1975: 333).

Nonetheless, the jury, like the Appeal Court Judges, attached rather direct relevance to Demeter's utterances on the tapes. Most notably, the trial Judge reread the transcript to the jury at their request during deliberation. Several points are problematic here. Though the rationale for allowing the tapes to be introduced was to bolster Szilagyi's evidence, they were heard as direct statements from Demeter as to his guilty mind. Consequently, Demeter's rights to remain silent and not to be made to incriminate himself were procedurally circumvented. Secondly, though they were gathered legally at the time of the investigation, the introduction of the Protection of Privacy Act would have made the secret interception of these taped conversations illegal and possibly inadmissible. Because no such law existed at the time they were made, the transcripts of the tape were not excluded. Another point relates to their language: most of the taped conversations were in Hungarian, and the transcripts consisted of English translations. The problem here is that many consisted of highly ambiguous utterances and were distorted by background interference. Since the jury was presented with English translations from the Hungarian, subtle inflections and idiomatic expressions were not directly detectable but were rendered by a third-party translation. Lastly, no overall record of the recordings was preserved; the police selected incriminating sections and erased the remainder, including passages that might have been favourable to Demeter (Jonas and Amiel, 1977: 187). Presumably, passages that tended to incriminate Szilagyi were also erased. What is distressing with respect to these all-important sources is that, contrary to the opinion of the Appeal Court, they do not contain direct statements that clearly demonstrate guilt. They contain ambiguous and suspicious utterances, elusive and suggestive statements. In every case, the hearer must read between the lines to infer guilt.

A Sampling of the Transcripts

The Appeal Court examined 17 short passages of conversation between Szilagyi and Demeter, some of which were only five or ten lines long and were recorded over a period of several weeks following the murder. As noted above, the Hungarian conversations were translated and were entered into the court record by having Szilagyi read them and, where required, comment on the ambiguities. This was usually imperative because, standing alone, the transcripts never contain statements by Demeter saying "I did it" or "I know who did it," but quite the opposite. Several of the most damaging transcripts are the following.

A. Transcript 1
DEMETER: . . . He, who left the scene left it of course covered in blood from head to toe because she was hit on the head seven times. I don't know who this is.
SZILAGYI: You don't know yourself.
DEMETER: Csaba, the hell I don't know. But it was done in such, so, such a terribly primitive and barbarian way that [inaudible] not at all. Now then the . . . the police are probably looking for him right now. The place is going to swarm with xxx [inaudible] (*R. v. Demeter*, 1976: 456).

Szilagyi told the court that when Demeter said "the hell I don't know," the emphasis was on "hell," not on "I," the implication being that Demeter did know something about the identity of the killer. In other words, though he says at first he does not know who the killer is, his second statement is a denial of this. Demeter's implication in the death is amplified in later utterances where worry is expressed about his conversations with various people he had consulted about getting rid of his wife. In transcript 4 he says

. . . all they need is one man who is willing to state under oath that I have been talking with him about such things or only that I asked him whether he knew such a person in order to charge me with murder (p. 457).

Demeter continues in the same vein in conversation 5:

The only thing they would like is that somebody say, "Yes Peter Demeter asked me if I would do it, but I said, no hard feelings, but no, or I wouldn't even insult you with this, that [inaudible] and he asked whether I knew someone, because I have no such connections" . . . This is enough to put me into the prisoner's box with the thing, that is called a conspiracy to cause the murder of so and so with an unknown, unknown associate (pp. 457-458).

As Jonas and Amiel point out, such utterances are consistent with Demeter's plan to murder his wife, but do not exclude the possibility advanced by the defense that she may have simultaneously been exploring the same fate for him. This is consistent with the hearsay account given by Dinardo, said to have originated with Eper. If the Eper story were true, this would make Demeter guilty only of conspiracy to murder that resulted in the abortive Dawes Road incident two days before the murder. But such a defense would hardly be credible, especially in view of the exclusion of Eper's stories to Dinardo. One can also imagine the incredulity of the jury if Demeter had taken the stand and claimed "I didn't do it, I only planned to do it."

The next major incriminating transcript concerns Demeter's speculation about how the matter was going to end.

B. Transcript 9

SZILAGYI: Peter, when will all this be over?

DEMETER: For you . . .

SZILAGYI: [inaudible]

DEMETER: For you, it will probably be over very soon, for me it will probably be over the day they find uh . . . the culprit or it will last forever. In short for you it is already over, because, and can't you understand that for you it was over long ago, it is only, only because of me?

SZILAGYI: Yes, well, if they find the culprit, then . . .

DEMETER: . . . then everything is over, because the culprit is either in connection with me . . .

SZILAGYI: Or he isn't.

DEMETER: . . . and then I get life, you see, which is twenty years about, or I don't know what; or he is not and then the case will be closed and I come out baby pink and smelling good, you see. [inaudible] not [inaudible] can't you see with your intelligence that, that they know very well that you haven't been there?

SZILAGYI: Yes.

Again, this transcript contains reasoning that is hard to attribute to an innocent man. Demeter says that the situation will end when the killer is found. If the killer is connected with Demeter, then Demeter will face a life sentence. The problem is obvious: why would an innocent man worry about being implicated unless he was party to the crime, and hence not innocent. Even if the murderer was one of Demeter's known associates, why would he automatically conclude that this would implicate him? After all, a man can kill another man's wife without the cooperation or collusion of the husband. Demeter seems to miss this, presumably because "the connection" he mentions is not merely his knowledge of or acquaintance with this person, but instructions which, if discovered, would have the effect of implicating him in murder. On the other hand, if the killer is unconnected with Demeter, he says he will come out "baby pink and smelling good." Here he seems to be in doubt as to whether the killer will be connected with him or not. If he were truly innocent, how could he have any doubts as to whether the killer is involved with him? Why does he have any worry about being baby pink and smelling good unless he has been involved in something illegal? These are the kinds of obvious common-sense inferences that are read between the lines to make sense of Demeter's reasoning. Though it is true that any number of alternative interpretations might have been offered, procedurally it was up to Demeter to provide the appropriate and true interpretation if adverse interpretations were incorrectly drawn.

Transcripts 10 through 13 contained allusions to conversations that, as explained by Szilagyi, involved various unstated murder scenarios. Alone, they are quite unconvincing. However, the last major transcript, like A and B above, appears intuitively inconsistent with any innocence or clear conscience on Demeter's part. Even though Demeter says he does not know the killer and that he has a few bones to pick with him, it appears that this may be because of the vicious and sloppy manner in which the killing was done. The conversation begins with Demeter advising Szilagyi of his innocence of everything except "collusion." The reference to "collusion" bolsters the interpretation that Demeter and Szilagyi had previously been meeting to plan something illegal.

C. Transcript 14

DEMETER: Consequently, you can't be attacked with anything except for collusion . . .

SZILAGYI: Yes.

DEMETER: . . . and you have nothing to that effect . . .

SZILAGYI: Okay, Peter, tell me one more thing. That guy, does he know me?

DEMETER: No, no.

SZILAGYI: He . . . you . . . okay . . . All right, that's enough.

DEMETER: But, but, this, this, if, if he doesn't know me, how would he know you?

SZILAGYI: Yes, okay.

DEMETER: Didn't you think of that?

SZILAGYI: Yes.

DEMETER: You understand? Now uh . . . uh . . . which one, the private eye? He obviously knows who you are, since he has found out through your car . . .

SZILAGYI: Yes, well naturally, Peter, not him but the last man, the man they are looking for.

DEMETER: No, no, no, this is not a telephone topic, because you see uh . . . I told you that in the uh . . . uh . . . uh . . . funeral parlour, that, that not even I . . .

SZILAGYI: Yes.

DEMETER: But whom I don't know, you don't know, you have to admit that, don't you?

SZILAGYI: Yes.

DEMETER: And, and I'd like to meet him myself because I have a few bones to pick with him.

SZILAGYI: What?

DEMETER: Well, I'd have a few bones to pick with him.

SZILAGYI: Yes, I understand, yes.

DEMETER: Now then, uh . . . uh . . . uh . . . I could do him in personally.

SZILAGYI: Yes.

This transcript, like the previous ones, may be consistent with Demeter's guilty mind, even though Demeter says about the killer that he could "do him in personally." It is difficult to hear this as the desire for vengeance from a bereaved husband when it is prefaced with the statement that Demeter has "a few bones to pick with him." Presumably a husband with a clear conscience would have more than bones to pick with his wife's killer. If we try to put ourselves in the shoes of the jurors, we must accept that Demeter acts like a person with something to hide, and fearful of being overheard when he says "this is not a telephone topic." The same sense of defensiveness is also detectable when he points out Szilagyi's vulnerability, what he can be "attacked with," namely collusion. Further, when asked about whether the killer is known to Szilagyi, Demeter is less than candid. He doesn't say "how do I know?" or "I haven't a clue," but "not even I [know]." Generally, we only use the construction "not even I" when a paradox or irony is involved. The paradox is that Demeter seems to be one who should know, but not even he who *should* know knows. In other words, if he were entirely in the dark about the matter, he would say "I don't know" as opposed to "not even I [know]. Consequently, he subtly communicates a sense of guilt in his words, his sentence construction, and his self-consciousness. Despite the fact that, on the face of it, the information in his statements denotes innocence, the other elements of his utterances indicate guilt. These strong impressions in transcripts 1, 9 and 14 that Demeter was connected with the killer, combined with his direct statements in transcripts 4 and 5, in which he expressed concern over a charge of conspiracy to murder, sealed the case, and despite the common-law principle of right to silence, sealed it with Demeter's own words. As noted earlier, though the transcripts were permitted initially as an *aide memoire* for Szilagyi, they progressively took on a life of their own as the trial jury and later the Appeal Court Judges scrutinized them as direct clues regarding Demeter's guilty mind.

Regina v. Demeter in Perspective

On May 9, 1977, nearly four years after the murder, the Demeter case ended when the Supreme Court of Canada unanimously dismissed the last appeals. The Court heard arguments as to whether the confession of Eper was admissible and whether the trial judge should have sequestered the jury earlier in the trial. The Court decided that the question of sequestering of the jury was out of its jurisdiction, since the Supreme Court of Canada may hear appeals involving errors in questions of law only. The discretion of the trial Judge to sequester or not is a factual matter, and errors involving such are examinable in the provincial courts of appeal where the matter had already been re-examined without consequence. As for the hearsay evidence, the lower court's view of Eper's confession was reconfirmed. Since his statement was not consciously made against his own immediate interest, there was no ground for an exception to the hearsay rule; and the alleged confession was properly excluded at the trial. Aside from a pardon, the last avenue of appeal under Canadian law had been exhausted.

Few cases have received the scrutiny given to the Demeter case. Aside from the lengthy judicial reviews in the appeal process, the case was sensationalized in the mass media throughout the trial. As a news story, it had few rivals. There were a brutal murder of a beautiful woman and tales of mistresses and lovers, underworld hoods, mysterious police informers, and large insurance policies. It was dramatized in a best selling book, *By Persons Unknown*, as well as in a full-length movie. As a criminal case however, it was in many respects highly atypical. Where most criminal matters are resolved with guilty pleas in a matter of minutes in the lower courts, this was one of the longest criminal trials in Canadian history, and certainly one of the most expensive. Estimates of salaries, expenses and fees for the detectives collecting evidence, for the judges at the various levels, for the court personnel at the preliminary inquiry, the trial, and the two levels of appeal, for the expert witnesses, for the various Crown prosecutors and the defense team certainly put the total bill in excess of $1,000,000.

Though the case is not very representative of most criminal matters, it exemplifies the higher court experience. It dealt with a very grave matter. The case was a contested case involving competing theories of how the facts ought to have been interpreted. The matter was decided in terms of the evidence, and the evidence, because it was frequently ambiguous and subtle, required careful sorting and scrutiny. The points of law raised were frequently complex and contestable.

Perhaps one of the most important features of the higher court trial is the frequency with which questions of law are re-examined and clarified. The higher courts witness a great deal of lawmaking in the form of case law decisions. By comparison, very little law is made in negotiated lower court guilty pleas. If any of the counts of appeal had been decided in favour of the defense, these would likely have become precedents for future cases. As it was, the trial judge was called on to clarify the Privacy Act in arriving at a decision over the admissibility of the taped conversations. He ruled that the Act could not retroactively make the interceptions illegal, that questions of the quality and completeness of the tapes did not affect their admissibility but their weight, and that the privileged communication between a lawyer and a client is not breached by electronic surveillance where the purpose of the communication is to mislead the police (i.e., not seek legal advice) (*R. v. Demeter*, 1975). The aggressive challenge of the existing laws by defense counsel, the application and development of jurisprudence by the Judge, together with the likelihood of appeal, tend to stretch the official participants to the limits of their knowledge and abilities, and consequently a more vigorous application of the law is likely to result.

One of the interesting features of this case is that, had it been tried in the US, much of the decisive evidence might possibly have been excluded. In the US, evidence that is gathered in an illegal manner cannot be entered against an accused in court; this rule was applied inconsistently in the area of electronic surveillance until 1968 (Carr, 1977). Though wiretapping and electronic surveillance are now allowed with judicial authorization (Parker, 1983: 377-378; 391ff.), the police operated in the Demeter case without any special legislative authorization. Indeed, Canadian law in this area was not clarified until Parliament passed the Protection of Privacy Act in 1974. Since the most damaging evidence involved the surreptitious tape recordings, an exclusionary rule might have scuttled the prosecution's case. As noted in the discussion of civil rights and their violation, the issue of police misconduct is treated under Canadian law as a separate issue from the question of the admissibility of the evidence gathered as a result of such conduct. Broadly speaking, this reflects much less concern with due process and misbehaviour on the part of criminal justice officials in Canada than in the US, and a greater preoccupation with the factual matters relating to the guilt or innocence of the accused. This goes hand in hand with the considerable latitude and power provided to the Crown prosecutor. As we have noted, the indictment was so loosely worded that a major element of the Crown's case provided by Virag's testimony could be factually disproved without exonerating the accused. Additionally, two of Demeter's co-conspirators in the murder plans, Stark and Szilagyi, were named at the pleasure of the Crown as Crown witnesses rather than as co-accused, and subsequently escaped prosecution. Had they been charged as co-accused they could not have been compelled to testify at the trial. Further, while the Crown did not introduce such witnesses until well into the trial, it was held that there was no basic change in the case against the accused since the indictment had been so loosely worded: "by person or persons unknown", and so there was no grounds for questioning the fairness of the trial.

Summary

Because higher court cases occur relatively infrequently, researchers have tended to pay little attention to them. However, from the point of view of those who are interested in legal reasoning, they are indispensable because they contribute disproportionately to the case law that interprets and amplifies the statutory law.

Secondly, unless we direct our attention to higher court trials we get little insight into the operation of laws in action. Knowing the Criminal Code and the principles of justice that underlie it are fundamental for understanding the process of justice, but these are not enough. Studies of higher court trials give some insight into how these legal resources are mobilized and developed in the particular set of factual circumstances surrounding individual cases. For example, while we are aware of the principle of the right to silence, we have seen in this particular case how transcripts of taped recordings involving the accused were introduced at trial virtually negating this right. Ericson's studies of the police (1981, 1982) stressed the significance of law as an "enabling" device employed by policemen to control cases and circumstances. The same lesson can be applied here. Law is not a hard and fast framework that stamps out dispositions like a mathematical deduction, but rather a set of enabling devices for creating and sorting alternative versions of reality, and a set that slowly evolves in response to new factual situations.

A third lesson to be drawn has to do with how the rules of evidence and procedure help shape the version of reality that goes to the jury. The jury is rarely asked to draw an inference from a set of black-and-white statements. The basis of the trial is that there are competing versions of reality. The jury must sort through competing statements, pieces of physical evidence, and testimony from people of mixed credibility. Rules of evidence selectively structure what is presented to the jury. For example, in this case, Dinardo's report of the alleged confession of Eper was excluded because it was hearsay and "highly improbable." However, Szilagyi's report of Demeter's plans to murder his wife and the transcripts from the taped conversations, which were frequently inaudible, incomplete, discontinuous and translated from Hungarian, were allowed in. The solution to the shortcomings of the transcripts was to allow the jury to weigh their value in light of their weaknesses. Yet this remedy was disallowed in the case of Eper's confession. Why not give the jury the same capacity to weigh the confession in light of its weaknesses? Clearly the trial jury attached enormous weight to the transcripts independently of the pretext by which they were introduced, that is, as an *aide memoire* to Szalagyi. One might speculate that the jury would have found Dinardo's account of Eper's story equally intriguing, yet the operation of the hearsay rule allowed the one but not the other version of reality to go to the jury. This suggests that the different safeguards against misleading testimony may artificially and incompletely reconstruct the facts put to the jury because they are inconsistent in the solutions they provide for the control of unreliable information. Hearsay leads to exclusion while doctored evidence goes to credibility.

A fourth lesson to be drawn from this case regards appeals. The appeal process identified a range of very unsatisfactory elements in the trial: among them being the judge's initial charge to the jury, the false testimony of police informer Virag, the implied accusation that Maloney coached Dinardo and the judge's failure to sequester the jury until after the media had published stories prejudicial to Demeter. Each of these was found objectionable but did not form the basis for a new trial because, in the framework of the appeal courts, this is warranted only if the errors lead to a miscarriage of justice. Since the appeal courts seemed to have treated Demeter's guilt as an open and shut matter, none of the irregularities could be viewed as consequential.

Yet the outcome of the trial might have been altogether different if these irregularities had been prevented. In point of fact, this would be an empirical matter to be decided by all the expense and labour of running a new trial. However, by the time the matter gets to the appeal court this possibility may be simply academic; the appeal court in effect second guesses what the decision of the jurors would be. If they foresee no change in the verdict, there has lawfully been no miscarriage of justice, despite the appearances to the contrary raised in appeals.

One final note of interest to students of the Demeter case: In October of 1983 while on day parole release, Demeter was charged with two counts of counselling someone to commit murder involving his cousin, and three counts of arson involving fires at the Demeter home in Mississauga.

FURTHER READING

Vincent Bugliosi and Kenneth Hurwitz, *Till Death Do Us Part: A True Murder Mystery.* New York: Bantam, 1979.

Marjorie Freeman Campbell, *Torso.* Toronto: Macmillan, 1974.

Demeter v. The Queen [1977], Vol. 34, *Canadian Criminal Cases,* (Second Series), pp. 137-143.

Ellen Godfrey, *By Reason of Doubt: The Belshaw Case.* Toronto: Clarke, Irwin, 1981.

Jacques Hébert, *I Accuse the Assasins of Coffin.* Montreal: Editions du Jour, 1964.

George Jonas and Barbara Amiel, *By Persons Unknown.* Toronto: Macmillan, 1977.

Desmond Morton (ed.), *The Queen v. Louis Riel.* Toronto: University of Toronto Press, 1974.

Gwynn Nettler, *Killing One Another,* Vol. 2 of *Criminal Careers.* Cincinnati: Anderson Pub., 1982.

E. W. Pelrine, *Morgantaler: The Doctor Who Couldn't Turn Away.* Agincourt: Gage, 1975.

Regina v. Demeter [1975], Volume 19, *Canadian Criminal Cases,* (Second Series), pp. 321-336.

Regina v. Demeter [1976], Vol. 25, *Canadian Criminal Cases,* (Second Series), pp. 417-476.

William Trent with Steve Truscott, *Who Killed Lynn Harper?* Montreal: Optimum, 1979.

CHAPTER 9

The Psychology of the Eyewitness

Introduction: The Legacy of Mistaken Identification

The Demeter case was problematic largely because there were no eyewitnesses to the murder. However, as we shall see, the presence of the eyewitness brings with it an entirely different set of problems and issues, primary among them the risk of convicting the accused on the strength of erroneous eyewitness testimony. In this chapter we shall review the problem of mistaken identification, some of the factors that contribute to it, as well as certain proposed solutions including the use of hypnosis and the polygraph. While there is no evidence for believing that mistaken identification occurs frequently, we have no shortage of cases where the falsely convicted are pardoned and sometimes compensated.

The most famous case involved the turn of the century convictions of Adolf Beck on charges of swindling women of their jewellery and valuables. As a result of the independent eyewitness accounts of ten women, he was sentenced in 1896 to a term of seven years. Two years later, Beck was released from jail after he showed that he had been mistaken for another man. However, in 1904 another series of similar offenses occurred in London and, in April, Beck was convicted once more and sentenced to jail for five years. Fortunately, the series of crimes occurred again in July while Beck was in jail. The real culprit was apprehended and convicted. Beck was declared innocent of the crimes of 1895 and 1904, and he was given a sum of five thousand pounds to help compensate him for the miscarriage of justice (Watson, 1924).

This sort of thing is not limited to turn of the century justice. In 1974 in England, the Devlin Committee was struck to investigate the problem of erroneous eyewitness identification that resulted in two false convictions. In a case of shoplifting, Luke Dougherty was convicted and sentenced to a term of 15 months for stealing three sets of curtains. After serving nine months, the identification evidence was overturned and he was subsequently given a payment of two thousand pounds for his experience. In a more serious case, Laszlo Virag was sentenced to 10 years for the theft of meter coin boxes, the use of a firearm to resist arrest and the wounding of a policeman. The eyewitness identification of him was refuted after he had served five years when the real culprit confessed; he was cleared and given 17,500 pounds for his trouble.

In a recent Nova Scotia case that came to national attention in 1982, Don Marshall was acquitted of a murder charge after spending eleven years in jail for a murder he did not commit. Marshall and an acquaintance attempted to rob two men in a park in Sydney, Nova Scotia. One of the "victims" stabbed Marshall's friend to death and blamed Marshall. False evidence given by several questionable witnesses helped to convict Marshall at trial. Since the evidence also indicated that Marshall may have perjured himself at the original trial, the appeal court that overturned Marshall's conviction seemed to suggest that his chances for financial compensation for wrongful imprisonment would be slim (*Calgary Herald*, May 11, 1983: 1-2).

In 1968 in the US, Charles Clark was given a new trial as a result of the destruction of the eyewitness testimony of the daughter of a store owner who had been shot dead in 1927 during a robbery. The daughter had pointed Clark out in a police lineup as the man who held the gun. Despite an alibi substantiated by his landlady, he was convicted and sentenced to life imprisonment in 1938 and spent the next 30 years in jail. He maintained his innocence throughout and even refused a pardon for good behaviour because to accept it would have implied an admission of guilt. "In 1968, the case was assigned to the Legal Aid and Defenders Association of Detroit. Attorneys for Clark poured through early transcripts and discovered that the victim's daughter had at one time said that she could not identify Clark as one of the robbers. She finally admitted that when she could not identify Clark, he was pointed out to her before the lineup and she was told by the authorities that he was the guilty man" (Loftus, 1979: 178). A new trial was granted in 1968, but the prosecutor dismissed the charge. In 1972, the governor of Michigan awarded Clark $10,000 for humanitarian consideration.

Lonnie and Sandy Sawyer underwent a similar experience. In 1975 they were convicted of a kidnapping of a store clerk. The clerk had given police a description of the abductors' car, an off-white 1965 Dodge Dart. The Sawyers were driving a Plymouth Valiant of the same year and colour. Though he had only seen his assailants for a very brief period, the clerk confirmed that the Sawyers were the kidnappers and, despite their corroborated alibis, they were subsequently convicted and sentenced to terms of 30-40 years. As a result of the work of a private detective, the real kidnapper was tracked down and made a confession. The Sawyers were pardoned in 1977 after two years in jail and after tens of thousands of dollars of investigative fees (Pearlman, 1977). In September 1982, William Bernard Jackson was released after having served five years in prison for multiple rape convictions. His release followed a 94-count indictment returned by a Columbus grand jury against a local doctor. Jackson resembled the doctor and was erroneously identified by witnesses as the culprit.

As indicated earlier, these sorts of cases occur relatively infrequently. The Devlin Report throws some light on this. The Report reviewed the record of all the identification parades or lineups held by the police in England and Wales in 1973. There were 2116 such lineups. These resulted in the positive identification of 944 suspects held by the police. Of these, 850 were prosecuted and about 700 were convicted. For 258 accused persons who were convicted, the sole evidence against them was positive, eyewitness testimony. The Report also points out that there were 188 lineups at which the witnesses wrongly identified one of the know innocent "controls" in the lineup. This represents a misidentification rate of 9% of all the lineups. Since the police knew beforehand who the real suspects were, those misidentified came to no harm. However, if the police had mistakenly apprehended an innocent subject, the misidentification rate would suggest that this person would nonetheless be picked out in 9 out of every 100 lineups. If we assume that there is a stable pattern of 258 persons convicted for every 2116 identification parades, this indicates a rate of about 12%. Hence, on the basis of these figures, the chance of an innocent person being wrongly identified and convicted by erroneous eyewitness testimony would be about .09 × .12 or one percent. This is, of course, an extremely high overestimate since it is premised on the random identification of suspects by the police and the total absence of any compelling alibis exhonerating the innocent. Also, it applies only to those cases in which the sole evidence is identification evidence. In point of fact, during the 30-year period from the mid-1940s to the mid-70s, only 38 cases of disputed identity were established in England. These included 16 cases that resulted in a free pardon, 20 cases quashed or acquitted following action by the Court of Appeal and two cases where the real offenders were discovered before the innocent were convicted. These figures, since they refer only to proven cases of misidentification, probably understate the problem. On the other hand, civil liberties groups received 17 allegations of wrongful identification from convicted persons in Britain in 1974. Again, these probably overstate the problem. Whether the figures are interpreted liberally or conservatively, everyone acknowledges that the frailties of eyewitness testimony pose a serious problem for criminal justice. In this chapter we will examine some of the areas that contribute to the unreliability of such testimony and some of the proposed safeguards and solutions.

The various cases described above show that our reliance on what people say they saw or experienced is subject to a whole range of distortions, interference and other problems. The first and most obvious is the psychological processes underlying perception and recollection. However, as we shall see, the fact that there is some fragility at the psychological level opens up the testimony to other more malevolent influences. As we see from the above illustrations, the convictions of Beck and Jackson appear to have been based on innocent misidentification. However, evidence suggests that Marshall and Clark went to jail thanks to police interference with witnesses.

In the Australian case of *Craig and The King* (1933: 44) Justices Evatt and McTiernnan outlined what is involved in what appears to be even the simplest identification:

An honest witness who says, "The prisoner is the man who drove the car," whilst appearing to affirm a simple, clear and impressive proposition is really asserting: (1) that he observed the driver, (2) that the observation became impressed upon his mind, (3) that he still retains the original impression, (4) that such impression has not been affected, altered, or replaced, by published portraits of the prisoner or by suggestions of third parties, and (5) that the resemblance between the original impression and the prisoner is sufficient to base a judgement not of resemblance, but of identity.

Though in the ideal case these five points present few real problems, evidence suggests that eyewitness testimony can be distorted at each of these steps and may result in some of the miscarriages of justice described above.

Factors Affecting Initial Perception

The initial observation of a criminal act by a bystander is often affected by a high level of stress. If one's life is endangered, a whole series of autonomic reactions occur in the nervous system producing changes in the heart rate, breathing and the flow of adrenalin. Robert Buckhout reports that experimental studies of perception under stress indicate that people are "less capable of remembering details . . . less accurate in detecting signals . . ." And while there will be good recollection of what initiated the threat, "memory for other details such as clothing and colours is not as clear; time estimates are particularly exaggerated" (1970: 25). This situation is compounded by other factors. Often the witness will not have a good opportunity to view the situation because of bad lighting, physical obstructions, poor eyesight or just the complexity, speed and suddenness with which the event transpired, and which divided the attention of the witness.

Any one of these circumstances could effectively invalidate the ability of the witness to observe as the Canadian case of *Regina v. Boyd* (1953) illustrates. In a prosecution for armed robbery an accused was acquitted on an order of the Ontario Court of Appeal after it was established that one of the bank tellers who had had an opportunity to view the robbery was not called as a witness. Though one teller did give evidence of identification, it was clear that the teller's attention was divided during the robbery since there had been five robbers. The accused had no previous record and provided evidence of work records in support of an alibi. The Court felt that the failure of other tellers to pick the accused out of a lineup cast doubt on the sole identification witness, and Boyd was acquitted (Wall, 1965: 112).

In another armed robbery case, *Rex v. Harrison* (1951), the conviction was overturned because, of the five witnesses to the crime, only three could identify the accused at the trial, and only one of these had been able to identify him originally. The court concluded that no witness had an opportunity to see the robber (Wall, 1965: 115). Without other incriminating evidence, the conviction could not be allowed to stand and Harrison was freed.

Factors Affecting Whether the Perception Registers

Though in most cases the witnesses are aware that a crime is transpiring, in many instances witnesses only learn *after* the fact that people and circumstances they had seen were involved in a criminal event. What before seemed insignificant takes on new importance — but often after the observations have slipped into oblivion and must therefore be reconstructed. This point has been well known to psychologists since the 1895 experiments of J. McKeen Cattell, who had students report details of people and circumstances encountered on their way of lectures. The reports, while frequently omitting description of things that must have been encountered, contained very confidently detailed descriptions of non-existent facts and situations. Our attention is selective and clearly without a motive or particular focus of orientation, very little of what we see and do is retained in our memories. To the extent that it is incomplete, the attempts at recall are more imagination than true recollection. The hazards posed for eyewitness identification are obvious. Problems also arise in the opposite situation, as when witnesses are able to provide strong identification of a defendant when, at the time of the observation, no crime had yet been committed, and when there was nothing to call particular attention to the behaviour of the individual. In a New York murder case, the accused was said to have been noticed by the town sheriff from a distance of 20 to 60 feet standing with a group of men on a street corner. Since the sheriff had no suspicion at the time that the person was involved in a crime, the Court refused to give much value to his report. Since there was "nothing to indicate that the witness bestowed anything approaching conscious and thoughtful observation upon any features of the man" then little weight could be attached to his testimony (Wall, 1965: 126).

Another area in which there are problems in the registering of observations concerns cross-race identification. Witnesses are more likely to identify a suspect on the basis of recollection of the skin colour only. In *R. v. Peterkin* the eyewitness had identified the accused, a black man, but was unable to specify any other details of physique, stature, age or the like. A psychologist was called "to testify to the fact that there are fewer identifying elements in a negro than in a caucasian man and that according to scientific tests it is very difficult for caucasians to identify negroids because to a white man they 'all seem to look alike'" (Starkman, 1978-79: 384). This sort of automatic stereotyping becomes injurious when eyewitnesses harbour prejudice against a group and are more liable to attribute criminal actions on the basis of this. Gordon Allport's study of prejudice is a good illustration. Allport asked subjects to briefly view a drawing showing several people on a train including a black man and white man who were engaged in a confrontation. Though the drawing shows that the white man is holding a razor, half the subjects reported seeing the razor in the hand of the black man. This reflects the fact that their original perception was biased by stereotypes about violence and race (Allport, 1975). As Robert Buckhout argues, the same kind of effect may come into play when a man reports on the behaviour of a woman driver (1970:26).

Delay and the Retention of Memory

Even assuming that the criminal activity was observed accurately, it is common knowledge that the evidence becomes more unreliable with the passage of time. This presents a formidable problem not only where there is a delay between the crime and the identification, but also where following arrest the normal court schedule puts months between the crime and the trial. Patrick Wall (1965: 127) suggests that if the suspect is positively identified shortly following the crime by witnesses with fresh memories, no harm is done in terms of false identification even though there may be long delays before trial. However, various changes occur over time. People who reported being unable to identify the criminal suddenly find they have little problem in doing so, and others who were initially quick to spot the suspect find he looks less and less like what they remember. Starkman (1978-79: 364) outlines the danger presented by this.

When a witness after many months finally makes an identification at trial, they may be simply repeating what in all probability they have done many times before at the time they observed the event, at the police station, at the preliminary inquiry and in private consultation with the Crown counsel before the hearing. And although their original perception has been influenced by countless factors they remain unaware of this distortion and consequently believe in the accuracy and correctness of their testimony.

What Starkman is pointing to here is not the ordinary biological decay of memory, but its transformation as a result of interaction with other people, or in the words of Justices Evatt and Tiernnan as reported above, the affecting, altering or replacement of the first impressions "by published portraits of the prisoner or by suggestions of third parties". This influence aggravates the already natural decay process and is the area of greatest worry in the production of unreliable evidence.

Influences of Third Parties

The influences of third parties on memory are many and varied. They include conscious attempts to slant the identification process, as well as unconscious and coincidental circumstances which have the same effect. When police wish to have a criminal suspect viewed by a witness, they may present the suspect in a lineup of 5 to 10 other people. A large body of case law records the attempts of the police to bias or prejudice the procedures by selecting the "control" members of the lineup in such a way as to highlight a known attribute of the suspect that is also characteristic of the wanted person. This frequently produces wrongful convictions.

> Following are examples of some of the more obvious abuses that have been committed by the police in conducting unnecessarily suggestive lineups: placing an Oriental suspect in a lineup containing only Whites; having a suspect in a lineup obviously different in hair color, or height, or weight, or age, or clothing, etc., from all other members of the groups; conducting a showup after the witness failed to identify the suspect in a lineup, followed by another lineup before the witness could positively identify the suspect; drawing attention to a particular person by stating, "Look closely at the man on the extreme right"; and allowing a suspect to be verbally identified by one witness in the presence of other witnesses (Yarmey, 1979: 153).

In America, the judicial response to these dangers resulted in the 1967 case of *United States v. Wade* in which the US Supreme Court held that pretrial identification was a "critical stage" in the trial process, that it was subject to abuse and unintentional suggestion and that the accused had the right to counsel at this stage of an inquiry. In the Wade case the accused was required after his arrest to participate in a lineup in the absence of his lawyer. He was positively identified by two employees of a bank that was robbed. However, the Court held that this constituted a denial of the right to counsel and required that the in-court identification of Wade had to be established on some basis other than the illegal lineup.

In the 1967 case of *Gilbert v. California*, the United States Supreme Court ordered a new trial for Gilbert based on the lower court's erroneous admission of identification evidence from an illegal lineup. Like Wade, Gilbert had been arrested for robbery and was required to participate in a lineup in the absence of his counsel. However, Gilbert appealed on the basis of a denial of due process. The unreliability of the Gilbert identification resulted from the fact that the lineup was held in an auditorium in front of 100 witnesses to numerous robberies. In their collective presence, the opinion quickly spread that Gilbert was the culprit. Because of the infectious character of such a group identification, it was found that Gilbert had been denied due process of law (Yarmey, 1979: 152). Gilbert was awarded a new trial.

The third important 1967 decision was the case of *Stovall v. Denno*. Stovall, a black suspect in a murder and stabbing case, was taken to the hospital in handcuffs for a "show-up" identification in front of the critically wounded female victim. A show-up is simply the presentation of a suspect in front of a possible witness or victim. In this case, she positively identified the suspect by sight and by the sound of his voice. The Court acknowledged that the show-up procedure was inherently suggestive to a witness, but held that in this case it was not *unnecessarily* suggestive and so did not cause an irreparable mistake in identification. The question as to whether the procedure involved a denial of due process had to be settled by viewing all the surrounding circumstances and the Court felt that, in view of the critical injuries of the victim, the procedure did not deny due process. The defense that Stovall was denied right to counsel at the show-up could not apply since that right was not established until the Wade decision was announced on June 12, 1967 and so could not be applied retroactively.

Later decisions tended to weaken the safeguards created by the 1967 cases. In the 1972 case of *Kirby v. Illinois*, it was held that the right to counsel only applied in "adversary judicial criminal proceedings" and so, unless the accused was already indicted, he had no right to counsel at the lineup. Consequently, the police in the US now often delay formal charging until *after* the accused has been identified in the lineup. In other cases, the emphasis has swung from a strict concern with due process to a greater concern as to whether the eyewitness evidence, whether or not obtained in a suggestive manner, is nonetheless reliable. The Court has focussed on five factors to decide the question of reliability: the opportunity of the witness to observe the criminal initially; the attentiveness of the witness at the time; the ability of the witness to describe the suspect; the certainty of the witness at the point of confrontation in the lineup or show-up; and the time elapsed between the crime and the identification. Canadian courts have been reluctant to create new safeguards such as those that exist in the US. The position in Canada appears to be that the weakness of eyewitness testimony is a factual matter to be decided by the jury with the benefit of cautions from the judge and cross-examination by defense counsel.

Aside from situations marked by suggestive lineups and show-ups, there are cases in which the police have in effect coached the witness in picking out the right suspect. The identification of Charles Clark discussed above is one such case. Another is the case of theft against Bundy in England in 1910. In this case, a witness whose original opportunity to view the accused was quite minimal admitted under cross-examination that he had been informed by the police that Bundy looked like the man they suspected. The Appeal Court rightly concluded that such evidence was "wholly valueless" (Wall, 1965: 114).

Though it has never been established by a court, commentators on the famous Sacco and Vanzetti case point to circumstances that suggest that the police influenced the memories of certain key witnesses. Sacco and Vanzetti, two Italian immigrants, were tried and convicted in 1921 in Massachusetts for murdering two men in a payroll robbery; both men were later executed. When arrested by police they were armed and Sacco owned a gun of the same calibre used in the murders. However, both had substantiated alibis for the day in question; Sacco had been to the Italian Consulate to apply for a passport and Vanzetti, a fish peddler, had been in Plymouth selling fish. At the trial the prosecution produced five witnesses who identified Sacco as one of the gunmen: Mary E. Splaine, Francis Devlin, Lola Andrews, Louis Pelzer and Carlos E. Goodridge. Surprisingly it was established that at the preliminary inquiry, Mary Splaine had indicated that she could not say whether she had seen Sacco or not. Lola Andrews and Louis Pelzer had each told police neither had seen enough to make an identification. And Goodridge had told three people he had not seen enough to identify anybody. Of the four witnesses who placed Vanzetti near the scene of the crime, one told a friend that at the sight of the gun he had ducked for cover and did not see anything. Nonetheless, the memories of all these witnesses mysteriously improved with age for each was confidently able to make a positive identification at the trial. In particular, Mary Splaine, who had seen the men for two or three seconds in the car as it drove by at a distance of 60-80 feet, provided an account that was uncanny in its details, especially for someone who at first was so uncertain. At the trial she gave the following description of Sacco:

> He was a man that I should say was slightly taller than I am. He weighed possibly from 140-145 pounds. He was a muscular - he was an active looking man. I noticed particularly the left hand was a good sized hand, a hand that denoted strength. . . . The left hand, that was placed . . . on the back of the front seat. He had a gray, what I thought was a shirt, - had a grayish, like navy color, and the face was what we would call clear-cut, clean-cut face. Through here [indicating] was a little narrow, just a little narrow. The forehead was high. The hair was brushed back and it was between, I should think, two inches and two and one half inches in length and had dark eyebrows, but the complexion was a white, peculiar white that looked greenish (in Frankfurter, 1927: 11-12).

Before his trial for murder, Vanzetti was implicated as a gunman in a separate robbery. The chief eyewitness in this case also experienced an improvement in memory. The witness told police on the day of the crime that he did not get a good look at the robbers and he repeated this two weeks later. After Vanzetti was arrested, the witness was taken to view him. By the time the case went to court the witness had changed his story.

> . . . at Vanzetti's preliminary hearing, Harding included in his description of the gunman the never-before-mentioned items of dark complexion, high cheek bones, red cheeks, hair cut close in back, and a trimmed mustache. Still later, at the trial, Harding added that the gunman had a high forehead, short hair, a rather broad face and a round bullet-shaped head. He also stated that he had gotten "a very good look" at the gunman. It need hardly be pointed out that these added descriptive features gradually began to depict Vanzetti remarkably well (Wall, 1965:94).

In his discussion of the case, Patrick Wall argues that it is not unusual for a witness to recall details that were initially omitted in a description. However, when in a highly publicized case all the key witnesses have enjoyed such remarkable "improvements" in their recollection, it is extremely likely that this is because of the influence of the police on the witnesses. Other commentators have noted the detectives' repeated showing of photos of the suspects to the witnesses effectively implanted and reinforced images that then became the basis for the apparent recollections. Presumably the witnesses, in attempts to be helpful, started to offer the investigators what they wanted to hear; the question "Is this the man?" came to be heard in reverse: "This is the man!" However, while not downplaying the importance of this subtle form of persuasion, the detail of descriptions given by Splaine and Harding suggest that rather more active coaching was involved in the Sacco and Vanzetti cases.

One last form of influence in addition to biased lineups and witness coaching concerns something more subtle: unconscious transference, which occurs where the victim of a crime transfers memories of faces and persons he is familiar with to the unknown assailant. Elizabeth Loftus reports a very convincing instance that involved an assault against an officer at an army base. After a drinking bout, the officer was attacked in his bed by a man with a gun. After a brief struggle, the man was disarmed but managed to flee. The victim indicated that he had never seen his assailant before but could probably identify him. Within a week, the officer had picked the suspect out in a lineup. The following day, the officer was involved in an automobile accident with an army sergeant, and in a second lineup involving both the original suspect and the sergeant, he picked out the latter, who was subsequently charged in the attack. The sergeant was acquitted, thanks in part to an explanation to the court of the process of unconscious transference. Loftus outlines how this probably operated in this instance.

When the victim saw Franklin at the time of the automobile accident, he may have looked familiar. The familiarity could have been due to a chance encounter someplace on the military base, as the two men often inhabited the same place. The familiarity that the victim experienced could have been incorrectly related back to the incident, causing the victim to believe that it was Franklin who had committed the assault (Loftus, 1979: 193).

Houts, in his book, *From Evidence to Proof* (1956), cites another case. Following the robbery of a ticket agent, a sailor was picked out of an identification lineup by the agent. The sailor provided a good alibi and was subsequently cleared in the matter. However, when the agent was questioned as to why he had indicated the sailor, he related that it was because his face looked familiar. It was eventually established that the sailor had frequently purchased tickets from the agent. This was the reason the sailor looked familiar and it was not because he had been spotted as the robber. The agent transferred the recollection of the face in his attempt to find the real bandit in the lineup. Houts cites another instance in which a client of an insurance company that had been robbed twice was erroneously identified by several employees as the wanted bandit. In the course of clearing up the case, it was established that he did indeed have a familiar face to the employees, though again, not because he was the robber, but because he had visited the office twice previously to negotiate loans on his insurance policies. Consequently, his face struck a familiar chord during the lineup. Cases of unconscious transference present a very real danger in eyewitness identification because the distortions they engender are unconscious and because, being partially based on correct recollections, they lend great confidence to the erroneous witness opinion. Further, Patrick Wall (1965: 122) suggests that the repeated exposure of the witness to the same suspect tends to make the procedure a self-fulfilling prophecy as the witness begins to think there is some familiarity in the suspect's features, and may unconsciously transfer recollections from previous lineups to the earlier crime scene and confidently identify the wrong person.

Strong Convictions about False Evidence

One of the disturbing features of much erroneous eyewitness identification is that it is held with such conviction and delivered with such confidence. A witness in a 1919 robbery case was asked to view a lineup in order to identify the criminal who had robbed him. He pointed out one person saying, "That's the man. I'll always remember to my dying day the faces of the guys who pulled guns on me." The problem was that he had pointed out a plainclothes detective who had nothing to do with the case. In the Adolf Beck case, we find a similar self-assurance. Fanny Nott, one of the victims reported with characteristic certainty her recognition of Beck:

... I went straight into the Court, and found the prisoner standing in the dock; I saw his back; I should know him among a thousand. I recognized him at once; I am quite sure he is the man . . . I identified him by his back at once at the Police Court. I was quite sure of him, and always have been.

Another witness, Rose Reece recounted:

. . . I do not remember if anything was said when I picked him out - his nose is most peculiar, and is one I could pick out of a thousand - his whole face is different from any other man I ever remember seeing . . . (Watson, 1924: 118)

Despite their self-certainty all these witnesses were mistaken. If the eyewitness experience is held dearly by the witness, it seems to be even more so by the jury, who repeatedly demonstrate a misplaced confidence in the process, and a substantial lack of sympathy even for accused who provide strong alibis for their whereabouts. Starkman summarizes some of the relevant cases:

Juries are unable to disregard the apparent certainty and believability of an eyewitness identification. They have believed eight witnesses who identified a defendant rather than 31 who swore he was not the guilty party. They have believed nine identifying witnesses, many of whom admitted they could be mistaken, rather than 40 completely respectable and disinterested alibi witnesses. They have believed a woman who identified the defendant as the man who raped her, even though she admitted asking the same man to stay with her until her husband came home. And they believed the victim of an assault who testified that he was able to recognize his assailant by the light caused by the flash of a gun which he had used and added that he was "as certain of that as he was of anything under heaven" (Starkman, 1978-79: 365-366).

These observations are strongly supported by experimental studies involving simulated jury decisions. Such studies involve batches of undergraduate students who are presented with the details of a criminal case and who are asked to make a finding of guilt or innocence in the manner of a real jury. A study by Loftus (1979) described the following facts: A store owner was robbed of $110 by a gunman who shot the storeowner and his grandchild. Two hours later the police arrested a suspect and at the trial the following facts were established. First of all, the real gunman was seen running into the suspect's apartment building; $123 was found in his room; there were ammonia traces found on the suspect's shoes and ammonia had also been used to clean the store floor; and lastly, paraffin tests revealed gunpowder particles on the suspect's body that would have been consistent with the recent use of a firearm. For its part, the defense put the suspect on the stand and he claimed his innocence; the money found was his own savings; since the accused worked as a delivery man he could have gotten ammonia on his shoes in any number of locations; and lastly, he claimed he had never fired a gun in his life. The student jurors were found to convict at the rate of 18%. In a second variation of the experiment, a new item of information was added: a store clerk who witnessed the shootings had positively identified the suspect as the gunman. Here 72% of the jurors voted guilty. In a third variation, it was established that this eyewitness had extremely poor eyesight. Instead of the normal 20/20 vision his was 20/400. Also, he did not have on his glasses on at the time of the crime. Strong medical evidence introduced by the defense indicated that he probably was unable even to register the details of the gunman's face. Though we would expect such evidence to completely undermine the reliability of the eyewitness, Loftus discovered it had only a marginal impact: the rate of guilty findings dropped from 72% to 68%. Only about 4% were prepared to discard the eyewitness testimony because of its inherent unreliability. This research confirms what numerous actual cases have reported: the testimony of the eye-witnesses and the perception and memory on which it is based, no matter how corrupti-ble or prone to distortion, are given enormous weight by jurors.

The Relationship between Language and Memory

To this point we have addressed our attention to problems in the processes of observa-tion and recollection that arise in the course of interaction between the witness and significant others in the justice process. However, experimental studies of memory indi-cate that language used to spark recollection can in part structure what is recalled. For example, R.J. Harris (1973) studied estimates of the height of basketball players by experimental subjects. Subjects were shown a photograph and asked either how tall or how short the player was. Estimates ranged from averages of 79 inches for those given the "tall" cue versus 69 inches for those given the "short" cue. However, everyone was exposed to the same player. Similar distortions were discovered in estimates of the length of a movie shown to the subjects. Estimates varied on average by 30 minutes between those asked how "long" versus how "short" the movie was. Loftus (1975) found similar results in estimates of the frequency of headaches. Subjects asked how "frequently" they experienced headaches reported an average of 3.19 per week. This contrasted with a figure of 2.2 per week for those asked how "occasionally" they experi-enced them. Consequently, even directly experienced events like headaches were sub-ject to distortion in recollection.

Loftus developed this problem in a series of celebrated studies of witness recollec-tions of car accidents. Subjects were shown a short film depicting a multiple car crash with a number of crucial questions covering pertinent details of the accident (did you see a broken headlight? did you see the car which turned left? did you see broken glass?). Half of the questions touched on details depicted in the film while the other half did not. For half the subjects, all the critical questions began with the words, "Did you see the . . ." as in "Did you see the broken headlight?" Clearly the definite article, "the," conveys the sense that there in fact was a broken headlight. Predictably, the results of the experiment confirmed that those subjects who were confronted with the definite article were more likely to report having seen something, whether or not it really oc-curred in the film, than those confronted with questions using the indefinite article (Loftus and Zanni, 1975: 86-88). In another study, Loftus showed subjects a film of an auto accident. Subjects were asked to estimate the speed of the cars during the accident. In this case, the verbs used to depict the speed were varied to convey different speeds. Some subjects were asked "How fast were the cars going when they contacted?" The verb contacted was replaced with "hit," "bumped," "collided" and "smashed." The results were increasingly higher estimates depending on the verb—from 32 m.p.h. for "contacted" up to 41 m.p.h. for "smashed" (Loftus and Palmer, 1974: 585-589). Clearly, the verbal cues used to retrieve the perception appeared to reconstruct what was actu-ally seen. When subjects were asked to return a week after the first experiment for a follow-up study, they were asked whether they had seen any broken glass in the crash. The film did not show any broken glass. Nonetheless, many more of those who had the week previously been given the sentence involving the verb "smashed," reported hav-ing seen glass than those given the cue word "hit." Since everyone watched the same film, we must conclude that the different recollections resided in the way the event was depicted in questioning after the fact. For example, the term "smashed," when used to describe accidents implies more things than were actually witnessed, including broken glass. In a related experiment, subjects watched a short film of an accident caused by a motorist making a right hand turn onto a highway without giving the traffic an opportunity to slow down. Two groups of subjects were asked different questions: One group was asked, "How fast was the car going when it ran the stop sign?"; the other, "How fast was it going when it turned right?" Then subjects were asked if they had seen the stop sign. Loftus discovered that the presumption of the first question, that is, that there was a stop sign, led subjects to subsequently believe that they had seen it all along. Those who did not receive the biased first question, did not in the second question recall seeing any stop signs, nor was there a stop sign in the film. Hence, merely asking subjects about a non-existent object increases the likelihood that the witness will later report it as having been there initially. This suggests some modification of traditional views of memory. In the traditional view, an experience is stored first in the short-term memory, then, if important or novel, practiced or repeated, it moves to long-term storage to be retrieved when required. The new view incorporates a feedback loop between what gets stored, what is subsequently as well as previously observed, and the conditions under which the information is retrieved.

The implications of this for studies of witnesses in criminal and civil cases are obvious. The images, feelings, cognitive representations and recollections that witnesses report are subject to flux and reconstitution. They are not simple playbacks like audiotapes. They are enhanced and enriched by subsequent events, including police questions about crime, and what gets reported in the newspaper or produced for television. All these can introduce presuppositions into the mind of the witness that contribute to a vivid reconstruction or transformation of what originally transpired. This is a doubly dangerous situation inasmuch as this transformation often occurs inadvertently, or unintentionally by virtue of the language or terms employed by those who are investigating, reporting, examining, summarizing, and adjudicating the events in question. Nonetheless, a number of safeguards have been proposed to deal with some of these problems.

Suggested Safeguards

Trial judges, appeal courts, commissions of inquiry, students of jurisprudence, and social psychologists alike have contemplated the weaknesses of eyewitness evidence and have described ways in which to minimize the risks associated with it. Some of the safeguards that have been identified are already operative while others are matters of contention. These safeguards include 1) ensuring that biases are minimized in the pre-trial and trial identification procedures and that tainted evidence is challenged or excluded; 2) seeking corroboration of eyewitness evidence; 3) strengthening the judge's charge to the jury; and 4) admitting the expert testimony of psychologists regarding perception and memory.

First, regarding the process of identification, it should be pointed out that appeal courts have quashed convictions in cases where the chief issue in the trial was whether the suspect was the right person and where there was some question as to the fairness and reliability of the method of identification. If it could be shown that the lineup or show-up was structured in such a way so as to make the suspect "stand out in a crowd" and to so bias the procedure that the identification was unreliable, the appeal courts have overturned the original conviction. Also, where an individual has been identified

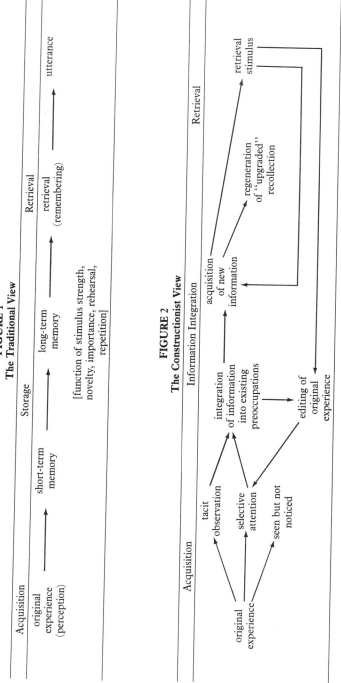

FIGURE 1
The Traditional View

Acquisition | Storage | Retrieval

original experience (perception) → short-term memory → long-term memory → retrieval (remembering) → utterance

[function of stimulus strength, novelty, importance, rehearsal, repetition]

FIGURE 2
The Constructionist View

Acquisition | Information Integration | Retrieval

original experience

tacit observation

selective attention

seen but not noticed

integration of information into existing preoccupations

editing of original experience

acquisition of new information

regeneration of "upgraded" recollection

retrieval stimulus

solely by virtue of his location in the witness box, and without a prior pretrial identification, this has been ruled a mere opinion and the conviction has been quashed. The courts have also heard evidence as to the *consistency* of witness statements, the *accuracy* of descriptions, the *certainty* during identification, as well as *mistakes* or *failures* in previous attempts to identify a witness. In the US the accused, if already indicted, has the right to counsel during such identification procedures. To date, Canadian courts have not found this safeguard necessary. Certain critics of the evidence of eyewitnesses have suggested that any testimony from such witnesses should be excluded by the trial judge, though this is thought by most to be too extreme a response (Woocher, 1977: 1000ff). The current practice is to let the jury assess the credibility of the witness and the value of such testimony in light of all the circumstances. The exclusion of such evidence might have the adverse affect of ruling inadmissible valid evidence. Courts in both the US and Canada have chosen instead to leave the question of the reliability and validity of such evidence for the jury to decide.

Corroboration is the second area where safeguards are sought. Corroboration is already required in Canada in cases of perjury, treason and forgery, and in cases of the unsworn testimony of children. Corroboration need not be the statement of a supporting witness, but could consist of physical evidence such as a fingerprint or the incriminating discovery of an item of clothing. The problem with an insistence on the necessity of corroboration is that there are situations in which identification by a single witness may be superior to that of two other witnesses, whether they agree or not. For example, a witness who knows the suspect beforehand, or has a better and/or longer chance to make an observation may furnish valid evidence whether it can be corroborated or not. For this reason, the Law Reform Commission of Canada opposed the requirement for corroboration. So too did Devlin's Committee in England, and for the same reason: the quality of evidence is not guaranteed by more than one witness; and so, to put such a requirement on the evidence of a prospective witness would be too much of a burden. Also, as in the first point, the weight to be given to any evidence is a question for the jury to decide. For the court to insist on corroboration would be to second-guess a factual question, which is, after all, the work of the jury. Lastly, the decision of the trial jury is open to inspection in the appeal court if there is evidence of a miscarriage of justice based on the unreliable testimony of a witness. Consequently, some safeguards are already in place and additional safeguards such as an exclusionary rule for uncorroborated evidence would automatically invalidate sound evidence merely because it might be uncorroborated. Lastly, many cases of false conviction have been supported by the corroborative testimony of numerous eyewitnesses, as in the case of Adolf Beck. Consequently, corroboration is no guarantee of the truth.

A third type of safeguard concerns the judge's instruction to the jury before deliberation and specifically the duty to advise the jury about problems of credibility and reliability in eyewitness testimony. Under Canadian law the judge was at one time required to instruct jurors that corroboration by a third party of a victim's complaint was advisable in order to find someone guilty of rape. Corroboration is still required for a series of other sexual offenses (Law Reform Commission of Canada, 1975b: 11). Also, judges are required to advise jurors of the risk of convicting on the strength of one eyewitness where the defendant has a substantial alibi or where the witness is vague or imprecise in what was observed (see Starkman, 1978-79: 375-77). Many critics are sceptical about the value of such instructions no matter how specific. Nonetheless, some jurisdictions have seen attempts to formalize and strengthen the judge's charge in order to underscore the risks of eyewitness testimony. The Michigan State Bar Committee

(1977) published a set of instructions to be used by judges in cases involving such testimony. The instructions specifically advise that the jurors should consider whether

... the witness had opportunity to observe the criminal acts and the person committing them, including the length of time available for observing; whether the witness had occasion to see or know the defendant before the incident; the distance between the various parties; the light or lack of light at the time; the witness' state of mind at the time of the offense; and other circumstances affecting the witness' opportunity to observe the person committing the offense. [Also] ... the identification made by the witness after the offense must be the product of his own memory. You may take into consideration any subsequent identification, the circumstances surrounding the identification, the certainty or lack of certainty expressed by the witness, the state of mind of the witness at the time, and other circumstances bearing on the reliability of the identification. You may also consider the length of time that elapsed between the occurrence of the crime and the time the witness saw the defendant as a factor bearing on the reliability of the identification (in Loftus, 1979: 189).

In Britain, the Devlin Committee also recommended that instructions to jurors be formalized and furthermore that they be required of judges by statute. Specifically, they would require that the judge warn of the danger of conviction on the basis of eyewitness identification unless the circumstances of identification were exceptional or the evidence was substantiated in other ways. Where exceptional circumstances were relevant, these would have to be brought to the jury's attention. And where there were no such circumstances and no other substantiation, the judge would be required to direct a verdict of not guilty. The Committee suggested that unsubstantiated eyewitness testimony that had nothing exceptional to recommend its reliability should not be considered as overcoming the reasonable doubt criterion in criminal cases. Critics of such rules point out that judges currently do point out problems in such testimony, that jurors are already aware of such things by virtue of common sense and that the weaknesses, if any, can be equally established during cross-examination. Also, the determination of what constitutes an exceptional circumstance would be a matter for the trial judge to determine, and so the legislation would unavoidably be returned to the discretion of the trial judge.

The final safeguard called for by the critics involves the admission of evidence from psychologists testifying to the fallibility of perception and memory. As a rule, the Courts in both the USA and Canada have resisted attempts by the defense to introduce such expert testimony. The 1973 decision of *United States v. Amaral* and the 1977 Canadian decision of *R. v. Audy* both dealt with cases of eyewitnesses to robbery whose observations were made under highly stressful circumstances. Defense counsel in both cases attempted to introduce testimony from psychology professors; both were refused permission, appealed on this basis and had the trial court decisions reaffirmed. The reasoning of the courts rested on the relevance of expert testimony. Expert testimony cannot be introduced to directly decide the guilt or innocence of the accused. The expert is allowed to introduce evidence that can assist the jury in deciding the matter and where the juror is unlikely to make a correct judgement without the help of such expertise.

It follows that if the testimony touches on matters the jury is already familiar with, there can be no special claim to expertise. Specifically, since experts are limited to the sorts of factors that can distort the processes of observation and recollection in normal individuals, they are no better judges of the capacity of the witness than ordinary jurors, especially since the judge's charge to the jury acts to remind the jury of such weaknesses. Psychologists of course emphasize that the ordinary juror and member of society, while not naive to such evidence, is still not suspicious enough of it. It is not clear that the justice system would be greatly improved by making sceptics of jurors, especially since the admissibility of such expert testimony would allow both the defense and the prosecution to call their own witnesses, one to challenge the reliability of eyewitness testimony, the other to confirm it. Such battles of the experts tend to erode public confidence in the scientific basis of the expert's profession, as in the case of psychiatry and psychiatric evidence. The exclusion of psychological evidence may be a blessing in disguise for the psychological profession. However, in certain areas, the testimony of psychologists might add something not within the experience of the ordinary juror as, for example, the problem of cross-racial identification and the problem of unconscious transference. In certain cases, evidence from psychological experts was permitted, though these are clearly exceptional. Generally, it has been held that experts on eyewitness identification could not add anything more than what is already available to the jury, or that it could not safeguard in any unique or special way the conviction of the innocent. However, this research may affect the legal process in a more subtle way: by alerting judges and defense counsel to the extreme vulnerability of observers in general to suggestions and distortions. In view of the relevant case law, as well as committees drafting reforms in this area, this is nonetheless the kind of thing that contemporary judges and lawyers are already aware of.

New Developments in Evidence: Are the Polygraph and Hypnosis Shortcuts to Truth?

In recent years a number of solutions to the problem of recollection have been advanced by psychologists and physiologists. These include the use of drugs to break down the defenses and presumably the deceptions of those who are wilfully misrepresenting the truth, the use of polygraphs to detect deceptive responses and the use of hypnosis to enhance the recollections of witnesses. Typically, hypnosis has been confined to the witnesses of crime while drugs and the polygraph have been used to screen suspects. In the previous sections we have examined problems with the recollection and reconstruction of witness memories. In this section, we will explore the utility of these new fields as they relate not only to witness recollection, but to the detection of deception in recollection. Also, we will look at the judicial response to these new fields.

Detecting Deception: The Polygraph

A whole range of "truth serums," including sodium amytal and sodium pentothal, have been advocated as medications that might be administered to suspects to force them to speak truthfully. This practice was premised on the belief that subjects could not maintain deceit while in a state of narcosis; this has not turned out to be the case. It is possible both to lie to others about one's innocence, and to be falsely convinced by others of one's guilt.

The polygraph, unlike the use of drugs, is a technique that measures the involuntary reactions of the autonomic nervous system. Changes in galvanic skin response, in heartbeat and breathing are associated with stress and anxiety. The polygraph operator questions the suspect about a number of things relating to a criminal event and the suspect's experiences. In the Lie Control Test, some questions are called "controls" because they are irrelevant to the episode in question: presumably the reactions of the innocent will be the same to both the relevant and the control questions. In another variation, the Guilty Knowledge Test, questions are asked and/or exhibits are presented that are calculated to produce a response only in the mind of a guilty party. For example, the suspect may be confronted with a series of photos of various crime scenes. The theory is that the innocent will register no special reaction to the key picture or pictures while the guilty person, because of a recollection, will show signs of physiological stress when the key picture or item is presented. The Guilty Knowledge Test is especially useful in clearing innocent suspects. D. T. Lykken (1980: 24-25) reports a 100% success rate in identifying the innocent in laboratory studies. Due to the ability of certain people to suppress stress signals, attempts to identify the guilty were less uniform, falling in the 80% to 95% range. Field studies of the Lie Control Test have not fared so well. Horvath (1977) and Barland and Raskin (1976) reported that such tests were powerful in uncovering the majority of the known guilty parties; however, the tests falsely led the examiners to conclude that approximately half of the known innocent subjects were guilty according to the "expert" interpretations of the stress signals. This led Nettler (1982c: 30) to advise that "if you are innocent, don't take the test." You have a 50-50 chance of being falsely accused! Nettler also points out that it is possible for the guilty to beat the lie detector test by inducing stress during the control questions in order to raise the stress signals into the range occurring during the relevant questions. For example, a subject may bite his or her tongue or tighten up and squeeze muscles to stimulate the autonomic nervous system and so throw off the polygraph readings. The implications of this are clear: contrary to the optimism that first greeted its advance, the polygraph is not infallible. There is no guarantee that a positive reading is evidence of a guilty mind, nor that a negative reading is evidence of innocence. The polygraph can be beaten by the guilty, and the innocent can be falsely convicted by it. However, this applies chiefly to the Lie Control Test and not the Guilty Knowledge Test. The former appears to be more subject to flights of interpretation and ought to be discounted in favour of the latter test, though even the latter should be viewed with some scepticism. Unfortunately, the Lie Control is the dominant test.

The interpretive problems with polygraph records are compounded by the fact that despite the efforts of regional associations, there has not evolved any recognized national standards for the operation of polygraph tests. In addition, most polygraph operators have only perfunctory training in the operation of the equipment and interpretation of the results.

In a submission to a US House of Representatives committee on the use of polygraphs, Professor Fred Inbau (1968) estimated that only about 20% of all polygraph examiners were truly qualified and that most operators had just several weeks experience at a training institute. In addition, the operator relies not only on the stress indicators in arriving at a conclusion, but on the general demeanour and attitude of the subject, hesitancy, tone of voice and any reluctance and lack of frankness in the responses. This has led critics to argue that the introduction of polygraph evidence at trial is highly questionable for it leads juries to abrogate their own assessment of credibility and truth for that of the polygraph expert (Wilner, 1977: 299). In other words, because the procedure has technological trappings, it wrongly leads the jurors to infer that it preempts their own assessments because it appears to be based on the output of a scientific machine as opposed to a clinician's interpretation of these results and subjective assessments of credibility. The same scientific halo effect makes it inadmissible to mention in court that an accused has either taken or refused to take a lie detector test. If the jury were told that the accused had taken a test but the results were barred from the court, the jury would probably conclude that the test showed the accused was guilty. Likewise, if the accused were reported to have refused to take a test, the jury would infer that he or she must have done so to avoid being caught (Wilner, 1977: 314). Consequently, courts in Canada and the US have refused to draw any inference from an accused's refusal to take a lie detector test. In point of fact, the main attraction of the use of polygraphs by police forces is probably not in establishing deception, but in encouraging confessions. Reid and Inbau (1966: 168) suggest that under the pressure of the test a confession is obtained in 50% to 70% of all polygraph cases. So while the results of the polygraph may be questionable, the operator is free to testify, not so much as an expert witness giving evidence of polygraphy, but as a person in authority who was told a confession.

In both Canada and the US, there has been an extreme reluctance on the part of the courts to grant much credence to polygraphy. In the US it is usually allowable only by mutual agreement of the prosecution and defense counsel. In Canada, the opinion of the courts was established in *R. v. Wong* (1978) and *Phillion v. The Queen* (1977). In Wong, the accused was charged along with several others with murder. Wong submitted to two polygraph tests, which resulted in testimony of the operators to the effect that Wong was telling the truth when he reported that he did not stab the deceased. However it was pointed out on appeal that whether he wielded the knife or not, the expert witness testimony failed to exclude Wong as a *party* to the offense. Furthermore, it was concluded on appeal that the trial judge should not have admitted the expert testimony of the polygraphers. Wong was awarded a new trial on issues irrelevant to polygraphy. The Wong case was decided before the important decision in *Phillion v. The Queen*. Phillion had been convicted of murder in the stabbing death of an apartment superintendent. Following his initial arrest, Phillion gave a confession to the police. At his trial, Phillion refused to testify and introduced evidence of a noted polygraph operator that, if believed, would have indicated that he was innocent and that he had lied during his earlier confession. During the polygraph test, Phillion was asked whether he had stabbed and killed the deceased. He replied no. The polygrapher's evidence, heard during a *voir dire*, was to have consisted of his expert opinion that, on the basis of the stress readings, he had found Phillion's answers truthful. The trial judge excluded the evidence on the basis that the jury might have placed too much weight on it. The Court of Appeal concluded that it had been rightfully excluded because while it was only opinion evidence it had been offered in such a way that it went right to the very question before the court. Expert opinion is only allowable where a factual matter is beyond the knowledge of the lay juror. It is supposed to enable the juror to overcome the lack of knowledge and to come to a factual decision, not to make the decision in place of the juror. In this case, the evidence would have had the effect of doing just that. One of the objectionable aspects of the expert evidence was that, if it had been admitted, it would have had the effect of allowing the accused to circumvent the courts and to say to a polygraph operator what he or she was unwilling to say directly in court. The higher courts found this extremely self-serving. In the Supreme Court of Canada, the exclusion of the evidence was upheld on the basis that it was hearsay. The expert was merely repeating secondhand a factual matter that was learned firsthand, and his repeating it was done to establish the truth of the statement (i.e. that Phillion was truthfully proclaiming his innocence). Consequently, in Canada there seems little future for the use of expert polygraph evidence in court to directly incriminate or exonerate an accused.

However, polygraphy will continue to be a useful procedure for the police in screening suspects and establishing leads that can independently speak to the culpability of the suspect.

Hypnosis, Suggestion and the Law

Hypnosis and polygraphy have been directed at different aspects of witness testimony. Polygraphy has been used principally to test the truthfulness of statements by suspects. By contrast, hypnosis has been used to restore weakly recorded memories and has been used with victims and suspects as well as with eyewitnesses. However, it is not a test of the truthfulness or accuracy of what they report during recall. There have been remarkable solutions to criminal cases tied to hypnosis. The famous Chowchilla kidnapping case in California in which a bus load of children was hijacked was solved by a witness's recall of a license plate during hypnosis. Similar cases have been solved all across North America by the successful jogging of memories through hypnosis. While the actual physiological basis of hypnosis is still a matter of dispute, it is nonetheless acknowledged that hypnosis is a peculiar state of consciousness between waking and sleeping in which the subject voluntarily suspends wilful behaviour at the instruction of a trusted superior. Under the influence of the hypnotist, subjects are reported to show evidence of increased tolerance for pain (anesthesia), loss of certain motor functions (catalepsy), selective memory impairment (amnesia), ability to recall experiences from childhood including birth trauma (age regression) and tolerance of auditory and visual hallucinations as well as other symptoms. For the purposes of criminal investigation, hypnosis has been drawn on to overcome memory loss whether this has come from a regression produced by trauma or fear, or from the natural process of memory decay.

A recent Canadian case, *R. v. Zubot* (1981), involved the use of hypnosis to enhance the memory of a witness who had overheard a conversation in a neighbour's yard on the day of his murder. The conversation was between the two culprits and included a reference to the first name of one of the men who was being asked by the other to help him lift the corpse. The witness identified the man in a series of police photos. Under hypnosis she also recalled the Christian name of one of the men mentioned in the conversation. The first culprit pleaded guilty to manslaughter, but Zubot went to trial on a charge of murder and was acquitted. Apparently the jury was not overly impressed by the hypnotically enhanced recollection. In other cases, the accused person has been hypnotized. This was allowed in *R. v. Pitt* (1968) where the accused, who was charged with murdering her husband, wished to be hypnotized to refresh her memory about details surrounding the event. In *R. v. Horvath* (1979) and *R. v. Booher* (1928) confessions were obtained by the use of hypnosis from suspects held in custody, were subsequently entered at trial, and in both cases were excluded from evidence. In the Horvath case, the suspect was a 17-year-old male charged with the murder of his mother. He was interrogated intensively by a police polygraph operator who through the use of hypnotic suggestion led him to "unburden himself." Justices Spence and Estey of the Supreme Court of Canada characterized the situation this way (R. v. Horvath, 1979: 2):

> In this case a 17-year-old accused, of unstable character, was "hammered" in cross-examination by two impressive police officers and then taken by a skilled interrogator through an examination which left him in a condition of complete emotional disintegration. No statement made by an accused under those circumstances could be imagined to be voluntary.

Horvath's confession was excluded and he was subsequently acquitted. In this case there is no suggestion by the Court that the involuntariness of the confession made it unreliable. The Court seemed more concerned with the fact that the involuntary induction of the hypnotic trance was a form of "moral violence" that abrogated the right to be silent. In the most recent case to be reported under Canadian law, the issue discussed was the whole question of fallibility and inherent untrustworthiness of hypnotically enhanced evidence. This was the case of *R. v. K.* (1979), a Family Court decision involving a juvenile who was charged with "a delinquency of criminal negligence causing death" following a car accident in which two persons were killed. The accused had no recollection of the events leading up to and following the accident, and agreed to undergo hypnosis to help restore recollection. Justice Garfinkel of the Manitoba Provincial Family Court refused during a *voir dire* to admit the evidence recalled under hypnosis. He noted that hypnosis was a "reduced state of consciousness characterized by a heightened susceptibility to suggestion." He add that hypnosis

is not infallible and there are difficulties in obtaining the truth from a hypnotized subject. The subject may give results which he feels will please the hypnotist and he may lie or distort the actual events. Further, the hypnotist could suggest a response or answer and easily affect the memory recall of the subject . . . the reliability of a memory recalled or refreshed by hypnosis has not been satisfactorily established and the evidence must be therefore excluded ([1979] 47 C.C.C. (2d) at p. 436).

Cases of the abuses of the types posed by Justice Garfinkel abound. In a 1978 Ohio case, *State v. Papp*, the accused was hypnotized to recall details surrounding a murder with which he was charged. While under hypnosis, he exhonerated himself and blamed another party. It was later shown that he was merely faking hypnosis. The 1977 California case of *People v. Ritchie* turned out likewise. A substantial amount of circumstantial evidence was brought against the accused in a murder case involving a 2½-year-old victim. Under hypnosis the accused "relived" the experience in dramatic detail and "recalled" facts that pointed to the guilt of his wife and cleared him. Because of inconsistencies in the evidence and its unreliability, it was excluded. Martin Orne (1981: 66) reports that in the case of *Leyra v. Denno* (1954) a conviction for murder was quashed when it was shown that a confession was involuntarily obtained from the accused by a psychiatrist who induced the subject, under hypnosis, into believing he had committed the murder. Orne argues that false confessions are sometimes elicited under the same psychological conditions that motivate innocent people to "confess" to well-publicized crimes. Consequently, there are no shortages of cases to illustrate the abuses that Justice Garfinkel suggested. Like the polygraph, hypnosis is not an infallible device: it can wrongly exonerate the guilty and can convict the innocent. Critics of hypnosis have argued that its use should be confined to criminal investigations which can establish independent evidence of guilt. Further suggested safeguards include the videotaping of the interaction between the hypnotist and subject; this will provide a way of independently assessing the risk of influencing a witness. Also, it has been suggested that the hypnotist should be excluded from the police investigating team in order to avoid the hypnotist's knowing what the police want to hear; to this end, Orne (1981: 99) suggested that all the communication between the investigators and the hypnotist should be written down and communicated via memoranda. Also, the prehypnotic interrogation should be videorecorded to ensure that the subject is not given cues that could distort the recollections during the hypnotic session. Critics of hypnosis have advised that adherence to these guidelines would minimize the potential for abuse of hypnotic evidence. For our purposes it is sufficient to note that the justice system is rightfully sceptical of the advances from the psychological sciences. The dangers in testimony are rarely the sorts of things that can be easily cured with liberal doses of truth serum, hypnosis or lie detector tests. Though each is viewed as a solution to an earlier problem, in many instances the medicine has been more harmful than the original disease.

Summary

In this chapter we have examined some of the miscarriages of justice that have arisen through erroneous eyewitness identifications. The sources of these errors are several: the wilful misleading of witnesses by third parties, the unwitting mislabelling of suspects by faulty identification procedures, and the psychological processes that contribute to the transformation and distortion of memory. These types of errors can be introduced in the initial perception of the events, in the identification parades, during the police interviews with witnesses, during the recollections and rehearsals with witnesses prior to the court appearance and during the actual courtroom testimony itself. Because of the serious consequences of such errors, critics of the justice system have suggested a number of special safeguards such as a standardization of procedures to ensure unbiased identifications, a requirement of corroboration, a strengthening of the judge's charge to the jury and a recognition of the expertise of psychologists on identification matters. Current judicial practice has shown itself to be sensitive to biases in lineups, the desirability of corroboration and the importance of the charge to the jury. However, this concern has not always resulted in the creation of formal guidelines. As for the admission of expert witnesses in the areas of perceptual psychology, polygraphy and hypnosis, the courts have been reluctant to revise the current rules of evidence and have instead relied on the traditional safeguards against erroneous conviction: the scepticism of juries, the force of cross-examination and the guidance of judicial instruction. And where these have failed, there has been recourse to the appeal courts, executive pardons and, in certain cases, humanitarian compensation for the unjustly imprisoned.

FURTHER READING

E.M. Borchard, *Convicting the Innocent: Errors of Criminal Justice*. New Haven: Yale University Press, 1932.

Patrick Devlin, *Report to the Secretary of State for the Home Department of the Departmental Committee on Evidence of Identification in Criminal Cases*. London: Her Majesty's Stationery Office, 1976.

A.N. Doob and H.M. Kirshenbaum, ''Bias in police lineups—partial remembering.'' *Journal of Police Science and Administration*, Vol. 1, 1973, pp. 287-293.

F. Frankfurter, *The Case of Sacco and Vanzetti*. New York: Little, Brown, 1927. (Reprinted in Universal Library edition, 1962).

Justice Society, *Compensation for Wrongful Imprisonment*. London, 1982.

Elizabeth F. Loftus, *Eyewitness Testimony*. Cambridge: Harvard university Press, 1979.

Gwynn Nettler, *Lying, Cheating, Stealing*, Vol. 3 of *Criminal Careers*. Cincinnati: Anderson Publishing, 1982.

N.R. Sobel, *Eyewitness Identification: Legal and Practical Problems*. New York: Clark Boardman, 1972 (1976 supplement).

David Starkman, "The use of eyewitness identification evidence in criminal trials." *Criminal Law Quarterly*, Vol. 21, 1978-79, pp. 361-386.

P.M. Wall, *Eyewitness Identification of Criminal Cases*. Springfield, Ill.: Charles C. Thomas, 1965.

A. Daniel Yarmey, *The Psychology of Eyewitness Testimony*. New York: Free Press, 1979.

CORRECTIONS

CHAPTER 10

Deterrence of Crime by Punishment

Punishment as Deterrence

In his study of the lifestyle of cheque forgers, John Klein formulated the problem of the cause of cheque forgery in an ironical way. Given that a skilful operator can defraud a string of banks of tens of thousands of dollars in a day's work, the question should not be "why do they do it?" but rather, "why don't we all do it?" (Silverman and Teevan, 1980: 335-347). Since the patterns of deception are easily learned and the risk of being apprehended on the spot are extremely low, "filthy lucre" is within the easy grasp of most intelligent people. However, all but a handful resist the temptation. The most common explanation of our fortitude is that we fear the consequences of doing otherwise. The prospect of the pain and the embarrassment of apprehension and punishment deters our criminal impulses. We also do not want to jeopardize our status and be ill thought of or despised by those who otherwise hold us in some regard. Hence both internal and external controls regulate our choices; but such constraints are not always foolproof. Sometimes our rational self-interest and an easy gain weighs heavier in the balance than the risks and approbation associated with being caught and punished. Consequently, the deterrent effect of law enforcement and the sentencing of offenders is based on a tension between the considerations of rational criminal behaviour in which crime pays as opposed to the risks of criminal behaviour in which getting caught hurts. This has been illustrated in a number of studies.

   In an investigation of student cheating, Tittle and Rowe (1973) asked students to evaluate the results of their own weekly multiple choice tests. The researchers graded the tests prior to handing them back to the students but made no marks on the papers.

As an indication of cheating they measured the difference between the scores they determined versus the credit the students gave to themselves. The point of the study was to
measure the effect of a moral appeal to be honest, which was given to one group versus
a direct threat that dishonesty would be penalized announced to another. The threat-
group was told that a student had been caught giving himself more credit than he was
due and so was being punished. Though the speech encouraging honesty had no effect
whatsoever, following the threat announcement the rate of cheating dropped from over
30% to 11% (Tittle and Rowe, 1973: 488-498).

   In a similar experiment conducted by Stanley Schachter, students were given an
opportunity to secretly enhance their grades by changing their choices on a self-corrected
test. Where Tittle and Rowe changed the student perception of risk in the external
environment, Schachter worked on the internal environment. Specifically, Schachter's
hope was to influence the rate of cheating by blocking the level of emotional arousal of
the students to inhibit anxiety and remorse. By feeding them small doses of chlorpro-
mazine, a depressant, disguised as a vitamin, Schachter doubled the level of cheating
over that of a control group (Schachter, 1971: 150-151). Because their ability to react
emotionally to the situation was impaired by the drug, the internal controls failed, and
consideration of deviant self-interest gained the upper hand. No doubt there are a number
of naturally occurring criminogenic conditions, ranging from congenital emotional dis-
orders to illicit drug- and alcohol-related reactions that produce the same effect. However,
as rationalists emphasize, when we inspect aggregate data the probability of criminal
behaviour can be calculated independently of considerations of individual pathology.

Rational Bases of Criminal Behaviour

The classical school of criminology associated with Cesare Beccaria (1738-1794) was
premised on the notion that crime is rational behaviour that must be controlled,
measure for measure by punishment. Deterrence was viewed as the primary objective
of law and punishment. In his time, Beccaria was extremely liberal: where his Italian
contemporaries called for uniformly severe and frequently barbaric sentences, he called
for punishments only so harsh as to offset the impulse to deviate from the norm. He
deplored the European customs of scalding and boiling, hanging, drawing and quartering, disfigurement, torture and burning. Late renaissance Europe had evolved only
moderately beyond the practice of crucifixion (Foucault, 1977: Ch. 1). Beccaria's 1764
treatise On Crimes and Punishment was influential in subsequently reforming the harsh
English and European penal codes. Beccaria's position was that criminals were free
moral agents, that they knew the difference between right and wrong, and that they
chose to do wrong because it was in some way more profitable than doing what was
right. Hence the response of the state should be to offset the gains of crime by specifying just as much punishment as would be required to make crime uninviting, while at
the same time preserving the liberty of law-abiding citizens. In addition to calling for
proportionate punishment, Beccaria called for the abolition of torture, of secret accusation and arrest and of politically motivated prosecutions. He argued that justice should
be administered uniformly and that the laws should be reformed to more specifically
describe the requirements of the crime. While his influence waned under the direction
of later biological criminologists, it continued to flourish among students of jurisprudence and is linked with reforms associated with our concept of mens rea, specifically
the rise of the insanity defense, the exception of children from criminal liability, and

the subsequent partial exception of juveniles. These changes were based on a revised conception of who could have free will, the concept at the core of Beccaria's work.

How relevant is the rationalist model to criminal behaviour? Though textbook writers under the influence of Social Darwinism tended to portray the criminal as pathologically imbalanced and morally degenerated, community studies like William F. Whyte's *Street Corner Society* have stressed the rationality and the "organization" of criminal careers. Whyte's gangsters amassed fortunes by promoting illegal gambling, prostitution, underground nightclubs and illicit booze. The risks engendered in such enterprises were reduced by bribing politicians and policemen and by dividing up territories between rival criminal organizations to minimize friction. Similarly, the use of bribery to minimize the fateful consequences of conviction for professional thieves has been studied in some detail in Sutherland's work on the professional thief. In addition to fixing charges by bribing public officials and police officers, the professional thief minimized prosecution by choosing victims who would be reluctant to call the police: for example, homosexuals who were being extorted or businessmen who had been the victims of a confidence game. Also, if under suspicion by private investigators, the professional thief would try to make deals with the insurance companies to return merchandise in exchange for having them not press charges (Sutherland, 1937).

Aside from the rationality of criminal behaviour for the practitioner, much criminal behaviour thrives because of the demands of consumers. This was especially true during the period of prohibition, but remains true today with respect to prostitution and illegal drugs. Donald Cressey's study of the Cosa Nostra points to the economic dimension of crime: "The America confederation of criminals thrives because a large minority of citizens demand illicit goods and services it has for sale" (1969: 294).

Rational crime is not limited to illegitimate businesses. Legitimate firms also are known to have manipulated the market to their advantage with far greater costs to the economy. According to Ramsay Clark crimes like tax evasion, monopoly pricing and consumer fraud gross billions of dollars annually.

> Illicit gains from white-collar crime far exceed those of all other crime combined . . . One corporate price-fixing conspiracy criminally converted more money each year . . . than all of the hundreds of thousands of burglaries, larcenies, or thefts in the entire nation during those same years. Reported bank embezzlements cost ten times more than bank robberies each year (1970: 38).

One of the best illustrations is the great e............................f leading American electrical manufacturing industry (inc......................................McGraw-Edison and Allis-Chalmers), who.......................................pricing on items like power generators and tr.................................Sherman Antitrust Act established that, ove.....................................prices had inflated the costs of such goods t.....................................1977). Establishment of guilt in such cases i.......................vestigators to be accountants as well as police and lawyers.

Aside from successfully organized illegal endeavours, how appropriate is the rationalist model for more low-level criminal behaviours? Here we are limiting our attention to crime involving property, money and other forms of wealth such as theft, robbery, extortion, fraud and forgery. One way of establishing the relevance of the model is to measure changes in the rates of crime as costs vary and so correlate the incidence of crime with changes in its profitability. A number of studies have examined such relationships and tend on the whole to confirm the rationality position.

Cobb, Krohm and Gunning: Crime as Income

At a conference sponsored by the American Enterprise Institute in 1972, several reports were presented by economists showing the gainfulness of different types of property crime. William E. Cobb (1975) presented an analysis of the gainfulness of theft and burglary (excluding robbery and petit larceny) for the city of Norfolk, Virginia for the years 1964 and 1966. Benefits of these crimes were estimated on the basis of the full face value of money stolen, and the adjusted value of the goods stolen. Cobb put this latter figure at 20% of the face value for jewellery and furs and 12% of the face value of clothing since thieves are typically able to turn over such merchandise only at a fraction of its market value. Cobb then adjusted the total benefit figure upwards by 50% to control for the underreporting of crimes and arrived at a benefit of $353,899 for 1964. Of this, it was assumed 18% went to juvenile offenders, who were excluded from the sample, leaving $290,339 for adult offenders. To calculate the costs, Cobb examined fines paid and length of time incarcerated. For the 60 thieves incarcerated, he determined that with their relative lack of education, in 1964 they would have been able to earn approximately $1.62 per hour, and given the high rate of unemployment for this group, they usually would have worked only 30 weeks per year. This income was forfeited for a total of 78.34 years served by the total group. He calculated the possible income from lawful employment over this 78 year period as a cost to be deducted, along with the fines, from the net income from theft in order to determine the marginal benefits of crime. The annual gross average legitimate income was calculated at $1,932 totalling $151,353. The total costs, including lost income plus fines of $2,460, amounted to $153,813.

TABLE 1
Profitability of Theft, Norfolk, Virginia, 1964

Benefits		
Adjusted Value of Stolen Goods	= $353,899	
Minus 18% (stolen by juveniles)	= 290,339	
Net Value		$290,339
Costs		
Average Annual Income Foregone by Imprisonment	= $ 1,932	
Annual Loss × 78.34 yrs. of Sentences Received	= 151,353	
Total of Fines	= 2,460	
Gross Costs (fines plus foregone income)		153,813
NET BENEFIT FOR THEFT		$136,526

Source: Cobb, 1975.

On this basis, the illegal income represented a gain of nearly 90% more on average than they might have expected from their lawful employment calculated at 30 weeks per year. Even assuming they worked 50 weeks per year, the group figure shows a net gain of 15% over and above the possible lawful earnings. Similar results were obtained for the 1966 data. Cobb concluded that this sort of crime pays — at least in Norfolk, Virginia for the period studied.

Gregory Krohm's study (1973) of the pecuniary incentives of burglary in Chicago during 1969 and J. Patrick Gunning Jr.'s study (1973) of burglary in Delaware in 1967 likewise tended to suggest that crime pays. Krohm calculated that in the short run each burglary nets the thief $36.70 versus a possible daily income of $23.30 for legitimate unskilled blue-collar work. However, since the thief is estimated to be out of the work force 65% of the time due to incarceration, compared to 7% unemployment for the legitimate worker, his or her adjusted benefit falls to just over half that of the legitimate worker. To offset this, Krohm argues that when the value of the prison services (i.e., room and board) are added to the income this again puts burglary in the profit column. Krohm also points out that there are significant differences between the risk of incarceration for juveniles compared to adults, which appear to to explain the greater incentive of burglary for juveniles. While an adult faces a chance of .0024 of going to jail for any single burglary, the chance for the juvenile is .0015. Krohm also calculated that the risk of imprisonment reduces the juvenile's average take by 32%, yielding $24.96 daily. Given the high rate of youthful unemployment in legitimate work (22%) and the minimum wages paid to juveniles, the net daily legitimate income is given as $9.06. According to Krohm, this makes burglary a most attractive option to juveniles. However, Krohm fails to control for the fact that most juveniles are far less efficient burglars and rarely enjoy the same measure of success as older counterparts. This would deflate the calculation of this average take and reduce the disparity between legitimate and illegitimate income.

The economic premise that crime occurs simply because it pays is not observed uniformly in empirical studies. For instance, Michael Sesnowitz (1972), who studied the returns to burglary in Pennsylvania in 1967, determined that the net take per burglary was $119 where the expected cost of imprisonment was $316, so that each burglary generated on average an expected cost to the thief the equivalent of a $197 loss. Clearly not all cost-benefit analyses fit the simple rationality model. The same counterintuitive finding was reported for an economic study of the incidence of arson. Where the economic model suggests that arson will occur at the bottom of the business cycles, reflecting attempts of businessmen to convert equity to cash, Spillman and Zak (1979) found no such relationships.

These studies are problematic at a more general level. Though they are based on a simple cost-benefit economic rationality, they are mistakenly premised on the positive marginal returns of crime versus work, and treat this difference as the reason for criminal behaviour. As Gunning says in his opening line, "The hypothesis to be tested in this paper is that the profits of professional burglary are high enough to induce persons, who would otherwise have been productive citizens, into a life of crime" (Gunning, 1973: 35). However when we see that Gunning's juveniles face 22% unemployment and that Cobb's adults face 40% unemployment (i.e. usually work only 30 weeks of the year) it is not feasible to focus on the marginal return of theft versus work. Given these patterns of underemployment, the criminals would appear to have lots of time to augment their legitimate income. For example, the 195 adults arrested in Cobb's study faced a total of 78.34 years in prison, or 4.8 months on average. In fact, most of the serious prison time was faced by 31 convicted felons, leaving the majority out of jail. As an alternative, it would make more sense to study the distribution of theft throughout the social classes to see if it is more prevalent where legitimate opportunities are curtailed (Gordon, 1971).

Clearly, from this perspective it would not matter if the marginal returns from crime were less than those from legitimate employment since they would not constitute competing mutually exclusive careers, but supplementary sources of income. In this context, the criminal response is rational in the economic sense, especially to the extent that legitimate earnings fail to meet the costs of subsistence. Nonetheless, there are problems with the approach at a more general level: as a model of behaviour, the rationality theory explains what amounts to a radical variation in behaviour (legitimate work or criminal theft) with a constant (the fact that in work or in crime we act rationally).

Since both crime and work have rational aspects, a better theory would describe the distribution of the two types of rational adjustment. Merton's anomie theory (1938), for example, argues that crime will be a mode of adaptation where legitimate opportunities for subsistence are blocked. In other words, a gap between one's aspirations and one's ability to reach them will breed crime. The roles of poverty and unemployment are not given any attention in the simple cost-benefit analyses, though in anomie theory these factors add a somewhat greater precision in identifying the social location of many property-related criminal activities.

Later studies improved on the initial cost-benefit studies by focussing on the changes in these patterns over time and by considering a larger number of variables. The hallmark of these later, more mathematically sophisticated studies has been their focus on the deterrent elements of choice situations. Where earlier workers stressed the income side of the equation, that is, the material returns from crime, the later work examined shifts over time in the risk of arrest, conviction and incarceration. This basic common element shows that decreases in the likelihood of punishment have correlated with increases in the incidence of a wide range of crimes.

Economic Models of Robbery, Violence and National Crime Rates

Studies by Tim Ozenne (1974) and Lee R. McPheters (1976) deal with US bank and non-bank robberies respectively. Ozenne studied losses from bank robberies from 1966 to 1970 in over 30 US states and demonstrated a correlation across states between the expected gross return and the expected penalty. His model predicted that states that were relatively profitable financial targets would experience increases in offenses relative to those less profitable target states. The prediction was tested by comparing rates of increase of bank robbery between two successive periods with the profitability on the base period (1974: 40). Ozenne's analysis supported the inference that where robbery pays, it happens more often. McPheters's analysis of non-bank robbery focussed on changes in four key variables between 1959 and 1971: a) the total non-bank robbery losses for the United States, b) the robbery rate per 100,000 population, c) the percentage clearance rate for robbery measured by the number of robberies solved by successful arrest, and d) the percentage rate of conviction for apprehended robbers. There were several suggestive findings. First, the real losses from robbery when adjusted for inflation between 1959 and 1971 dropped in value by one third. Robbery became on the whole less profitable. This would have been especially true since demographic changes suggest that the number of robbers increased: hence, each robber netted less. By contrast, the robbery rate increased by over 450% during the period. Notably, the success of the police and the courts fell behind as witnessed by the clearance and conviction rates. Where 42.5% of robberies were cleared by arrest in 1959, under 25% were cleared by arrest in 1971. The rate of conviction dropped by more than half from 64.8% to 31.5%. McPheters noted that changes in the robbery rate were more closely related to the drop in the clearance rate, that is, the rate of arrest. The sharp drop in the probability of apprehension apparently offset the shrinking gain from robbery. Where McPheters stressed the risks to crime, Ozenne stressed the profitability. The work of both broadly supports the value of rationalist or economic approach.

Similar conclusions were drawn from a study of violent crimes in New York City by Shlomo and Revel Shinnar (1975). Following Avi-Itzhak's (1973) focus on safety crimes — homicide, rape, assault, robbery and burglary — the Shinnars showed a strong correlation over the period 1940 to 1970 between increased victimization rates and such changes in the criminal justice system as the decrease in convictions, the decreased use of prisons, and the shortening of prison sentences. The effects of the changes in the justice system contribute over and above the increased incidence in crime due to increases in urbanization and density. The Shinnars argued that between 1960 and 1970, while the total crime picture expanded by 300%, 185% of the change correlated with shifts in policy towards more humane (i.e., non-custodial) handling of offenders (1975: 603-604).

At the same time, the chance of being the victim of a violent crime shifted. "At the crime rates reported 20 or 10 years ago, an inhabitant of Brooklyn or even Manhattan had a 90% chance of never being the victim of a violent crime" (1975: 583). In 1970, the chances of an inhabitant of Manhattan being at least once the victim of a violent crime were 84%. If burglaries (break and enter) are included, the figure jumps to 99%. If we examine robbery alone (including mugging), a 1935 inhabitant of Manhattan had a 2% lifetime risk of being robbed. In 1970, this jumped to 70% (1975: 600). Similarly, the risk to the assailant dropped sharply. The Shinnars computed this risk by dividing the unadjusted figure for all index crimes by the number of persons in prison. This gives a figure of .35 for New York State in 1960, but it drops to .06 in 1970. This results from the fact that the number of violent crimes increased sixfold during that decade while the prison population hardly changed at all (1975: 584). Though there has been an international movement to reduce the size of prison populations, New York State decreased the practice of incarceration more rapidly than other jurisdictions and experienced a distinctively high growth in serious crime. The solutions to the crime problem offered by the Shinnars, though crude, are well in line with the expectations of rationality theory.

> If we send every convicted mugger and robber to prison for five years, we could reduce this type of violent crime by a factor of five. . . . If we improve police work, and the efficiency of the criminal justice system as a whole, we might increase the probability of a mugger getting convicted for each crime to 20% (the value now prevailing in England). Then, a net prison stay of three years would do the same job. Either we increase the length of stay . . . or we increase the probability of a criminal getting convicted and sent to prison for every crime he commits (pp.605-606).

Of course, this might mean doubling the number of jails, though it is argued the costs of this would be offset by the savings from a reduction in serious crime. This prison alternative is not very savoury when one considers that the US already has the highest rate of incarceration among Western nations and has prison populations that are massively overrepresented by the country's poor and minority groups.

The classic study by Isaac Ehrlich (1973) of the economic determinants of participation in illegitimate activities is very broad in scope. Ehrlich examined variations in all the major crimes across states in the United States in 1940, 1950 and 1960. Using techniques developed by economists for analyzing complex relations he was able to separate the effects of a number of different variables in order to determine their individual degree of association with criminal behaviour. They include the following. (a) The crime rate, the dependent variable, was measured for evidence of immediate effects by other variables and for delayed effects. (b) A measure was taken of the probability of apprehension and imprisonment based on the number of offenders in jail for each offense category. (c) The average sentence per offense was recorded. (d) Measures were taken of median family incomes as well as (e) the percentage of families below one-half the median income. (f) The percentage of nonwhites in the population was measured as well as (g) rates of unemployment and labour force participation for urban males aged 14 to 24. (h) The level of education and (i) degree of urbanization were also determined. The major findings included the following:

1. "The rate of specific crime categories, with virtually no exception, varies inversely with estimates of the probability of apprehension and punishment . . . and with the average length of time served in state prisons" (1973: 545).
2. Crimes against property (robbery, burglary, theft) were found to vary with the degree of income inequality, though there were relatively small effects of income inequality on crime against the person, particularly rape and murder.
3. All specific crime rates were positively related to the percentage of nonwhites in the population.

Other indications in the data suggest that the labour force participation of young men "insulates" them from participation in crime. Though the insulation effect on crimes involving property are ambiguous, the degree of labour force participation appears to be negatively related with crimes against the person. Lastly, the probability of catching and convicting serious criminals was found to be positively related to the expenditure on the police and negatively related to the crime rate. Indeed, Ehrlich estimated that "a one percent increase in expenditure on direct law enforcement would result in about a three percent decrease in all felony offenses" (1973: 558). In his conclusion, Ehrlich, unlike Cobb, Krohm, Gunning and the Shinnars, is sensitive to the lower-class economic factors that make criminal careers attractive. If society wants to create disincentives toward crime, the role of social mobility must not be ignored in favour of more police. This is especially relevant since Ehrlich found that the efficiency of the police in solving crimes was inversely related to the size and density of the population.

> Our empirical investigation also indicates that the rates of all felonies, particularly crimes against property, are positively related to the degree of a community's income inequality, and this suggests a social incentive for equalizing training and earning opportunities across persons, which is independent of ethical considerations or any social welfare function. Whether it would pay society to spend more resources in order to enforce existing laws would then depend not only on the effectiveness of such expenditure in deterring crime, but also on the extent to which alternative methods of combating crime pay (1973: 561).

Avio and Clark: Severity of Punishment versus Certainty of Apprehension

Research on the deterrence of criminal behaviour has been undertaken with Canadian data by Avio and Clark (1976; 1978). In a study of the risks of property crime in Canada from 1970 to 1972, they confirmed most relationships that had already been established elsewhere. Specifically, there was a negative relationship between the crime rate for robbery and breaking and entering and the probability of apprehension. Similarly, there was a negative relationship between conviction rates for robbery and theft, though surprisingly no association in the case of fraud and break and enter. In addition, calculations of opportunity costs as projected by unemployment and income inequality seemed to have no effect on the incentives to steal. A 1971 study of property offenses in Ontario amplified the relationship between apprehension and severity of punishment. Unlike most earlier studies, which reported that the probability of arrest, *as well as* the length of incarceration (or severity of punishment) are negatively related to specific crime rates, Avio and Clark (1978) found no relationship with respect to the length of sentence. Notably, a different measure of sentence length was used — the expected sentence. Rather than examine the sentence rate for offenders *released* during the period under study, they examined sentences of offenders *convicted* during the period — adjusted for the current amenities of early release and parole and utilization of earned remission opportunities (time suspended for good behaviour). Avio and Clark concluded that arrest is a greater deterrent to crime than the severity of the sentence. Presumably, the trauma and stigma of arrest are known to be onerous and to be relatively certain while the consequences of sentence can be quite vague, especially in view of the variability in sentences, the delay between arrest and conviction, the likelihood of charge reduction during the court phase and the prospects of early release. Consequently, the Canadian research confirms generally the economic or rationalist model of criminal behaviour, but qualifies the relationship between deterrence and the certainty versus the severity of punishment.

The economic or rationalist models of crime have enormous implications for devising the optimal response to criminal behaviour. If justice policies were framed on the basis of Avio's work, swiftness and certainty of apprehension and expediency in the trial phase would be given priority. By contrast, basing policy on the work of the Shinnars would lead to a stress on massive prison expansion and long fixed periods of incarceration. Lastly, Ehrlich's work oscillates between a bolstering of police resources, a step inherently limited by city size and population density, and economic and educational reforms aimed at accelerating the employment of disadvantaged groups in order to eliminate the sources of criminal manpower. For the most part, economists have examined property offenses under the rationalist model and have often identified areas of interest shared by most social theorists, specifically, the relevance of income inequality as a condition of much criminal activity. However, economists and sociologists tend to part company when it comes to the most harmful crime, murder, and the possible deterrent effect of the death penalty.

The Rate of Murder and the Penalty of Death: *Sellin v. Ehrlich*

The sociological case for the relationship between murder and the use of capital punishment has been developed principally in the works of Thorsten Sellin. Sellin argues that, contrary to popular belief, the existence and the use of the death penalty have no discernible consequences for the would-be murderer and so have no effect on the homicide rate. Sellin's position is based on a number of observations. First, an examination of the homicide rates in clusters of American states, some of which have abolished and some of which have retained capital punishment, does not reveal differences in the homicide rate which the deterrence theory would predict. Since the states are geographically contiguous, Sellin reasons that they are matched on relevant socioeconomic factors

TABLE 2
Homicide Rates per 100,000 Population
in Contiguous American States with and without the Death Penalty 1920-1974

Abolitionist Jurisdictions		Retentionist Jurisdictions		
Michigan		Ohio	Indiana	
5.29		5.69	4.68	
Rhode Island	Maine	Connecticut	Massachusetts	New Hampshire
1.85	1.69	2.28	1.93	1.35
Wisconsin	Minnesota	Iowa	Nebraska	
1.83	2.03	1.79	2.69	
		Kansas†	Missouri	Colorado
		4.02	7.79	5.71

†Kansas was an abolitonist state until 1935.
Source: Based on T. Sellin, *The Penalty of Death*, 1980, pp. 144-155. The figures were aggregated from five-year totals covering the period 1920-1974.

that might influence the crime rates and so extraneous variables are presumably controlled for.

According to Sellin, where the threat of capital punishment is present, there is no obviously lower homicide rate as expected. Though this matching strategy has been criticized because no controls were actively demonstrated, Baldus and Cole (1975) have identified a number of key similarities in the matched groups, which show common patterns of labour force participation, unemployment, age structure, per capita income and per capita government expenditures.

Sellin's critics have identified problems in his research. Since he samples these matching states at random, there is no demonstration for the United States as a whole that retentionist states and abolitionist states have comparable homicide rates. Such a comparison would require controls on a whole range of criminogenic factors aside from the existence of capital punishment, and Sellin has avoided any attempts at sophisticated statistical techniques. Indeed, in all his comparisons there are no tests of statistical differences (see Avison, 1981). However, Sellin does not rest his conviction on similarities between abolitionist and retentionist states alone.

In addition to examining the relationship between the use or disuse of the death penalty and its consequence for the homicide rate, Sellin has also studied the effect of differences in actual use of execution between jurisdictions and changes in homicide rates stemming from a state's abolition and reinstatement of capital punishment. Examination of the number of executions over the period 1920-1974 in retentionist states shows that executions, which were relatively frequent at the start of the period trail off over time to become virtually non-existent in the early 1970s (Sellin, 1980: 144-171). Contrary to what deterrent theory would suggest, there is no clear inverse relationship with the crude homicide rate. On the contrary, Sellin's data show that the homicide rate remains relatively constant with high points in the 1920s, a low in the 1940s and new high points in the late 1960s and early 1970s. This is true for both abolitionist and retentionist states and suggests that the homicide rate is affected primarily by something other than executions, but again there are no controls in Sellin's data for factors that might be confounding or repressing a deterrent effect.

Sellin's observations have been borne out by other researchers. Karl F. Schuessler (1952), who studied American national data from several decades prior to 1950, found no association between the homicide rate and the use of capital punishment. Chambliss (1969: 361- 363) examined the period 1951 to 1966 and found that the number of executions nationwide dropped from 105 in 1951 to just one in 1966. However, the murder rate remained fairly constant during this period, varying between 4.5 to 5.6 per 100,000 population, with an average of about 4.9 (1969: 363). This is again contrary to the deterrent model.

Sellin's last kind of evidence concerns the repeal and the reintroduction of the death penalty on homicide rates in 11 American states. This provides an unique quasi-experimental test of deterrence. Sellin discovered that the abolition of capital punishment was not associated with a rise in murder and that its reintroduction did not bring about any decline (Sellin, 1959: 34-38). Similar observations have been noticed for other jurisdictions, including Canada (Fattah, 1976: 34). In a similar vein, Leonard Savitz (1958) examined the capital crime rates in Philadelphia immediately before and after well-publicized trials at which the defendants were sentenced to death. Savitz focussed on the trials rather than the executions because frequently the executions were announced in brief news releases buried in the back pages of the newspapers, while the trials all received prominent front-page coverage. Apparently, the lesson of capital punishment was lost on the would-be criminals who carried on despite the graphic reminders about the consequences of such crimes for those apprehended.

This type of media effect on behaviour is not clear cut. If the public forms an attachment to the media figures, the death of such figures can affect the behaviour of some members of the public. This was dramatically illustrated in a study of the impact of fictional television stories on the patterns of suicide in the US by David Phillips. Phillips (1982) discovered that following soap opera suicide stories, there were increases in the rates of suicide, especially among women, as well as an increase in single-vehicle motor crashes. Obviously the suicide of even a fictional character to whom one has been attached influences one's behaviour, and on the aggregate level this results in fluctuations in suicidal behaviour. Perhaps the key to the difference between the findings of Savitz and those of Phillips is that would-be murderers do not read the papers, and if they do, they do not identify with convicted criminals in the same way that an audience identifies with soap opera heroes.

An interesting sidelight to the study of executions was the discovery by Sellin (1980: 55-68) that black offenders tended to face the death penalty far more frequently than white offenders for the same crime, especially when the victim was white. Bowers and Pierce (1980) reported similarly that bias exists across a number of American states in cases of interracial homicide. For example, in Texas a black person who kills a white person is 87 times more likely to be sentenced to death than a black who kills another black. A white who kills a white is twice as likely to face the death sentence as a white who kills a black. Obviously, the deaths of whites are avenged more aggressively. As Sellin and Bowers and Pierce have noted, the differential execution pattern raised serious doubts about the principle of equality before the law.

The Econometric Approach

In 1975, Isaac Ehrlich published the first of a series of controversial studies of the deterrent effect of capital punishment that jarred the political as well as the academic world.

Ehrlich's approach, models and conclusions differed in every respect from those of Sellin. Sellin's work was never directed at establishing a relationship between murder and some independent variable, but was devoted for reasons of humanitarian conviction to showing the absence of a relationship, particularly between capital punishment and the commission of capital crimes. By contrast, Ehrlich's work was motivated by the promise of including violent crime under the economic model developed for property crimes. Ehrlich's strategy was to devise a way of measuring the cost of crime to the would-be criminal, to measure variations in such costs, and to determine whether the crime supply, in this case homicide, varied with the cost as the law of supply and demand dictates. He argued that the greater the cost (i.e. risk) to the criminal, the less the demand for the commodity, in this case, murder. The principal cost identified by Ehrlich was the probability of execution or "execution risk." Where Sellin found no evidence for deterrence, Ehrlich (1975: 398) reported that "the empirical analysis suggests that on the average the tradeoff between the execution of an offender and the lives of potential victims it might have saved was of the order of magnitude of one for eight for the period 1933-67 in the United States." This conclusion had enormous policy implications because it was published while the US Supreme Court was debating the constitutionality of capital punishment in the case of *Gregg v. Georgia* (1976) (i.e., whether the death penalty *per se* invariably constituted cruel and unusual punishment). Commentators have noted that "several Supreme Court justices based their decisions supporting the constitutionality of the death penalty on the possibility that it might deter" (Levine, Musheno and Palumbo, 1980: 390). In the Canadian Parliamentary debates that resulted in the abolition of the death penalty in Canada, Ehrlich was cited by the retentionists as proving that capital punishment works. Ehrlich's conclusion was based on calculations of the probability of arrest, conviction and execution for murder from 1933 to 1967 in the United States. His results confirmed the economic model: as the risk of arrest, conviction and execution declined, the murder rate increased. Because of the enormous policy implications of his discoveries, Ehrlich's study was closely scrutinized and experienced a number of severe criticisms from criminologists, economists and statisticians.

For example, Bowers and Pierce (1975) pointed out that the deterrent effect was illusory inasmuch as the effect disappeared when the extremely low rates of execution after 1964 were excluded. They reproduced Ehrlich's analysis calculating the effects for various time periods and concluded that "all empirical support for the deterrent effect of capital punishment disappears when the five most recent years are removed from the time series that Ehrlich selected for analysis" (1975: 198). For the time series prior to this, the relationship between the risk of execution and the rate of murder was positive — quite the opposite of what deterrent theory would predict.

Other problems identified by critics included a sharp reverse in the findings when alternative but equally plausible methods of representing the variables and their relationships were undertaken (e.g. using normal values versus logarithms) (Passell and Taylor, 1977; Baldus and Cole, 1975). Questions were also raised about the validity of the historical rate. The FBI data on which Ehrlich based his analysis were said to be of mixed quality. In the 1930s, they were compiled from 400 agencies, while in more recent years some 8,500 agencies were filing criminal statistics; consequently, the critics charged that the data would be inherently unreliable due to the changes in patterns of reporting (Hann, 1976). Another criticism of the FBI source was that it consisted of aggregate national data, which by its nature would be insensitive to fluctuations at the regional or state level. As a result, a deterrent effect in one location might be swamped by a murder epidemic in another, especially since not all states permitted the death penalty. A better test would be a comparison of states that both allowed capital punishment and used it versus those states for legal or simply humanitarian grounds did not execute offenders. Baldus and Cole (1975) rated this as a mark of superiority of Sellin's work over Ehrlich's.

Another very important question raised regarding Ehrlich's work related to a failure to examine the socioeconomic accelerators of murder. While the focus of Ehrlich's model was on how execution risk controlled the murder rate, critics argued that it was necessary to study some of the social conditions of murder because such conditions appeared to vary simultaneously with changes in execution risk. Where Ehrlich identified changes in execution risk as a cause of changes in the murder rate, critics claimed that both murder and execution could be related to another factor, so that the deterrent effect was a mistaken identification of the cause or direction of effect.

In fact, Ehrlich (1975: 17) observes in his conclusion that "the results of the empirical investigation indicate that the rate of murder and other related crimes may also be reduced through increased employment opportunities." In other words, unemployment as well as the execution rate appear to correlate inversely with the rate of homicide. As noted in our examination of Ehrlich's 1973 work, conditions of unemployment and poverty are structural precipitators of crime. While the relationship between poverty and theft is obvious, the relationship between homicide and poverty, though initially problematic, becomes more obvious when we consider that the single most frequent source of homicide in Canada from 1957 to 1965 was armed robbery (Favreau, 1965: 100-103). Though not relevant in every case, socioeconomic factors are far too important to ignore. In addition, a replication of Ehrlich's earlier 1973 study by Forst (1977) indicated that demographic differences between various states also affected the crime rates. Factors like migration, population density and rates of broken homes were better correlates of homicide than Ehrlich's deterrence variables.

In addition to Forst, other attempts have been made to replicate Ehrlich's findings without success. Passall and Taylor concluded, after reanalyzing Ehrlich's data, that his methods and data "do not permit any inference whatsoever about the deterrent effect of the death penalty" (Bedau and Pierce, 1976: 359). The National Research Council report in America filed by Klein, Forst and Filatov argued that "the strongest social scientific conclusion that can be reached at this time" is that the deterrent effect of capital punishment is an unresolved question (1978: 358-59).

In a Canadian test of Ehrlich's position, Avio (1979) examined the relationship between the rate of execution and the murder rate. Avio argued for a number of reasons that the Canadian data were more valid than the American. Particularly, the federal jurisdiction over the courts made the death penalty available across the entire country, unlike the US. The data on executions were recorded on a per-case basis and the Canadian Criminal Statistics Act of 1876 assures greater uniformity of reports. Avio's work nonetheless failed to establish any inverse relationship between the execution risk and the murder rate, and tended to support the failures of other studies to establish the conjecture that severe punishment offsets the rewards of murder and depresses its rate of occurrence.

An earlier test of the period 1965-1970 by C.H.S. Jayewardene (1977) did establish a significant inverse relationship between the expected execution rate and the homicide rate, but overlapped with the five-year period of moratorium where executions were prohibited — beginning in 1967. Also, the relationship only held when Canada was viewed as a whole; some provinces experienced a decrease in homicide following the trial period of abolition.

TABLE 3
Murders, Convictions and Expectancy of Punishment
1965-1970

Year	Murder Rate per 100,000 Population	Recommendations for Capital Punishment Following Conviction for Murder†	Expectancy of	
			Life Imprisonment	Non-Life Jail Term
1965	1.5	.2%	16.8%	20%
1966	1.3	.2%	16.2%	18.1%
1967	1.6	.1%	15.9%	19.4%
1968	1.8	—	17.1%	21.7%
1969	1.9	—	14.1%	22.3%
1970	2.3	—	13.5%	24.6%

†All sentences were commuted to life imprisonment.
Source: C.H S. Jayewardene, *The Penalty of Death*, 1977: 86.

In addition to murder, the national rates for all violent crimes increased during this period (some more rapidly than murder). As Fattah (1972) pointed out, such observations undermine any confidence in the association between murder and the abolition of hanging. Fattah argued that a whole series of global changes occurred in the social fabric, which contributed to the changes in the homicide rate. These changes were associated with a rise in reports of all violent crimes including attempted murder, wounding, assault, rape and robbery. There were also substantial variations in the rate between provinces from 1962 to 1970, which led Fattah (1972: 191-194) to conclude that the ban on hanging had no discernible consequences for homicide and that ''these rates are conditioned by other factors than the death penalty.'' Among these many changes was the introduction of legal aid. Jayewardene (1977: 60) argues that the existence of legal aid precipitated more aggressive prosecution policies, which in turn fostered a higher likelihood that unexplained sudden deaths would be labelled murder, that suspects would be sought, bargains made, and weak cases downgraded:

> With this orientation, the number of recorded murders would increase. So would the proportion of cases remaining unsolved. The proportion of cases resulting in a conviction of murder would decrease, and the proportion of cases resulting in a conviction of manslaughter would increase (p. 60).

Consequently, the changes in the rate of homicide could merely reflect changes in labelling practices by the police. As Jayewardene notes, when increases in the rate of murders known to the police are compared with the conviction rate for murder, the conviction rate does not drop over time as deterrent theory would suggest, but tends to remain the same or to vary independently of increases in the murder rate.

TABLE 4
Murder Rates and Conviction Rates for Murder
in Canada 1961-1970

Year	Murders Known to the Police†	Proportions Convicted
1961	1.2	.4
1962	1.4	.7
1963	1.4	.6
1964	1.4	.6
1965	1.5	.7
1966	1.3	.5
1967	1.6	.5
1968	1.8	.4
1969	1.9	.6
1970	2.3	.9

†per 100,000 population seven years and over
Source: Jayewardene, 1977: 60.

Canadian Policy on the Death Penalty

The Parliamentary debates that finally abolished the death penalty in 1976 were not the first on this question. During the First World War, Robert Bickerdike spearheaded an abolitionist movement that saw a series of private member's bills to abolish hanging defeated in 1914, 1915 and 1917. His followers introduced similar bills over the next decade (Jayewardene, 1977: 100-102). Following the lead of Great Britain, Canadians reopened the question in 1953. A joint committee of the Canadian Senate and House of Commons was established to investigate capital punishment, corporal punishment and lotteries. In 1956, it recommended in favour of the retention of hanging, but suggested a number of reforms, including abolition of the death penalty for accused under 18 years of age, full disclosure of the Crown case to the accused, the provision of legal counsel, a required plea of not guilty for murder cases and the right of automatic appeal (Chandler, 1976: 18). During this period, the great majority of executions were commuted to life imprisonment; the commutation of death sentences to life imprisonment has been common throughout the twentieth century (Favreau, 1965). In 1967, the House of Commons placed a formal five-year moratorium on the death sentence, except for murders of police officers and prison guards killed in the line of duty. This position was reaffirmed in 1973 by a second vote and, following a similar 1969 vote in Britain, the death penalty was abolished in Canada in 1976. It remains on the books in most US jurisdictions, though executions are extremely rare. The last executions took place in Canada at the Don Jail in Toronto in the early hours of December 19, 1962 when Ronald Turpin and Arthur Lucas were hanged for murder (Anderson, 1973: 78). Between 1950 and 1965 about 70 percent of all capital convictions in Canada were commuted, and from 1963 to 1976 all death sentences were commuted to life imprisonment. The new laws in 1976 replaced the hanging penalty with fixed periods of incarceration of 25 years before eligibility for parole in the case of first-degree murder and 10 years in the case of second-degree murder.

Requirements for an Optimum Deterrent Effect

Though the empirical evidence is quite uneven, few criminologists would deny that, at least in principle, the fear of punishment inhibits criminal behaviour. The problems emerge when this abstract relationship is implemented in practice. A whole range of conditions mediate the relationship and tend to swamp the effect. For this reason there is no fail safe way of testing for the effects of deterrence. A range of factors separate the would-be criminal from his just deserts. For example, do the knowledge of punishment and the risks of apprehension reach the prospective criminal? Certainly the knowledge of sanctions is communicated to the first-time offender and has a *specific* inhibiting or deterrent effect on his subsequent contemplation of criminal acts. And certainly incarceration incapacitates the criminal by removing the opportunity for most crimes. However, what most people are interested in is the *general* deterrent effect — the influence of knowledge about punishment communicated to the population at large through the punishment of individual offenders. This is the more important target area in most studies of deterrence. Presumably deterrence works not merely by incapacitating the small group that gets caught, but by warning the others of the consequences.

However, in exacting any particular type of punishment, another consideration is germane, especially in developing social policies on deterrence. This concerns the *marginal* deterrent effect, that is, the advantage of one kind of punishment over another. For example, studies of the deterrent effect of capital punishment really are studies of the degree to which execution is a *greater* deterrent to murder or a marginally more effective deterrent than life imprisonment. Consequently, in deciding what responses should be made to crime, we are usually concerned with the general, marginal effects of different crime control strategies. Should we fine offenders or lock them up? Should we build prisons or mental hospitals? Should we boil all offenders in oil as a lesson to crime-prone youth; or should we create conditions for full employment, which make petty thievery unattractive? Should we hang murderers, or merely deploy more detectives to ensure that serious criminals are tried and jailed swiftly? Should we emphasize the certainty of arrest by posting rewards for information and beefing up the use of informants, or overcrowd the prisons to ensure the severity of punishment of those who are caught and convicted? At another level, are we prepared to overlook the civil rights of citizens in order to allow the police greater latitude in arresting suspects? Each of these dilemmas is premised on some notion of how deterrence operates in the society and each has enormous implications for how the finite resources of society are expended to control crime.

The deployment of resources also has a feedback aspect, inasmuch as it reinforces the perceived importance of the crimes it is deployed against. Campaigns against prostitutes that round up hookers *en masse* reinforce the idea that prostitution surely needs cleaning up, and the same applies to raids on homosexual bathhouses. On the other hand, the failure to investigate and prosecute corporations and their officers for financial crimes reinforces the impression that there is little here which requires attention. This feedback also operates at the behavioural level. If we adopt a pro-incarceration approach and lock up offenders for long periods of time, we may in the short-term deter crime simply by incapacitation. Indeed few studies of deterrence separate specific deterrence from general deterrence or the deterrent effect versus the incapacitation effect (Cousineau, 1973). Given the harsh conditions of prison life, and the opportunities for acquiring criminal skills and contacts (Letkemann: 1973), the very expensive incarceration option may ensure more criminal behaviour further down the line.

The mere existence of a sanction does not guarantee that criminal impulses will be dissuaded or countered; on the contrary, it may aggravate the situation. Therefore, a number of conditions must be satisfied if the existence of legal punishment is to intimidate would-be criminals while respecting the rights of law-abiding citizens. While not an exhaustive list, some of the relevant factors include the following: a) there must be some effective communication of the sanction to the targeted group, that is, the criminals, and those aspiring to such callings; b) the criminals ought to have a sensitivity or aversion to the risk of crime; c) the risk of apprehension, conviction and punishment must be real or likely; d) the punishment must be serious or painful enough to rationally create an aversion to the prospects of conviction without being so detrimental to the offender as to negate the possibility of rehabilitation; e) the punishment must be swift enough to be connected with the transgression that provoked it; and f) the deterrent factor must be a politically prudent choice that optimizes the control of the criminal target group while at the same time safeguarding the liberties and aspirations of the other sectors of society.

Communication

The communication of what is risked by violating the law is done for the most part via the sentencing of criminals in court. While few members of the lay public have a good grasp of sentence maximums, normal sentence lengths or the value of fines for different crimes, everyone shares a broad understanding that serious crimes like murder entail substantial prison terms while illegal parking will result in a fine. The media publicity given today to important criminal trials reinforces this knowledge, as did the public floggings or executions in previous eras. The use of the pillory and the stocks, which persisted even in 19th-century Canada, also assured the communication of public approbation over deviant behaviour, as did the branding of adulterers and vagrants in earlier periods.

The secrecy with which the penal services in Western countries have conducted capital punishment, disciplinary floggings and regimentation of the lives of convicts, has tended to sanitize punishment, leaving the barbarity and cruelty of these conditions for the novelist to recapture (Capote, 1965; Caron, 1978). By contrast, what is communicated by the judiciary in the courts is the fact that convicted criminals spend time in jail and lose their liberty, not what this deprivation means in terms of the prison experience.

One notable attempt to bridge this gap was the introduction of first-time juvenile offenders to the realities of prison life in the "Scared Straight" program at Rahway Prison in New Jersey. Batches of trouble-prone juveniles were sentenced by juvenile judges to visit a group of "lifers" to have explained to them some of the brutalities of inmate life: sexual exploitation, murder, terrorism and suicide, as well as the primitive 19th-century plumbing and the forced architectural confinement. Though the Scared Straight program appears to have had little long-term effect on the juveniles (Finckenauer, 1982), the graphic documentary based on it has had a significant impact in communicating information to the general public on quality-of-life aspects of the modern prison environment.

One of the few other times members of the public have an opportunity to learn of the inhumane conditions of prisons is in the aftermath of prison riots and prison hostage-taking incidents. But even here, prisoner grievances are frequently censored to guarantee the public integrity of the administration positions (Culhane, 1979). This primary area of the communication of sanctions and the establishment of their credibility in the minds of would-be offenders is glossed over in most studies of deterrence (Henshel and Carey, 1975).

Aversion to Threats of Punishment

The deterrence process central to the economic-rational theory of behaviour is based on an idealized and perhaps overly reflective decision-maker. The criminal is viewed in the same light as the consumer who does comparison shopping to maximize savings. Where the consumer watches for clearance sales, bargains and loss leaders, the would-be criminal monitors clearance rates, conviction rates and penalties. Obviously, this is not done in either case with any great precision. The criminal reacts to subjective information about risk given by such things as news reports of police crackdowns, arrests of accomplices, police patrols and changes in the vulnerability of victims.

However loose this process is, it requires a modicum of reflection and planning. There are several problems with it, however. First of all, not all crimes are rationally planned. Sociologists who have looked for the deterrent effect of execution on murder rates frequently point out that murder is often an expression of extreme emotion undertaken with little reflection of the risk involved or deliberation about the consequences. By contrast, other criminal behaviours are undertaken as a means to an end, as, for example where the cheque forger or embezzler (Nettler, 1982a: 109-112) undertakes his task with careful planning, flair and sophistication in order to support a lifestyle high on the hog. Chambliss (1969: 368-372) suggests that instrumental crimes are more sensitive to threats of punishment than expressive or impulsive acts. It follows that tests of deterrence ought to reflect these different types of behaviour and their respective vulnerability to inhibition. Consequently, we might find robbery-related murder deterred by severe punishment to a greater degree than intrafamilial murder; or we might expect driving offenses deterred to a greater degree than crimes of violence. For example, in his study of a crackdown on parking offenders, Chambliss found a sharp decline in violations when the authorities increased the magnitude of fines and aggressively towed away repeat offenders (1969: 388-93). The cost and inconvenience of getting caught clearly outweighed the short-term benefit of the violation.

In addition to the emotional dimension of the behaviour, there are marked variations in the capacity of offenders to clearly weigh the consequences of crimes whether they be instrumental or affective. The psychopath, sociopath, and schizophrenic tend to be overrepresented in prison populations. An examination of the 85 capital murder cases in Canada from 1957 to 1965 revealed a very high number of defendants who were mentally debilitated. Of the 68 defendants who were examined by psychiatrists, approximately 44% were found to be schizoid, schizophrenic, hysterical, suffering from hallucinations, emotionally unstable, psychopathic, psychotic, chronic alcoholic or of substandard intelligence (Favreau, 1965: 100-103). This indicates that for a significant part of the criminal population, we cannot make the usual assumption about their rationality. Our assumptions about the inhibiting effects of threat and the perception of risk may be mistaken for this subpopulation. The same may apply to those whose normally sound judgement is corrupted by addiction to heroin or other habit-forming drugs. These conditions neutralize the inhibitory aspects of the fear of punishment.

One of the factors that contributes to persistent juvenile delinquency is the absence of strong familial ties and good role models. In addition, control theorists argue that the capacity to resist temptation is distorted by disruptions in the process of socialization.

According to control theorists, juveniles who are crime-prone are qualitatively differ-ent from their contemporaries: they tend to lack a positive self-concept; they lack long-term goals and realistic objectives; they are more prone to frustration and less tolerant of it and so develop patterns of immediate gratification; they are less attached to their parents, and less committed to school and conventional activities (Nettler, 1978: 306-315). The overall impact of these psychological dimensions is that many juvenile delinquents lack internal containment and self-control of their impulses. Again, for the subsample of the criminal population in this condition, the risk of punishment does not carry the same value as for the average person, and so the deterrent process will have less success with these criminals than with others.

Certainty and Severity of Punishment

If would-be criminals were absolutely assured of punishment, the threat of reprisal would surely affect their behaviour, provided of course that the punishment was signifi-cant and that it could not be delayed inevitably. Problems arise when there are doubts attached to these conditions. Waldo and Chiricos (1972) found that undergraduate stu-dents who felt it was unlikely that someone involved in petty theft or someone using marihuana would get arrested were also the ones most likely to steal or to use drugs. In other words, where the probability of punishment was perceived as low, the criminal behaviour was greatest.

Generally speaking, research indicates that lower crime rates are associated with high rates of crimes cleared through arrest, especially in the areas of the more rational offenses (for example, theft and parking violations) as opposed to things like impaired driving. As for severity, it is generally thought that the certainty of apprehension is more important than the severity of punishment (Teevan, 1976). While punishment has to be distasteful to deter, where the probability of apprehension is very low, the penalty becomes abstract and lacks any subjective relevance. The relatively low clear-ance rates for property crimes and the vagaries of the judicial processing of those appre-hended contribute to a lowering of the certainty of punishment. These factors appear to be more influential than how grave the punishment will actually be. Indeed Fattah (1976: 47) suggests that "the social stigma attached to punishment is more powerful as a general deterrent than the length of incarceration." Indeed, the primary worries of juveniles who were asked to rate the things that inhibited them from a range of crimes were, in order of importance, what the family would think, the risk of losing a job, the shame of the court appearance, and finally, the actual punishment (Fattah, 1976: 81). It appears that, above a certain threshold, changes in the penalty become meaningless; the more important factor is the status losses associated with arrest. Hence, severity, while relevant, is of secondary importance compared with certainty.

Other factors relating to changes in severity concern the possibility of increasing the crime rate if penalties become extreme. It has been argued that if the penalty for sexual assault or robbery were life imprisonment, the criminal might be motivated to murder his victims to eliminate any chance of their testifying against him. After all, having drawn one life term for sexual assault, the added life term for murder might be viewed as redundant. The witness may be murdered at no greater liability to the criminal.

On the other hand, if penalties are severe, there is always a reluctance among jurors to convict an offender where it is felt that the punishment to follow would be too extreme. Jurors have often let the guilty go free because convictions involved execution.

Summary

One of the goals of punishment and imprisonment is deterrence. Deterrence is effective where it offsets the benefits or profitability of crime by assuring the criminal of retributions for his conduct. Presumably we deter because we are prepared to be retributive to those who violate laws. However, the relationship between the deterrent influence of punishment and the choice of criminal behaviour is complicated by a number of intervening conditions. Policies that are not communicated cannot deter. The punishment must be meaningful in several respects. It must be serious enough to offset the behaviour of the would-be criminal, yet not so extreme as to prevent convictions by juries or to endanger the lives of victims and witnesses. Also, it must be meaningful to the criminal in the sense that it is seen as certain to occur because of the probability of arrest and conviction. It must be meaningful also in the sense that the penal treatment will be seen to be punitive. Deterrence theory assumes a fairly rational and calculating would-be criminal. However, this assumption is not equally applicable to all criminals. Some are less calculating than others. Also, the model of rationality is not equally applicable to all crimes. The fear of punishment is more liable to inhibit instrumental crimes than expressive crimes. Lastly, in evolving systems of response to crime, deterrence is not the only consideration. The decision to retain or abolish the death penalty, for example, is not premised simply on the belief that it may or may not deter killers. Ethical considerations are also involved, as are considerations of retribution, incapacitation and the protection of society. These are areas that deserve more serious scrutiny.

FURTHER READING

K.L. Avio and C.S. Clark, *Property Crime in Canada: An Econometric Study*. Toronto: University of Toronto Press, 1976.

David Chandler, *Capital Punishment in Canada*. Toronto: McClelland and Stewart, 1976.

Erickson, M.L., J.P. Gibbs and G.F. Jensen, "The deterrence doctrine and the perceived certainty of legal punishments." *American Sociological Review* 42 (1977): 305-17.

James O. Finckenauer, *Scared Straight and the Panacea Phenomenon*. Englewood Cliffs: Prentice-Hall, 1982.

Robert G. Hann, *Deterrence and the Death Penalty: A Critial Review of the Research of Isaac Ehrlich*. Ottawa: Solicitor General, 1976.

G.F. Jensen, "Crime doesn't pay: Correlates of a shared misunderstanding." *Social Problems* 17 (1969): 184:201.

G.F. Jensen, M.L. Erickson and J.P. Gibbs, "Perceived risk of punishment and self-reported delinquency." *Social Forces* 57 (1978): 57-78.

Gwynn Nettler, *Responding to Crime*, Vol. 4 of *Criminal Careers*. Cincinnati: Anderson Publishing, 1982.

H. Lawrence Ross, *Deterring the Drinking Driver: Legal Policy and Social Control*. Lexington: Lexington Books, 1982.

F.E. Zimring and G.J. Hawkins, *Deterrence: The Legal Threat in Crime Control*. Chicago: University of Chicago Press, 1973.

CHAPTER 11

Correctional Services in Canada

The previous chapter dealt with the role of deterrence in preventing crime. However, the actual institutions, processes and structures which undertake this role have never been labelled explicitly with deterrence in mind. Rather than a Department of Punishment and Deterrence we have the Correctional Service of Canada (CSC) and the National Parole Board (NPB). The Correctional Service of Canada was established in 1979 by combining the Canadian Penitentiary Service (CPS) and the National Parole Service (NPS). The CPS was responsible for the federal penitentiaries and the NPS was mandated to supervise parolees from the federal system. Today the NPB makes decisions respecting the granting of parole to applicants from federal and provincial institutions, though some provinces have their own parole boards to review applications from those in provincial jails. This leaves to the CSC the job of incarcerating offenders as well as supervising those who have geen granted some form of conditional release. In this chapter we shall examine the major phases in the correctional sequence, from sentencing to incarceration to conditional release, and the different objectives and records of performance in each of these areas.

Correctional services in Canada are a highly controversial and an enormously costly area of justice. Though they amount to only 21% of federal spending on the whole justice system (Chretien, 1982: 113), federal estimates for 1983-84 put the price tag of the federal correctional services at $667,023,000 (Correctional Services Canada, 1983: 8) while the provinces spend an equivalent amount (Canadian Centre for Justice Statistics, 1983: 7). This puts the annual combined costs at well over one *billion* dollars. Despite this there seems to be an enormous public and professional cynicism about the utility of correctional services (Martinson, 1974). This is backed by a string of inquiries into prison use that have recurrently called for prison reform and for the rehabilitation of offenders. As Gosselin outlines in his study of *Prisons in Canada* (1982) this "paper chain of reports" began in 1849 and continued with reports in 1876, 1920, 1936, 1937, 1965, 1970 and 1973 and ended most recently in 1977. Included were the famous Archambault (1938), Fauteux (1965) and Ouimet (1969) reports, each of which called for progressive reform of correctional services, and each of which retraced many of the recommendations of its predecessors with little consequence (Gosselin, 1982: 30-31). We begin our examination of the correctional sequence with a description of the sentencing process.

Sentencing

Accused persons face a range of sentencing options upon conviction for a crime. These include an option of fine or time in jail, sentences of under two years to a provincial jail, incarceration in a reformatory or training school for juvenile offenders, a penitentiary sentence for those serving a sentence of over two years, a suspended sentence, an order of probation or a discharge of the conviction. Generally speaking, the length of sentence determines whether the accused is incarcerated in a provincial jail or in a federal penitentiary. Sentences of two years or longer typically result in federal incarceration while those that are shorter lead to provincial incarceration. The federal penitentiaries typically house more serious offenders, and are marked by greater interpersonal stress and a stricter regime. However, they also tend to have better defined inmate rights and better recreational and training facilities. Recent agreements between the federal government and the provinces have resulted in the ability of institutions at one level to transfer inmates to the other level, for medical or humanitarian reasons. For example, women sentenced to jail terms over two years are frequently transferred to a local provincial institution rather than to the Women's Prison in Kingston, Ontario. Similarly, provincial inmates may be transferred to a federal institution for medical or psychiatric reasons.

Probation orders, suspended sentences and discharges are methods of exerting control over convicted offenders where the option of paying a fine is thought to be too lenient yet where incarceration is viewed as too harsh. Under a probation order an offender is required to keep the peace and be of good behaviour and to report regularly to a probation officer. In addition, the accused may be required to follow certain stipulations outlined by the judge in the order such as abstaining from alcoholic use, seeking employment, not owning or carrying a weapon, making restitution to a victim or returning before the court on request. A probation order can continue in force for a maximum of three years. Often the probation order will indicate what jail sentence the convicted person is avoiding by complying with the terms of probation. In these cases, the sentence is suspended but may become activated if the convicted person fails to comply with the terms of the probation order. A discharge can also be given in place of a jail sentence if the judge feels that it is in the best interests of the accused and not contrary to the public interest. The discharge, in effect, wipes out the record of the conviction. The discharge may be absolute or conditional. A conditional discharge is a discharge that becomes effective subject to compliance with some requirement specified by the judge. For example, a discharge may be conditional upon making restitution to a victim. Though discharges, suspended sentences and probation orders have slightly different requirements (see Criminal Code of Canada, Sections 662, 633 and 664), these options are generally designed to minimize the incarceration of first-time offenders who commit relatively minor offenses. Lastly, it is important to distinguish probation from parole. Probation is a form of release made possible by a court order *prior* to incarceration while parole is a form of early release available to those already in jail. Consequently, probation is a sentencing option while parole is a form of preparing an inmate for re-assimilation into society after a term of imprisonment. Having reviewed these sentencing options, we can now consider how frequently each is exercised.

TABLE 1
Court Sentences Given For Indictable Offenses, 1973*

	Number	Per Cent of Total
Option of fine	12,983	31.8
Jail under one year	10,008	24.5
Jail one year and over	2,086	5
Reformatory and Training School	1,011	2.5
Penitentiary under two years	7	–
Penitentiary 2-5 years	1,267	3.1
Penitentiary 5-10 years	305	0.7
Penitentiary 10-14 years	66	0.1
Penitentiary 14 years and over	30	0.07
Life Imprisonment	40	0.19
Indeterminate Preventive Detention	3	–
Capital Punishment commuted to Life Imprisonment	1	–
Suspended Sentence without probation	2,355	5.7
Suspended Sentence with probation	9,599	23.5
Total	40,761	100

* Excludes Quebec and Alberta.
Source: Canada Year Book (1980-81).

Table 1 suggests that in 1973 about 4.2% of those convicted of indictable offenses went to federal penitentiaries. Under 30% went to provincial jails. Evidence for 1981-82 indicates that over half of the admissions to provincial jails had sentences less than one month, about one in five was sentenced from one to three months, and only about one in twenty was sentenced to over twelve months. The median average sentence was one month (Canadian Centre for Justice Statistics, 1983: 3). Note that these figures include both first-time and repeat offenders, and that they include only those convicted of indictable, as opposed to summary conviction, offenses.

In addition, there has been a trend away from the use of incarceration in sentencing, especially in less serious offenses. For example, if we examine the period 1964 to 1973, the incarceration rate for theft dropped from 33% to 21%, while for the more serious offense of robbery (which is a form of theft using violence or the threat of violence), the rate remained the same (see Table 2).

One of the chief concerns in studies of sentencing is the lack of uniformity in sentences across different provinces, between rural and urban areas and across different magistrates and judges in any one location. For example, John Hogarth's study, *Sentencing as a Human Process* (1971), documented great disparities in the use of different sentencing options across the various provinces. Some provinces had three times the use of suspended sentences (with and without probation) of other provinces. Some provinces incarcerated over half those convicted, compared to about one-third in other provinces (Hogarth, 1971: 11). Hogarth found similar variations among a sample of 71 Ontario

TABLE 2
Incarceration Rate as a Percentage of Convictions:
Canada, 1964-1973

Year	Incarceration Rate	
	Robbery	Theft
1964	89	33
1966	85	29
1968	90	29
1970	90	23
1972	88	21
1973	87	21

Source: Chretien, 1982: 108.

magistrates. Though each was consistent in the type of sentence given to similar offenders, the magistrates appeared to vary significantly among themselves. Hogarth suggested that he could predict the sentence in a case much more accurately on the basis of knowledge about the judge's attitudes, values and beliefs than he could on the basis of the facts of the case. Lastly, Hogarth discovered that magistrates in rural parts of Ontario tended to be more lenient in sentencing similar offenders than their counterparts in the urban areas. To the extent that the facts of the cases were similar, the observations about differences in sentence are grave. However, critics of this type of research suggest that the degree to which cases in different areas and before different judges are similar is open to question. For example, Chiricos and Waldo (1970) suggest that when one controls for criminal record and the seriousness of the offense, alleged differences arising from extralegal attributes tend to diminish or disappear. Similarly, Hagan's study of the incarceration of native people in Alberta suggests that there is little evidence that natives are sentenced more punitively than others (Hagan, 1975). Nonetheless, a high rate of native incarceration in provincial institutions results from default of payment of fines (Hagan, 1974). In other words, the burden of fines seems to be inordinate for natives and results in extremely high rates of incarceration. In addition, Hagan (1974) discovered that native (versus white) status was correlated with previous arrests and that low socioeconomic status was associated with the seriousness of the initial charge. This suggests that natives faced more serious charges than whites and tended to face them with more significant criminal records. Consequently, differential treatment for natives operated prior to the sentencing appearance. Contrary to these findings, research in the United States suggests that even controlling for the offense type and criminal record, differences appeared at the point of sentencing as natives received harsher penalties than whites (Hall and Simkus, 1975), as did blacks compared to whites (Lizotte, 1978).

In addition to the influence of extralegal factors on sentence severity, there is a whole grey area in which the social characteristics of the offender result in class biases in sentencing. For example, Warner and Renner (1978) found that the severity of sentences depended not solely on criminal record and the seriousness of the charge, but on gender and employment status. Mandel (1983a) reviewed a series of Canadian sentencing decisions in which social worth as calculated by employment status, social status and community contributions, has been invoked to justify less harsh sentencing of offenders. This policy, which has become part of the case law regarding sentencing, obviously works to the detriment of the unemployed and the lower status. The conflicting penal objectives of denunciation of the crime, rehabilitation of the offender and deterrence of potential offenders allow the judiciary to punish the poor in the name of denunciation while treating the well-to-do with kid gloves in the name of rehabilitation. This is evidenced in the recurrent idea that high-status offenders have suffered enough by virtue of the publicity of a trial and, consequently, do not require a punitive period of incarcerartion. This may amount to a self-fulfilling prophecy in that the lenient treatment of prominent offenders prevents their dislocation from society, thereby resulting in evidence of rehabilitation, while the poor, who bear the brunt of incarceration, experience dislocation, problems of reintegration and higher rates of recidivism. In light of this, Mandel suggests that imprisonment should be viewed not so much as a way of preventing crime, but of maintaining the social order which is marked by class inequalities. Put briefly, of all those who contravene the law, those sections of society most marginal in terms of their productivity in the context of capitalist entreprise become the chief candidates for imprisonment during the sentencing sequence. This is made possible by the enormous latitude given to the judiciary in arriving at a sentence and the desirability of tailoring justice to the specific circumstances of the crime and the offender. While the idea of devising a punishment to suit the crime is laudable, the systematic class bias that taints the sentencing process is objectionable in a democratic state. It violates the expectation that the law be applied uniformly. Similarly, the requirement of uniformity before the law should not be subverted because of changes in government policy that *create* unemployment in the name of defeating inflation. Notably those persons most liable to imprisonment are currently from the age group most likely to face unemployment as a direct result of the recession and government measures to offset inflation. Recall from the analysis of econometric models of crime and deterrence that low levels of employment opportunity were associated with high levels of criminal conduct. This suggests that since the employment record of the accused figures strongly in the sentencing decision, macroeconomic factors, which have different effects on different classes, can introduce class distortions in the decision to incarcerate.

Prisons in Canada

Historical research indicates that prisons are a relatively recent method of social control in western countries. In 18th century Europe, there was a wholesale reliance on execution for a range of grave as well as minor offenses. There was also enormous ingenuity in devising painful methods of execution and torture. Capital punishment was inflicted by hanging, drawing and quartering, by burying, burning or stoning, by boiling or by drowning. Minor offenses were met with fines, though offenders were also frequently forced on public display in the stocks. Whipping, mutilation and branding were also widely used for a range of offenses. Banishment, or transportation to the colonies, was likewise employed until the mid-19th century (Edmison, 1976). Nonetheless, research indicates that even in the harshest periods of penal history there were significant variations between different countries and over time in each country (see Knafla, 1981). The existence of capital punishment and even sentencing did not guarantee executions. In fact, from the mid-18th century onwards European justice started to liberalize. This took many forms including a new attitude towards the treatment of the convicted. Rather than brutalizing the convicted by torture or execution, places of confinement were built. They were termed "penitentiaries" because they were thought to promote penance, contrition and reformation. They provided isolation of the individual to promote contemplation in order to foster moral reform, as well as work, in order to avoid the idleness that was thought to promote crime. Religious orders had, from the middle ages, employed similar systems of individual confinement to overcome difficulties of conformity experienced by their members. Reflecting this tradition, the individual cells in the now civil system were often termed "reformatories" (Gosselin, 1982: 58). Kingston Penitentiary, which opened in 1835 with a capacity of 370 inmates, initially confined the inmates in some of the smallest cells ever constructed in the New World: six feet eight inches long by two and a half feet wide and six feet high. These cages were marginally expanded as later Canadian penitentiaries built cells four feet wide by eight feet long by eight feet high. Calder (1981: 301) indicates that inmates in the first Canadian penitentiaries were typically locked up for 12 hours per day.

The organization of life within the penitentiary system evolved from models developed in the US. In 1829, the Cherry Hill Penitentiary in Philadelphia, Pennsylvania, devised a system characterized by individualized cell lock-ups, a regime of required labour, religious counselling and inmate isolation. Under the Auburn model, developed in New York State, prisoners were isolated at night, but put to work collectively during the day, albeit under a regime of strict silence. The Pennsylvania system was adopted widely in Europe while the Auburn system was adopted throughout North America.

In British North America there existed little public concern over serious crime until the 1820s, when there was a significant influx of immigrants, most notably from Ireland. The religious, class and value differences between the new and the previous settlers promoted a concern for social control and incarceration (Bellomo, 1972).

By the time of Confederation in 1867 three penitentiaries had been built in Canada: at Kingston, Ontario, St. John, N.B., and Halifax, N.S. Other regional penitentiaries appeared in Montreal in 1873, Stoney Mountain, Manitoba in 1876, New Westminster, B.C. in 1878 and Prince Albert, Saskatchewan in 1911 (Griffiths, Klein and Verdun-Jones, 1980: 204). Though contemporary social critics find enormous problems with the nature and effects of modern penitentiaries, these institutions were at least in their inception superior to the physical brutalities that characterized earlier forms of punishment and were more rational in terms of classifying and separating different types of offenders. Baehre (1977) suggests that the jails that preceded the age of penitentiaries threw together in common quarters the insane, the misfit, the career criminal, the debtor, the prostitute, the young and those detained for trial.

With the new penal philosophy came a more rational classification of offenders, as well as more constructive employment of the inmates' time. Nonetheless, life remained purposefully harsh for those behind bars. Discipline was enforced by the use of corporal punishment, isolation and deprivation of privileges. The penitentiary food and routine were disturbingly unvaried. Cell plumbing was unknown and inmates used night buckets and washed infrequently. To make matters worse, communicable diseases, such as typhoid fever, proved to be a dire problem in prisons. On the social side, inmates were sometimes subjected to physical brutalities and immoral treatment by the penitentiary operators and inmate mail was capriciously intercepted (Calder, 1981: 306-307). Predictably, inmates staged many disturbances. For example, a riot broke out in 1867 at the Halifax Penitentiary and troops were summoned to restore order. A similar revolt was forestalled in 1889 at Kingston Penitentiary when fully armed troops were paraded in the prison yard in anticipation of the disturbance. In 1886 in Montreal at St. Vincent de Paul Penitentiary over 40 inmates participated in an incident in which several prisoners seized prison officials and their revolvers and narrowly missed freeing themselves but for the show of force of a battery of armed guards (Calder, 1981: 313). However enlightened the new penitentiaries were on paper, they created punitive and stressful experiences for the inmates and motivated the same sort of violent demonstrations against authority that are witnessed in contemporary penitentiary situations.

The Modern Prison Picture

Where pre-Confederation Canada had three penitentiaries, the current system has 62. These are divided about equally between maximum, medium, minimum and community correctional services. In 1979-80 the average daily count of inmates at the federal level was just over 9,000. Of those actually in prisons (as opposed to a community correctional centre) approximately 40% were in maximum security, 47% in medium security and 13% in minimum security (Gosselin, 1982: 130). In 1979-80 approximately 6,700 people were on parole or mandatory supervision from federal institutions (National Work Group on Justice Information and Statistics, 1981: 7). By comparison with American institutions, Canadian penitentiaries are relatively small with maximum inmate populations under 500 (Bowker, 1982: 396ff). In addition to inmate populations, the prisons are operated by correctional staff. In 1978/79, for approximately 9,500 inmates there were about 8,000 correctional workers, or about 83 staff for every 100 inmates (Chretien, 1982: 118).

In terms of the national rate of imprisonment, historical and comparative data indicate that Canadians have traditionally incarcerated a higher proportion of their fellow citizens than most other democracies except the US.

TABLE 3
Rates of Persons in Adult Prisons
Per 100,000 Total Population:
Selected Countries: 1900, 1960 and Recent Year

	1900	1960	1970	Recent Year
Canada	81.9	96.5	90.3	96.9 (1980)
Australia	52.9	77.9	90.0	63.3 (1980)
England-Wales	81.7	58.1	80.2	85.1 (1980)
France	64.9	61.6	59.5	66.7 (1980)
Japan	–	77.2	46.0	43.0 (1978)
Netherlands	143.3	28.3	17.7	24.6 (1978)
USA	128.8*	192.9	175.8	207.3 (1978)

Note: The estimate of average daily population is usually based on a calendar year or fiscal year end, or census estimate.
* 1890
Source: Chretien, 1982: p. 104.

The Canadian rate of incarceration between 1890 and 1980 has not fluctuated consistently up or down over time, but has tended to remain fairly stable, reaching its highest point during the Great Depression and its lowest point at the turn of the century (Chretien, 1982: 100).

The Regime of Incarceration

The immediate point of incarceration is to remove offenders from society so as to deprive them of their liberty. However, removal to jails and penitentiaries is associated with a host of other pains. The physical conditions of incarceration include loss of privacy, physical restriction to the prison and control of movement within it, confinement in limited spaces and overcrowding, as well as the routinization of experience. These are not so much effects of imprisonment, as correlates of physical confinement (McKay et al, 1979). Sykes (1958) suggests that loss of liberty is painful not merely because of physical confinement, but because of the psychological sense of rejection by and isolation from the free community. The incarcerated are not merely removed from society but deprived of access to and support from family and friends. Contrary to the design, the loss of liberty does not make those incarcerated in penitentiaries into penitants.

Sykes (1958: 65-78) cites several further areas of deprivation that accompany loss of liberty: deprivation of access to goods and services, deprivation of heterosexual relations, deprivation of autonomy and deprivation of security. Part of one's liberty in the free community is the right to own material goods: furniture, a car, a stereo, records, books, clothing, food, liquor and the like. Except for some clothes, the inmate is separated from these material goods as well, and more importantly is separated from the status and ego value that such material goods can furnish. By way of replacement, the inmate is entitled to the material goods and services provided by the institution, to institutional food, institutional entertainment, furniture and bedding. Regarding the loss of heterosexual contact, Sykes points out that this can be enormously stressful not merely because sexuality is a basic human need, but because the homosexuality that is fostered in the absence of heterosexuality calls into question the inmate's self-conception, and fosters coercive and exploitive relationships. Programs of conjugal visits available to some inmates who are seeking re-assimilation into the free community lessen the stress associated with this area of deprivation, though, as we shall see, this may give rise to other areas of tension.

Loss of autonomy and loss of security are further pains of imprisonment. Autonomy is lost by subjecting inmates to the rigid and repetitive daily timetabling of events, the fixed scheduling of meals, work time, free time and exercise, the begrudging deference to authority and control by institutional rules. It is further exacerbated by a lack of control over institutional procedures and decisions for early or conditional release. Also, the penitentiary authorities may shuffle an inmate from one institution in one region to another one elsewhere without the inmate's consent; in 1980-81, this, in fact, was the largest source of inmate complaints (Correctional Investigator, 1982). But there are other areas where lack of control creates stress: delay of and/or interference with mail and visits, lack of access to desired medical care, random searches of cells for contraband, harrassment, movement of cell assignment, disregarded claims for injury and lost property, unsatisfactory treatment by staff and lack of meaningful programmes.

In addition to lack of autonomy, a loss of the sense of security comes with incarceration. Despite inmate solidarity, the penitentiaries house some of society's most violent individuals. One of the problems of being the victim of inmate violence is that the victim is under pressure from other inmates to avoid bringing the problem to the prison staff. A victimized inmate is expected to deal with this problem by an act of revenge. Alternatively, the inmate can seek to be removed from the general population to either a protective custody or a dissociation unit, both of which entail further limitations of movement, contact and institutional freedom. The threat of violence and the lack of legitimate methods of dealing with it contribute to an underlying and pervasive atmosphere of insecurity. This insecurity is reflected in the record of penitentiary violence. In discussing program effectiveness, Correctional Service Canada (1983: 19) reported some trends in security-related incidents. In the three-year period from 1979 to 1982, there were approximately 27 murders and 10 known attempted murders in federal penitentiaries. During the same period there were approximately 150 major assaults on inmates by other inmates and 35 major assaults on staff. There were approximately 155 attempted suicides, 40 completed suicides and 18 hostage-taking incidents (also see McKay et al, 1979: 43). Since the daily penitentiary population over this period averaged approximately 9,000 inmates, these rates of violence are enormously high compared to those for the general population. However, they are probably not surprising given the makeup of the penitentiary population and the deprivations under which this population lives.

Adaptation

In 1940 Donald Clemmer published his study of *The Prison Community*, in which he identified a process of socialization to prison life by which inmates developed patterns of mutual dependence, mutual reliance and a shared outlook. The development of this inmate subculture was identified as the chief reason for inmate incorrigibility. The inmate code as described by Sykes and Messinger (1970: 402-403) specified a number of rules to be observed by inmates: don't interfere with other guys, don't squeal, don't lose your head, be cool, don't exploit other inmates, don't be weak, and don't be a sucker. In addition to this set of shared rules, studies of inmate subculture identified some of the special terms or argot developed to describe the roles and experiences of prison inmates. As Sykes (1958: 84) noted, "prison argot . . . provides a map of the inmates social system." Inmates in the New Jersey prison studied by Sykes distinguished between "rats" or "squealers" who snitched for personal gain as opposed to "center men" who cooperated with institution officials, including informing on other inmates, because they shared the administration's perspective on the inmates. In the domain of exchanges of what little materials and possessions that were allowed to inmates, a distinction was drawn between the "gorilla" and the "merchant." The "gorilla" exploited the weaker inmates by thieving their goods while the "merchant" set himself up as a hustler of institutional stores and contraband. "Wolves, punks and fags" characterized the various sexual roles played by different inmates in homosexual contacts. "Ballbusters, real men, hipsters and toughs" characterized different personality styles reflecting various kinds of accommodations to the trials and tribulations of everyday life in the institution. In his autobiographical account of life behind bars in various Canadian institutions, Roger Caron (1978) provides a small glossary of inmate argot among prison inmates today. One of the key functions of argot is that it allows subcultural members who share it to map the world in the same way, and, like a vernacular language or accent, to distinguish from the expressions people use whether they are part of the inmate subculture or not (Wieder, 1974).

Theories of the Inmate Subculture

There are two important sources of the inmate subculture. The first, called the importation model, argues that the backgrounds of inmates are already similar prior to incarceration, that those who find themselves behind bars have already experienced a common rejection of normative lifestyles in addition to a well-developed subculture of violence (Thomas and Foster, 1973). The second theory, called the deprivation model, does not deny the common background and experience of inmates, but complements it. This theory, as outlined in Goffman's study of *Asylums* (1961), argues that total institutions, that is, institutions that provide for the total lifestyle and care of individuals, whether in prisons, mental hospitals, army boot camps or boarding schools, produce mortification of inmates by virtue of the standardization of procedures required when large batches of inmates are controlled by a small number of staff. Mortification, the sense of profound anxiety and ego insecurity, results from stripping away from individuals their privacy, autonomy, personal belongings, freedom of movement, sense of security and other external social supports. This is usually done without any malicious intent, the chief factor being organizational expediency. In response to such circumstances, individuals devise various defensive strategies to neutralize the effects of and to insulate themselves from the institution or to attack and/or coopt its agents. For Goffman, the convict code is a strategy to recover some of the sense of integrity, meaningfulness, self-direction and control that is removed by virtue of the standardization within total institutions. The inmate solidarity, the antagonism of the institution's staff, the subversion of its aims and the cooption of its materials, supplies and programs return some measure of control to those who have otherwise been stripped of it, and with this measure of control, some sense of autonomy and self-worth.

Total institutions must foster basic creature comforts. However, MacKay et al (1979: 53ff) indicate that the provision of creature comforts must extend beyond the provision of rudimentary shelter and food. Incarceration must be responsive to the full range of comforts and stimulations that are fundamental to human experience. They identify several requisites of comfort: 1) recognition status, or ego's need to obtain a sense of worth from others; 2) dominance, or ego's need to have others respond to his ideas and plans; 3) independence; 4) protection-dependency, or ego's needs to have others protect his interests; 5) love and affection; and lastly, 6) physical comfort. In terms of Goffman's account of total institutions, inmates in most prisons are liable to be given a modicum of physical comfort by the institution but little in the way of personal recognition, personalized attention, independence, protection or affection. On the other hand, the underlife in total institutions is rarely fully adequate for developing sound and equitable substitutes for these things. This is reflected in the high rates of violence and pathology described earlier. One area of prison life that has become increasingly problematic in this regard in the past decade and a half is the prison riot.

Disturbances in Canadian Penitentiaries

Disturbances and riots by inmates of federal penitentiaries and provincial jails are becoming increasingly frequent. In the 42-year period between 1932 and 1974, there were 65 major incidents in federal institutions, or about 1.5 per year (McGuigan et al, 1977: 5). For the 10-year period 1971-1980, there were 193 disturbances, of which 68 were classified as violent (Ellis, 1982: 3) giving annual figures of 19.3 and 6.8 disturbances per year. This means that considering violent incidents alone, disturbances were occurring about four-and-one-half times as frequently during the 1970s compared to the prior period. The 1970s also witnessed some of the most violent and costly disturbances in Canadian history. In April 1971, inmates rioted, seizing control of the Kingston Penitentiary and six guard hostages (Desroches, 1974). A number of sex offenders, child abusers and squealers were chained to chairs in a circle under the central dome of the institution and were systematically beaten and tortured by the other inmates. Two died as a result of the ordeal. Before the institution was recaptured with the help of the army, prisoners tore apart the concrete and steel cell blocks. Similarly, in the summer of 1982, at the Archambault institution in Montreal, three guards were killed and two of the inmate leaders committed suicide during the most violent riot in Canadian penal history. In the spring of 1983, $2.5 million damages were done in the wake of a riot at the Prince George provincial institution in BC, and $5 million damages were done at Matsqui Institution, also in BC, in 1981 (Aubin et al, 1983).

In the US similar watershed riots occurred. In 1971, at the maximum-security institution at Attica in New York State, scores of prisoners were shot dead by national guardsmen who stormed the overcrowded institution to restore order. In 1980, the worst prison riot in US history occurred at the penitentiary at Sante Fe, New Mexico. Inmates inflicted over $60 million in damages to the prison, and, in addition, tortured dozens of sex offenders and squealers with blow torches and cruel physical beatings, killing 33 of them (Reid, 1981: 45). Both the Attica and Santa Fe institutions are over twice the size of Canada's largest penitentiaries.

In his study of Canadian penitentiary disturbances during the 1970s, Desmond Ellis (1982) points out several of their important characteristics. First of all, they occur disproportionately at the maximum as opposed to the medium security level: the maximum security institutions reported five times as many incidents as the medium security institutions (Ellis, 1982: 7). Secondly, though they changed in character, they occurred more and more frequently toward the end of the decade compared to the beginning. Ellis notes that the later disturbances, while more frequent, involved fewer inmates on average at each incident and the incident took a shorter time period to resolve.

The 1977 McGuigan inquiry into penitentiary disturbances suggested that the cause of these disturbances was a lack of discipline and a breakdown in authority within the institutions. The argument advanced was that the open rivalry between guard unions, inmate committees and the prison administration calls into question the legitimacy of the institution and its rules and programmes, and erodes the inmates' inhibitions about bucking the institution. Add to this the deprivations and the perceived arbitrariness of institutional decisions which motivate inmates to reject the regime. Throw in an increasing number of lifers and long-sentence inmates, inmates who have little to lose from a disturbance. Finally, add a rapid turnover in the post of wardens and a shortage of experienced guards. These various elements constitute a recipe for increasing defiance of prison authority and with it, the violent and destructive outbursts that have marked the maximum-security institutions for the past decade and a half.

Several of these items were critical in events preceding the 1971 riot at the Kingston Penitentiary. According to the Swackhamer inquiry (1971), tension was extremely high before the riot because of programme curtailment. The Kingston Penitentiary was shortstaffed because of the transfer of staff to the new maximum security institution at Millhaven. Also a general shortage of staff in the system caused an in-transfer of many inmates from medium security institutions. The staff retained at Kingston was, on the whole, less experienced, and poorly equipped to deal with the large number of discipline problems confined at Kingston. To make matters worse, the warden's repeated communications to the Solicitor General about the explosive atmosphere at Kingston and the need for special assistance were disregarded (Ellis, 1982: 17-18).

Ellis argues that the McGuigan inquiry's solutions to the problem of disturbances and the Solicitor General's response to them are questionable. The then Solicitor General, Francis Fox (1977), expressly rejected some proposals that would have given individual wardens more autonomy in dealing with their institutions, proposals that would have counteracted the trend toward an anonymous bureaucratic administration. In other words, centralization of policy contributes to the grass root sense that the warden is just a 9 to 5 civil servant relaying messages from Ottawa, and that nobody is really in charge. The turnover in the top personnel administering the institutions reinforces this view. While these factors appear to create conditions favourable to prison riots, Ellis stresses the importance of another feature of the bureaucratization of prisons. Ellis (1982: 24-25) argues that the variable that best corresponds to the changing pattern of disturbances during the 1970s is the number of rules and reforms added to or modified by the penitentiary bureaucracy. The number of rules and reforms of penitentiary administration reflects the distribution of disturbances throughout the 1970s very closely. While reforms and regulations are designed with the idea of bringing practices in line with institutional and public policy ideals, they have the unintended consequence of creating staff insecurity, of creating banks of inmate grievances and of creating disorganization in the prison subculture. These changes produce an "increase in the probability, not just of disturbances, but of disturbances involving violence" (Ellis, 1982: 25). This applies even to such reforms as the Living Unit designed to facilitate domestic contacts between inmates and their families.

If Ellis is correct about the source of prison disturbances, the future of prisons is not bright. Public concern over high-profile criminals like the child slayer, Clifford Olsen, is creating a call for more punitive penal treatment. Similarly, there is a trend toward the construction of super-maximum security institutions, which will virtually isolate inmates in controlled, solitary environments until their release. The changes, whether as reforms or more punitive regimes, will multiply the rules and regulations, will create new role difficulties for guards, will subject inmates to the latest popular penal philosophy, will bottleneck more of the serious violent offenders in prison for longer periods and thereby create the elements required to foster more violent disturbances.

Release from Prison

The formal objective of correctional services in Canada is to administer sentences imposed by the courts and to prepare inmates for their eventual return to the community as responsible citizens (Correctional Service Canada, 1983: 10). This objective expressly reflects a move away from the medical model of incarceration, which lies at the foundation of the idea of incarceration as rehabilitative treatment. The medical model suggests that criminals are sick or maladapted creatures who require therapeutic intervention to change their behaviour, and that this need forms the basis of the deprivation of their liberty. The McGuigan report (1977: 37) rejected this approach and suggested that the programmes devised for prison inmates create opportunities for them to initiate their own course of personal reformation. This shifted the onus for reformation from the institutions and its programmes to the shoulders of the inmates. This stance differs from the earlier Archambault report of 1938 and the Fauteux report of 1956, which stressed the necessity for penitentiaries to rehabilitate and reform inmates (Griffiths, Klein and Verdun-Jones, 1980: 240). A similar trend away from rehabilitation was expressed in the Law Reform Commission study of *Imprisonment and Release* (1975c), which questioned the ability of prisons to foster rehabilitation. The Law Reform Commission argued that imprisonment should be imposed only in the most serious circumstances to separate a dangerous offender from society, to denounce the values expressed by reprehensible criminal behaviour or to control offenders who ignored other sanctions imposed by the courts. The Commission did not denounce rehabilitation, it merely argued that this should not be a reason for depriving someone of liberty, especially in view of the lack of evidence that prisons, as currently organized, are rehabilitative in a systematic way. As noted, correctional philosophy has moved to a position which creates opportunities for inmates to better themselves while at the same time both carrying out the sentence of the courts and preparing the inmate for reassimilation into the community.

What is the overall effectiveness of incarceration? Does prison work? To the average person these would seem to be straightforward questions, yet in view of the differing objectives of incarceration, it is necessary to identify performances in terms of the various institutional objectives. As a method of protecting the public by depriving the offender of liberty, one measure of success of prison is the percentage of those incarcerated who remain in custody until lawfully released, or stated as a measure of failure, the number of unlawful departures or escapes from correctional custody. Correctional Service Canada (1983: 20) reports that from 1978 to 1982 the average annual figures show just over 20 escapees per 1000 inmates. This average figure is composed of scores of walk-away escapes from minimum security institutions (over 150 per 1000 in 1981-82), to a tiny handful of escapes from the maximum security institutions (about 1.8 per 1000 in 1981-82). Assuming the motive to escape is similar at both types of institutions, the maximum security rates obviously show a virtually impenetrable regime of containment. On the other hand, from a public policy perspective, where security is least stringent and where the greatest number of offenders go unlawfully at large, they pose the smallest hazard to the public. In other words, the minimum security inmates are by definition the least dangerous, although they are the group most frequently to escape custody.

Aside from the immediate protection of the public through the incarceration of offenders, what evidence is there of a longer term protection, or in the words of the mandate of Correctional Services, what evidence is there that offenders are "prepared" to return to the community? One measure is the rate of recidivism, that is, the percentage of institutional releases who are re-admitted to penitentiary as a result of another conviction at a later date. Correctional Service Canada suggests that "if recidivism is going to occur, it usually takes place within five years; and more commonly two" (1983: 21). Examining evidence from the six years between 1972 and 1977 suggests that the recidivism rate dropped slightly from 31% of those released in the year 1972 to 27% of those released in 1977 (Correctional Service Canada, 1983: 21). It is very difficult to draw conclusions about programme effectiveness from this change. One of the inherent problems with measures of recidivism is that the shorter the period of measurement, the smaller the rate of recidivism. Consequently, when we compare the performance of recent populations with those of previous populations, we tend to have a more complete record of how an earlier group has performed, while a more recent group, which shows less evidence of unlawful behaviour, may subsequently return to crime. To control for this, we ought to compare recidivism during equivalent periods of time. Presuming that this has in fact been done in the 1972 and 1977 periods, the apparent reduction in the rate of recidivism is significant. However, it may have several sources.

It may reflect changes in the outlook of the individual offender by which he presumably avoids or reduces his unlawful behaviour, or at least takes greater steps to avoid getting caught. Alternately, it may reflect changes in the behaviour or makeup of the police, the judiciary and/or the parole authorities resulting in less crime being officially recognized and/or the greater use of non-penitentiary sanctions for those who are apprehended. However, as we saw in our discussion of the police, despite relatively stable conviction records for indictable offenses, there has been a significant increase in the per capita size of police forces, making the certification of crime more probable, and consequently making the return of repeat offenders to penitentiary more likely. Yet in terms of recidivism, the opposite has occurred. In addition, in our discussion of deterrence, we saw that major policy shifts do not exert significant effects on criminal behaviour as witnessed by the abolition of capital punishment. In that case, research indicated that changes in the frequency of crimes appeared to be controlled by global factors such as the economy and the age profile of a population. The lesson to be drawn is that the minor decrease in the rate of recidivism between 1972 and 1977 probably has little to do with changes in the operation of the penitentiary and its effects on inmates, and more to do with factors beyond its control, such as the aging of the penitentiary population. For whatever reasons, the trend toward a decrease in the recidivism rates, while not grounds for being optimistic about penitentiary treatment, is certainly not grounds for pessimism.

In addition to confinement within an institution, the correctional service operates a series of conditional release programmes which fulfill a variety of aims. We shall examine what these programs consist of and how they operate.

Conditional Release

Temporary Absence. This programme of short-term release may be granted after an inmate has served six months or one-sixth of the sentence (whichever is longer). These may be escorted or unescorted releases and are given for a variety of reasons. About three quarters are designated as "rehabilitative" and involve such things as attendance at sport activities, community service projects or family visits. These are pursued to help the inmate reintegrate into the community. The rest are given for medical, humanitarian or administrative reasons. Despite the drain on manpower, about three quarters of all TAs are escorted (Working Group, 1981: 5). Generally, the warden of a penitentiary may grant an escorted TA for up to five days: in certain circumstances, the warden and the NPB may grant unescorted TAs for rehabilitative purposes for up to 72 hours each quarter. In each case, the release is conditional upon a decision that it will not constitute an undue risk to society. About 50,000 TAs are granted annually, and about half of all inmates will receive at least one TA. The *Solicitor General's Study of Conditional Release* indicates that only 0.5% of cases between 1976 and 1980 ended in outright failure; that is, about 15 cases per year result in a failure to return and a declaration that the inmate was unlawfully at large (Working Group, 1981: 5).

Day Parole. There is little systematic information regarding this form of release. Day parole may involve residence in a minimum security penitentiary, accommodation in a halfway house, or private accommodation in a private residence in the community. Consequently, day parole can take many forms; under some arrangements inmates will be released from prison during the day for work, or may be de facto fully paroled with requirements to periodically report to correctional officials. Day parole can be granted after an inmate has served one-sixth of the sentence and is generally granted for a four-month period, and may be renewed, but the inmate's day parole programme will not last longer than 12 months. During 1976-1980 about 15,000 day paroles were granted and the majority concluded without incident; 18% were terminated by correctional authorities for unsatisfactory and/or illegal inmate behaviour (Working Group, 1981: 6). Up until 1973, TAs were awarded at the warden's discretion and were frequently given back to back, providing for six-day releases. In 1977, Parliament introduced the minimum eligibility requirement for TA and limited unescorted TAs to 72 hours per quarter. With these restrictions, the utilization of the TA programme has dropped since 1978 to about one third of its previous level (Working Group, 1981: 49). At the same time, the utilization of day parole has increased dramatically. Both day parole and TA provide a number of functions and effects: they allow the wardens to reward and encourage the good conduct of inmates; they provide a break from incarceration while still maintaining control over the inmate; they can be used to relieve institutional tension and overcrowding; they provide evidence of the inmate's responsibility while at large on a limited basis; they can be used to mitigate harsh sentences, to allow inmates to participate in community employment or treatment opportunities. The *Solicitor General's Study of Conditional Release* suggested that there ought to be greater utilization of TAs "to offset the debilitating effects of incarcertion, to provide a 'break' from imprisonment, and to reduce overall levels of institutional tension" (Working Group, 1981: 52). The study also deplored the wide disparities between regional utilization of these programs. The Working Group similarly criticized the lack of clear guidelines for eligibility and the lack of reasons given for refusal.

Full Parole. In 1959, the Parole Act was proclaimed by Parliament establishing the NPB, and creating opportunities for conditional release under supervised parole. Parole replaced a form of release created at the turn of the century under which certain offenders were returned to the community under a "ticket of leave" (Griffiths, Klein and Verdun-Jones, 1980: 258-59). Under the provisions of parole, inmates generally are eligible for consideration after serving one third of their sentences; those granted parole usually serve approximately 40% of their sentence. However, not everyone who serves the required time seeks or is granted parole. In fact, only about 33% of those who had satisfied the time requirement in 1979-80 had received parole by 1981 (Working Group, 1981: 7). As Macnaughton-Smith (1976) pointed out, prior to recent changes in the law, that slight freedom granted to parolees was extremely precarious for an offender whose parole was revoked for failure to observe its conditions by commission of an indictable offense. Such individuals were returned to prison to serve all of the sentence that remained outstanding before parole, and simultaneously lost all of the statutory remission of sentence that had already been awarded before parole, and which would have resulted in early release whether parole had been granted or not. This meant that offenders who experienced parole revocation would be returned to prison to serve out their sentences without any credit or allowance for either the successful time spent on parole or for the earned remission gained before parole. Changes in the law now give credit for the good time spent on parole. Also, as of 1977, the NPB could recredit the earned remission previously accumulated by the inmate prior to parole, though they appear to be reluctant to do so (Working Group, 1981: 88). These changes have removed some of the more objectionable aspects of the handling of parole violations.

Part of the revisions of the parole legislation effectively extended parole coverage to those who would have been released early by virtue of the earned remission of sentences. Time reduced under this programme is served under mandatory supervision, which will be described below. Those who are awarded parole by the NPB are subject to supervision by a parole officer. They may be required to remain in the area designated by the parole office and, in some jurisdictions, to report periodically to the police. In addition, they are forbidden to carry or own a gun, cannot incur debts or marry and are required to work or seek work. Generally, parolees undergo three stages of supervision involving periods of intensive, active and finally periodic contact with parole supervisors. Transitions between the levels of supervision reflect the decreased perception of risk to the community posed by the parolee as well as the parole officers' case loads. Since most parole officers handle case loads in excess of 100 parolees, and are required to undertake extensive paper work in processing and monitoring those under supervision (Working Group, 1981: 78-79), it has been suggested that little therapeutic benefit can really be expected from such contacts, and that they are little more than an administrative control of releases, creating opportunities for self-help.

At any time there are some 3000 persons under supervision by the NPB. Most periods of parole last between one and two years. Some 1500 to 2000 inmates are awarded parole annually. What is the success rate of parole? First of all, it must be noted that parole may be revoked for breaking one of the administrative conditions of release mentioned earlier. In addition, parole may be revoked to "protect society" (Parole Act, 16 (1)), or may be revoked where the parole officer strongly suspects that the parolee has committed a crime. Lastly, parole is forfeited outright where a criminal charge has been laid against the parolee. However, in certain non-criminal cases the revocation is for only a day or two where, for instance, there is evidence of excessive drinking or some transitory disorder. The Parole Act allows the parole officer to cancel revocation of parole for up to 14 days after initial decision. After that, a formal hearing is held by the NPB to determine if there are grounds to revoke parole. This flexibility allows the parole officer control over short-lived problems without jeopardizing the parolee's status permanently.

If we examine the percentage of a cohort of inmates who have been granted parole and who are returned to penitentiary before the end of the supervisory period, we have some measure of the success, or rather, the failure rate of this programme. Note that this measure gives a fairly conservative indication of success because it counts as failures those who have merely violated the administrative conditions of release, as well as those who have broken the criminal laws. The *Solicitor General's Study of Conditional Release* reports that "the return rate for full paroles granted in 1973-75 (of which almost all have now been completed) average 26% (including 16% for new criminal convictions). An additional 4 to 5% of parolees later returned to penitentiary on a new criminal charge" at a later date (Working Group, 1981: 7). This suggests a success rate of 75 to 80%. Similar figures are reported by Correction Service Canada for 1975-1982 (1983: 22). They suggest that the majority of those who qualify under the NPB selection for parole are, for whatever reasons, successful in avoiding revocation of their conditional release. From a public policy perspective, this record is grounds for confidence in parole, despite its shortcomings.

Remission and Mandatory Supervision. In the mid-1970s, correctional services switched from a mixed programme of earned and statutory remission of sentence to a fully earned remission programme. Currently, inmates can earn credit for positive behaviour at a rate of 15 days per month and can thereby accumulate a reduction of incarceration of up to a maximum one-third of their sentence. The reduction is served in the community under mandatory supervision. Of the fifteen possible days of credit per month, ten are awarded for participation in work or educational programmes, and five are for acceptable conduct. In practice, about 90% of inmates earn all possible remission (Working Group, 1981: 9). Notably, remission is not subject to NPB approval and so it applies without systematic screening of cases. Given the high rates of remission generated, it has ceased to work as a positive incentive utilized to direct inmate behaviour as much as a punishment for unfavourable conduct. Consequently, it has lost the notion of being "earned" at all (Working Group, 1981: 84-85). Despite this, earned remission is a check against the harshness of judicial sentences and the conservatism of NPB decisions. Where the judiciary calls for a long period of imprisonment and where the NPB rejects motions for release at one-third of the sentence, earned remission allows the inmate to capitalize on the opportunity for release at two-thirds of the sentence on the basis of acceptable prison behaviour.

There are about 2500 releases under this programme annually. These constitute about 60-65% of all full releases from penitentiary. Of all the various conditional release programmes, mandatory supervision has the least favourable record. Figures for 1976-1978 indicate a return of inmates to prison for violation of the terms of release of just under 40% (Working Group, 1981: 10). Just under 10% of those released after successfully completing the period of MS were eventually convicted and returned to penitentiary.

Mandatory supervision is clearly the area where offenders can count on their own behaviour for early release independently of parole and TA opportunities. However, automatic release under MS indicates that those who qualify are frequently the least able to care for themselves. This contributes to the controversy over MS and led the NPB to try to rearrest dangerous offenders immediately following release on MS. This practice of "gating" has been tested in the courts and pronounced illegal. MS remains the most contentious of CSC's programmes.

The controversial nature of MS is, in fact, one of its most interesting facets. It is controversial to NPB because the Board is constantly being blamed for the failures of offenders released on MS, although it has no hand in and cannot prevent these releases, even if it believes the offender will be a physical threat when released. It is controversial to offenders because they consider remission as "time off" their sentence (as it was before 1970) and they resent having to serve the remitted portion under supervision, subject to revocation (especially for non-criminal behaviour), after their release. It is controversial to the police, who because they deal with MS violations in the form of arrests, regard the overall program as a failure. It is controversial to parole officers because of the resentment and hostility of offenders which make supervision difficult and unpleasant. Parole officers also have to deal with other problems caused by or associated with MS, such as the paperwork and frustration involved in "revolving door" cases, lack of release plans and even, for some, a sense of personal risk from MS cases. Finally, it is controversial to penitentiary authorities who have to live with the "returns" from MS, revoked offenders who are often bitter and difficult to deal with (Working Group, 1981: 90).

Despite its failure to change the behaviour of so many inmates, MS remains an important aspect of the correctional programme. For that 50-60% who never have further contacts with the correctional service after a period of MS, it permits a small measure of self-direction and opportunity for self-control. These things, as noted earlier, are essential for the preservation of the inmate sense of autonomy and worth.

Summary

The use of incarceration as a form of social control has been a relatively recent social invention originating in systematic form in the mid-19th century. While we find deplorable many of the features that accompany the deprivation of liberty, from a longer-term perspective the treatment of convicted persons has certainly improved, though very slowly. We have devised numerous sentencing options to prevent or minimize incarceration and have developed community-oriented penal programmes to facilitate early and/or conditional release. Both types of programmes are designed to divert convicted persons from prisons. The programmes have not always been applied uniformly across the country and have not always been borne equally by offenders of different socio-economic status. Also, the judiciary has frequently "compensated" for early release by giving longer prison terms than they would otherwise in order to offset sentence reductions (Working Group, 1981: 89). These discrepancies obviously must be rectified under more responsible public policy whether the initiative is taken by Parliament, or by the violent protests of the inmates of the correctional institutions.

The confinement of inmates in prisons to carry out the sentence of the court often contradicts the preparation implied by the mandate to return inmates to the society as useful citizens. In other words, we try to prepare the inmate for lawful reassimilation into society by separation from society. Yet the effects of imprisonment and the learned institutional dependency that is fostered by long sentences militate against inmate adaptation after release. The other side of the coin is that early release of poorly adjusted offenders may renew the danger to the public which was the ground for removal and separation in the first place. Despite this contradiction, the records of penitentiary recidivism and the successfully completed conditional release programmes are far from being bleak. While recidivism and programme failures are at times substantial, on the whole these various programmes must be counted as successful in engendering satisfactory conduct from the majority of participants. Given the conditions of financial restraint through the 1980s we should expect greater public accountability of the correctional and parole services, and a greater reliance on the less debilitating and cheaper forms of penal control, the community-based correctional services.

FURTHER READING

Claire Culhane, *Barred From Prison*. Vancouver: Pulp Press, 1979.

Luc Gosselin, *Prisons in Canada*. Montreal: Black Rose, 1982.

Curt T. Griffiths, John F. Klein and Simon N. Verdun-Jones, *Criminal Justice in Canada*. Vancouver: Butterworths, 1980.

Brian Grosman, *New Directions in Sentencing*. Toronto: Butterworths, 1980.

James L. Hackler, *The Great Stumble Forward*. Toronto: Methuen, 1978.

Peter Macnaughton-Smith, *Permission to be Slightly Free*, Law Reform Commission of Canada. Ottawa: Supply and Services, 1976.

W.T. McGrath (ed.), *Crime and Its Treatment in Canada*, Second Edition. Toronto: Macmillan, 1976.

Gwynn Nettler, *Responding to Crime*, Vol. 4 of *Criminal Careers*. Cincinnati: Anderson, 1982.

Roger Ouimet, *Report of the Canadian Committee on Corrections*. Ottawa: Queen's Printer, 1969.

Harold Pepinsky, *Crime Control Strategies*. New York: Oxford University Press, 1980.

Sue Titus Reid, *The Correctional System: An Introduction*. New York: Holt, Rinehart and Winston, 1981.

Robert R. Ross and Paul Gendreau (eds.), *Effective Correctional Treatment*. Toronto: Butterworths, 1980.

CHAPTER 12

The Future of Canadian Justice

Introduction: The Criminal Law Review

In 1982 Jean Chretien, then Minister of Justice, released *The Criminal Law in Canadian Society*, a report prepared by the Federal Department of Justice. It contained a statement of the scope, purpose and principles of the criminal law and suggested guidelines for the complete revamping of the existing Code. This follows the thrust of the Law Reform Commission of Canada which was created by Parliament in 1970 to remove the anachronisms in the Criminal Code and to update it with respect to the contemporary social values and issues. Canada's first Code was approved by Parliament in 1892 and was revamped in 1955. The contemplated reconstruction of the Code is far more fundamental than that which occurred in 1955. It is an attempt to fundamentally reconceive what the criminal justice system ought to be doing in our society. The point of departure for the public discussion of the changes is the body of reports, working papers and studies conducted under the auspices of the Law Reform Commission. These studies deal with the basis of the criminal law, sentencing, incarceration, deterrence, aspects of criminal procedure, specific types of offenses, the laws of evidence, administrative and regulatory law, and so on. In this discussion we will examine the current program for change developed by the Criminal Law Review in light of some of the problems and issues in Canadian justice raised in earlier chapters. Given the consensus shared by all the federal political parties that the existing Code needs to be modernized, we can be fairly confident that the Code will be overhauled even if there is a change in the makeup of the government.

The Purpose of the Criminal Law

The Criminal Law Review initiated by Chretien identifies the purpose of the criminal law and the justice system as twofold: the pursuit of security and justice. By security the Review refers to "the preservation of the peace, prevention of crime [and] protection of the public." By justice is meant "equity, fairness, guarantees for the rights and liberties of the individual against the powers of the State, and the provision of a fitting response by society to wrongdoing" (Chretien, 1982: 40). In its discussion of these two objectives, the Review takes a conservative approach to changes in the justice system.

To begin with, the Criminal Law Review is extremely pessimistic regarding the ability of correctional services to rehabilitate offenders or protect the public. Consequently, the chief strategy devised to control crime is to improve policing in order to increase the certainty of offenders being detected and arrested. As shown in our discussion of the police this sector already enjoys the lion's share of funding in the justice system. This policy then calls for more of what we already have. In addition, according to the Law Review proposals, the purpose of criminal sanctions will be limited officially to retribution or punishment, with deterrence, incapacitation and rehabilitation confined to unintended by-products of corrections, by-products for which the system would no longer be accountable. This could mean that the performance of correctional services would be measured by whether confinement is painful, not whether it deters, incapacitates or rehabilitates.

Under this approach, the penal experience in Canada, which has been criticized frequently for its callous and brutal treatment of offenders, and which, in the jaundiced eye of public opinion, has been viewed as a dismal failure, can now be viewed as a howling success simply because its mandate may be limited to retribution. This approach is shortsighted. If we focus in the short run exclusively on retribution in the name of justice, we may do a disservice to the public in the long run in the area of security. Offenders who are returned to society without preparation and adjustment will be grave hazards to public safety on their release. Consequently, the identification of retribution as the sole purpose of criminal punishment would be narrow and regressive, and would be harmful to society in the long run, and contrary to public security, one of the basic purposes of justice.

The Proper Scope of Criminal Law

The Criminal Law Review argues that since criminal prosecution is the most coercive and punitive form of social control, it ought to be used parsimoniously, that the Code ought to be confined to the most serious harms in the society, and that where there are other forms of control, such as civil remedies or regulatory laws, these ought to be invoked. In our discussion of the policing of harmful business conduct, we saw that entrepreneurs and corporations were able to create harmful products, unsafe worksites and toxic emissions without criminal liability. So, too, in our discussion of biases in lawmaking, we saw how the narcotics laws were written to target low-status users while high-status traffickers were covered by non-criminal legislation. What this suggests is that in the name of parsimony, we risk maintaining the system of regulatory law for the rich and criminal law for the poor. However, the Criminal Law Review expressly recognizes this problem, when it suggests that criminal liability ought not to be confined to individuals.

It is not necessary or desirable to confine the criminal law to acts committed by individuals against other individuals; rather, it is advisable to clarify and give greater consideration to the liablity of organizations, and individuals working within organizations, where serious harm to an individual or to the general good is caused or threatened (Chretien, 1982: 48).

In order to see that future changes in the law reflect this sentiment, several things will have to happen simultaneously. First, if we consider the conduct of business organizations, Parliament will have to rewrite the anti-combines legislation in order to make it easier to curb monopolistic business practices. Business monopolies by definition undermine competition and encourage artificially high prices to consumers. Current legislation is virtually unenforceable, as witnessed in its inability to curb the concentration of ownership in a number of industries including newspaper publishing and the petroleum industry. If Parliament is going to entertain legislation bringing harmful business conduct into the criminal field, it should also revise the existing penal legislation regarding business, chiefly the Combines Investigation Act.

A second area requiring attention was raised in our discussion of the lawful excuses that may be offered in court in response to criminal charges arising from harmful business conduct. The excuses related to the *mens rea* or mental element required in establishing criminal culpability. Since, aside from price fixing and bid-rigging, most harms are the unintended side effects of normal business strategies, we require clarification in the law to determine when conduct is reckless or negligent and the extent to which due diligence and mistake of fact can be offered as excuses for harmful conduct. In our discussion of the possible lawful excuses that might be offered in these business cases, it was suggested that the stringent requirement of a guilty mind made it highly unlikely that criminal law could be utilized as a penetrating control of business harms.

Consequently, it would appear that Parliament should confirm that criminal liability will extend to business conduct where there is evidence that it is reckless, careless or negligent. Also, the responsibility for business behaviours should fall on the individual actors, and not be deflected to a legal fiction, the corporation, which by design is meant to prevent individual liability. By providing for individual accountability, executives are liable to be more careful and diligent, knowing that, if a criminal charge arises, their names, and not the corporation's, will be called at trial.

The third point to be made is that, in addition to recognizing that organizations may be sources of serious harmful conduct, there must also be recognition that the justice system itself can create harms. Just as there are victims of crime, so too there are victims of justice. This problem has arisen in several different chapters. For example, failure of the police to uphold laws regarding the civil rights of suspects seems to carry no liability for the police. The remedy section of the Charter is specifically vague on redressing these harms. Injured parties are referred to a court of competent jurisdiction to get whatever justice seems appropriate in the circumstances. If specificity is the mark of good law, the remedy section could certainly use some rewriting. Also, there must be greater accountability for the type of crimes documented by the McDonald Commission. The Criminal Law Review cannot call for control of organizational harms, and then exempt attention from an organization in which there was a breakdown in the rule of law, merely because this was a police organization. In a democratic society this type of lawlessness is doubly pernicious by reason of its occurrence within government. It cannot be allowed to use that status to have itself exempted from control. This was in fact what happened in the case of RCMP crimes. The government commissioned an inquiry to gather facts, the inquiry discovered lawlessness and the government refused to act. In fact, when private citizens attempted to initiate prosecutions, these were stayed by the Crown. Consequently, victims of a government organization had no initial protection under the law and were subsequently denied redress for this in the courts.

Other areas where justice organizations have acted harmfully involve false convictions and prosecutions. Don Marshall, who spent eleven years in jail for a murder he did not commit, has no legal recourse against the system that unjustly deprived him of his freedom. In cases such as this, a pardon may be granted by the Governor in Council and financial compensation may or may not be given. However, it is not something that anyone is presently lawfully entitled to. A parallel situation involves someone who is maliciously prosecuted. In Toronto, in 1983, nurse Susan Nelles was prevented by the courts from launching a civil suit against the Provincial Attorney General and her Crown prosecutors in a murder case involving poisonings at Toronto's Sick Children's Hospital. The charges were dismissed at a preliminary inquiry for a lack of evidence, but only after Nelles had spent enormous sums on her defense and had undergone tremendous personal mortification. Where victims of crime have access to victim services and compensation boards, victims of justice, like Nelles and Marshall, are virtually without protection from government organizations. In order for there to be balance in the systen, there must be formal processes of redress for the victims of justice.

Harm and Morality

The Criminal Law Review suggests that "the major criterion for determining what conduct merits response from the criminal law is whether the conduct causes or threatens serious harm to individuals or society" (Chretien, 1982: 3). As we noted in earlier chapters, what counts as harmful is not always straightforward. While it is a truism that such "core crimes" as murder, assault and robbery are harmful, the real issues confronting the public are far more subtle. They concern what *counts* as murder, assault and robbery. Does abortion count as murder? Does a prescription of a lethal dose of painkiller given to the terminally ill count as murder? The Criminal Law Review appears to be operating on the assumption that society is based on a discrete set of common core values that must be reflected in the law. However, there is little evidence of such values aside from the feeling that what is wicked and reprehensible should be outlawed.

As a result, the types of things that appear in a penal code will reflect the moral interests of those groups or persons who control the creation of legislation, making criminal those things that count as wicked and reprehensible for them. Notably, the Law Reform Commission's study of *The Limits of Criminal Law* (1979) suggested that pornography ought to remain subject to control under the criminal obscenity law. Presumably, other victimless crimes such as gambling, prostitution and narcotics use ought to remain crimes in that these too offend "core values." What is disturbing here is that we stress the relevance of harm as a criterion for criminalizing conduct, yet treat as evidence for the harm the simple fact that the conduct is viewed as immoral and unorthodox from the perspective of the dominant class or interest group. This appears to have been the case in the criminalization of opium use, as well as in the case of prohibition. In order to minimize the criminal code from becoming an ideological tool employed by dominant groups to warehouse their values and to denigrate the morality of minority groups, it is imperative that the harmfulness be construed very concretely.

It should not be enough that, because our personal morality finds some conduct offensive, this is sufficient to criminalize it. Consequently, if pornography, narcotics use and/or prostitution are demonstrably harmful, then criminalizing them would be consistent with the objective of maintaining public security. However if they are merely distasteful, disgusting, unorthodox or things that we do not value highly, they should be beyond the scope of criminal justice. Let them be controlled by citizens or community groups by their own choices and initiatives and by education and public discussion. Criminalizing services for which there are substantial public demands does not promote justice; it merely creates incentives for criminal entrepreneurs, artificially boosts the costs of such services and creates illicit pools of untaxed wealth. Here the harm may be greater than the unorthodox conduct that it was meant to control.

Unfortunately, on the question of harms and values, the Law Review is inconsistent: it rightfully stresses the necessity for harm, yet at times seems to suggest that conduct contrary to dominant values also may be criminized:

> The concept of justice, as well as imposing constraints on the manner in which the state can act, also imposes a positive duty in requiring the criminal law to respond to certain forms of conduct: anything short of such a response would imply an inappropriate attitude to the public interest or societal value attacked by that conduct. (Chretien, 1982: 48)

Presumably, according to this position, an obscene performance or a gambling arrangment could be criminalized independently of any demonstration of harm to the public. It would be criminalized not to to prevent a harm, but, in the words of the Review, to prevent justice from showing "an inappropriate attitude." This possibility is ripe for abuse by dominant groups who would use society's most coercive method of social control, the criminal law, to impose their values on others. An insistence that harm be proven and demonstrated would curb this type of bias.

Justice, Necessity and Economy

In discussing the limits on the powers and sanctions of the law, the Criminal Law Review identified three central considerations: justice, necessity and economy. The principles of justice involve chiefly the rules of criminal procedure devised to protect the individual from the state. These include the principle of the rule of law, the presumption of innocence, the right not to be deprived of liberty without due process, the right to a fair trial and freedom from cruel and unusual punishment. Also included are the rules of evidence which provide for protection against self-incrimination, establishment of all the elements of the offense by the prosecution, and so on. In other words, the principles encoded in the rules of criminal procedure and the rules of evidence provide the framework for the implementation of justice.

The second principle is that the invocation of the criminal law should only occur when necessary.

> For some offences, necessity, like justice, will require anything but restraint (in the sense of leniency). For other offences and offenders, the circumstances, viewed from the perspective of justice and necessity, may dictate a restrained approach. (Chretien, 1982: 49)

This lofty principle aggravates the questions of equity raised in earlier chapters. Since there are no guidelines for restraint, there is no guarantee of uniformity before the law. Government and business offenders can be shown restraint while low-status offenders bear the harsh, "necessary" treatment of criminal prosecution. Unless restraint is paired with a uniform application of law, this principle will only upgrade inequality from an informal to a formal dimension of law.

Economy is the final principle. This principle holds that justice must be administered with a sense of financial responsibility. There must be limits to the numbers of police officers and penitentiaries that the justice system calls for. Just as we have restraint in other sectors of society during periods of financial crisis, the justice system must also operate more efficiently and show restraint. This is the financial counterpart to the earlier considerations of the criminal law as a device to be used parsimoniously, only where there exists evidence of real and substantial harm, and only when necessary. This principle has become imperative in recent years when the costs of justice have come to be measured, not in the millions, but in the billions of dollars.

The Application Principles

Having identified the purposes of the criminal law, its scope and the principles governing it, the Criminal Law Review then specifies 12 further principles by which the objectives of law should be applied. The manner in which they are written suggests that they may form the preamble to a revised Criminal Code. If implemented, these measures would go some distance in further democratizing the Canadian system of justice.

Purpose of the Criminal Law

The purpose of the criminal law is to contribute to the maintenance of a just, peaceful and safe society through the establishment of a system of prohibitions. sanctions and procedures to deal fairly and appropriately with culpable conduct that causes or threatens serious harm to individuals or society.

Principles to be Applied in Achieving this Purpose

The purpose of the criminal law should be achieved through means consonant with the rights set forth in the Canadian Charter of Rights and Freedoms, and in accordance with the following principles:

(1) the criminal law should be employed to deal only with that conduct for which other means of social control are inadequate or inappropriate, and in a manner which interferes with individual rights and freedoms only to the extent necessary for the attainment of its purpose;

(2) the criminal law should clearly and accessibly set forth:

(i) the nature of conduct declared criminal;

(ii) the responsibility required to be proven for a finding of criminal liability;

(3) the criminal law should also clearly and accessibly set forth the rights of persons whose liberty is put directly at risk through the criminal law process;

(4) unless otherwise provided by Parliament, the burden of proving every material element of a crime should be on the prosecution, which burden should not be discharged by anything less than proof beyond a reasonable doubt;

(5) the criminal law should provide and clearly define powers necessary to facilitate the conduct of criminal investigations and the arrest and detention of offenders, without unreasonably or arbitrarily interfering with individual rights and freedoms;

(6) the criminal law should provide sanctions for criminal conduct that are related to the gravity of the offence and the degree of responsibility of the offender, and that reflect the need for protection of the public against further offences by the offender and for adequate deterrence against similar offences by others;

(7) wherever possible and appropriate, the criminal law and the criminal justice system should also promote and provide for:
  (i) opportunities for the reconciliation of the victim, community, and offender;
  (ii) redress or recompense for the harm done to the victim of the offence;
  (iii) opportunities aimed at the personal reformation of the offender and his reintegration into the community;

(8) persons found guilty of similar offences should receive similar sentences where the relevant circumstances are similar;

(9) in awarding sentences, preference should be given to the least restrictive alternative adequate and appropriate in the circumstances;

(10) in order to ensure equality of treatment and accountability, discretion at critical points of the criminal justice process should be governed by appropriate controls;

(11) any person alleging illegal or improper treatment by an official of the criminal justice system should have ready access to a fair investigative and remedial procedure;

(12) wherever possible and appropriate, opportunities should be provided for lay participation in the criminal justice process and the determination of community interests. (Chretien, 1982: 4-6)

Prospects for Change

1. Harm and Criminalization

One of the recurrent themes from previous chapters has been that we tend to over-criminalize morality offenses and to undercriminalize harmful business conduct. If the focus of the criminal law is going to be confined to "serious harm," as the Criminal Law Review suggests, this could result in a realignment of the criminal law to control truly dangerous conduct which would mean no more Toronto gay bath raids, no more "crackdowns" on prostitution, no more busts of movies like Caligula or Last Tango in Paris, nor seizures of Lady Chatterly's Lover, and no more revolving door trials for Dr. Morgentaler. Presumably, we would see an end to the enforcement of morals through criminal law control.

In the extreme case this could result in a decriminalization of a number of morals offenses including prostitution, pornography and narcotics use, as well as certain homosexual and gambling offenses. Presumably, this would not lead to a total absence of regulation, but merely an absence of regulation through criminal law. There is a lesson in how we currently control abortion, i.e., making it illegal to procure a miscarriage other than through an approved hospital therapeutic abortion committee. This solution has thrown the issue of abortion into the lap of local communities, making abortions available, but unequally so, across Canada. In a similar vein, we might expect there to be provincial variations in the extent to which morality is controlled by local legislatures and city halls. The decriminalization of morals offenses does not prevent such steps as the provincial or municipal licensing of things like prostitution and gambling. Nor does it prevent retention of criminal control over the truly harmful aspects of morality offenses such as procurement of children for pornography or the operation of a motor vehicle while under the influence of narcotics.

On the other hand, the focus on real harm could bring such acts as the reckless environmental dumping of toxic chemicals and the sale of unsafe products into the scope of criminal justice. This of course will prove to be political dynamite because, if interpreted widely, it could lead to the criminalization not only of acts like dumping mercury into public waters but also of manufacturing and selling carcinogenic products such as cigarettes. On the face of it, it seems very unlikely that Parliament would decriminalize prostitution while depriving millions of their nicotine rush. However, it is paradoxes such as these which must be clarified if the Criminal Law Review is to succeed in achieving a more balanced approach to the criminalization and decriminalization of conduct. This issue is unavoidable since harm has been given central importance in devising the scope of criminal law.

2. Discretion and Accountability

In principles two through five the Criminal Law Review is very forceful in stressing the importance of procedural safeguards in invoking criminal charges. The principles cover the specificity of law, the burden of proof, and the question of civil rights. These are devises for ensuring the fair application of law. However, principles eight through eleven expand the accountability of justice personnel and may prove to be more important in addressing problems raised in earlier chapters. Principles eight and nine cover sentencing. They stress the need for a uniformity of sentences across Canada, as well as a need for avoiding incarceration wherever possible. These steps, if implemented, may prove to be far more revolutionary for judicial behaviour than the Charter of Rights and Freedoms. Judicial behaviour in the area of sentencing is infrequently reviewed and so is rarely accountable to public sentiments or public policy in any systematic way.

Principles ten and eleven call for controls on discretion and abuse of process, respectively, and call for procedures to respond to or redress such situations. Presumably, a serious control of discretionary behaviour would offset such abuses as malicious prosecution, overcharging by the police, illegal police conduct, denial of civil rights and arbitrary penal treatment (that is, with respect to things like parole and earned remission, and involuntary transfers between institutions). Also, victims of justice would, under the eleventh principle, have a specific procedure to redress illegal or improper treatment. Presumably such procedures, unlike police reviews of police misconduct, would be independent of internal organizational influence and would be accompanied by powers to give meaningful compensation for mistreatment as well as to reverse illegal or improper situations. Presumably, the more vigorously such situations can be addressed, the less the likelihood that, in the long run, these will arise. If cases of abuse of process are successfully identified and forcefully corrected, the justice personnel involved will be given great incentives to avoid repetitions of these acts, which ought to result in a more balanced administration of law in the long run. However, this will involve an historic break with the enormous discretion currently granted to Crown prosecutors, police investigators and correctional authorities. Yet, to the extent that such discretion has contradicted the principle of the uniform and fair application of law, this break is both warranted and desirable.

3. Corrections

While the Criminal Law Review is on the whole pessimistic about changing the behaviour of offenders in the correctional sequence, several principles give guidance on what might be achieved through sentencing and incarceration. In principles six and seven, deterrence, compensation of victims, reconciliation between victims and perpetrators of crime, individual reformation and community reintegration of the offender are all touched upon. This suggests that the Criminal Law Review, despite its claims, sees more in corrections than simple retribution. While this view is laudable, it would seem reasonable that, given the enormous costs of federal correctional facilities, the Law Review ought to entertain radically different procedures for depriving offenders of their liberty. The current maximum security prisons seem better derived from the architecture of modern zoos than the 19th-century Auburn correctional facility.

Most of the stressful features of penitentiary life seem to be *inadvertent* consequences of the way in which we organize the social interaction of inmates. In principle, imprisonment is removal from society and deprivation of the choices to organize one's time and experience according to one's career, strategies and objectives. In fact, it amounts to co-housing with the vicious, under the care of the antagonistic in accord with the objectives of the indifferent. These concentration camps of marginal humanity are counterproductive to the establishment of individual responsibility and self-management. Corrections are not something for which prison has been expressly designed.

When we contemplate the dull regimentation of penitentiary life, the unproductive boredom and repetition, the deprivation of the basic trappings of self-respect and self-responsibility, any number of alternatives seem more promising, including resettlement in penal colonies in the north, house arrest and/or impressment into public service (such as civil defense, municipal construction and forestry work). Penal service should not by definition be destructive of the offender's ego and self-reliance, nor should it be physically or mentally cruel or abusive. It should be a curtailment of liberty and a negation of personal choice with respect to participation in the market and the political life of free citizens, while fostering independence and self-reliance.

A lesson in the physical destruction of the Kingston Penitentiary by inmates in 1971 should not be lost on the Criminal Law Review. While the construction of the penitentiary reflected state of the art thinking about penology then, it no longer is viewed as appropriate or effective. Fundamentally different social arrangements need to be considered.

Conclusion

In the coming years there will be a basic rewriting of the Canadian criminal law. This will effect the entire operation of the criminal justice system. In order to protect the security of the public we have argued that the attention of the law must be confined to demonstrably harmful conduct. Also, to protect the public in the long run, the correctional sequence requires far more attention than the Criminal Law Review appears prepared to give it. In order to promote justice, the behaviour of criminal justice personnel needs to be made far more accountable, and where harmful or unfair, needs to be subject to formal redress. The various principles outlined by the Criminal Law Review can allow the attainment of security and social justice. However, the degree and direction of change will depend on the public initiative in the political process.

REFERENCES

Aaronovitch, S. and K. Aaronovitch. 1947. *Crisis in Kenya.* London: Lawrence and Withorp

Adachi, Ken. 1976. *The Enemy That Never Was.* Toronto: McClelland and Stewart

Allport, Gordon. 1975. *The Psychology of Rumor.* New York: Russell and Russell

Anderson, Frank W. 1973. *Hanging in Canada.* Aldergrove, B.C.: Frontier Publishing

Aubin, Benoit et al. (June 6) 1983. *Inside Canada's Prisons.* Toronto: *Maclean's Magazine* 16-22

Avi-Itzhak, B. and R. Shinnar. 1973. "Quantitative models in crime control" 1 *Journal of Criminal Justice* 185-217

Avio, K.L. 1979. "Capital punishment in Canada: a time series analysis of the deterrent hypothesis" 12:4 *Canadian Journal of Economics* 647-676

Avio, K.L. and C.S. Clark. 1976. *Property Crime in Canada: An Econometric Study.* Toronto: University of Toronto Press

Avio, K.L. and C.S. Clark. 1978. "The supply of property offenses in Ontario: evidence on the deterrent effect of punishment" 11:1 *Canadian Journal of Economics* 1-19

Avison, William. 1981. Review of *The Penalty of Death* (Sellin) 6:4 *Canadian Journal of Sociology* 541-42

Baehre, Rainer. 1977. "Origins of the Penitentiary System in Upper Canada" 69 *Ontario History* 185-207

Baldus, D.C. and J.W. Cole. 1975. "A comparison of the work of Thorstein Sellin and Isaac Ehrlich on the deterrent effect of capital punishment" 85 *Yale Law Journal* 170-86

Banton, Michael P. 1974. "Police" 14 *Encyclopedia Britannica Fifteenth Edition.* Chicago: Benton 662-671

Barland, G.H. and D.C. Raskin. 1976. *Validity and Reliability of Polygraph Examinations of Criminal Suspects.* U.S. Dept. of Justice, Report 76-1. Salt Lake City: Dept. of Psychology, University of Utah. Cited in Nettler, 1982a

Bartlett, Donald L. and James B. Steele. 1973. *Crime and Injustice.* Philadelphia: Philadelphia Inquirer

Beccaria, Cesare. 1764. *Essay on Crimes and Punishment.* Translated by Henry Paolucci, 1963. Indianapolis: Bobbs-Merrill

Becker, Howard S. 1963. *Outsiders.* New York: Free Press of Glencoe

Bedau, H. and C. Pierce (eds.). 1976. *Capital Punishment.* New York: AMS Press

Bellomo, J.J. 1972. "Upper Canadian attitudes towards crime and punishment, 1832-51" 64 *Ontario History* 11-26

Berger, Thomas. 1982. *Fragile Freedoms: Human Rights and Dissent in Canada.* Toronto: Clarke, Irwin

Berns, Walter. 1979. *For Capital Punishment: Crime and The Morality of the Death Penalty.* New York: Basic Books

Bertrand, Robert J. 1981. *The State of Competition in the Canadian Petroleum Industry* (Seven Volumes) Ottawa: Supply and Services

Black, Donald and Albert Reiss. 1970. "Police control of juveniles" 35 *American Sociological Review* 63-77

Black, Donald J. 1970. "Production of crime rates" 35 *American Sociological Review* 733-748

Blumberg, Abraham. 1969. "The practice of law as confidence game: Organizational cooptation of a profession" in William J. Chambliss (ed.). *Crime and the Legal process.* New York: McGraw-Hill 220-237

Blumberg, Abraham, S. 1979. *Criminal Justice.* Revised Edition. New York: New Viewpoints

Borchard, E.M. 1932. *Convicting the Innocent: Errors in Criminal Justice.* New Haven: Yale University Press

Borovoy, Alan. 1975. "Comment" in W.S. Tarnopolsky (ed.). *Some Civil Liberties Issues of the Seventies.* Agincourt: Carswell 117-121

Bowers, W.J. and G.L. Pierce. 1975. "The illusion of deterrence in Isaac Ehrlich's research on capital punishment" 85 *Yale Law Journal* 187-208

Bowers, W.J. and G.L. Pierce. 1980. "Arbitrariness and discrimination under post-Furman statutes" 26 *Crime and Delinquency* 563-635

Bowker, Lee H. 1982. *Corrections, The Science and The Art.* New York: Macmillan ✔

Box, Steven. 1981. "The social construction of official statistics on criminal deviance" Chapter 6 in *Deviance, Reality and Society.* Second Edition. London: Holt, Rinehart and Winston

Boydell, Craig L. and Ingrid A. Connidis (eds.). 1982. *The Canadian Criminal Justice System.* Toronto: Holt, Rinehart and Winston

Boydell, Craig L., Paul C. Whitehead and Carl Grindstaff (eds.). 1982. *The Administration of Criminal Justice in Canada.* Toronto: Holt, Rinehart and Winston

Brannigan, A. and J.C. Levy. 1983. "The legal context of plea bargaining" 25:4 *Canadian Journal of Criminology* 399-420

Brecher, Edward M. 1972. *Licit and Illicit Drugs.* Boston: Little, Brown

Brodeur, Jean-Paul. 1981. "Legitimizing police deviance" in Clifford Shearing (ed.). *Organization Police Deviance.* Toronto: Butterworth 127-160

Buckhout, Robert. 1970. "Eyewitness testimony" 231:6 *Scientific American* 23-31

Bugliosi, Vincent and Kenneth Hurwitz. 1979. *Till Death Do Us Part: A True Murder Mystery.* New York: Bantam

Calder, W.A. 1981. "Convict life in Canadian federal penitentiaries, 1967-1900" in Louis A. Knafla (ed.). *Crime and Criminal Justice in Europe and Canada.* Waterloo: Wilfred Laurier University Press 297-318

Calgary Herald. (May 16) 1983. Editorial: "Acid-rain talk cheap" 2

Callwood, June. 1981. *Portrait of Canada.* Toronto: Doubleday

Cameron, Mary Owen. 1969. "Shoplifters who become data" in William J. Chambliss (ed.). *Crime and the Legal Process.* New York: McGraw-Hill 174-188

Campbell, Marjorie Freeman. 1974. *Torso.* Toronto: Macmillan

Canada Year Book. Annual. Ottawa: Supply and Services

Canadian Centre for Justice Statistics. 1983. 3:1 *Juristat Service Bulletin* 1-8

Canadian Civil Liberties Education Trust. 1974. "Due process safeguards and Canadian criminal justice" in Craig L. Boydell, Paul C. Whithead and Carl F. Grindstaff (eds.). *The Administration of Criminal Justice in Canada*. Toronto: Holt, Rinehart and Winston 155-185

Capote, Truman. 1965. *In Cold Blood*. New York: Random House

Carlen, Pat. 1976. *Magistrate's Justice*. London: Martin Robertson

Caron, Roger. 1978. *Go Boy! Memoirs of a Life Behind Bars*. Toronto: McGraw-Hill Ryerson

Carr, James G. 1977. *The Law of Electronic Surveillance*. New York: Clark Boardman

Carson, W.G. 1982. *The Other Price of Britain's Oil*. Oxford: Martin Robertson

Chambliss, William J. (ed.). 1969. *Crime and the Legal Process*. New York: McGraw-Hill

Chambliss, William J. 1974. "The state, the law and the definition of behavior as criminal or delinquent" in Daniel Glaser (ed.). *Handbook of Criminology*. Chicago: Rand McNally 7-44

Chambliss, William J. and Robert Seidman. 1982. *Law, Order and Power*. Second Edition. Reading, Mass.: Addison-Wesley

Chan, A.B. 1983. *Gold Mountain*. Vancouver: New Star Books

Chandler, David. 1976. *Capital Punishment in Canada*. Toronto: McClelland and Stewart

Chapman, Terry L. 1976. *The Drug Problem in Western Canada 1900-1920*. Unpublished MA Thesis, The University of Calgary

Chiricos, Theodore and Gordon Waldo. 1970. "Punishment and crime: An examination of some empirical evidence" 18 *Social Problems* 200-217

Chretien, Jean. 1982. *The Criminal Law in Canadian Society, Report of the Criminal Law Review*. Ottawa: Department of Justice

Cicourel, Aaron. 1968. *The Social Organization of Juvenile Justice*. New York: Wiley

Clark, Ramsay. 1970. *Crime in America*. New York: Simon and Schuster

Clarke, Kenneth L., Richard Barnhorst and Sherrie Barnhorst. 1977. *Criminal Law and the Canadian Criminal Code*. Toronto: McGraw-Hill Ryerson

Clemmer, Donald. 1940. *The Prison Community*. Boston: Christopher

Clinard, Marshall B. and Peter C. Yeager. 1980. *Corporate Crime*. New York: Free Press

Cobb, William E. 1973. "Theft and two hypotheses" in Simon Rottenberg (ed.). *The Economics of Crime and Punishment*. Washington, D.C.: American Enterprise Institute for Public Policy Research 19-30

Connidis, Ingrid A. 1979. "Problem in the use of official statistics for criminal justice research" 21:4 *Canadian Journal of Criminology* 397-415

Cook, Shirley. 1969. "Canadian narcotics legislation, 1908-1923: A conflict interpretation" 6 *Canadian Review of Sociology and Anthropology* 36-46

Correctional Investigator. 1982. *Annual Report of the Correctional Investigator, 1980-1981*. Ottawa: Supply and Services

Correctional Services Canada. 1983. *1983-84 Estimates Expenditure Plan*. Ottawa

Courtis, M.C. 1974. "The police and the public" in Craig L. Boydell, Paul C. Whithead and Carl F. Grindstaff (eds.). *The Administration of Criminal Justice in Canada*. Toronto: Holt, Rinehart and Winston 115-125

Courtis, M.C. and I. Dussuyer. 1970. *Attitudes to Crime and the Police in Toronto*. Toronto: Centre of Criminology Publication, University of Toronto

Cousineau, D.F. 1973. "A critique of the ecological approach to the study of deterrence" 54 *Social Science Quarterly* 153-158

Cressey, Donald. 1969. *Theft of the Nation: The Structure and Operations of Organized Crime*. New York: Harper and Row

252   REFERENCES

Culhane, Claire. 1979. *Barred From Prison*. Vancouver: Pulp Press

Cumming, Elaine, Ian Cumming and Laura Edell. 1965. "Policeman as philosopher, guide and friend" 12 *Social Problems* 276-286

Desroches, Fred. 1974. "The April 1971 Kingston Penitentiary riot" 18:1 *Canadian Journal of Criminology and Corrections* 317-331

Devlin, Patrick. 1958. *The Criminal Prosecution in England*. New Haven: Yale University Press

Devlin, Patrick. 1959. *The Enforcement of Morals*. London: Oxford University Press

Devlin, Patrick. 1976. *Report to the Secretary of State for the Home Department of the Departmental Committee on Evidence of Identification in Criminal Cases*. London: Her Majesty's Stationery Office

Devons, Ely. 1965. "Serving as a juryman in Britain" 28 *Modern Law Review* 561-570

Dion, Robert. 1982. *Crimes of the Secret Police*. Montreal: Black Rose

Doob, A.N. and H.M. Kirshenbaum. 1973. "Bias in police lineups — partial remembering" 1 *Journal of Police Science and Administration* 287-293

Duster, Troy. 1970. *The Legislation of Morality: Law, Drugs and Moral Judgement*. New York: Free Press

Edmison, J. Alex. 1976. "Some aspects of Nineteenth Century prisons" in W.T. McGrath (ed.). *Crime and Its Treatment in Canada*. Second Edition. Toronto: Macmillan 347-369

Ehrlich, Isaac. 1973. "Participation in illegitimate activities: A theoretical and empirical investigation" 81:3 *Journal of Political Economy* 521-565

Ehrlich, Isaac. 1975. "The deterrent effect of capital punishment: a question of life and death" 65:3 *American Economic Review* 397-417

Ellis, Desmond. 1982. *Canadian Penitentiaries During the Years 1971-1980*. LaMarsh Research Program Reports on Violence and Conflict Resolution. Downsview, Ont.: York University

Empey, LaMar and Maynard L. Erikson. 1966. "Hidden delinquency and social status" 44:4 *Social Forces* 546-554

Erickson, M.L., J.P. Gibbs and G.F. Jensen. 1977. "The deterrence doctrine and the perceived certainty of legal punishments" 42 *American Sociological Review* 305-317

Erickson, Patricia. 1980. *Cannabis Criminals: The Social Effects of Punishment on Drug Users*. Toronto: Addiction Research Foundation

Ericson, Richard V. 1981. *Making Crime: A Study of Detective Work*. Toronto: Butterworth

Ericson, Richard V. 1982. *Reproducing Order: A Study of Police Patrol Work*. Toronto: University of Toronto Press

Ericson, Richard V. and Patricia M. Baranek. 1982. *The Ordering of Justice: A Study of Accused Persons As Dependants in the Criminal Process*. Toronto: University of Toronto Press

Erikson, Kai T. 1966. *Wayward Puritans*. New York: Wiley

Erikson, Maynard. 1973. "Group violations, socio-economic status and official delinquency" 52:1 *Social Forces* 41-52

Ermann, M. David and Richard J. Lundman. 1982. *Corporate Deviance*. New York: Free Press

Evans, Robert. 1973. *Developing Policies for Public Security and Criminal Justice*. Ottawa: Economic Council of Canada

Fattah, E.A. 1972. *A Study of the Deterrent Effect of Capital Punishment with Special Reference to the Canadian Situation*. Ottawa: Information Canada

Fattah, E.A. 1976. "Deterrence: a review of the literature" in the Law Reform Commission of Canada, *Fear of Punishment*. Ottawa: Supply and Services Canada 1-20

Favreau, Guy. 1965. *Capital Punishment: Material Relating to Its Purpose and Value*. Ottawa: Queen's Printer

Ferguson, G.A. and D.N. Roberts. 1974. "Plea bargaining: Directions for Canadian reform" 52:4 *Canadian Bar Review* 497-576

Finckenauer, James O. 1982. *Scared Straight and the Panacea Phenomenon*. Englewood Cliffs, N.J.: Prentice-Hall

Ford, Daniel F. and Henry W. Kendall. 1975. "Catastrophic nuclear reactor accidents" in The Union of Concerned Scientists (ed.). *The Nuclear Fuel Cycle*. Cambridge: MIT Press 70-119

Forst, B.E. 1977. "The deterrent effect of capital punishment: a cross-state analysis of the 1960s" 61 *Minnesota Law Review* 743-67

Fotheringham, Alan. 1982. *Malice in Blunderland*. Toronto: Key Porter Books

Foucault, Michel. 1977. *Discipline and Punish*. Translated by Alan Sheridan. New York: Colophon Books

— Fox, Francis. 1977. *Response of the Solicitor-General to the Parliamentary Sub-Committee Report on the Penitentiary System in Canada*. Ottawa: Supply and Services

Frankfurter, F. 1927. *The Case of Sacco and Vanzetti*. Boston: Little, Brown (reprinted in Universal Library edition, 1962)

Friedenberg, Edgar Z. 1980. *Deference to Authority: The Case of Canada*. White Plains, N.Y.: M.E. Sharpe

Friedland, M.L. 1978. *Cases and Materials on Criminal Law and Procedure*. Fifth Edition. Toronto: University of Toronto Press

Gall, Gerald L. 1982. *Civil Liberties in Canada Entering the 1980's*. Toronto: Butterworth

Geis, Gilbert. 1974. *One Eyed Justice*. New York: Drake Publishing

Geis, Gilbert. 1977. "The heavy electrical equipment anti-trust case of 1961" in G. Geis and R.F. Meier (eds.). *White Collar Crime*. Revised Edition. New York: Free Press 117-132

— Geis, Gilbert and Robert F. Meier. 1977. *White Collar Crime*. Revised Edition. New York: Free Press

Gervais, Charles Henry. 1980. *The Rumrunners: A Prohibition Scrapbook*. Thornhill: Firefly Books

Glasbeek, Harry J. and Michael Mandel. (August) 1979. "The crime and punishment of Jean-Claude Parrot." *Canadian Forum* 10-14

Glassner, Barry. 1982. "Labelling theory" in M.M. Rosenberg, R.A. Stebbins and A. Turowetz (eds.). *The Sociology of Deviance*. New York: St. Martin's Press

Godfrey, Ellen. 1981. *By Reason of Doubt: The Belshaw Case*. Toronto: Clarke, Irwin

Goff, Colin and Charles E. Reasons. 1978. *Corporate Crime in Canada*. Scarborough: Prentice-Hall

Goffman, Erving. 1961. *Asylums*. New York: Doubleday

Gofman, John W. and Arthur R. Tamplin. 1979. *Poisoned Power*. Revised Edition. Emmaus, Pa.: Rodale Press

Gold, Martin. 1966. "Undetected delinquent behavior" 3:1 *Journal of Research in Crime and Delinquency* 27-46

Goldfarb, Ronald. (November 1) 1969. "Prisons: The national poorhouse" *The New Republic* 15-17

Gonick, Cy. 1975. *Inflation or Depression?* Toronto: James Lorimer

Gordon, David. 1971. "Capitalism, class and crime in America" 3:3 *Review of Radical Political Economy* 51-75

— Gosselin, Luc. 1982. *Prisons in Canada.* Montreal: Black Rose ✓

Gray, James H. 1972. *Booze: The Impact of Whiskey on the Prairie West.* Scarborough: New American Library

Greenaway, W.K. and S.L. Brickey (eds.). 1978. *Law and Social Control in Canada.* Scarborough: Prentice-Hall

Greenspan, Edward L. (ed.). Annual. *Martin's Annual Criminal Code.* Agincourt: Canada Law Book Ltd.

Griffiths, Curt T., John F. Klein and Simon N. Verdun-Jones. 1980. *Criminal Justice in Canada.* Vancouver: Butterworth

Grosman, Brian. 1969. *The Prosecutor.* Toronto: University of Toronto Press

Grosman, Brian. 1975. *Police Command: Decisions and Discretion.* Toronto: Macmillan

Grosman, Brian (ed.). 1980. *New Directions in Sentencing.* Toronto: Butterworth ✓

Gunning, J. Patrick. 1973. "How profitable is burglary?" in Simon Rottenberg (ed.). *The Economics of Crime and Punishment.* Washington. D.C.: American Enterprise Institute for Public Policy Research 35-38

Gusfield, Joseph. 1963. *Symbolic Crusade: Status Politics and the American Temperance Movement.* Urbana: University of Illinois Press

Gyorgy, Anna. 1979. *No Nukes.* Boston: South End Press

Hackler, James L. 1978. *The Great Stumble Forward.* Toronto: Methuen

— Hagan, John. 1974. "Criminal justice and Native people: A study of incarceration in a Canadian province" *Canadian Review of Sociology and Anthropology.* Special Edition 220-236

Hagan, John. 1975. "Law, order and sentencing: A study of attitude in action" 38 *Sociometry* 374-384

Hagan, John. 1977. *The Disreputable Pleasures.* Toronto: McGraw-Hill Ryerson

Hagan, John. 1982. "The corporate advantage: A study of the involvement of corporate and individual victims in a criminal justice system" 60 *Social Forces* 993-1022

Hagan, John, Ilene Nagel and Celesta Albonetti. 1980. "The differential sentencing of white-collar offenders in ten federal district courts" 45 *American Sociological Review* 802-820

— Hall, E.L. and A.A. Simkus. 1975. "Inequality in the types of sentence received by Native Americans and Whites" 13 *Criminology* 199-222

Hall, Jerome. 1969. "Theft, law and society: The Carrier's case" in William J. Chambliss (ed.). *Crime and the Legal Process.* New York: McGraw-Hill 32-50

Hann, Robert G. 1976. *Deterrence and the Death Penalty: A Critical Review of the Research of Isaac Ehrlich.* Ottawa: Research Division of the Solicitor General of Canada

— Harding, Jim. 1976. "Mercury Poisoning" 11:7 *Canadian Dimension* 14-23

Harris, R.J. 1973. "Answering questions containing marked and unmarked adjectives and adverbs" 97 *Journal of Experimental Psychology* 399-401

Hart, H.L.A. 1963. *Law, Liberty and Morality.* Stanford: Stanford University Press

Hartnagel, H.F. and D. Wynne. 1975. "Plea negotiation in Canada" 17 *Canadian Journal of Criminology and Corrections* 45-56

Hébert, Jacques. 1964. *I Accuse the Assassins of Coffin.* Montreal: Editions du Jour

Helder, Hans. 1979. *The Police, Case Negotiation and the Para-legal System.* Unpublished MA Thesis, Centre of Criminology, The University of Toronto

Henshel, Richard L. 1979. "Will police disruptive tactics leave only the facade of democracy?" 4:2 *Canadian Journal of Sociology* 167-171

Henshel, Richard L. 1983. *Police Misconduct in Metropolitan Toronto: A Study of Formal Complaints.* LaMarsh Research Program on Violence. Downsview, Ont.: York University

Henshel, Richard L. and S.H. Carey. 1975. "Deviance, deterrence and knowledge of sanctions" in R.L. Henshel and R.A. Silverman (eds.). *Perception in Criminology.* Toronto: Methuen 54-73

Heumann, Milton. 1978. *Plea Bargaining: The Experience of Prosecutors, Judges and Defense Attorneys.* Chicago: University of Chicago Press

Hills, Stuart L. 1980. *Demystifying Social Deviance.* New York: McGraw-Hill

Hogarth, John. 1971. *Sentencing as a Human Process.* Toronto: University of Toronto Press

Holt, Simma. 1964. *Terror in the Name of God.* Toronto: McClelland and Stewart

Horvath, F.S. 1977. "The effect of selected variables on interpretation of polygraph records" 162 *Journal of Applied Psychology* 127-136

Houts, Marshall. 1956. *From Evidence to Proof: A Searching Analysis of Methods to Establish Fact.* Springfield, Ill.: C.C. Thomas

Howard, Ross and Michael Perley. 1980. *Acid Rain: The North American Forecast.* Toronto: Anansi

Hutchison, George and Dick Wallace. 1977. *Grassy Narrows.* Toronto: Van Nostrand Reinhold

Inbau, Fred E. 1948. *Lie Detection and Criminal Interrogation.* Second Edition. Baltimore: Williams and Wilkins

Inbau, Fred E. 1968. *Testimony for Use of Polygraph as Lie Detectors by the Federal Government,* Hearing Before a Subcommittee of the House Committee on Government Operations, 88th Cong. 2d Sess. Pts. 1-5

Irwin, Ronald. 1981. Chairman of the House of Commons Sub-Committee on Acid Rain. *Still Waters: The Chilling Reality of Acid Rain.* Ottawa: Supply and Services

Jackson, Michael. (December) 1982. *Sentences That Never End: The Report on the Habitual Criminal Study.* Faculty of Law, University of British Columbia, Mimeo 1-188

Jacobs, Paul. 1979. *Paul Jacobs and the Nuclear Gang.* Documentary Film (Distributed by New Time Films)

Jayewardene, C.H.S. 1977. *The Penalty of Death: The Canadian Experience.* Lexington: Lexington Books

Jeffrey, C.R. 1957. "The development of crime in early English society" 47:March-April *Journal of Criminal Law Criminology and Police Science* 647-66. Reprinted in William J. Chambliss (ed.). *Crime and the Legal Process.* New York: McGraw-Hill 1969, 12-31

Jensen, G.F. 1969. "Crime doesn't pay: correlates of a shared misunderstanding" 17 *Social Problems* 184-201

Jensen, G.F., M.L. Erickson and J.P. Gibbs. 1978. "Perceived risk of punishment and self-reported delinquency" 57 *Social Forces* 57-78

Jonas, George and Barbara Amiel. 1977. *By Persons Unknown.* Toronto: Macmillan

Juristat Service Bulletin. (June) 1982. "Homicides of police officers in Canada" 2:3

Justice Society. 1982. *Compensation for Wrongful Imprisonment.* London: Justice Publication

Kalven, Harry and Hans Zeisel. 1966. *The American Jury.* Boston: Little, Brown

Kaplan, Robert. 1981. "Foreword" *The Young Offenders Act, Highlights, 1981.* Ottawa: Supply and Services

Kaufman, Fred. 1979. "Judges' rules and administrative directions to the police" in *The Admissibility of Confessions.* Third Edition. Toronto: Carswell 386ff

Kelling, George L., Tony Pate, Duane Dieckman and Charles E. Brown. 1974. *The Kansas City Preventive Patrol Experiment.* Washington, D.C.: Police Foundation

Kelling, George L. and David Fogel. 1978. "Police patrol, some future directions" in Alvin W. Cohn (ed.). *The Future of Policing.* Beverly Hills: Sage 153-181

Kennedy, Mark. 1976. "Beyond incrimination" in William J. Chambiss and M. Mankoff (eds.). *Whose Law, What Order?* New York: Wiley 54-65

Kirkpatrick, A.M. and W.T. McGrath. 1976. *Crime and You.* Toronto: Macmillan

Klein, John F. 1976a. "The dangerousness of dangerous offender legislation: forensic folklore revisited" 18 *Canadian Journal of Criminology and Corrections* 109-122

Klein, John F. 1976b. *Let's Make A Deal.* Lexington: Lexington Books

Klein, John F. and Arthur Montague. 1980. "Cheque writing as a way of life" in Robert A. Silverman and James J. Teevan Jr. (eds.). *Crime in Canadian Society.* Second Edition. Toronto: Butterworth 335-347

Klein, L.R., B.E. Forst and V. Filatov. 1978. "The deterrent effect of capital punishment: an assessment of the estimates" in A. Blumstein, J. Cohen, and D. Nagin (eds.). *Deterrence and the Death Penalty: A Critical Review of the Research of Isaac Ehrlich on Deterrent and Incapacitative Effects.* Washington, D.C.: National Academy of Sciences 336-360

Knafla, Louis A. (ed.). 1981. *Crime and Criminal Justice in Europe and Canada.* Waterloo: Wilfred Laurier University Press

Knapp Commission (New York City). 1973. *The Knapp Commission Report on Police Corruption.* New York: Braziller

Kolko, Gabriel. 1963. *The Triumph of Conservatism.* New York: Free Press of Glencoe

Krohm, Gregory. 1973. "The pecuniary incentives of property crime" in Simon Rottenberg (ed.). *The Economics of Crime and Punishment.* Washington, D.C.: American Enterprise Institute for Public Policy Research 31-34

La Fave, W. 1965. *Arrest: The Decision To Take a Suspect Into Custody.* Boston: Little, Brown

Laskin, John B., Edward L. Greenspan and J. Bruce Dunlop. 1982. *Canadian Charter of Rights Annotated.* Aurora: Canada Law Book

Law Reform Commission of Canada. 1974. *Discovery in Criminal Cases.* Ottawa: Information Canada

Law Reform Commission of Canada. 1974-75. *Fourth Annual Report.* Ottawa: Information Canada

Law Reform Commission of Canada. 1975a. *Report on Evidence.* Ottawa: Information Canada

Law Reform Commission of Canada. 1975b. *Report on Corroboration.* Ottawa: Information Canada

Law Reform Commission of Canada. 1975c. *Imprisonment and Release.* Ottawa: Supply and Services

Law Reform Commission of Canada. 1976a. *Criminal Responsibility for Group Action.* Ottawa: Supply and Services

Law Reform Commission of Canada. 1976b. *Studies on Imprisonment.* Ottawa: Supply and Services

Law Reform Commission of Canada. 1977. *Our Criminal Law.* Ottawa: Supply and Services

Law Reform Commission of Canada. 1978. *Report on Sexual Offenses.* Ottawa: Supply and Services

Law Reform Commission of Canada. 1979. *Limits of Criminal Law: Obscenity. A Test Case.* Ottawa: Supply and Services

Letkemann, Peter. 1973. *Crime as Work.* Englewood Cliffs: Prentice-Hall

Levine, J.P., M.C. Musheno and D.J. Palumbo. 1980. *Criminal Justice: A Public Policy Approach.* New York: Harcourt, Brace and Javanovich

Liason. (July-August) 1979. "Criminal crossword" 5:7, 6-11

Lindesmith, Alfred. 1959. "Federal Law and Drug Addiction" 7 *Social Problems* 48-57

Lindesmith, Alfred. 1965. *The Addict and the Law.* Bloomington, Ind.: Indiana University Press

Lizotte, A.J. 1978. "Extra-legal factors in Chicago's criminal courts: Testing the conflict model of criminal justice" 25 *Social Problems* 565-580

Loftus, Elizabeth F. 1975. "Leading questions and the eyewitness report" 7 *Cognitive Psychology* 560-572

Loftus, Elizabeth F. 1979. *Eyewitness Testimony.* Cambridge, Mass.: Harvard University Press

Loftus, Elizabeth F. and J.C. Palmer. 1974. "Reconstruction of automobile destruction: an example of the interaction between language and memory" 13 *Journal of Verbal Learning and Verbal Behavior* 585-589

Loftus, Elizabeth F. and G. Zanni. 1975. "Eyewitness testimony: the influence of the wording of a question" 5 *Bulletin of the Psychonomic Society* 86-88

Lummus, H. 1937. *The Trial Judge.* St. Paul, Minn.: Foundation Press

Lykken, D.T. 1979. "The detection of deception" 86 *Psychological Bulletin* 47-53

Lykken, D.T. 1980. "Polygraphic interrogation: the applied psycho-physiologist" in A. Gale and J. Edwards (eds.). *Physiological Correlates of Human Behavior.* London: Academic Press

Maas, Peter. 1973. *Serpico.* New York: Viking Press

MacKaay, E. 1976. *The Paths of Justice.* Montreal: Group de Récherche en Jurimetric, Université de Montreal

MacKay, A. Wayne. 1982. *The Canadian Charter of Rights: Law Practice Revolutionized.* Halifax: Faculty of Law, Dalhousie University

Macnaughton-Smith, Peter. 1976. *Permission To Be Slightly Free.* Law Reform Commission of Canada. Ottawa: Supply and Services

Mancuso, Thomas S., Alice Stewart and George Kneale. 1979. "Radiation exposures of Hanford workers dying from cancer and other causes" 33:5 *Health Physics* 369-385

Mandel, Michael. 1983a. "Imprisonment, class and democracy in contemporary Canadian capitalism." Toronto: Osgoode Hall Law School, Mimeo

Mandel, Michael. 1983b. *Law and Social Order Part I.* Toronto: CBC Transcripts

Mann, William E. and John A. Lee. 1979. *RCMP vs The People.* Don Mills, Ont.: General Publishing

Manning, Peter. 1971. "The police: Mandate strategies and appearances" in Jack Douglas (ed.). *Crime and Justice in America.* Indianapolis: Bobbs-Merrill 149-194

Manning, Peter. 1979. *Police Work: The Social Organization of Policing.* Cambridge, Mass.: MIT Press

Martinson, Robert. 1974. "What works? Questions and answers about prison reform" 35: Spring *Public Interest* 22-54

Mather, Lynn. 1979. *Plea Bargaining Or Trial? The Process of Criminal Case Disposition.* Lexington: Lexington Books

Mazur, Allan. 1981. *The Dynamics of Technological Dispute.* Washington, D.C.: Communication Press

McBarnet, Doreen. 1981. *Conviction: Law, The State and the Construction of Justice.* London: Macmillan

McDonald Commission. (August) 1981. *Royal Commission of Inquiry Concerning Activities of the Royal Canadian Mounted Police.* Second Report: Freedom and Security Under the Law (Vol. 1 and 2), Third Report: Certain RCMP Activities and the Question of Government Knowledge (Vol. 1). Ottawa: Supply and Services

McDonald, Lynn. 1969. "Crime and punishment in Canada: A statistical test of the conventional wisdom" 6 *Canadian Review of Sociology and Anthropology* 212-236

McGrath, W.T. (ed.). 1976. *Crime and Its Treatment in Canada.* Second Edition. Toronto: Macmillan

McGrath, W.T. and M.P. Mitchell (eds.). 1981. *The Police Function in Canada.* Toronto: Methuen

McGuigan, Mark. (August) 1983. *The Position of the Attorney General of Canada on Certain Recommendations of the McDonald Commission.* Ottawa: Department of Justice

McGuigan, Mark et al. 1977. *The Parliamentary Sub-Committee on Penitentiary Disturbances.* Ottawa: Supply and Services

McKay, H.B., C.H.S. Jayewardene and Penny B. Reedie. 1979. *The Effects of Long-Term Incarceration.* Ottawa: Supply and Services

McKay, Paul. 1983. *Electric Empire: The Inside Story of Ontario Hydro.* Foreward by Ralph Nader. Toronto: Between the Lines Press

McLeod, R.M., J.D. Takach and M.D. Segal. 1981. *Breathalyzer Law in Canada,* Revised Edition. Toronto: Carswell

McPheters, Lee R. 1976. "Criminal behavior and the gains from crime" 14 *Criminology* 137-152

Merton, Robert K. 1938. "Social structure and anomie" 3 *American Sociological Review* 672-682

Michigan State Bar Special Committee on Standard Jury Instructions. 1977. *Michigan Criminal Jury Instructions.* Ann Arbor, Mich.: Institute of Continuing Legal Education

Morand, Justice Donald R. 1976. *Ontario Royal Commission Into Metropolitan Toronto Police Practices.* Toronto: Queen's Printer

Morton, Desmond (ed.). 1974. *The Queen v. Louis Riel.* Toronto: University of Toronto Press

Munro, John C. 1982. *The Elimination of Sex Discrimination from the Indian Act.* Ottawa: Supply and Services

Murphy, Emily. 1922. *The Black Candle.* Toronto: Thomas Allen

Nagel, Stuart. 1970. "The tipped scales of American justice" in Abraham S. Blumberg (ed.). *Law and Order: The Scales of Justice.* Chicago: Aldine-Transaction

National Transportation Safety Board. 1983. *Marine Accident Report: Capsizing and Sinking of the Ocean Ranger.* Washington, D.C.: U.S. Government Publications

National Work Group on Justice Information and Statistics. 1981. *Correctional Services in Canada 1978/79 1979/80.* Ottawa

Nawaz, Mohammad. 1978. *Pot Smoking and Illegal Conduct*. St. Catherines, Ont.: Diliton Publishing

Nettler, Gwynn. 1978. *Explaining Crime*. Second Edition. New York: McGraw-Hill

Nettler, Gwynn. 1982a. *Lying, Cheating, Stealing*, Volume 3 of *Criminal Careers*. Cincinnati: Anderson Publishing Co.

Nettler, Gwynn. 1982b. *Responding to Crime*, Volume 4 of *Criminal Careers*. Cincinnati: Anderson Publishing

Nettler, Gwynn. 1982c. *Killing One Another*, Volume 2 of *Criminal Careers*. Cincinnati: Anderson Publishing

Newman, Donald J. 1956. "Pleading guilty for consideration" 46 *Journal of Criminal Law Criminology and Police Science* 780-790

Newman, Donald J. 1966. *Conviction: The Determination of Guilt or Innocence Without Trial*. Boston: Little, Brown

Newman, Peter C. 1978. *The Bronfman Dynasty*. Toronto: McClelland and Stewart

Nonet, Phillipe and Philip Selznick. 1978. *Law and Society in Transition: Toward Responsive Law*. New York: Harper and Row

Novick, Sheldon. 1969. *The Careless Atom*. Boston: Houghton Mifflin

Oppenheimer, B.S. 1937. "Trial by Jury" 11 *University of Cincinnati Law Review* 141

Orne, Martin. 1981. "The use and misuse of hypnosis in court" in M. Tonry and N. Morris (eds.). *Crime and Justice: An Annual Review of Research* Volume 3. Chicago: University of Chicago Press 61-104

Ouimet, Roger. 1969. *Report of the Canadian Committee on Corrections*. Ottawa: Queen's Printer

Ozenne, Tim. (January) 1974. "The economics of bank robbery" 3 *The Journal of Legal Studies* 19-51

Parker, Graham. 1983. *An Introduction to Criminal Law*. Second Edition. Toronto: Methuen

Passell, P. and J.B. Taylor. 1976. "The deterrence controversy: a reconsideration of the time series evidence" in H. Bedau and C. Pierce (eds.), *Capital Punishment*. New York: AMS Press 359-371

Passell, P. and J.B. Taylor. 1977. "The deterrent effect of capital punishment: another view" 67 *American Economic Review* 445-51

Pawlick, T. (June) 1980. "The silent toll" 4:8 *Harrowsmith Magazine* 33-49

Pawlick, T. and D. Matthews. (June) 1980. "It can happen here" 4:8 *Harrowsmith Magazine* 40-41

Pearlman, S. (August) 1977. "The Sawyer brothers" *Good Housekeeping* 82-88

Pelrine, E.W. 1975. *Morgentaler: The Doctor Who Couldn't Turn Away*. Agincourt: Gage

Pepinsky, Harold E. 1980. *Crime Control Strategies*. New York: Oxford University Press

Phillips, David P. 1982. "The impact of fictional television stories on U.S. adult fatalities: new evidence on the effect of the mass media on violence" 86:6 *American Journal of Sociology* 1340-1359

Piliavin, Irving and Scott Briar. 1964. "Police encounters with juveniles" 70 *American Journal of Sociology* 206-214

Radway, Kenneth. 1979. "Judge shopping" in James L. Wilkins (ed.). *Prosecution and the Courts*. Toronto: Centre of Criminology 661-684

Rashke, Richard. 1981. *The Killing of Karen Silkwood*. Harmondsworth: Penguin

Reasons, C.E. 1982. "Organizational crimes" in M. Michael Rosenberg, Robert A. Stebbins and Allan Turowetz (eds.). *The Sociology of Deviance*. New York: St. Martin's Press 150-170

Reasons, C.E. and William I. Perdue. 1981. *The Ideology of Social Problems*. Sherman Oaks, CA: Alfred Publishing

Reasons, C.E. and R.M. Rich (eds.). 1978. *The Sociology of Law: A Conflict Perspective*. Toronto: Butterworth

Reasons, C.E., L.L. Ross and C. Paterson. 1981. *Assault on the Worker*. Toronto: Butterworth

— Reid, John E. and Fred E. Inbau. 1966. *Truth and Deception: The Polygraph Lie Detector Technique*. Baltimore: Williams and Wilkins

Reid, Sue Titus. 1979, 1982. *Crime and Criminology*. New York: Holt, Rinehart and Winston. Second Edition, 1979 (Third Edition, 1982)

Reid, Sue Titus. 1981. *The Correctional System: An Introduction*. New York: Holt, Rinehart and Winston

— Reiman, Jeffrey H. 1979. *The Rich Get Richer and the Poor Get Prison*. New York: Wiley

Reiss, Albert. 1971. *The Police and the Public*. New Haven, Conn.: Yale University Press

Rice, A. Clayton. 1982. "The right to counsel" in Gerald L. Gall (ed.). *Civil Liberties in Canada Entering the 1980s*. Toronto: Butterworth 191-221

Right to Privacy Committee. 1983. "The legal score to January 12, 1983" 3:1 Toronto: *Action* 6

Rosenberg, M. Michael, Robert A. Stebbins and Allan Turowetz (eds.). 1982. *The Sociology of Deviance*. New York: St. Martin's

Ross, H. Laurence. 1982. *Deterring the Drinking Driver: Legal Policy and Social Control*. Lexington: Lexington Books

Ross, Robert R. and Paul Gendreau (eds.). 1980. *Effective Correctional Treatment*. Toronto: Butterworth ✓

Rothman, David J. 1971. *The Discovery of the Asylum*. Boston: Little, Brown

Rumbaut, Ruben and Egon Bittner. 1979. "Changing conceptions of the police role: A sociological review" in Norval Morris and Michael Tonry (eds.). *Crime and Justice, An Annual Review of Research*. Volume 1. Chicago: University of Chicago Press 239-288

Ryerson Polytechnical Institute (eds.). 1982. *Readings in Sociology: A Critical Perspective*. Toronto: Concept Press

Salhany, Roger. 1978. *Canadian Criminal Procedures*. Third Edition. Agincourt: Canada Law Book

Savan, Beth. 1983. *Law and Social Order Parts III and IV*. Toronto: CBC Transcripts

Savitz, Leonard D. 1958. "A study of capital punishment" 49 *Journal of Criminal Law, Criminology and Police Science* 328-341

Schachter, Stanley. 1971. *Emotion, Obesity and Crime*. New York: Academic Books

Schmeiser, Douglas A. 1974. *The Native Offender and the Law*. Law Reform Commission of Canada. Ottawa: Supply and Services

Schuessler, Karl F. (November) 1952. "The deterrent influence of the death penalty" 284 *The Annals of the American Academy of Political and Social Science* 54-63

Schurgin, A.S. and T.C. Hollocher. 1975. "Radiation Induced Lung Cancers Among Uranium Workers" in The Union of Concerned Scientists (ed.). *The Nuclear Fuel Cycle*. Cambridge: MIT Press 9-40

Selected Trends in Canadian Criminal Justice. 1979. Prepared for Federal-Provincial Conference of Ministers Responsible for Criminal Justice. Ottawa: Solicitor General

Sellin, Thorsten. 1959. *The Death Penalty: Report for the Model Penal Code Project of the American Law Institute.* Philadelphia: American Law Institute

Sellin, Thorsten. 1980. *The Penalty of Death.* Beverly Hills: Sage

Sesnowitz, Michael. 1972. "The returns to burglary" 10 *Western Economic Journal* 177-81

Shearing, Clifford D. (ed.). 1981. *Organizational Police Deviance.* Toronto: Butterworth

Shearing, Clifford D., F. Jennifer Lynch and Catherine J. Mathews. 1979. *Policing in Canada: A Bibliography.* Ottawa: Solicitor General

Shinnar, Shlomo and Reuel Shinnar. 1975. "The effects of the criminal justice system on the control of crime: a quantitative approach" 9 *Law and Society Review* 581-611

Silverman, Robert and James L. Teevan (eds.). 1980. *Crime in Canadian Society.* Second Edition. Toronto: Butterworth

Simon, Rita James. 1965. "Trial by jury: a critical assessment" in Alvin W. Gouldner and S.M. Miller (eds.). *Applied Sociology: Opportunities and Problems.* New York: Free Press

Sinclair, Upton. 1906. *The Jungle.* New York: Doubleday

Skolnick, J. 1966. *Justice Without Trial.* New York: Wiley

Snider, Laureen. 1978. "Corporate crime in Canada: a preliminary analysis" 20 *Canadian Journal of Criminology* 142-168

Snider, Laureen. 1982. "The criminal justice system" in Dennis Forcese and Stephen Richer (eds.). *Social Issues: Sociological Views of Canada.* Scarborough: Prentice-Hall 345-439

Sobel, N.R. 1972 (1976 Supplement). *Eyewitness Identification: Legal and Practical Problems.* New York: Clark Boardman

Spillman, T.C. and T.A. Zak. 1979. "Arson: an economic phenomenon?" 23:2 *American Economist* 37-43

Spitzer, S. 1975. "Toward a Marxian theory of deviance" 22 *Social Problems* 638-651

Starkman, David. 1978-79. "The use of eyewitness identification evidence in criminal trials" 21 *Criminal Law Quarterly* 361-386

Stenning, Philip C. 1982. *Legal Status of the Police.* Law Reform Commission of Canada. Ottawa: Supply and Services

Stewart, Walter. 1977. *Strike!* Toronto: McClelland and Stewart

Sudnow, David. 1965. "Normal crimes" 12 *Social Problems* 255-276

Sutherland, Edwin. 1937. *The Professional Thief.* Chicago: University of Chicago Press

Sutherland, Edwin. 1969. "The diffusion of sexual psychopath laws" in William J. Chambliss (ed.). *Crime and the Legal Process.* New York: McGraw-Hill 74-97

Sutherland, Edwin H. and Donald R. Cressey. 1966. *Principles of Criminology.* Seventh Edition. (Ninth Edition, 1974; Tenth Edition, 1978.) Philadelphia: T.B. Lippincott

Swackhamer, J.W. (Chairman). 1971. *Report of the Commission of Inquiry Into Certain Disturbances at the Kingston Penitentiary During April 1971.* Ottawa: Solicitor General

Swift, Jamie. 1977. *The Big Nickel.* Kitchener: Between the Lines Press

Swigert, Victoria Lynn and Ronald A. Farrell. 1980-81. "Corporate homicide: Definitional processes in the creation of deviance" 15 *Law and Society Review* 161-182

Sykes, Gresham M. 1958. *The Society of Captives.* Princeton: Princeton University Press

Sykes, Gresham M. and S.L. Messinger. 1970. "The inmate social code" in Norman Johnston, Leonard Savitz and Marvin Wolfgang (eds.). *The Sociology of Punish-*

ment and Corrections. Second Edition. New York: John Wiley 401-408

Szasz, Thomas. 1974. *Ceremonial Chemistry.* Garden City, N.Y.: Anchor

Tarnopolsky, Walter S. 1975a. *The Canadian Bill of Rights.* Second Edition. Toronto: McClelland and Stewart

Tarnopolsky, Walter S. (ed.). 1975b. *Some Civil Liberties Issues of the Seventies.* Toronto: Carswell

Tarnopolsky, Walter S. and Gerald A. Beaudoin. 1982. *The Canadian Charter of Rights and Freedoms: Commentary.* Toronto: Carswell

Taylor, Ian. 1981. *Law and Order: Arguments for Socialism.* London: Macmillan

Taylor, Ian. 1982. "Moral enterprise, moral panic and law and order campaigns" in M.M. Rosenberg, R.A. Stebbins and A. Turowetz (eds.). *The Sociology of Deviance.* New York: St. Martin's 123-149

Teevan, James J. 1976. "Deterrent effects of punishment for breaking and entering and theft" in Law Reform Commission of Canada. *Fear of Punishment.* Ottawa: Supply and Services 121-149

Tepperman, Lorne. 1977. *Crime Control.* Toronto: McGraw-Hill Ryerson

Thio, Alex. 1978. *Deviant Behavior.* Boston: Houghton-Mifflin

Thomas, Charles W. and Samuel C. Foster. 1973. "The importation model perspective on inmate social roles: An empirical test" 14:1 *Sociological Quarterly* 226-234

Thomas, Jim. 1982. "New directions in deviance research" in M.M. Rosenberg, R.A. Stebbins and A. Turowetz (eds.). *The Sociology of Deviance.* New York: St. Martin's 288-318

Thornberry, Terence. 1973. "Race, socioeconomic status and sentencing in the juvenile justice system" 64:1 *The Journal of Criminal Law and Criminology*, 90-98

Tigar, M.E. and M.R. Levy. 1977. *Law and the Rise of Capitalism.* New York: Monthly Press

Tittle, Charles and Allan Rowe. 1973. "Moral appeal, sanction threat and deviance: an experimental test" 20 *Social Problems* 488-98

Torrey, Lee. (8 November) 1979. "The accident at Three Mile Island" *New Scientist* 424-427

Torrey, Lee. (24 April) 1980. "Radiation cloud over nuclear power" *New Scientist* 197-199

Tremeear, W.J. 1902. *The Criminal Code and the Law of Evidence in Canada.* Toronto: Law Book Publishers

Trent, William with Steven Truscott. 1979. *Who Killed Lynn Harper?* Montreal: Optimum

Troyer, Warner. 1977. *No Safe Place.* Toronto: Clarke, Irwin

Trudeau, Pierre Elliott (ed.). 1956. *The Asbestos Strike.* Translated by James Boake from La grève de l'amiante. Toronto: James Lewis and Samuel, 1974

Turk, Austin. 1969. *Criminality and Legal Order.* Chicago: Rand McNally

United States Congress House Committee on Government Operations. 1974. *The Use of Polygraphs and Similar Devices by Federal Agencies.* Washington, D.C.: U.S. Government Printing Office

Utz, P. 1978. *Settling the Facts: Discretion and Negotiation in the Criminal Courts.* Lexington Books

Vaz, Edmund W. 1976. *Aspects of Deviances.* Scarborough: Prentice-Hall

Vaz, Edmund and Abdul Lodhi (eds.). 1979. *Crime and Delinquency in Canada.* Scarborough: Prentice-Hall

Verdun-Jones, Simon N. and F.D. Cousineau. 1982. "A critical analysis of plea bargaining in Canada" in C.L. Boydell and I.A. Connidis (eds.). *The Canadian*

Criminal Justice System. Toronto: Holt, Rinehart and Winston 177-199

Vincent, Claude L. 1979. *Policeman.* Toronto: Gage

Waldo, G. and T. Chiricos. 1972. "Perceived penal sanctions and self-reported criminality: a neglected approach to deterrence research" 19 *Social Problems* 522-540

Wall, Patrick M. 1965. *Eyewitness Identification in Criminal Cases.* Springfield: Charles C. Thomas

Waller, Irvin and Janet Chan. 1974. "Prison use: A Canadian and international comparison" 17 *Criminal Law Quarterly* 47-72

Warner, A. and K.E. Renner. 1978. "The standard of social justice applied to an evaluation of annual cases appearing before the Halifax courts" 1 *Windsor Yearbook of Access to Justice* 62-80

Watson, Eric R. 1924. *The Trial of Adolf Beck.* Toronto: Canada Law Book Company

Weeks, Robert P. (ed.). 1958. *Commonwealth vs. Sacco and Vanzetti.* Englewood Cliffs, N.J.: Prentice-Hall

Weller, Phil and the Waterloo Public Interest Research Group. 1980. *Acid Rain, The Silent Crisis.* Waterloo: Between the Lines Press

Westley, William A. 1953. "Violence and the Police" 59 *American Journal of Sociology* 34-41

Westley, William A. 1956. "Secrecy and the Police" 34 *Social Forces* 254-257

Wexler, Mark N. 1974. "Police culture: A response to ambiguous employment" in Craig L. Boydell, Paul C. Whitehead and Carl F. Grindstaff (eds.). *The Administration of Criminal Justice in Canada.* Toronto: Holt, Rinehart and Winston 126-151

Whitaker, Reginald. 1969. *Drugs and the Law: The Canadian Scene.* Toronto: Methuen

Whyte, William F. 1955. *Street Corner Society.* Chicago: University of Chicago Press

Wieder, Lawrence D. 1974. *Language and Social Reality: The Case of Telling the Convict Code.* The Hague: Mouton

Wilkins, James L. 1975. *Legal Aid in the Criminal Courts.* Toronto: University of Toronto Press

Wilkins, James L. (ed.). 1979. *The Prosecution and the Courts.* Toronto: Centre of Criminology, University of Toronto

Wilkins, James L. Forthcoming. *Ducks in a Row: The Practice of Prosecution.*

Wilkins, James L. and Fern Jeffries. 1971-72. " 'Due process safeguards and Canadian criminal justice': A critique" 14 *Criminal Law Quarterly* 220-235

Williams, Jay R. and Martin Gold. 1972. "From delinquent behavior to official delinquency" 20:2 *Social Problems* 209-229

Wilner, Norwood S. 1977. "Polygraphy: short circuit to truth?" 29 *University of Florida Law Review* 286-317

Wilson, James Q. 1968a. *Varieties of Police Behavior.* Cambridge, Mass.: Harvard University Press

Wilson, James Q. 1968b. "The police and the delinquent in two cities" in Stanton Wheeler (ed.). *Controlling Delinquents.* New York: John Wiley

Woocher, Frederic D. 1977. "Did your eyes deceive you? Expert psychological testimony on the unreliability of eyewitness identification" 29 *Stanford Law Review* 969-1030

Working Group. 1981. *Solicitor General's Study of Conditional Release.* Ottawa: Supply and Services

Worthington, Thomas S. 1980. "The use of hypnotically enhanced evidence" 27:4 *International Journal of Clinical and Experimental Hypnosis* 402-416

Yarmey, A. Daniel. 1979. *The Psychology of Eyewitness Testimony.* New York: Free Press

Zimring, F.E. and G.J. Hawkins. 1973. *Deterrence: The Legal Threat in Crime Control.* Chicago: University of Chicago Press

Case References

Canadian Cases

Attorney General of Canada v. J.V.C. Lavell and *Isaac et al and Bedard* [1974] S.C.R. 1349

Brownridge v. The Queen [1972] 7 C.C.C. (2d) 417

Demeter v. The Queen [1977] 34 C.C.C. (2d) 137

Hogan v. The Queen [1975] 18 C.C.C. (2d) 65

Kienapple v. The Queen [1974] 15 C.C.C. (2d) 524

Moore v. The Queen [1978] 43 C.C.C. (2d) 83 (S.C.C.)

O'Connor v. The Queen [1966] 4 C.C.C. 342

Pappajohn v. The Queen [1980] 52 C.C.C. (2d) 481

Phillion v. The Queen [1977] 33 C.C.C. (2d) 535

Re Copeland and McDonald et al [1979] 42 C.C.C. (2d) 334

Re Dowson and The Queen [1982] 62 C.C.C. (2d) 286

R. v. A [1976] 25 C.C.C (2d) 474

R. v. Agozzino [1970] 1 C.C.C. 380

R. v. Audy [1977] 40 C.C.C. (2d) 188

R. v. Ballageer [1968] 3 C.C.C. 353

R. v. Beaudry [1967] 1 C.C.C. 272

R. v. Benolkin et al [1977] 36 C.C.C. (2d) 206

R. v. Booher [1928] 4 D.L.R. 795

R. v. Boyd [1953] 105 C.C.C. 146

R. v. Brown [1972] 8 C.C.C. (2d) 227

R. v. Carker [1967] S.C.R. 114, 2 C.R.N.S. 16

R. v. Craig [1974] 22 C.C.C. (2d) 212

R. v. Demeter [1975] 19 C.C.C. (2d) 321

R. v. Demeter [1976] 25 C.C.C. (2d) 417

R. v. Drybones [1970] S.C.R. 282; 3 C.C.C. (2d) 303

R. v. Dubois [1960] 32 C.R. 187

R. v. Gaff [1980] 12 C.R. (3d) 188

R. v. Giesbrecht [1980] 11 C.R. (3d) 342

R. v. Gray [1962] 132 C.C.C. 337

R. v. Harms [1944] 81 C.C.C. 4

R. v. Harrison [1951] 100 C.C.C. 143

R. v. Hogan [1980] 11 C.R. (3d) 328
R. v. Horvath [1979] 93 D.L.R. (3d) 1
R. v. Johnston and Tremayne [1970] 4 C.C.C. 64
R. v. K. [1979] 47 C.C.C. (2d) 436
R. v. McNamara et al [1981] 56 C.C.C. (2d) 193
R. v. Peterkin [1959] 125 C.C.C. 228
R. v. Pitt [1968] 68 D.L.R. (2d) 513
R. v. Quon [1949] 92 C.C.C. 1
R. v. Shanower [1972] 8 C.C.C. (2d) 527
R. v. Siggins [1960] 127 C.C.C. 409
R. v. Springer [1975] 24 C.C.C. (2d) 56
R. v. Steeves [1964] 1 C.C.C. 166
R. v. Taylor [1970] 1 C.C.C. (2d) 321
R. v. Weightman and Cunningham [1977] 37 C.C.C. (2d) 303
R. v. Wilmot [1940] 74 C.C.C. 1
R. v. Wong (no. 2) [1978] 4, Western Weekly Reports. 468
R. v. Zamal et al [1964] 1 C.C.C. 12; 42 C.R. 378; 1 O.R. 224 (C.A.)
R. v. Zubot [1981, unreported] Medicine Hat Court of Queen's Bench, Madame
    Justice Heatherington, October, 1981. See M. McKinely and Ric Dolphin,
    "Hypnosis for the Prosecution," *Alberta Report*, Nov. 13, 1981, p. 36.

Non-Canadian Cases

Australia

Craig and the King [1933] 49 Commonwealth Law Reports 429

England

Fagan v. Commission of Metropolitan Police [1969] 1 Q.B. 439
R. v. Dudley and Stephens [1884] 14 Q.B.D. 273

U.S.A.

Fuller v. Preis [1974] 77 A.L.R. (3d) 301
Gilbert v. California [1967] 38 U.S. 263; 87 S. Ct. 1951
Gregg v. Georgia [1976] 96 S. Ct. 21909
Kirby v. Illinois [1972] 406 U.S. 682; 92 S. Ct. 1877
Leydra v. Denno [1954] 347 U.S. 556
Miranda v. Arizona [1966] 10 A.L.R. 974
People v. Ritchie [1977] (No. 36932, Super. Ct., Orange County, California, 4/7/77)
Rochin v. California [1952] 342 U.S. 165
State v. Papp [1978] (No. 78-02-00229, Com. Pleas Ct., Summit County, Ohio, 3/23/78)
Stovall v. Denno [1967] 38 U.S. 293; 87 S. Ct. 1967; 18 L. Ed. (2d) 1199
U.S. v. Amaral [1973] 48 F. (2d) 1148 (9th Cir.)
U.S. v. Wade [1967] 388 U.S. 218; 87 S. Ct. 1926

NOTE: Students who are interested in exploring case law will find that it is cited differently from most academic sources. Judgements reported during or following the state's prosecution will appear as Rex or Regina versus the name of the person in question. On appeal, the name of the defendant appears first. Usually this is followed by the year in which the decision is reported, followed by the volume and series of the publication, then the page at which the judgement begins. *R. v. Horvath* [1979] 93 D.L.R. (3d) 1 is read as Regina and, or Regina versus, Horvath, 1979, Volume 93 of the *Dominion Law Reports*, the Third Series beginning at page one. Most cases reported here are available in *Canadian Criminal Cases* (or C.C.C.), *Criminal Reports* (C.R.) or *Supreme Court Reports* (S.C.R.), which can be consulted at any faculty of law.

INDEX

law enforcement record 50-51
lawyers 103-09
legal aid 85-86, 89, 104-06, 108, 155,
    176, 212
Letkemann, P. 214
Levine, J.P., M.C. Musheno and
    D.J. Palumbo 210
Lizotte, A.J. 222
Loftus, E. 176, 182-86, 189
Loftus, E. and J.C. Palmer 185
Loftus, E. and G. Zanni 185
Lummus, H. 136
Lykken, D.T. 191

M

Macdonald, J.A. 41
MacKaay, E. 153, 156
Mackenzie King, W.L. 12-13, 16
Macnaughton-Smith, P. 233
Mancuso, T.S. 116
Mandatory supervision 225, 234-35
Mandel, M. 62-65, 106, 108, 131,
    222-23
Manning, P. 54, 57
Marshall, D. 176, 177, 242
Martinson, R. 219
Marxism 2, 7
Mather, L. 144
McBarnet, D. 151
McDonald, L. 59-60, 61
McDonald Commission 29-30, 58,
    62-66
McGuigan, M. 62
McKay, H.B. 226, 227, 228
McLeod et al. 96-97
McNamara et al. 130-31
McPheters, L. 204-05
media 11, 13-14, 28, 45-46, 69, 109,
    209, 215
mens rea 29-30, 35, 127-28, 130,
    143-44, 200, 241
mercury poisoning 121-22
Miranda 72-74, 77, 78
mistake of fact 26-27, 129, 241
mistaken identification 175-77
M'Naghten rule 33-34
monopolies 111, 112, 241
Moore 70
moral crusade 11-12

moral entrepreneurs 7 ff., 13, 17, 18-19
Morand commission 55, 57-58
Morgentaler, 154
motivation 29, 158
murder 31, 49, 95, 101, 158-59 ff.,
    207-13, 227
Murphy, E. 14, 15

N

Nagel, S. 107
negligence 37, 121, 128, 241
negotiated guilty pleas 136 ff.
Nelles, S. 242
Nettler, G. 26, 34, 38, 191, 216, 217
Newman, D.J. 136
Newman, P. 10
normal crimes 141
Norman law 21
Novick, S. 123
Nuclear Liability Act 123
nudism 22-23

O

obscenity 38
occupational death and injury 101-02,
    114-19, 121-22
Ocean Ranger 115
O'Connor 80-81, 82, 83, 84
Opium and Drug Act 13
Oppenheimer, B.S. 154
order maintenance 53
organized crime 10, 22, 201
Orne, M. 194-95
Ouimet report 51, 220
Outerbridge, W. 131
overcharging 137-39
Ozenne, T. 204-05

P

Pappajohn 27-28, 129
Parker, G. 4, 31, 34-36, 70, 73
parole 207, 221, 225, 232-34
partial exclusionary rule 72 ff.
Passell, P. and J.B. Taylor 210
Pawlick, T. 116
Pawlick T. and D. Matthews 117
Pelrine, E.W. 154
penal sanction 1, 19, 219 ff.
penitentiary 224 ff.

Phillion 192
Phillips, D. 209
Piliavin, I. and S. Briar 59
plea bargaining 97, 135 *ff.*, 154
police culture 54–57
police deployment 59–61
police deviance 29–30, 54–58, 62–66,
    77–78, 84–85, 118
police strikes 61
politicality 1, 19, 25, 95
poll tax 2
pollution as deviance 119–22
polygraph 192 *ff.*
pornography 38, 242, 246
presumption of innocence 70, 243
prison 205, 223–26
prison effectiveness 231 *ff.*
prison life 226–28, 247
prison riots 224–25, 228–30
proactive policing 52
probation 220–21
prohibition 8–11, 201
prostitution 22–23
psychiatrists 11, 190, 216
psychopathy 34, 216
public defender 104–06

Q
Quon 149

R
racism 14–17
Radway, K. 135
rape 26–29
Rashke, R. 114, 116
ratio of police to citizens 48
rational model of crime 201, 202–04
RCMP 29, 46–47, 58, 61–66, 138
reactive policing 52
reasonable excuse 27–28, 81–82
Reasons, C.E. 85, 119
Reasons, C.E., L.L. Ross and
    C. Patterson 37, 95
recidivism 231–32
recklessness 30, 128, 241
reforms 6–7
rehabilitation 40–41, 140, 215, 230, 240
Reid, J.E. and F. Inbau 192

Reid, S.T. 40, 46, 53, 55, 56, 57, 73, 78,
    136, 229
Reiman, J. 100, 101, 103, 106, 108
Reiss, A. 52
reliability of eyewitnesses 181
remission 207, 233–35
res judicata 149
restitution 144, 148
restraint 38
retribution 38–40, 240, 247
right to counsel 78–85, 180–81, 188
right to silence 70, 77, 157, 167, 171,
    194
Rochin 77–78
Rothman, D.J. 40
rules of evidence 156–57, 173

S
Sacco and Vanzetti 181–82
Salhany, R. 156
Savan, B. 121, 124
Savitz, L. 209
Saxon law 21
"scared straight" program 215
Schachter, S. 200
Schmeiser, D.A. 107
Schuessler, K.F. 209
Schurgin, A.S. and T.C. Hollocher 115
Section 115 63, 85
Sellin, T. 207–09
sentencing 33, 38–41, 56, 106–09, 136,
    140, 144, 146–47, 150–51, 155,
    215, 220–23, 230, 245–46
Sesnowitz, M. 203
severity of punishment 206–07, 217 *ff.*
sexual assault 28–29, 33, 95
sexual psychopaths 11
Shearing, C. 29
sheriffs 46–47
Shinnar, S. and R. Shinnar 205
Silkwood, K. 114–15
Silverman, R. and J. Teevan 199
similar facts evidence 144
Simon, R. 154
Sinclair, U. 7
Snider, L. 114
socialism 2
specificity 1, 19, 112, 200, 241, 246
Spillman, T.C. and T.A. Zak 203

Holt, Rinehart and Winston of Canada, Limited

ISBN 0-03-92162: